SWITZERLAND

'Switzerland awaits your visit; wherever you decide to go, and however you decide to travel, you will leave with marvellous memories.'

Norman Renouf

About the Guide

The full-colour introduction gives the author's overview of the country, together with suggested itineraries and a regional 'where to go' map and feature to help you plan your trip.

Illuminating and entertaining cultural chapters on local history, food and drink, politics, tourism and the craft of woodcarving give you a rich flavour of the country.

Planning Your Trip starts with the basics of when to go, getting there and getting around, coupled with other useful information, including a section for disabled travellers. The Practical A–Z deals with all the essential information and contact details that you may need while you are away.

The regional chapters give public transport and driving information. The author's top 'Don't Miss' ✪ sights are highlighted at the start of each chapter.

A language and pronunciation guide, ideas for further reading and a comprehensive index can be found at the end of the book.

Although everything listed in this guide is personally recommended, our authors inevitably have their own favourite places to eat and stay. Whenever you see this Author's Choice ★ icon beside a listing, you will know that it is a little bit out of the ordinary.

Hotel Price Guide (*see also* p.48)

Luxury	CHF 500 and above
Expensive	CHF 250–500
Moderate	CHF 100–250
Inexpensive	up to CHF 100

Restaurant Price Guide (*see also* p.50)

Very expensive	CHF 60 and above
Expensive	CHF 40–60
Moderate	CHF 25–40
Inexpensive	up to CHF 25

About the Author

Born and educated in London, **Norman Renouf** became a travel writer and photographer in the early 1990s. He has written numerous guides and articles covering destinations in Europe from the Arctic Circle to Gibraltar and as far east as Moscow, St Petersburg and Tallinn. He has been visiting Switzerland since the mid-1960s, and has developed a thorough knowledge of the cities, mountain villages and culture of the country. He currently resides in southern Spain.

1st edition published 2010

01 INTRODUCING SWITZERLAND

Top: Alpine meadow above Mürren, Bernese Oberland

Above: Town Hall, Basel

Switzerland is a sparkling wonderland known for its breathtaking scenery. With more than 70 per cent of its land covered by the Alps, it is famous for its alpine resorts and winter sports opportunities. However, this small, landlocked country has far more to offer visitors than mountains and snow. There are also numerous lesser-known valleys, villages and towns with their own unique characteristics and traditions. The country's cultural diversity, shown in language, architecture and cuisine, is also a major attraction. The large swathe of central, north and eastern Switzerland, with Zürich both the largest city and the country's financial centre, is dominated by the German influence. Contrastingly, the French style of life is predominant in the western and southwestern regions, with Geneva and Lausanne being the main cities. Interestingly, the Valais area divides its loyalties. Altogether different, though, is the only region in Switzerland below the Alps – Ticino. Sunnier and more luxuriant in its flora, it is Italian in character and has a strong Mediterranean feel. In parts of Graubünden, in the southeast of the country, Romansch traditions and language still thrive.

As might be expected, such diversity demands a flexible political system. Bern, on the central plains, is the capital of the Swiss Confederation and the seat of the federal government that governs under a constitution accepted on 29 May 1874. The country is divided into 26 cantons, three of which are divided into half-cantons, which each have their own constitutions and elected regional assemblies.

Above: Astronomical Clock, Bern

Right: Zürich cityscape, featuring the spires of the Fraumünster (left) and St Peter's

Being so small, Switzerland is one of the easiest countries in Europe in which to travel. It is easily possible to go north to south in three to four hours, and west to east in about eight hours by train. It has a fully integrated public transport system (including trains, buses and lake steamers) that is clean, efficient and runs on time regardless of sometimes extreme weather conditions. This is supplemented by private transportation systems such as funiculars, gondola cars, cable cars and cog-wheel railways.

It has to be said that Switzerland is an expensive country to visit. But one thing you can be guaranteed in Switzerland is that you will always get value for money. Swiss hospitality is world famous, and the service and attention that you will receive in the hotels, restaurants and cafés will be exemplary. Everything is done to make your stay as comfortable as possible and the attention to detail in some hotels is extraordinary. Many of the hotels have been run by the same family for generations, so visitors return time and again, knowing that they will be returning to a familiar place that will offer them consistent levels of comfort and service.

Switzerland has so much to offer – beautiful alpine scenery, cultured cities and towns, skiing, snowboarding and adventure sports, idyllic lakes, luxurious hotels and spas, and wonderful restaurants and cafés. However you decide to spend your time, you will leave with many happy memories.

Where to Go

Northwestern and **northeastern** Switzerland are dominated by two cities, **Basel** and **Zürich** respectively. Each region has its own interesting local towns and characteristics.

Bern, the capital of Switzerland, has a rather different atmosphere to other Swiss cities, combining a beautifully preserved medieval centre with much culture. On a clear day there are magnificent views from the city to the huge mountain peaks of the **Bernese Oberland**, where you will find the most varied and eclectic experiences of any of Switzerland's mountain regions.

Central Switzerland is dominated by Luzern and its beautiful lake. From here you can take a trip up Mount Pilatus, and enjoy a ride on the world's first revolving cable car, Engelberg's Titlis Rotair.

The **Lake Geneva** region offers the cosmopolitan city of Geneva, attractive towns on the northern side of the lake, the important cheese-making village of Gruyères and the charming mountain village of Les Diablerets, with its exciting mountain-top adventures.

Mountain-lovers will delight in what can be found in the **Valais**, too. Here, every side valley is totally different: there are international resorts such as Zermatt; rural Lötschental, with its quaint traditions; and Crans-Montana, which hosts major golf tournaments. Wherever you go you will find idyllic alpine scenes.

Ticino, the only region south of the Alps, has no towering mountains, but the warmer climate, Italian character and beautiful lakes more than make up for this.

Graubünden, in the far southeast, is different again. It is home to the affluent resort of St Moritz, which attracts the A-list celebrity crowd every winter. In complete contrast, is tiny Scuol, which has the most interesting public spa in Switzerland. Wherever you go in Graubünden, and whenever you go, you are sure to come across some of the most delightful scenery in Switzerland, totally unspoilt by mass tourism.

Top: Old bakery sign, Luzern

Above: The Lällekönig, Basel

Below right: Train arriving at Kleine Scheidegg

Chapter Divisions

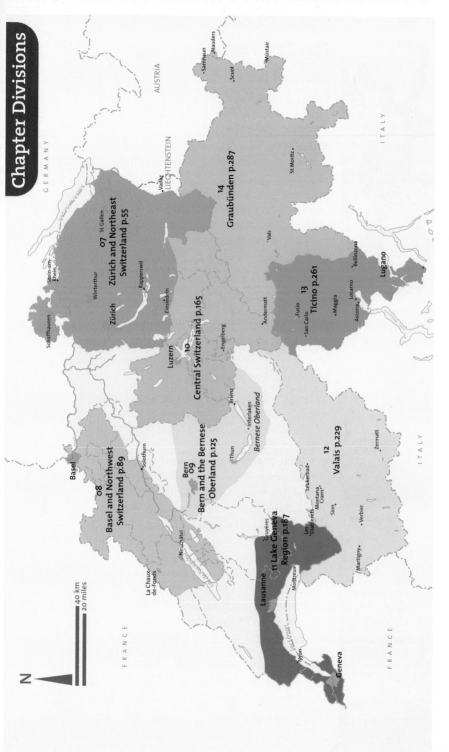

N

40 km
20 miles

GERMANY

AUSTRIA

LIECHTENSTEIN

FRANCE

ITALY

Schaffhausen

Stein-am-
Rhein

Winterthur

Zürich

07 St Gallen
Zürich and Northeast
Switzerland p.55

Rapperswil

Einsiedeln

Vaduz

Samnaun
Nauders

Scuol

Müstair

14
Graubünden p.287

Vals

St Moritz

Basel

08
Basel and Northwest
Switzerland p.89

Solothurn

Neuchâtel

La Chaux-
de-Fonds

Luzern

10
Central Switzerland p.165

Engelberg

Brienz

Interlaken

Bern

09
Bern and the Bernese
Oberland p.125

Thun

Bernese Oberland

Andermatt

13
Ticino p.261

Fusio

San Carlo

Maggia

Bellinzona

Locarno

Ascona

Lugano

Lausanne

11 Lake Geneva
Region p.187

Gruyères

Les
Diablerets

Montreux

Nyon

Geneva

Leukerbad

Montana
Crans

Sion

Verbier

12
Valais p.229

Zermatt

Martigny

FRANCE

ITALY

Top Ten Places to Visit

Cities and Towns

01 **Bern**, wander around the medieval Old Town, with its arcades, colourful fountains, ornamental clock and, of course, its famous BärenPark (Bear Park), p.127

02 **Luzern**, this beautiful city has a charming lakeside location. One of its many unusual attractions is the famous Kapellbrücke (Chapel Bridge), p.167

03 **Geneva**, Switzerland's most cosmopolitan city has an intriguing history, is the European headquarters of the United Nations, has the magnificent Mont Blanc as its backdrop and is home to the symbolic Jet d'Eau fountain on the lake, p.189

04 **Basel**, dominated by the fast-flowing Rhine, this city – at the junction of three countries – has numerous museums and art galleries and charming little wooden ferries that cross the river, p.91

05 **Montreux**, has a spectacular lakeside location close to the famous Lavaux vineyard terraces and musical connections because of its Jazz Festival and former resident, Freddie Mercury. The Château de Chillon is nearby, p.217

Above: Freddie Mercury memorial, Montreux

Below: St Martin, Basel Cathedral façade

Opposite top: Glacier at Zermatt

Opposite bottom: Chapel Bridge, Luzern

Mountain Resorts and Valleys

06 **Zermatt**, dominated by the massive Matterhorn mountain, Switzerland's most emblematic landmark, this car-free village has become a world-famous resort with hotels, restaurants and designer shops, p.254

07 **Bernese Oberland**, undoubtedly home to the most diverse range of mountain experiences in Switzerland – from lake steamers to a revolving restaurant at 9,744ft (2,970m), p.140

08 **Saas-Fee**, has an entirely different ambience to near neighbour Zermatt. This charming, car-free village is set in a natural bowl surrounded by huge peaks and boasts the highest revolving restaurant in the world at 11,483ft (3,500m), p.251

09 **Lötschental**, not one of Switzerland's best-known attractions, this beautiful, remote, ascending and attenuating valley is surrounded by towering mountains and the area has many unique traditions, p.248

10 **Scuol**, deep in the heart of the Lower Engadine valley in Graubünden, this small village has capitalized on its naturally warm waters by developing the most unusual public spa in the country. Wallow in an outdoor jacuzzi while the snows falls, and experience the Roman-Irish spa – one of only two in Switzerland, p.295

*Right: The spectacular
setting of the
Drehrestaurant,
Saas-Fee*

Mountain Experiences

There is a huge array of aerial cableways, but some mountain resorts have gone to unusual lengths to be different. Few things in Switzerland are as exciting as sitting in a revolving restaurant, enjoying mountain cuisine, while slowly being turned 360 degrees so that you can enjoy an ever-changing scene of alpine peaks.

Aerial Cableways

• Engelberg has the Titlis Rotair, which takes you up – and around. Its interior revolves, allowing you stunning views of the landscape. Not an experience for the fainthearted, p.183
• Samnaun, at the far eastern end of the Lower Engadine valley, has a double-decker cable car, p.302

Mountain-top Revolving Restaurants

• The most famous of these, and there are not very many, is the Piz Gloria at Schilthorn, used as a location in the James Bond movie, *On Her Majesty's Secret Service*. At an elevation of 9,744ft (2,970m), and reached on the cableway via Mürren, it offers spectacular views across the valley to the high peaks of the Bernese Oberland and even Jungfraujoch itself, pp.158–9
• At Saas-Fee they do things slightly differently, but the results are even more spectacular. An inside-the-mountain funicular, the Metro-Alpin, takes you up the last leg of the trip to 11,483ft (3,500m), where the world's highest revolving restaurant, Drehrestaurant, is set amongst some of the highest peaks in Switzerland, p.252

Itinerary 1:
Bernese Oberland

This five-day trip takes in the highlights of this amazing region.

Day 1 From **Interlaken** take a lake steamer to **Brienz** and then a Brienz Rothorn Bahn steam train to **Rothorn Kulm**. Return to Interlaken for the evening.

Day 2 Travel to **Mürren**, then take the cable car up to **Schilthorn** before returning on it to the valley station. Then take the bus to the **Trümelbach Falls**. After enjoying your time at the falls, take the bus to Stechelberg and then the cable car will whisk you back to Mürren.

Days 3–5 Spend three days based in **Grindelwald** and explore this diverse area – **Männlichen**, **Kleine Scheidegg**, the wonders that are found at **Jungfraujoch** (take things slowly because of the thin air, *see* p.154) and perhaps a hike from **Grindelwald First**.

Above: Brienz Rothorn Bahn steam engine

Below: Schreckhorn mirrored in Bachalpsee, First, Grindelwald

01 Introduction | Itineraries

Itinerary 2: The Valais

An interesting eight-day trip that explores many of the attractions and landmarks in this valley.

Day 1 The tour begins in the charming village of **Saas-Fee**, which is car-free. Ascend to the world's highest revolving restaurant, Drehrestaurant, for lunch, after which explore the village.

Days 2–3 Travel to **Zermatt** (also car-free) and spend two days admiring the **Matterhorn** from various perspectives, including from a helicopter, which takes you close to the summit.

Days 4–5 The next destination, **Lötschental**, is a place to relax. Enjoy a gentle hike up to the **Grundsee** lake or take the cable car to **Lauchernalp**, where you will find the fabulous mountain restaurant, Hockenalp.

Day 6 Move on to **Leukerbad** and partake of the various spa experiences found at the Lindner Alpentherme – particularly the Roman-Irish baths.

Days 7–8 The series of valleys in **Val d'Anniviers** are unlike others in the Valais. The villages here have many interesting cultural traditions, including cowfighting.

Below: Matterhorn, Zermatt

Right: Typical chalet in the Valais

Below: Peaceful village of Saas-Fee

Itinerary 3: Western Switzerland

This week-long tour takes in diverse aspects of the area.

Day 1 No trip to **Montreux** is complete without a visit to the **Château de Chillon**. Then a stroll along the charming waterfront promenade in Montreux will introduce you to Freddie Mercury's influence here.

Days 2–3 Make your way to **Lausanne**. This city has many facets to its character, not least some fabulous hotels. A trip across the lake to **Evian-les-Bains** is always fun. Also, the **Lavaux vineyard terraces** are just to the west.

Day 4–5 Spend the next two days in **Bern**. The heart of the city is one of the finest examples of medieval civic architecture in Europe.

Day 6 Solothurn is a small, aristocratic old town that is pleasant to stroll around. Be sure not to miss the Altes Zeughaus (Old Arsenal Museum).

Day 7 With its French ambience and lakeside location, **Neuchâtel** is a delightful city with a complex history. It also boasts the most unusual high-tech hotel in Switzerland, the Hôtel Palafitte.

Above: Lavaux vineyard terraces
Below: Château de Chillon
Opposite: Bern cityscape

*Above: Hauptbahnhof
and tram, Zürich*

*Below: Flower Clock,
Geneva*

Cultured Cities

Switzerland's towns and cities have their fair share of festivals and unique cultural attractions.

- **Basel**, a city influenced by three countries, it has more museums than any other place in Switzerland, p.91
- **Bern**, once the home of Einstein, it boasts the Zentrum Paul Klee, a museum dedicated to the artist, p.127
- **Geneva**, a bastion of French culture, the Swiss Reformation and a city of international importance due to the presence of the United Nations and the International Red Cross, p.189
- **Luzern**, home to the KKL (Culture and Congress Centre) and hosts the world-famous Summer Festival, p.167
- **Montreux**, has a worldwide reputation as a centre for arts and culture, hosting many annual events and festivals, p.217
- **Zürich**, Switzerland's largest city, which played a leading role in the Swiss Reformation, has the most famous, and most expensive, shopping street in the country – Bahnhofstrasse. There are numerous galleries in the Old Town, p.57

CONTENTS

18

Reference

Contents

History

02

Prehistory

To view Switzerland's prehistory you can visit the Cotencher caves in the canton of Neuchâtel (*www.latenium.ch*), where flint tools and the bones of a Neanderthal woman and 62 animal species dating back 60,000 years have been discovered. However, evidence of human existence dating back about 150,000 years and a flint tool believed to be 100,000 years old have been found in the country.

The Romans and the Dark Ages

The Roman influence in Switzerland began in the period around 50 BC and lasted until about AD 400, and during that time they set about fortifying areas along the Rhine and settling cities such as Basel, Chur, Geneva, Lausanne and Zürich. Their rule was challenged by migrating tribes moving from east to west, until eventually they were forced to withdraw south of the Alps. Now Switzerland was peopled by tribes of different cultures and who spoke different languages.

The Dark Ages, from around 400 to 1000 was a period when wealthy landowners, the nobility and the church vied for power. The influence of Christianity, which had been brought to the country by the Romans, increased, through the network of monasteries that spread throughout the country. In 962, King Otto 1 of Germany was declared emperor of what was to become the Holy Roman Empire by Pope John VII.

Middle Ages

The year 1291 is an important date in Swiss history as it is regarded as the point at which the Swiss Confederation began. Three rural communities, that of Uri, Schwyz and Unterwalden, known as the League of the Three Forests, formed an alliance to defend against attackers who would threaten their power. This alliance grew over the next two centuries, and its troops became feared throughout Europe.

The Reformation

As in the rest of western Europe, the 16th century in Switzerland was a time of discontent when, as a result of a proposed reformation of the Catholic church, Christendom was divided and Protestants denounced the rule of the Pope. In Switzerland, what started with the teachings of Martin Luther in Germany, Zwingli in Zürich (*see* p.63) and Calvin in Geneva, caused a split in the country. The more progressive areas, including Zürich, Basel, Bern and Geneva adopted the new ways, while the conservative rural areas retained their Catholicism.

While the underlying factor in the divide that occurred within the country was religion, other issues, such as social structure, were factors and there were widespread riots.

17th Century

The Thirty Years War (1618–48) had a profound effect on the Swiss Confederation. The war had caused great destruction and at one time or another during the conflict most European nations were involved. Significantly, the Swiss

Confederation had remained neutral and its members acknowledged that despite many fundamental ideological differences, they were stronger and more protected within their alliance than standing alone. The Confederation's neutral stance in relation to the Thirty Years War was the catalyst for an established policy of neutrality. The Treaty of Westphalia, which ended the thirty-year conflict, officially declared that Switzerland was independent from the Holy Roman Empire.

However, despite not involving itself in conflicts outside its borders, there were tensions within the country, both social and religious, that caused outbreaks of violence in the latter 1600s.

18th Century

This century was initially one of change and advancement in terms of new industries, such as clockmaking, textiles and agricultural developments. There was much discussion and exchanges of ideas between intellectual groups, both within the country and with other European nations. However, the developments were not beneficial for all. Many rural people found themselves without work due to the changes in the farming industry.

Towards the end of the century, events in France proved to be a major turning point in Switzerland's, indeed the whole of Europe's, history. There had been close ties between the Swiss and the French for almost three hundred years, and young Swiss mercenary soldiers (*see* p.250) were sent to serve the king of France. However, tragedy struck in 1792 when, defending the French king during the French Revolution, a whole detachment of mercenaries was massacred. The French Revolution stirred the people of western Switzerland, who supported the principles of liberty, fraternity and equality and parts of the Confederation were taken over by the French in 1793. In a further effort to protect itself from other European countries, France took over other areas of Switzerland in 1797. In 1798, despite an attempt at resistance, Bern fell to the French and the old Confederation was at an end and the Helvetic Republic was established. The government of the new republic was Swiss, but they had to accept some rulings dictated by the French and their policy of neutrality was broken when they entered into an alliance with the French and supplied them with troops. However, the Helvetic Republic proved to be shortlived, and following a civil war the cantonal system was reinstated.

19th Century

The period from 1815 to 1848 was an unsettling one for the country, even leading in 1847 to a civil war, when seven Catholic cantons attempted to break away from the rest of the country. However, the Sonderbund War (*sonderbund* meaning 'separate alliance' in German) was brought to a quick halt after only 26 days due to the actions of the federal army under the leadership of General Henri Dufour. This led to a period of reflection that ended in 1848 with the new Federal Swiss Constitution, emulating that of the USA, with 25 (there are now 26) more or less autonomous cantons. Despite revisions in 1874 and 1999, essentially the same system still prevails (*see* pp.24–5.)

20th and 21st Centuries

The 20th century saw many changes in Switzerland. In terms of the economic situation, agriculture gave way to industry. Post-Second World War, as in many other European countries, technical advances fed economic growth, and Switzerland's multi-faceted economy, including tourism of course, was well placed to succeed. Overall it was a prosperous century, with most people having a high standard of living.

For more information on Switzerland's foreign policy and its place within Europe during this time and in the 21st century, see pp.26–7.

Topics

03

Swiss Political System

The Swiss take their democracy very seriously indeed. Their 'Direct Democracy' system based on the 1848 Swiss Federal Constitution, which limits federal influence on domestic policies, is unique in the world. The federal state has three different levels of government: the Confederation, the cantons and the communes.

The Confederation

The Confederation, the highest level of government, has three branches of power – the Executive, Legislative and Judicial.

The **Executive** branch, considered one of the world's strongest, is formed by the Swiss Federal Council, a seven-member executive council operating as both a collective presidency and cabinet, elected by the United Federal Assembly to serve a four-year term. Both the president of the Confederation – a more or less ceremonial position as head of government who is considered first among equals and chairs the Swiss Federal Council – and the vice-president of the Federal Council are elected to concurrent one-year terms also by the Federal Assembly.

The **Swiss Federal Council** has been a source of great stability since its formation in 1848. Always elected at the same time, it is a coalition of the major parties elected in the same ratio. For many years it has consisted of the same four parties: the Free Democratic Party, the Social Democratic Party, the Christian Democratic People's Party and the Swiss People's Party. This system has become known as the 'magic formula'.

The **Legislative** level, known as the United Federal Assembly, has two chambers, the Council of States and the National Council.

The **Council of States** represents the 26 cantons and has 46 representatives – two each for the 20 full cantons and one each for the six half cantons. The rules of voting for these representatives vary from canton to canton.

The **National Council** has 200 members that are voted for every four years by the population. Representation is in direct proportion to the number of inhabitants in each canton; usually this leads to few changes in the parties' elected members.

The **Judicial** level is the **Supreme Court**, which itself has three branches: the Federal Supreme Court based in Lausanne, which has 60 judges, 30 full-time, 30 part-time; the Federal Insurance Court based in Luzern; and the Federal Criminal Court based in Bellinzona.

The Cantons

There are 26 cantons, 20 full ones and six half ones, and they represent the original states that combined to form, and cede parts of their sovereignty to, the Confederation in 1848.

The Communes

The cantons are divided into communes. Besides being given responsibilities by the Confederation and their respective cantons, communes also have limited powers of their own.

Direct Democracy

The system of referenda has been an integral part of the Swiss political system since the 1848 constitution. However, its roots go back to the Reformation (*see* p.63).

With regards to the **Federal Constitution**, either full or partial revisions have to be approved by a majority of the electorate. Amendments in relation to joining international organizations and federal laws that are not related to the constitution but are expected to be in law for more than a year are subject to the approval of both the cantons and the people.

In fact, any citizen is entitled to try to make amendments to the constitution. Unsurprisingly, it is a convoluted process. Initially, 100,000 signatures must be found within an 18-month period. Then, if it so wishes, the Swiss Federal Council can offer a counter suggestion, which is usually a form of compromise. Both this and the proposed amendment are voted for nationally on the same day. It is necessary to achieve a majority of both the cantons and the popular votes for it to be approved.

Also, any citizen can challenge enacted laws. They have to collect 50,000 signatures not more than 100 days after the law has been passed. This automatically triggers a national vote and the decision as to whether the law stands or is repealed is based on the majority of the voters.

Women's Voting Rights

For a country that goes to great lengths to ensure democratic rights for its citizens, it is surprising how long it took for women to achieve the right to vote in Switzerland.

As far back as 1886 women in Zürich unsuccessfully petitioned for the right to vote. After the First World War it was one of the main issues in the General Strike. Although the central government stalled on the issue, between 1919 and 1921 several cantons, including Geneva, Basel and Zürich, rejected the issue at referenda. After the Second World War even the more progressive cantons failed to grant women the right to vote.

In 1957 there was a breakthrough when Basel allowed women to vote, but only on a local level. A national referendum was held in February 1959 but once again men voted against it with a 67 per cent to 31 per cent majority, with the 'no' vote considerably higher in some cantons. However, progress was made in the French-speaking cantons of Geneva, Neuchâtel and Vaud, who voted to allow women to vote in referenda at cantonal and local levels. It wasn't until seven years later, though, that a German-speaking canton, Zürich, followed suit.

The issue was raised again in 1962 when Switzerland was considering joining the European Council and signing up to the European Convention of Human Rights. Even so, it wasn't until early in 1971 that women's right to vote was accepted nationally by a 66 per cent to 34 per cent majority, but as more cantons accepted the rights locally, others still resisted. Women were first elected to Parliament in the same year and a referendum on equal rights for men and women was passed in 1985.

To see how far Switzerland was behind other countries on this issue, the Soviet Union introduced the right for women to vote in 1917, the USA in 1920, the United Kingdom in 1928 and France and Italy in 1944 and 1945, respectively.

Swiss Neutrality

The policy of neutrality in foreign and defence policies is broadly accepted within Switzerland, but the country does have armed forces and military service is compulsory for males. In 2001 voters approved deployment abroad for Swiss troops in conjunction with UN or Organization for Security and Co-operation in Europe (OSCE) peacekeeping missions.

An understanding not to participate in wars between other countries and a state of permanent neutrality is one of the utmost principles of Switzerland's foreign policy. The origins of this go back way before this stance was formalized. Some suggest that it can even be traced back to the 1291 Oath of Mutual Protection, where an absence of a centralized government and the necessity of creating a power balance between diverse groups meant that it was a matter of self-interest.

Others refer to the advice of Nicholas of Flüe (1417–87), a saint, who suggested that Switzerland should not get involved in the affairs of others. Effectively, Switzerland has been neutral since the early 16th century. Having been beaten by the French in the Battle of Marignano in 1515, the following year the Swiss undertook a policy of neutrality. This held even through the **Thirty Years' War**, from 1618 to 1648, which ravaged central Europe. In 1674, as a consequence of facing a dispute with France, Switzerland recognized its limitations and self-interest by an official declaration of its neutrality by the council of the Swiss Confederation. Not only did this stop any wars with other countries, just as importantly it maintained social harmony in a country comprised of citizens who not only spoke German, French and Italian but who also had cultural ties to those countries.

Switzerland, therefore, became the first European country to declare neutrality. Subsequently other countries have taken a similar stance: Sweden in 1815, the Republic of Ireland in 1921, Finland in 1948 and Austria in 1955.

The **Treaty of Paris** in 1815 – a conference on post-Napoleon international relations – was when other European powers officially recognized Swiss neutrality. It was agreed that the country would not participate in military wars and the inviolability of Swiss territory was guaranteed. This was recognized in international law at the **Hague Convention** of 1907.

After the **First World War** Switzerland joined the League of Nations (later to become the United Nations), and although it agreed to participate in officially imposed sanctions it was relieved of this obligation in 1938.

Second World War

The Second World War presented Swiss neutrality with many challenges. Not only was it surrounded by Germany and Italy, who were fighting the Allies, but also by Austria and France, who housed troops from the Allied countries. In the face of this, Switzerland mobilized its army, preparing to defend its territory. Although Switzerland tried to maintain neutrality, neither side respected Swiss air space and Allied planes actually dropped bombs on Switzerland.

An important aspect of neutrality is that countries wishing to be neutral must also respect the spirit as well as the letter of that neutrality. The behaviour of Swiss institutions, particularly the national bank, private bankers and manufacturers, has been questioned as they exploited loopholes to trade with Nazi Germany. That, and the fact that it closed its borders to refugees, causing much consternation to Jews, has led to questions as to whether Switzerland's actions actually prolonged that war.

Post-Second World War to the Present Day

Subsequent to the Second World War Switzerland began to redefine its neutrality to allow it to participate in peacekeeping activities. Soon after, Swiss troops were used to help keep the ceasefire between South and North Korea.

In 1996 Switzerland joined **NATO's Partnership for Peace**; as there was no question of Swiss military participation it didn't conflict with the country's long-standing policy of neutrality. It sent unarmed peacekeeping troops to Kosovo in 1999 as part of a humanitarian action, but remained totally neutral when NATO attacked Serbia and Montenegro in the same year without a UN mandate. Even with a UN mandate, Switzerland will only allow transit rights for humanitarian reasons.

A referendum in 2001 approved two important changes to the Swiss military's role. Firstly, it allowed troops to be armed while on international peacekeeping duties; the first time this was put into action was in Kosovo in 2002. Secondly, it permitted Swiss troops to become a part of joint military training exercises with other nations.

Tourism – the Lure of Alpine Peaks

Swiss tourism was begun by affluent British mountaineers who discovered the peaks of the Bernese Oberland, and other ranges, in the early 19th century. Although it was the Swiss Meyer brothers who first climbed the majestic Jungfrau and the Finsteraarhorn, in 1811 and 1812 respectively, the so-called Golden Age of Alpinism, from 1854 to 1865, saw British mountaineers, often with Swiss and French guides, conquer many major alpine summits. Most notably, **Alfred Will**, who climbed the Wetterhorn in 1854 and, in 1865, **Edward Whymper's** ill-fated success at the Matterhorn, in which three noted British climbers and a guide perished.

In 1857, leading British alpinists gathered in London and formed the **Alpine Club**, which became the world's first mountaineering club and also somewhat of a gentlemen's club. This is not surprising really considering that most of the British alpinists were upper-class, well educated and wealthy.

This era was followed by what is now known as the Silver Age of Alpinism, from 1865 to 1882, when many of the peaks left unclimbed from the Golden Age were ascended, often by Britons. The fact that Queen Victoria holidayed in Luzern in 1868 further enhanced the country's appeal.

In addition, the alpine climate was considered especially helpful to those afflicted with tuberculosis and through the early part of the 20th century people coming to Switzerland to convalesce formed another aspect of tourism.

Infrastructure Development

Such tourism called for the development of a suitable infrastructure. Beginning in the mid-19th century, the building of suitable hotels and mountain huts began as

Sir Arthur Conan Doyle

Doyle made his mark on the Bernese Oberland in two, quite different, ways. Firstly, he orchestrated the demise of his fictional hero, Sherlock Holmes, at the Reichenbach Falls in Meiringen in 1893. Secondly, a year later, he was the first Englishman to take part in alpine skiing.

did mountain transportation construction, in what was a difficult environment. By the late 1800s many mountain train lines had been developed and opened including those at **Pilatus** (*see* p.180) in 1889, the **Gornergrat** (*see* p.257) in 1898 and, most incredibly, the **Jungfraubahn** that leads up through the inside of the Eiger to Jungfraujoch, the highest train station in Europe (*see* p.153). It was also necessary to vastly improve transalpine communications and in the same era the **Gotthard Rail Tunnel** and the **Simplon Tunnel** were opened. During the 10-year construction of the Gotthard Tunnel 200 workers were killed.

Sir Henry Simpson Lunn (1859–1939), founder of Lunn Poly, one of the UK's largest travel companies, played his part in the development of tourism in Switzerland. He organized the first educational tours, formed the **British Public Schools Alpine Sports Club** in 1905 and three years later founded the **Alpine Ski Club**, another gentlemen's organization.

Such affluent visitors needed to be provided with accommodation of a standard that would be acceptable to them and, with typical Swiss attention to detail, grand and illustrious hotels opened their doors, not just in the mountain villages but also in the cities. In many instances these establishments took advantage of the natural hot-water springs and incorporated spas.

These hotels offered then, as they do today, the highest levels of comfort, excellent restaurants and an array of facilities in which visitors could indulge. The other important factor they offered was continuity. Many of the hotels were family-run by generation after generation and often guests would return annually, comforted by the fact that they could take the same room and that the same table would be reserved for them at breakfast, lunch and dinner. This level of service continues in many hotels to this day.

Railway communications were extended all over the country and were fully electrified as early as the 1950s. These rail lines formed the basis of the integrated **Swiss Travel System** (*see* p.45), which is still the envy of the world.

Nevertheless, what can be termed 'mass tourism' didn't begin until well after the Second World War. Even as late as the mid-1960s what are now internationally recognized resorts, such as Grindelwald (*see* p.147), were just small villages.

A Country For All Seasons

Mountain resorts realized that they could appeal in summertime too and started developing new attractions. In 1927 the first aerial cable car opened at **Mont Blanc**. The resorts competed with each other to develop unusual attractions and, as a

Swiss Luxury

Switzerland is famed worldwide for its luxurious hospitality and this is reflected in the fact that there are, in this small country, over 120 5-star hotels. This is about one for every 65,000 people – one of the highest ratios, if not the highest, in the world.

result, no two places offer the same facilities. Wherever possible cable cars etc. were developed to take visitors to elevations where skiing is possible year-round. A perfect example of this is in **Zermatt**, where the Klein Matterhorn combination of gondola/cable cars (*see* p.257) is the highest in Europe. Nearby, **Saas-Fee** does things a little differently, using a combination of cable car and funicular inside a mountain to take visitors to the highest revolving restaurant in the world (*see* p.252). Other places developed unusual cable cars – **Samnaun** (*see* p.301) offers a double-decker cable car and **Engelberg** has the Titlis Rotair (*see* p.183), which not only ascends to high peaks but has an interior that revolves as it does so. **Les Diablerets** has its own cable car attraction: its Glacier 3000 (*see* p.226) takes visitors up to an environment where you can take a snow bus across the glacier or ride on the world's highest bobsleigh track. Most famous, though, is the **Schilthorn Cableway** (*see* p.157), which leads up to the Piz Gloria revolving restaurant that featured so spectacularly in the James Bond movie *On Her Majesty's Secret Service*.

Having developed such an enviable infrastructure, the next thing to do was to attract visitors. Not content to just market itself to Europeans, Switzerland searched the world to find new guests, such as the Japanese. It continues to do so, with a concentrated effort being made to attract the Chinese to these amazingly attractive alpine playgrounds.

The marketing people are also trying to attract visitors from India. This is because a number of Bollywood movies are shot on location in the Bernese Oberland due to the fact that filming in Kashmir (where previously many Bollywood movies were made) is now incredibly difficult because of the dispute over this region between India and Pakistan. So Indian visitors are being encouraged to visit Switzerland to see where their favourite films were made. There is even a Bollywood restaurant, decorated with numerous movie posters, at **Jungfraujoch** (*see* p.153).

Switzerland has not come by its excellent reputation for hospitality without much hard work and setting consistently high standards in everything it does. And, having such an enviable infrastructure, it doesn't easily change its successful format for tourism. In fact, change is slow here, and that's one of its most important attributes as visitors can return, time and time again, safe in the knowledge that they are guaranteed levels of unsurpassed comfort and familiarity.

Woodcarving Tradition

Woodcarving in Switzerland has traditionally been centred in the Bernese Oberland, specifically the village of **Brienz**, located at the eastern end of the pretty lake of the same name. This craft, the least-known aspect of Brienz's fame for tourists, dates back to the early Middle Ages when the combination of long, dark, winter nights and a plentiful supply of suitable Linden wood encouraged the citizens to practise the art of woodcarving. It wasn't until the early 19th century, however, that a man called **Christian Fischer** (1790–1848) started selling carved bowls and figures of animals and people to tourists, mainly the British. Fischer started local schools, encouraging young people to take up carving, and by the time of the 1851 and 1859 international fairs in London, Brienz woodcarvings had become world famous.

Today, the most famous name for woodcarvings is **Huggler Woodcarvings**, (*www.huggler-woodcarvings.ch*). The origins of this famous family-run company date back to **Kaspar Huggler** (1806–46), who started his career in the workshop of Christian Fischer. He passed his skills down to his son, **Johann Huggler** (1834–1912), who not only started the company but became known as the 'king of woodcarvers' in Brienz and whose surviving carvings of statues and groups are revered to this day.

In 1915 it was Johann's son, **Hans Huggler** (1877–1947), after studying at the Academy of Art in Munich, who introduced what is still one of Huggler's bestsellers: Christmas nativity scenes based on 'real' people of that era in Brienz. These days, more than 10 master carvers and their apprentices, who undertake a four-year course, take great pride and infinite care in producing genuinely hand-carved images out of solid blocks of wood that are astounding in their detail. What's more, as trends change they are encouraged to use their creativity to produce new designs that are becoming more modern.

Since 1884 Brienz has also been home to the **School for Wood Sculpture** (*www.holzbildhauerei.ch*), the only school of its kind in Switzerland for woodcarving. Operated by the canton of Bern since 1928, this offers comprehensive basic and advanced training that leads to a masters diploma.

Cuckoo Clocks

Brienz is also home to cuckoo-clock creators working for **Lötscher** (*www.loetscher.ch*), which was founded in 1920 and to this day is the only genuine brand of Swiss cuckoo clock in the world. (It is important here to distinguish between the colourful chalets made by Lötscher and the generally dark-brown and much more bland-looking cuckoo clocks from the Black Forest in Germany.) The clocks are made using Linden wood that has been aged for three years. This is an expensive process but ensures that the wood will not crack in humid or dry air. All of the pieces of these lovely clocks, typically either of a Brienzer or Emmenthaler chalet, are hand-made and hand-carved. The individual parts are then shipped to a factory near Zürich to be assembled, with a mechanical movement that is chain-driven in either a one- or eight-day cycle with a cuckoo call, gong strike and different melodies on the half-hour and hour. Lötscher doesn't have any retail outlets of its own, but its clocks are sold at Huggler stores and throughout Switzerland.

Food and Drink

04

Eating Out

Switzerland, with the exception of Ticino, more or less follows the eating habits of other northern European countries. Hotels usually serve breakfast – often in sumptuous buffet form – from around 7am to 10.30am; lunch is taken between midday and 2pm and dinner starts early, often at 6.30–7pm. That meal is usually a starter, main course and dessert – with the latter offering a choice between a trolley of mouthwatering desserts or amazing cheese selections.

Restaurants come in all shapes and sizes, from serious Michelin-starred ones down to mountain huts that only open between March and October. At the top of the range, few countries can better Switzerland, and such restaurants, either independent or as an integral part of hotels, offer opulence, service that is second to none and the most beautifully prepared and presented dishes. All of this, though, comes at a price. There are organizations, such as Les Grandes Tables de Suisse, *www.grandestables.ch*, and Relais & Chateaux, *www.relaischateaux.ch*, that promote such restaurants. Switzerland has produced some **world-famous chefs**, such as Anton Mosimann, and the country also attracts young chefs anxious to make their mark in their own particular culinary styles; these can be found on the Jeunes Restaurateurs d'Europe website, *www.jre.net*.

Besides these, you can find almost any type of restaurant in the major cosmopolitan **cities** of Basel, Geneva, Zürich and Luzern, with a wide range recommended in the respective chapters. In other places the selection will be much more limited, with regional specialities, lake fish such as perch and the usual cheese dishes being the order of the day.

On the other hand, the **mountain restaurants** (*bergrestaurants*) usually don't have any competition, and the dishes are more than likely to be fondue, raclette and *rösti*, with the occasional plate of dried meat as a worthy and tasty alternative. The smallest types of restaurant are the '**mountain huts**', charming places full of ambience that are usually only open outside the winter months and only locally known. Although the menu is invariably limited, the dishes are wholesome, home-cooked and delightful.

Ticino

As usual, things are different in Ticino, the Italian-speaking canton south of the Alps. The cuisine is heavily influenced by the northern Italian regions of Lombardy and Piedmont, with dinner being an appetizer (*antipasto*), followed by a first course (*primo*), most often pasta, and a second course (*secondo*), usually a meat dish. The meal culminates with cheese then a dessert, possibly *torta di pane* (a bread cake) or *torta della nonna* (a sugar tart), often ending with a *grappa* or *nocino*, a walnut-based liqueur.

The local restaurants are rather different, too, with *osterie*, *canvetti* and grottos being popular. All are simple restaurants with the last usually consisting of a simple kitchen and a small dining room, often with tables outside in the garden, featuring local produce.

Menu Reader

English	German	French	Italian
Breakfast			
Bacon	*Speck*	*Bacon*	*Bacon*
Cereals	*Getreideflocken*	*Céréales*	*Fiocchi di ceriali*
Eggs	*Eier*	*Oeufs*	*Uova*
Fried Eggs	*Setzeier*	*Oeufs poêlés*	*Uova al tegame*
Jam	*Konfitüre*	*Confiture*	*Confettura*
Sugar	*Zucker*	*Sucre*	*Zucchero*
Salads			
Caesar salad	*Cäsarsalat*	*Salade César*	*Insalata alla Cesare*
Green salad	*Grüner Salat*	*Salade verte*	*Insalata verde*
Mixed salad	*Gemischter Salat*	*Salade mâlée*	*Insalata mista*
Meats			
Chicken	*Huhn*	*Poulet*	*Pollo*
Duck	*Ente*	*Canard*	*Anitra*
Ham	*Schinken*	*Jambon*	*Prosciutto*
Sirloin steak	*Entrecote*	*Entrecôte*	*Costata di manzo*
Fillet Steak	*Filetsteak*	*Filet grille*	*Bistecca di filetto*
Rabbit	*Kaninchen*	*Lapin*	*Coniglio*
Roast beef	*Ochsenbraten*	*Rôti de boeuf*	*Arrosto di manzo*
Roast lamb	*Lammbraten*	*Rôti d'agneau*	*Arrosta d'agnello*
Roast pork	*Schweinsbraten*	*Rôti de porc*	*Arrosto di maiale*
Turkey	*Truthahn*	*Dinde*	*Tacchino*
Veal cutlet	*Kalbskotelett*	*Côte de veau*	*Costoletta di vitello*
Venison	*Rehkotelett*	*Chevreuil*	*Capriolo*
Fish and Shellfish			
Calamari	*Kalmare*	*Calmars*	*Calamari*
Cod	*Kabeljau*	*Cabillaud*	*Merluzzo*
Crab	*Taschenkrebs*	*Tourteau*	*Granciporro*
Fillet of Sole	*Seezungenfilets*	*Filets de sole*	*Filetti di sogliola*
Lobster	*Hummer*	*Homard*	*Astice*
Mussels	*Miesmuscheln*	*Moules*	*Cozze*
Octopus	*Krake*	*Poulpe*	*Polpo*
Oysters	*Austern*	*Huîtres*	*Ostriche*
Plaice	*Scholle*	*Carrelet*	*Platessa*
Prawns	*Hummerkrabben*	*Crevettes*	*Gamberi imperiale*
Salmon	*Lachs*	*Saumon*	*Salmone*
Scallops	*Jakobsmuscheln*	*Coquilles St Jacques*	*Conchiglie dei pellegrini*
Seafood	*Meeresfrüchte*	*Fruits de mer*	*Frutti di mare*
Shrimps	*Garnelen*	*Crevettes*	*Gamberetti*
Sole	*Seezunge*	*Sole*	*Sogliola*
Swordfish	*Schwertfisch*	*Espadon*	*Pesce spada*
Trout	*Forelle*	*Truite*	*Trota*
Tuna	*Thunfisch*	*Thon*	*Tonno*
Turbot	*Steinbutt*	*Turbot*	*Rombo*
Vegetables			
Asparagus	*Spargel*	*Asperges*	*Asparagi*
Assorted vegetables	*Gemüseplatte*	*Légumes variés*	*Verdure assortite*

English	German	French	Italian
Boiled potatoes	Salzkartoffein	Pommes à l'anglaise	Patate lesse
Broccoli	Brokkoli	Brocolis	Broccoli
Carrots	Karotten	Carottes	Carote
Cucumbers	Gurken	Concombres	Cetrioli
Green peas	Erbsen	Petits pois	Piselli
Lettuce	Kopfsalat	Laitues	Lattughe
Mixed vegetables	Mischgemüse	Macédoine de légumes	Macedonia de legumbres
Mushrooms	Kaiserlinge	Champignons	Ovoli
New potatoes	Neue Kartoffein	Pommes nouvelles	Patate novelle
Onions	Zweiben	Oignons	Cipolle
Roast potatoes	Geröstete	Pommes rôties	Patate arrosto
Spinach	Spinat	Épinards	Spinaci
Tomatoes	Tomaten	Tomates	Pomodori

Desserts

Apple pie	Apfelpie	Pie aux pommes	Torta di mele
Apple strudel	Apfelstrudel	Strudel aux pommes	Srudel di mele
Assorted pastries	Auswahl an Backwerk	Pâtisserie assortie	Pasticceria assortita
Cake	Torte	Gâteau	Torta
Fruit salad	Obstsalat	Fruits rafraîchis	Macedonia di frutta
Ice cream	Sahneeis	Glace à la crème	gelato de crema
Rice pudding	Reisauflauf	Gâteau de riz	Dolce di riso
Rumbaba	Baba mit rum	Baba au rhum	Babà al rum
Vanilla ice cream	Vanille-Eis	Glace à la vanille	Gelato di vaniglia

Fruit

Apple	Apfel	Pomme	Mela
Apricot	Aprikose	Abricot	Albicocca
Banana	Banane	Banane	Banana
Grapefruit	Grapefruit	Pamplemousse	Pompelmo
Grapes	Trauben	Raisins	Uva
Lemon	Zitrone	Citron	Limone
Orange	Apfelsine	Orange	Arancia
Peach	Pfirsich	Pêche	Pesca
Pear	Birne	Poire	Pere
Pineapple	Ananas	Ananas	Ananas
Strawberry	Erdbeere	Fraise	Fragola
Watermelon	Wassermelone	Melon d'eau	Cocomero

Bread-related

Cheese sandwich	Käsebrot	Sandwich au fromage	Panino al formaggio
Ham sandwich	Schinkenbrot	Sandwich au jambon	Panino al prosciutto
Roll	Semmel	Petit pain	Panino
Rye bread	Roggenbrot	Pain de seigle	Pane di segale
Sandwich	Sandwich	Sandwich	Panino
Slice of bread	Brotschnitte	Tranche de pain	Fetta di pane
Toast	Röstbrot	Toast	Pane tostato

Alcoholic Drinks

Beer	Bier	Bière	Birra
Bottled beer	Flaschenbier	Bière en bouteilles	Birra in bottiglia
Liqueur	Likör	Liqueur	Liquore
Local wine	Landwein	Vin de pays	Vino nostrano
Red wine	Rotwein	Vin rouge	Vino rosso

English	German	French	Italian
Table wine	Tischwein	Vin de table	Vino da pasto
White wine	Weissewein	Vin blanc	Vino bianco
Non-alcoholic Drinks			
Cappuccino	Cappuccino	Cappuccino	Cappuccino
Coffee	Kaffee	Café	Caffè
Coffee (black)	Kaffee Schwarzer	Café noir	Cafè nero
Coffee (milk)	Milchkaffee	Café au lait	Caffelatte
Fruit juice	Fruchtsaft	Jus de fruits	Succo di frutta
Ice	Eis	Glace	Ghiaccio
Lemonade	Limonade	Citronnade	Limonata
Milk	Milch	Lait	Latte
Mineral water	Mineralwasser	Eau minérale	Acqua minerale
Tea	Tee	Thé	Tè
Water	Wasser	Eau	Acqua
General Terms			
Bill (check)	Rechnung	Addition	Conto
Breakfast	Frühstück	Petit déjeuner	Prima colazione
Lunch	Mittagessen	Déjeuner	Colazione
Dinner	Abendessen	Diner	Pranzo
Dining room	Speisesaal	Sale à manger	Sala da pranzo
Glass	Glas	Verre	Bicchiere

Swiss Specialities

Owing to its native French, German and Italian influences – not to mention the cultural influx from around the world in places like Zürich and Geneva – Switzerland has a wide and interesting range of gastronomic tastes.

In most places, outside Ticino, **fondue** and **raclette** melted cheese dishes are popular, as is *rösti* – the Swiss version of hash brown potatoes often found in combination with sausages or the like. Certain **regions** also have their own favourites: fillet of perch and lake trout around Geneva; local sausage on a bed of leeks and potatoes in Lausanne; in Bern look for smoked pork, sausage and *sauerkraut*; minced veal in cream sauce and *rösti* is a favourite in Zürich; and the Italian-style cuisine of polenta, risotto and pasta can be found in Ticino. In the larger cities Spanish restaurants are surprisingly popular. It should not come as a surprise, either, that the presence of the United Nations and other international organizations in Geneva has benefited that city with numerous restaurants offering cuisine from around the world.

Cheese

Switzerland is, of course, famous for its cheeses, and more than 450 varieties are produced in the country. Cheesemaking is a major industry in Switzerland because 80 per cent of the cultivated land is not suitable for arable farming and it is therefore used to graze livestock. This has led to centuries of cheesemaking traditions where, even today, more than 1,200 village dairies are still in operation.

Altogether, just about half the milk produced in Switzerland is made into cheese. Cows' milk is used to make about 99 per cent of all the cheeses produced, the rest comes from sheep and goats' milk. What's more, Swiss cheese is made without the addition of any artificial additives.

Swiss cheese can be broken down into the following categories:

Extra hard and **hard**: Sbrinz – sometimes claimed to be the oldest European cheese, Emmentaler, Gruyères.

Semi-hard: Valais raclette, Appenzeller, Vacherin Fribourgeois.

Soft: produced from pasteurized milk and can be broken down into two sub-categories; **soft mould-ripened**, such as Brie, Camembert, Tomme, and **smear soft**, such as Reblochon, Münster and Limburger.

Cream cheese: cottage cheese, Mozzarella.

You can watch the cheesemaking process in action at certain dairies, such as those in Engelberg (see p.185) and Gruyères (see p.225).

Chocolate

Unlike with cheese, there is not an obvious answer as to why Swiss chocolate has become so famous worldwide. It certainly doesn't have the tropical climate necessary for growing cocoa, neither has it ever had any colonies in Africa or South America that do.

Columbus had recognized that the Mayas used cocoa beans to make a drink – but only for the aristocratic males – and as a currency. Hernando Cortes, the conquistador of the Aztecs, first brought the beans back to Europe in around 1528. In the early 17th century, French royalty brought cocoa back to their country, where it became a status symbol due to its cost, and from there its use gradually spread throughout the rest of Europe.

It wasn't until the then mayor of Zürich, Heinrich Escher, brought it back from Brussels in 1697 that it came to Switzerland, but even then it was only used by the influential guilds until the city council banned it early in the next century. Some time later, Italians introduced the drink to the general population of the country and by 1750 the first chocolate factory opened in what used to be a paper mill close to Bern. The fact that it used to be a paper mill is significant, as chocolate manufacturing at that time needed plenty of fast-flowing water to power the machinery. These conditions were plentiful in the country. Another advantage Switzerland had, and has, is that its central position in Europe places it at the crossroads of trade routes.

It wasn't until 1792 that the first chocolate shop opened, and that was in Bern. Thirty-three years later, in 1825, the oldest factory still in operation was opened near Vevey, on the shores of Lake Geneva, by **François-Louis Cailler**. Having learnt the business in Italy, he was the first to invent the process of making chocolate into bars. Keeping it in the family, his son-in-law, **Daniel Peter**, also made his mark on the business by creating milk chocolate.

A better-known name, **Philippe Suchard**, started production in the 19th century when chocolate was still an expensive item. He set about improving production methods. So much so, that in 1851 at the Great Exhibition in London, and at the Paris Universal Exhibition four years later, his chocolate won gold medals. By the early 1880s his business was so efficient that he produced half of all chocolate in Switzerland and, finally, chocolate became more affordable.

Around this time **Rodolphe Lindt** opened a factory in Bern and he introduced further manufacturing advances. In 1899 Lindt sold his business to Rudolf Sprüngli, whose shop is still going strong in Zürich (*see* p.66). In the same year, **Tobler**, famous for the Toblerone bar, opened his factory, also in Bern.

These days most of the major brands, with the exception of Lindt-Sprüngli, are owned by large conglomerates.

Drinks

Wine is one of Switzerland's best-kept secrets (see *www.swisswine.ch*), and it's not surprising, as it is estimated that 95 per cent of the production is consumed in the country itself.

The long, narrow Valais, with over 13,000 acres (5,250ha) and 20,000 growers and 700 winemakers, is the most productive region, producing a third of the country's output. It has a diverse range of grapes, with the red Dôle and white Fendant being the most popular. Humagne is one of the more classic red wines; it also comes in a very tasty white vintage, and the white Petite Arvine is particularly fine. The area around Geneva is home to a variety of both red and white wines, in about equal quantities. Its neighbour to the north, the Neuchâtel and three lakes region, produces Pinot Noir reds, a tasty rosé and the most well-known white wines come from the Chasselas grapes. The Vaud, between Geneva and the Valais, produces a quarter of Switzerland's wines and has 26 different appellations of origin including the famous Dézaley, dating back to the medieval Cistercian monks. Ticino and the more popular Aigle vintages, in the south, have 90 per cent of their vineyards planted with Merlot, but be sure to try the increasingly popular Merlot Blanco. German Switzerland, roughly speaking from Basel, Zürich, Schaffhausen, St Gallen

Buying Alcohol

Even in the larger cities, trying to buy alcoholic drinks to take away outside of the regular shopping hours, especially on Saturday afternoons and all day Sunday, is very difficult. However, one company has taken advantage of a loophole in shopping restrictions that allow shops to open every day, and long hours too, if they are part of a railway station complex. Accordingly, **Drinks of the World**, *www.beerworld.ch*, has shops in the RailCity complexes in Basel, Bern, Luzern and Zürich, which are open daily 9am–10pm. The stores sell the widest selection of beers – both national and international – to be found in Switzerland, and also a good selection of wines and spirits, all at competitive prices.

and across to Graubünden, grows 75 per cent Pinot Noir grapes, with the whites mainly Riesling-Sylvaner.

Swiss **beer**, generally, is of the lager variety. Feldschlösschen, owned by Carlsberg, is the largest brewer with its own-name brand, and is far and away the leading selling beer with 24 per cent of the market. The company also owns Cardinal, with a market share of 11 per cent, and other regional brands such as Gurten, Hürlimann and Valaisanne. Regionally, Appenzeller lays claim to an ever-growing number of less commercial tastes. In the larger cities brewery-pubs are now making a showing, with their own esoteric beers.

Those wanting something more potent should try the famous **liqueurs** such as Marc, Kirsch, Pflümli and Williamine, some of which are used to strengthen fondues.

Planning Your Trip

05

When to Go

In terms of cost, the price of accommodation in towns and cities tends to stay reasonably constant throughout the year. However, the ski resorts operate on a seasonal basis. High season is Christmas and New Year, and February to mid-April. Low season is early December to before Christmas, January after New Year and late April.

Some hotels/transportation links/attractions are only open at certain times of the year, so make sure you check before you travel.

Climate

For such a small country, Switzerland has an extremely diverse climate. In July it might reach 96°F (36°C) at low levels of altitude yet be snowing at 10,000ft (3,000m); equally, in early October it might be snowing heavily in the west in Graubünden yet be quite pleasant in Basel on the eastern side of the country. It can be warm and pleasant in cities like Zürich as early in the year as March and in the middle of winter at snow- and ice-covered skiing resorts the sun can be surprisingly hot.

Quite simply, whenever and wherever you go in Switzerland you are likely to encounter many climate changes. That said, in the summer months at lower altitudes it is likely to be pretty warm during the day; in the skiing resorts you can expect a good covering of snow and ice through to the end of March.

Weather forecasts can be checked on www.meteoswiss.admin.ch, the Swiss weather organization, and average snow condition information can be found on www.my switzerland.com and regional/resort websites.

Packing

With such a variable climate, you need to be well prepared. During spring, summer and autumn it is best to take a mix of clothes, including a warm jacket for excursions to the tops of mountains. In winter, much warmer attire is required, especially a waterproof jacket, warm trousers, hat, gloves, scarf, etc. At any time of the year you will need good walking shoes, preferably hiking boots. A backpack is useful too; as with hiking boots, the selection in Switzerland is far better than elsewhere.

Whatever time of year you visit you need to protect yourself from the sun. Be sure to take sunscreen, sunglasses and an appropriate hat.

Calendar of Events

Late January

Cartier Polo World Cup on Snow, St Moritz, www.polostmoritz.com. The top polo teams from four continents battle it out on the frozen lake at glittering St Moritz.

February/March

Carnival in Basel, Luzern and Zürich. A time when the Swiss become distinctly un-Swiss; strange and fantastic masks and costumes complement carnival musicians (Guggenmusigen) making as much noise as they can while people dance away the winter.

Late March to early April

Luzern Festival Ostern, www.lucernefestival.ch. A festival of sacred and concert music, with events held in the city's churches and the Concert Hall of the Culture and Convention Centre.

Mid-June

Art 34, Basel, www.artbasel.com. Considered one of the leading art events in the world, with galleries from Europe, America, Asia and Australia presenting art from the 20th and 21st centuries.

Late June to early July

New Orleans Jazz, Ascona, www.jazzascona.ch. One of Switzerland's most famous jazz festivals. It features the world's top artists and takes over the beautiful lakefront of this lovely town.

Early to mid-July

Montreux Jazz Festival, www.montreux jazz.com. This annual festival mixes jazz, blues, rock, reggae and soul with Brazilian and African sounds, including 300 free concerts.

Mid-August to mid-September

Luzern Festival, www.lucernefestival.ch. Nearing its 70th year, this is a festival of classical music that features the world's most famous orchestras, conductors and soloists.

Early September

Omega European Masters, Crans-Montana, www.omegaeuropeanmasters.com. One of the major tournaments on the PGA European Tour, this golf event takes place at 4,921ft (1,500m) with views of Mont Blanc and the Matterhorn.

Mid-September

Knabenschiessen, Zürich, www.knaben-schiessen.ch. One of Zürich's oldest festivals and Switzerland's largest fair.

Tourist Information

Switzerland Tourism, *www.myswitzerland.com*, operates the following offices:

In the UK and Ireland

Switzerland Tourism, 30 Bedford Street, London WC2E 9ED, **t** (freephone) 00800 100 200 30, *info.uk@myswitzerland. com*.

In North America

USA

Swiss Center, 608 Fifth Avenue, New York, New York 10020 **t** (toll free) 011800 100 200 30, *info.usa@myswitzerland.com*.

Canada

926 The East Mall, Toronto, Ontario M9B 6K1, **t** (toll free) 1 800 794 7795, *info.caen@my switzerland.com*.

Obviously if you plan to take part in specific activities such as skiing etc., you will need to make sure that you pack the appropriate clothing and equipment.

Festivals

Switzerland is a country of numerous and colourful festivals, religious, cultural and local. Information on these celebrations can be found at *www.myswitzerland.com* and *www.kadmusarts.com*, for musical and art festivals.

Consulates and Embassies

In the UK

Swiss Embassy

16–18 Montagu Place, London W1H 2BQ, **t** (020) 7616 6000, *www.eda.admin.ch/london_emb*.

Consulates General

c/o Thorburn & Co. Ltd., Church House, Deansgate, Manchester, M3 2GP, **t** (0161) 330 033.

255C Colinton Road, Edinburgh EH14 1DW **t** (0131) 441 4044.

8 The Horse Park, Boneybefore, Carrickfergus, County Antrim BT38 7ED, **t** 2890 32 16 26.

PO Box 368, Helvetia Court, South Esplanade, St Peter Port, Guernsey, **t** 1481 710267.

In the USA

Swiss Embassy

2900 Cathedral Avenue NW, Washington, D.C., 20008-3499, **t** (202) 745 7900, *www.swissemb.org*.

Consulates General

1349 West Peachtree Street, NE Suite 1000, Atlanta, Georgia 30309-3555, **t** (404) 870 2000, *vertretung@atl.rep.admin.ch*.

737 N. Michigan Avenue, Suite 2301, Olympia Center, Chicago, Illinois 60611-2615, **t** (312) 915 4500, *chi.vertretung@eda. admin.ch*.

Wells Fargo Plaza, 1000 Louisiana, Suite 5670, Houston, Texas 77002-5013, **t** (713) 650 0000, *vertretung@chi.rep.admin.ch*.

11766 Wilshire Boulevard, Suite 1400, Los Angeles, California 90025, **t** (310) 575 1145, *los.vertretung@eda.admin.ch*.

633 Third Avenue, 30th Floor, New York, New York, 10017-6706, **t** (212) 599 5700, *nyc.vertretung@eda.admin.ch*.

456 Montgomery Street, Suite 1500, San Francisco, California 94104 **t** (415) 788 2272, *sfa.vertretung@eda.admin.ch*.

In Canada

Swiss Embassy

5 Marlborough Avenue, Ottawa, Ontario K1N 8E6, **t** (613) 235 1837, *www.eda-admin.ch/canada*.

Consulates General

1572 Dr Penfield, Montreal, Quebec H3G 1C4, **t** (514) 932 7181, *mon.vertretung@eda.admin.ch*.

154 University Avenue, Suite 601, Toronto, Ontario M5H 3Y9, **t** (416) 593 5371, *tor.vertretung@eda.admin.ch*.

790–999 Canada Place, Vancouver, British Columbia V6C 3E1, **t** (604) 684 2231, *van.vertretung@eda.admin.ch*.

In Switzerland

UK Embassy

Thunsstrasse 50, 3000, Bern 15, **t** 031 359 7700, *www.ukinswitzerland.fco.gov.uk*.

UK Consulates General

Mrs Sue Kinoshita, Avenue Louis Casai 58, 1216 Cointrin, Geneva, t 022 918 2400, info@britishembassy.ch.

UK Vice Consulates

Dr Alan Chalmers, Gewerbestrasse 14, Innovation Centre, 4123 Allschwil, Basel t 061 483 0977, basel@british-vice-consulate.ch.

Mrs Sandra Darra MBE, Montreux-Vevey, t 021 943 3263.

Mr Peter Steimie, Via Pretorio 22, 6900 Lugano, t 091 950-0606, lugano@british-vice-consulate.ch.

Mr Andrew Bushnell, rue des Fontaines, 3974 Mollens, Valais, t 027 480 3210, sion@british-vice-consulate.ch.

Mr Antony McCammon, Hegibachstrasse 47, 8032 Zürich, t 01 383 6560, zurich@british-vice-consulate.ch.

US Embassy

Sulgeneckstrasse 19, 3007 Bern, t 031 357 7011, http://bern.usembassy.gov.

US Consulates General and Agencies

US Consular Agency, c/o US Mission, 11, rte de Prégny, 1292 Chambésy, Geneva, t 022 840 5160, Geneva-CA@state.gov.

US Consular Agency, Dufourstrasse 101, Zürich, t 01 422 2566, zurich-CA@state.gov.

Canadian Embassy

Kirchenfeldstrasse 88, 3005 Bern, t 031 357 3200, bern@international.gc.ca.

Entry Formalities

For citizens of Europe, the American continent, Australia, New Zealand and Japan visas are not required (exceptions may apply) for visits of less than three months.

A valid passport is required, and must be valid for three months past the travelling dates.

Disabled Travellers

Switzerland is very user-friendly for disabled visitors. Stations and trains are always being improved to include lifts, ramps and wheelchair-accessible toilets, and wheelchair-bound passengers can use the trains if the wheelchair is not larger than 2.3ft (70cm) wide, 3.93ft (120cm) long and 3.6ft (109cm) high. On all Intercity and most EuroCity and fast trains special wheelchair compartments are available in 2nd class; on older trains space will be available in the luggage carriage.

If you give notice at least 1 hour before the train leaves (call toll-free t 0800 00 71 02 and be present on the designated platform at least 10 minutes before departure), the wheelchair will be raised into the train by a

Useful Contacts

Access Travel, 6 The Hillock, Astley, Lancashire M29 7GW, t (01942) 888844, www.access-travel.co.uk. Travel agent for disabled people: special air fares and car hire.

Alternative Leisure Co., 165 Middlesex Turnpike, Suite 206, Bedford, MA 01730, t (718) 275 0023, www.alctrips.com. Holidays abroad for disabled people.

COMPAGNA, Lutherstrasse 20, 8004 Zürich, t 044 240 08 58, www.compagna.ch. A volunteer organization that will, for reasonable rates, pick up passengers at stations and accompany them if required.

Emerging Horizons, www.emerginghorizons.com. International on-line travel newsletter for people with disabilities.

Mobilise, Ashwellthorpe, Norwich NR16 1EX, t (01508) 489 449, www.mobilise.info. Assistance for those travelling by car from the UK.

Mobility International USA, 132 E. Broadway, Suite 343, Eugene, OR 97401, t/TTY (541) 343 1284, www.miusa.org. Information on international educational exchange programmes and volunteer service overseas.

RADAR (Royal Association for Disability and Rehabilitation), 12 City Forum, 250 City Road, London EC1V 8AF, t (020) 7250 3222, www.radar.org.uk. Information and books on travel.

SATH (Society for Accessible Travel and Hospitality), 347 Fifth Avenue, Suite 605, New York NY 10016, t (212) 447 7284, www.sath.org. Travel and access information; also details other access resources on the web.

Schweizerische Paraplegiker Vereinigung (Swiss Paraplegic Association), Kantonsstrasse 40, 6207 Nottwill, Switzerland, t 041 939 5400, www.spv.ch. Offers advice about car hire for the disabled.

Mobilift, which are available at more than 150 stations. Guide dogs travel free.

Hotels and certain restaurants with special features for the disabled are marked with a wheelchair symbol in the Swiss Hotel Guide, which is available from the Swiss tourist authorities. Alternatively, check *www.swiss hotels.ch*, and then click on 'hotels' in the navigation bar and then 'hotel guide'. By checking the field 'suitable for wheelchairs', the system will then list all suitable properties.

Health, Insurance and EHIC Card

Up-to-date health and vaccination advice for travellers to Switzerland can be found on the following websites: in the UK, *www.fco.gov.uk* and *www.nathnac.org*; in the USA, *www.cdc.gov/travel*; and in Canada, *www.hc-sc.gc.ca*. Make sure you consult these websites at least a couple of months before you are due to travel so that you can arrange for any vaccinations in time.

As there is not a state medical health service in Switzerland, medical treatment must be paid for – and it is expensive. Therefore, it is highly advisable to take out insurance cover against personal accident and sickness (you may be asked for proof of it before treatment) – as well as loss or damage to luggage and personal effects and cancellation charges. Note that if you plan to take part in certain sporting activities, such as skiing, snowboarding, etc., you need to make sure that your insurance covers you. The websites above have information on insurance.

UK residents should obtain a **European Health Insurance Card** (EHIC) before leaving the UK. Switzerland has an agreement with the EU, and the card entitles you to certain free and reduced-cost treatment. To obtain a card go to *www.ehic.org.uk*. For detailed information about what the card entitles you to see *www.nhs.uk*.

Maps and Publications

The maps in this guide are for orientation only; to explore in detail invest in a good, up-to-date map before you arrive. There are many online stores from which to obtain good maps or you can try the following shops:

Stanfords, 12–14 Long Acre, London WC2 9LP, t (020) 7836 1321, *www.stanfords.co.uk*.

The Travel Bookshop, 13 Blenheim Crescent, London W11 2EE, t (020) 7229 5260, *www.thetravelbookshop.com*.

Traveler's Choice Bookstore, 2 Wooster Street, New York, NY 10013, t (212) 941 1535.

Money and Banks

Switzerland is not a member of the European Union, and the Swiss franc (CHF) is the official currency, with 100 *centimes* equalling one franc. Notes come in denominations of CHF 10, 20, 50, 100, 200 and 1,000. Coins come in denominations of 5, 10, 20 and 50 *centimes* (half-franc) and CHF 1, 2 and 5.

Banks are usually open Monday–Friday 8.30–4.30pm, but once a week they usually extend these hours. Traveller's cheques and Eurocheques are widely accepted in Switzerland, credit cards are accepted more or less everywhere and ATM machines are prevalent throughout the country.

Getting There

By Air

From both the UK and the USA/Canada, many major scheduled national airlines, such as British Airways and Swiss, can whizz you straight to Geneva, Zürich and Basel. In addition, there are many budget airlines that operate services to Switzerland. It is important to note that no-frills airlines are not always the cheapest, above all on the very popular routes at peak times. One of the benefits of the no-frills revolution that is not always appreciated is not so much in their own prices but in the concessions they have forced on the older, mainstream carriers (British Airways, Swiss). It is always worth comparing no-frills prices with those of the main airlines.

Fly Rail Baggage and Check-In at the Train Station

Fly Rail Baggage greatly simplifies your journey into Switzerland. Your luggage can be registered from each airport worldwide, regardless of the carrier, to your destination in Switzerland. On the return journey, you can check-in your luggage at your train station of departure and pick it up again at the destination. What's more, over 35 train stations in Switzerland issue boarding passes.

By Car and Motorcycle

For travellers arriving by road, Switzerland is linked to Europe's extensive motorway network. You need to plan your route carefully and be clear about the kind of roads that you will be travelling on, as some of the mountain roads and passes are difficult to drive and are not recommended if you are not experienced in driving on these sorts of roads. It is important that you check the weather conditions prior to your departure and en route, as conditions can change quickly.

For information on the necessary licence, documentation, insurance and equipment needed to drive in Switzerland consult the motoring organizations: **AA**, *www.theaa.com*, or **RAC**, *www.rac.co.uk*, and **AAA**, *www.aaa.com*, in the USA. These websites will also provide information on the laws of the road in Switzerland. The **Swiss Touring Club**, *www.tsch.ch*, also provides this information (in German/French/Italian), along with up-to-date reports on road conditions, road closures, whether alpine passes are open (travel over many of the mountain passes is restricted to certain times of the year), etc.

See p.45 for more information on 'Getting Around By Car and Motorcycle'.

By Train

Eurostar and TGV Trains from Paris

Basel, Bern, Geneva and Zürich can be reached by first taking the **Eurostar**, *www.eurostar.com*, train from London St Pancras to Paris Gare du Nord. From there Bern and Geneva can be reached on a **TGV** service, *www.sncf.fr*, from Paris, Gare de Lyon; and from Paris Gare de l'Est, trains go to Basel and on to Zürich.

Tickets and rail passes can be purchased in the UK from **Rail Europe**, 1 Lower Regent Street, London, t 08448 484 064,

Airline Carriers
From the UK

Bmibaby, t 0905 8 28 28 28, *www.bmibaby.com*. From Birmingham, Cardiff, Manchester and East Midlands to Geneva.

British Airways, t 0844 493 0 787, *www.britishairways.com*. From Heathrow, Birmingham and Manchester to Geneva and Zürich, and from Heathrow to Basel.

easyJet, *www.easyjet.com*. From both Gatwick and Luton to Geneva and Zürich.

Flybe, t 0871 700 2000, *www.flybe.com*. From Southampton to Geneva.

Jet2, t 0871 226 1 737, *www.jet2.com*. From Leeds Bradford to Geneva.

Ryanair, *www.ryanair.com*. From Stansted to Basel.

Snowjet, t (020) 8652 1222, *www.snowjet.co.uk*. Seasonal flights from Stansted to Sion and Gatwick to Geneva.

Swiss, t 0845 601 0956, *www.swiss.com*. From Heathrow, Birmingham and Manchester to Geneva and Zürich, from Heathrow to Basel and from City Airport to Zürich.

From North America

Air Canada, *www.aircanada.ca*. From Toronto (Canada) to Zürich.

American Airlines, *www.aa.com*. From New York to Zürich.

Continental Airlines, *www.continental.com*. From New York (Newark) to Zürich.

Delta, *www.delta.com*. From Atlanta to Zürich.

Lufthansa, *www.lufthansa-usa.com*. From Boston, Chicago, Denver/Detroit, Los Angeles, San Francisco, Toronto (Canada), Vancouver (Canada) and Washington D.C. via Frankfurt to Basel, Geneva and Zürich.

Swiss, *www.swiss.com*. From Boston, Chicago, Los Angeles, Miami, Montreal (Canada), New York (Newark), Washington D.C. to Zürich and from Miami and New York (Newark) to Geneva.

www.raileurope.co.uk (open Mon–Fri 10–6 and Sat 10–4).

Tickets and rail passes can be purchased in North America from **Rail Europe, t** 1 877 257 2887 or 1 800 4-EURAIL in the USA and 1 800 361-RAIL in Canada, *www.raileurope.com*.

Many tickets and passes are also available through *www.myswitzerland.com*.

Getting Around

Switzerland is such a small country, and the transportation system so comprehensive and fast, that there will be few instances when travellers feel the need to fly between destinations in the country. While internal flights do operate, by the time you factor in waiting around at the airport etc., the train is often just as quick.

Swiss Travel System (STS)

This is a thoroughly integrated system that includes **train services**, the famed **postbus** system and a series of **boat services** on the beautiful Swiss lakes, which are all immaculately clean and punctual – regardless of the weather conditions. The trains run every hour, or even half hour, and connections are easy and, usually, only require a few minutes of changing time. More impressively, in this, the densest public transport system in the world, timetables are even coordinated to allow changes from one form of transport to another with the least possible delays.

See pp.46–7 for information on the train passes available.

The **Schweizerische Bundesbahnen, SBB** (Swiss Federal Railways), *www.sbb.ch*, has a marvellous website that allows you to plan trips – on trains, buses and even boats – confidently, even sometimes telling you what platform you need to be on.

The famous yellow **postbuses**, *www.postbus.ch*, with their distinctive horn sound, either connect with train services or operate where there are no train services. Tickets can usually be purchased on the bus, but sometimes it is necessary to reserve in advance. Consult the website.

By Car and Motorcycle

See p.44 'Getting There By Car and Motorcycle' for further information and for details of which websites to consult for information on driving in Switzerland (preparing your vehicle (if you are driving your own), necessary equipment, tolls, etc). There is also information for UK travellers on *www.fco.gov.uk* and in the US on *http://travel.state.gov*. Swiss traffic regulations are strictly enforced so it is vital that you are familiar with the laws and rules of the road.

Generally, car hire is expensive in Switzerland so you may be better off booking from home. Car hire companies with branches in Switzerland include **Avis**, *www.avis.ch*, **Europcar**, *www.europcar.ch* and **Hertz**, *www.hertz.ch*.

Petrol stations are typically open 8am–10pm. Outside of these hours, look for one of the many self-service stations, some of which accept credit cards but most of which take CHF 10 or CHF 20 notes. Petrol stations located away from major cities and towns are often closed on Sunday.

Bear in mind that some city/town centres and villages are car-free and often finding somewhere to park in city/town centres is extremely difficult and expensive.

By Bicycle

Cycling is extremely popular in Switzerland. Every region, town and city has cycle routes and there are nine long-distance routes that cross the country consisting of 3,300km of signposted paths that mostly keep you away from traffic. Tourist information offices can give you information and maps, and also see *www.veloland.ch*.

The **Swiss Cycling Federation** website, *www.cycling.ch*, gives details (in German only) of road regulations for cyclists and you should familiarize yourself with them. If you are taking your own bike with you it is advisable to buy a bicycle insurance sticker (*velo-vignette*), which costs about CHF 5 and is available at post offices, bicycle shops and other outlets. This covers you for third-party insurance and the sticker should be attached to the bicycle. This is not compulsory for tourists making occasional visits, but it is highly recommended.

It is very easy to hire a bike. One of the most prevalent companies is **Rent-a-Bike**, *www.rent-a-bike.ch*, which has over 100 outlets, many at railway stations. They usually have a range of bikes for you to choose from, including electric cycles and tandems at some branches. It is best to reserve in advance, particularly during busy times of the year, such as the summer.

Train Passes

There is an almost bewildering array of train passes available. Here's a selection. (2009 prices.)

Passes Available in Europe

InterRail Global Pass

Interrail, www.interrailnet.com, offers the InterRail Global Pass and InterRail One Country Pass Switzerland, available only to European citizens or those who have lived in Europe for at least six months. (Prices are in euros.)

Validity	Adult 1st	Adult 2nd	Youth 2nd
10 days in 22	489	359	309
5 days in 10	329	249	159
1 month consec.	809	599	399
22 days consec.	629	469	309

InterRail One Country Pass Switzerland

Validity	Adult 1st	Adult 2nd	Youth 2nd
8 days in a month	309	229	149
6 days in a month	255	189	123
4 days in a month	188	139	90
3 days in a month	147	109	71

Passes Available in Europe and North America

Anyone who is neither a permanent resident of Switzerland nor the Principality of Leichtenstein is eligible to buy any of the tickets below. No photo is needed, but you must present your passport.

Swiss Pass

Explore the entire country with a Swiss Pass. (Prices are in GB pounds.)

Validity	Adult 1st	Adult 2nd	Youth 2nd
4 days	229	153	115
8 days	332	221	166
15 days	402	286	201
22 days	464	309	232
1 month	510	340	255

The pass is valid on the legendary scenic routes and is also accepted on the public transportation systems of 38 Swiss town and cities. Swiss Pass holders also receive many discounts on mountain-top excursions and other services, and the price also includes a Swiss Museums Pass, which permits free entry to around 450 museums and exhibitions.

Swiss Flexi Pass

This ticket is ideal for people who do not plan on travelling every day. The Swiss Flexi Pass is valid for the amount of days you have purchased within one month (3, 4, 5 or 6 days that do not need to be consecutive). (Prices are in GB pounds.)

Validity	Adult 1st	Adult 2nd	Child 2nd
3 days in a month	220	146	73
4 days in a month	266	178	89
5 days in a month	308	205	103
6 days in a month	351	234	117

On the days you choose to activate your Swiss Flexi Pass, you will enjoy the same advantages as a Swiss Pass holder.

Swiss Card

Visitors who plan to stay mainly in one region of Switzerland should opt for the Swiss Card. Not only does it include transfers from the border or airport to your destination and back, it also offers a 50% discount on all trips made by train, boat, postbus and most mountain trains and cable cars between the first and second transfer day. The Swiss Card has a maximum validity of one month. The first and last transfers must be completetd by the end of the day, and each transfer has to be as direct as possible. (Prices are in GB pounds.)

Adult 1st	Adult 2nd	Child 2nd
150	107	54

Swiss Half Fare Card

With the Swiss Half Fare Card you can travel at half the fare on trains, buses, boats and some cable cars. You buy ordinary individual tickets for the journey you wish to make, and, producing the Swiss Half Fare Card, you only pay half the fare. The card is valid for one month and is appropriate for shorter journeys within Switzerland. It costs £58.

Passes Available in North America

The tickets mentioned below are available to citizens and permanent residents of North America. If you are planning on travelling in other countries as well as Switzerland, consider the Eurailpass family of ticket plans. Although not as comprehensive in Switzerland as the Swiss Pass family of tickets, they give you unlimited train travel in 20 countries through the extensive 100,000-mile rail network of Europe.

Eurail Global Pass

Valid for adults over 26, or youths 25 or under. (Prices are in US dollars.)

Validity	Adult 1st	Youth 2nd
15 days	511	322
21 days	662	429
1 month	822	535
2 months	1161	755
3 months	1432	933
10 days within 2 months	603	393
15 days within 2 months	792	515

Eurail Select Pass Three Countries

Design your own tailor-made pass choosing from 23 countries. Valid for adults over 26, or youths 25 or under. (Prices are in US dollars.) Passes valid for four or five countries are also available.

Validity	Adult 1st	Youth 2nd
5 days in 2 months	319	207
6 days in 2 months	352	230
8 days in 2 months	417	270
10 days in 2 months	483	313

Scenic Journeys

Switzerland offers a variety of special excursions by train, bus and boat that affords visitors the opportunity to sit back and admire the scenery. Most of the journeys are too long to do a same-day return trip, so factor this in when planning your itinerary. Below are a few examples of what's on offer; see www.myswitzerland.com for details of other trips.

The **Glacier Express**, www.glacierexpress.ch, perhaps the most famous of these trains, runs between Zermatt and St Moritz. It operates year-round, and takes approximately 8 hours in each direction. This is an unforgettable trip. From the comfort of a panorama car, you will watch in wonder as you pass over 291 bridges, through 91 tunnels and over the Oberalp Pass at 6,670ft (3,033m). Passengers may also feast on the culinary delights served up in the attractive dining car.

The **Bernina Express**, www.rhb.ch, offers spectacular scenery and a chance to cross into another country. It departs, year-round, from Chur and passes through St Moritz before beginning its ascent – on gradients of 1 in 14.25 without the aid of rack and pinion tracks – up to the Bernina Pass at 7,621ft (2,323m). It then descends through the Poschiavo Valley to Tirano, Italy. From June to October, passengers have the option of continuing on, by postbus, to Lugano. Services operate daily in both directions, with the trip to Tirano taking 4¼ hours each way, and the trip from Chur to Lugano taking 9 hours each way.

The **Lago Maggiore Express**, www.lago maggioreexpress.com, is a lengthy trip through fascinating landscapes and involves travel by boat and train. The round-trip can be started in a number of places. For example, you can start the journey in Locarno, travelling by boat to the Borromeo Islands and then across the lake to Stresa, Italy. From there, you take an express train to Domodossola, Italy, before boarding the FART train for a wonderfully beautiful trip through the Centovalli back to Locarno.

You can buy a one-day ticket, or there is a two-day ticket option, where you can stay overnight in one of the towns on the itinerary (accommodation not included in ticket price) and you also get unlimited travel on Lake Maggiore.

The **Golden Pass Line**, www.goldenpass.ch, takes you past scenic lakes and majestic mountains on its way from Montreux, on Lake Geneva, to Luzern, on Lake Luzern. Along the way it passes through Interlaken where, if the weather is favourable, you may get breathtaking views of the highest peaks in the Bernese Oberland. The trip can be taken in either direction, with the Montreux to Interlaken leg and the Interlaken to Luzern leg each taking about 3¼ hours.

The **William Tell Express**, www.wilhelmtell express.ch, operates only in the summer. It consists, uniquely, of a turn-of-the-century paddle-wheel steamer voyage from Luzern to Flüelen, followed by a train excursion through the high St Gotthard peaks, down to the lush garden city of Lugano, Ticino.

Hotel Price Categories

Prices are for a double room in high season.
luxury CHF 500 and over
expensive CHF 250–500
moderate CHF 100–250
inexpensive up to CHF 100

Where to Stay

Most Swiss hotels are members of the **Swiss Hotel Association**, which issues a Swiss Hotel Guide in book form, or you can check their website, *www.swisshotels.ch*. Their hotel ratings are deluxe (★★★★★), first class (★★★★), tourist class (★★★), standard (★★) and basic (★). Prices are set for single and double rooms according to the star rating and season, with the latter being rather variable, and with a continental breakfast usually included in the price. There are several organizations of groups of hotels such as **Alpine Classics**, *www.alpineclassic.ch*; **Swiss Budget Hotels**, *www.rooms.ch*; **Idyll Hotels**, *www.idyll hotels.com*; **Hotels Selection Suisse**, *www.selection-suisse.ch*; and **Swiss Deluxe Hotels**, *www.swissdeluxehotels.com*, all of which are worth looking at.

There are also other organizations, generally at a lower standard than hotels, which are well worthy of consideration. **Bed and Breakfast Switzerland**, *www.bnb.ch*, speaks for itself; **Tourism Rural**, *www.tourisme-rural.ch*, offers accommodation in farmhouses and rural homes between the Jura and the Alps; information about youth hostels can be found at **Swiss Youth Hostels**, *www.youthhostel.ch*; and **Swiss Backpacker News**, *www.backpacker.ch*, issues a magazine with information about less expensive accommodation.

Specialist Tour Operators

Here is just a very small selection of the many tour operators that offer trips to Switzerland.

In the UK

Crystal, t 0870 166 4971, *www.crystalholidays. co.uk*. Skiing holidays all over Switzerland for all levels of skier.

Inghams, t (020) 8780 4433, *www.inghams. co.uk*. Ski, snowboarding and lake and mountain holidays.

Powder Byrne, t (020) 8246 5300, *www.powder byrne.com*. Family skiing holidays to Arosa, Crans-Montana, Flims, Grindelwald, Klosters and Zermatt.

The Swiss Holiday Company, t 0844 901 1100, *www.swissholidayco.com*. Tailor-made itineraries, guided hiking, trekking and cycling tours.

Treyn Holidays By Rail, t (01904) 73 49 39, *www.treynholidays.co.uk*. Escorted rail holidays.

In the USA and Canada

Continental Journeys, Sherman Oaks CA, t 800 601 4343, *www.continentaljourneys.com*. Feature several escorted tours.

Magic Switzerland, t 800 337 9477, *www.magic switzerland.com*. Online agent that will create individual itineraries.

Alpine Hikers, 1203 Loren Drive, Prescott, AZ 86305, t 503 459 3940, *www.alpinehikers.com*. Self-guided and guided hiking tours.

Prime Travel, 1852 Marine Drive, W. Vancouver, BC, V7V 1J6, t 604 925 1212, *www.prime-travel.com*. 'Discover Switzerland' tours.

In Switzerland

Swiss Safari, Dorfstrasse 5, CH-7404, Wolfisberg, t 032 636 05 03, *www.swiss safari.com*. Tailor-made holidays, including golfing holidays and honeymoons.

Practical A–Z

06

Children

Switzerland is a natural wonderland for children. The mountains themselves are a big attraction, as are the many different forms of transport, such as funiculars and cog-wheel trains. There are many family-friendly resorts and hotels that offer a wide variety of different activities for children to keep them occupied, while attractions such as the **Tell-Freilichtspiele** (William Tell Open-Air Theatre), Interlaken (*see* p.143), the **Freilichtmuseum** (Swiss Open-Air Museum), Ballenberg (*see* p.161) and **Swissminiatur**, Ticino (*see* p.272) will be enjoyable for them.

The **Swiss Travel System Family Card** is issued free, and entitles children under the age of 16 to travel free (at least one parent has to travel with the children).

Crime and the Police

Switzerland has one of the lowest crime rates of all industrialized countries, so crime is not a big concern for visitors to Switzerland, especially outside the cities. Just take the usual precautions of ensuring that your money, valuable documents and luggage are safe.

In the event of an emergency you can contact the police, *www.swisspolice.ch*, on the emergency number t 117.

Eating Out

See box below for price categories in this book. For information on Swiss food and wine specialities, dining out and a menu reader, *see* **Food and Drink**, pp.31–8.

A service charge is added to bills in hotels and restaurants so there is no need to leave an extra tip, although many people round the bill up and leave a little extra.

Restaurant Price Categories

Price categories are based on a two-course meal for one person without wine.
very expensive over CHF 60
expensive CHF 40–60
moderate €25–40 CHF 25–40
inexpensive under CHF 25

Switzerland's smoking laws for restaurants and cafés are a little confusing and vary from canton to canton. Some allow smoking in a designated area. It's best to check before you light up.

Electricity

The current used in Switzerland is 220 volts (50 cycles), and most power sockets are designed for three-pin round plugs. However, the standard continental-type plug with two round pins is attached to most small appliances. Those from North America will need a travel converter if their small appliances cannot be adjusted between 110 and 220 volts.

Gay and Lesbian Scene

Most of Switzerland's cities have lively gay communities. The Switzerland Tourism website, *www.myswitzerland.com*, has information on bars, clubs, restaurants and events. You can also subscribe to a newsletter and download podcasts.

Health and Emergencies

Police t 117
Ambulance t 144 (not in all areas)
Fire Brigade t 118
Emergency road service t 140
Helicopter rescue Rega t 1414 /
    Air Glaciers t 1415

If you go to a **chemist's** (*apotheke, pharmacie, farmacia*) and it is closed, there should be a note on the front door informing you of the nearest open one.

Internet Facilities

In all the main cities and towns there are Internet cafés, with varying rates; a minimum of CHF 5 for about 15 minutes is common. In most of the MANOR department stores, often in the electrical department, there are computers with Internet facilities – although you have to stand – offering better rates.

Many hotels also have an Internet Corner or Small Office facilities, but be sure to check first what rates they charge as they can sometimes be excessive.

Public Holidays

1 January New Year's Day
2 January (regional)
March/April Good Friday and Easter Monday
1 May Labour Day (regional)
May Ascension Day
May Whit Monday
May/June Corpus Christi (regional)
1 August Swiss National Day
25 December Christmas Day
26 December Boxing Day

Language

Switzerland has four national languages. German, spoken in a variety of dialects but written in high German, is used in the north, central and eastern areas; French is spoken in western Switzerland; Italy is the language of Ticino in the south of the country; and Romansch – a derivative of Latin – is spoken in the southeastern region of Graubünden (Grisons). English is widely spoken in all the major cities and towns, and much of the country.

For tips on pronunciation and lists of useful words and phrases, see **Language**, pp.304–306.

Media

Swiss News, the national English journal, www.swissnews.ch, is a monthly newspaper giving a wide range of news about Switzerland in English.

World Radio Switzerland, www.world radio.ch, 101.7 FM in Geneva, is a leading English-speaking radio station.

Almost all hotels now have satellite TV that features CNN, SKY News, BBC Prime and other similar programmes.

English newspapers and the Herald Tribune are widely available at airports, train stations and other places, on the same day as publication in the largest cities and the next day in other, smaller, places.

The Swiss government has a news agency, www.swissinfo.ch, informing visitors in English, German, French, Italian, Spanish, Portuguese, Japanese, Chinese and Arabic about current events in both the country and the world in the form of text, photos and podcasts.

Post

Post offices, in general, are open Mon–Fri 8–12 and 2–5. However, in large cities they can also open on Saturday 8.30–12, and those located in shopping centres are usually open the same hours as the centre. See www.swiss post.ch.

Shopping

In the large cities and towns shops are usually open Mon–Fri 8.30–6 approximately, with some closing slightly earlier on Saturday. In smaller towns and villages it is still the custom to close between midday and 2pm. On Sunday the only places you are guaranteed to find a selection of shops open are at Geneva and Zürich airports and railway stations, and the railway stations at Bern and Luzern. With a very few, although growing, number of exceptions, no shops will be open elsewhere.

Tax-free shopping: in Switzerland there is 7.6% VAT (sales tax) on goods that is included in the price, and foreign visitors are entitled to a refund of VAT on goods of a value of CHF 400 or more through the Global Refund system, www.globalrefund.com. Shops participating in this scheme prominently display the TAX-FREE SHOPPING sign.

Switzerland is famous for many products, but perhaps none more so than Swiss watches with names like Rolex, Tag Heuer, Rado, Patek Philippe and Victorinox, as well as Swatch at the other end of the market. The **Fédération de l'Industrie Horlogère Suisse** (Federation of the Swiss Watch Industry), rue d'Argent 6, 2501-Bienne, t 032 328 0828, www.fhs.ch, is the regulatory body for the industry, and links to every Swiss watchmaker are found on its website. Obviously, there are numerous retail outlets for Swiss watches, but the most famous such company in Switzerland is **Bucherer**, www.bucherer. com, which has branches in Basel, Bern,

Victorinox – A Quintessential Swiss Story

A world-renowned institution, this company was begun in 1884 by cutler, Karl Elsener, great-grandfather of the present director. The business thrived and became the official supplier of pocket knives to the soldiers of the Swiss Army, with the first batch being delivered in 1891. Elsener subsequently developed a lighter, more elegant knife with more features for use by officers; the 'Officers' and Sports Knife was legally registered in 1897, which later becomes known as the Swiss army knife. In 1909, following the death of his mother, Karl Elsener chose her name, Victoria, as the company name. In that same year he also designed the now famous white cross and red shield logo that has become a symbol of Swiss quality. Twelve years later, in 1921, stainless steel was incorporated into the manufacture of the knives. 'Inox', the international designation for stainless steel, was appended to the company name, and 'Victorinox', the present name, was created. Throughout the years the Swiss army knife has been continuously redesigned, with new features added to meet the evolving needs and preferences of consumers in both military and private markets.

The Victorinox Swiss army knife has become a design icon. The New York Museum of Modern Art and the State Museum for Applied Art in Munich, Germany, have selected the Victorinox 'SwissChamp', consisting of 64 individual parts, weighing only 6½oz (185g) and with 33 different features, for exhibit in their collections on excellence in design.

Victorinox now produces a diverse range of products including knives with memory sticks, and their latest innovation is Swiss army watches. As the knives did before them, they have attained an international reputation for reliable, high-performance, stylish products – at a reasonable price.

Wenger SA had been a smaller competitor to Victorinox, supplying knives to the Swiss army since 1893, and subsequently producing its own range of watches. In 2005 Victorinox purchased the company, with the main aim of keeping production of the Swiss army knife in Switzerland. However, rather than incorporate it into the company, the Wenger brand has been retained.

Geneva, Interlaken, Lausanne, Luzern, Lugano, St Gallen, St Moritz, Zermatt and Zürich.

Swiss **knives** are also world-famous, and the **Victorinox**, *www.victorinox.ch*, name is seen everywhere in Switzerland. **Wenger**, *www.wenger-knife.ch*, also produces official Swiss army knives. (*See* box above.)

Cuckoo clocks, too, are synonymous with Switzerland and the attractive chalet-style ones that you see in all the main souvenir shops are almost certainly hand-carved at the **Lötscher**, *www.loetscher.ch*, premises in Brienz. Brienz is famous for its woodcarvers and **Huggler**, *www.huggler-woodcarvings.ch*, produces most of the beautiful pieces on display in the souvenir shops. (*See* p.30.)

Schweizer Heimatwerk, *www.heimatwerk. ch*, is a good alternative source for souvenirs as it offers the best design in contemporary Swiss handicrafts in the form of household items, home décor accessories, jewellery, clothes and toys. They have six shops, two in the city centre of Zürich and two at the airport, and are represented in Basel and at Geneva airport.

Turning to food, Swiss **cheese**, too, is internationally famous and comes in many tasty guises. The **Switzerland Cheese Marketing** organization, *www.switzerland-cheese.com*, leaves no holes uncovered in its interesting coverage of the topic on its website. Who can resist, either, Swiss chocolate made by such famous companies as Lindt, *www.lindt.com* and Suchard?

Sports and Activities
Winter Sports

In the winter Switzerland is, of course, famous for its skiing and other winter sports activities and is a popular destination for those who love to **ski**, **snowboard**, **toboggan**, etc. There are resorts suitable for everyone, from adrenalin junkies to families, and for all levels of ability. All resorts have ski schools that can get you started or help you improve your skills. Exploit the local knowledge of the instructors in the resort and the staff at the local tourist information office and mountain guides' bureau as to suitable ski runs for your level of ability and fitness.

As with any activity that is going to take you into the mountains, your safety is paramount. So check local weather conditions (tourist information office/mountain guides' bureau, *www.meteo schweiz.ch*) and consult the daily avalanche bulletin (**t** 187 or *www.slf.ch*, the website for the Federal Institute for Snow and Avalanche Research). Always seek advice from local experts before considering skiing off-piste.

Whatever activity you are taking part in, always make sure that you are properly prepared, equipped and clothed.

Summer Activities

In the summer, **mountain biking** and **hiking** are particularly popular. There are many marked hiking and walking trails, and there are routes suitable for all levels of ability and fitness. The **Swiss Hiking Federation**, *www.swisshiking.ch* (German/French), has information on all aspects of walking and hiking in the country. Ask in the local tourist office for their advice on suitable routes, as they will be familiar with the area. Many tourist organizations conduct guided walks and hikes, and you may prefer to do this rather than setting out on your own.

If you do decide to set off independently, you must check the weather as conditions can change very quickly. The local tourist information office will have weather forecast details and you can check on *www.meteo schweiz.ch*. (See also avalanche warning information above.) Ensure that you have an up-to-date map with you, any necessary equipment and food and drink, and that you are suitably clothed for the conditions that you are likely to encounter. Don't hike or walk alone and always make sure that someone knows where you're going, what time you set off and let them know when you return.

Swimming and **watersports** are popular at the lakeside resorts. Be aware of any safety signs regarding the suitability of swimming in certain areas and to be on the safe side check at the local tourist information office for details of suitable bathing spots.

Professional Sports

Football is well supported, especially in the larger cities; the European Football Championship, EURO 08, was held in Switzerland and Austria. **Ice hockey**, too, has plenty of enthusiasts, and Switzerland plays host to major events on the European professional **golf** and **tennis** circuits. (Tennis player Roger Federer, holder of 15 Grand Slam singles titles, more than any other male player, comes from Basel.)

Rather incongruously, Switzerland, a country far away from the world's oceans, actually won the 2003 and 2007 **America's Cup** yacht race, with the Société Nautique de Genève's Alinghi syndicate.

Telephones

Dialling from the UK

International access code 00 and country code 41 plus the area code (excluding the leading 0) and then the number.

Dialling from the USA or Canada

International access code 011 and country code 41 plus the area code (excluding the leading 0) and then the number.

Dialling from Switzerland

For the UK dial the country code 0044 followed by the area code (excluding the leading 0) and then the number.

For the USA and Canada, country code 001 followed by area code and number.

Dialling inside Switzerland

The full area code (including the leading 0) must precede the number.

Most Swiss public payphones can only be used with a Swiss **phone card**, the PTT-Taxcard, which comes in denominations of CHF 5, 10 and 20 and is available at post offices, newsagents and railway stations, etc.

There is usually a very heavy surcharge for telephone calls made from your **hotel room**, especially for international calls.

Other useful numbers: **t** 111 domestic operator; **t** 1141 international operator.

Time

Switzerland operates on a time system one hour ahead of the United Kingdom, and six hours ahead of Eastern Standard Time, USA.

Tipping

Tips are automatically included in all hotel and restaurant bills. It is customary to give a small tip (10–12%) for special services, such as luggage handling, and to taxi drivers.

Toilets

Wherever you go in Switzerland, whether public or private facilities, these will be immaculately clean and well maintained.

Women Travellers

Female travellers are unlikely to be harassed. Common sense should be used when travelling on public transport and walking at night.

Zürich and Northeast Switzerland

Zürich and northeastern Switzerland may not have high mountain peaks; in fact, with one or two exceptions, the scenery is pleasant rather than dramatic. However, this area has much else to offer. Zürich, one of the three main entry points to Switzerland by air, is full of interest and belies the bland reputation it might at one time have had. What's more the winters here can be milder and shorter than in the rest of the country. Culturally, too, the city has its surprises, as does nearby, and far lesser-known, Winterthur.

The Stiftbibliotek (Abbey Library) at St Gallen is a must-see, and one of the absolute delights of a visit to this part of the country is to have an early lunch at André Jaeger's spectacular Rheinhotel Fischerzunft restaurant in Schaffhausen. Then, just a few steps away from the front door, board a boat for a gentle cruise along the Rhine to the attractive town of Stein am Rhein.

07

Don't miss

⭐ **Stained-glass windows**
Fraümunster, Zürich
p.62

⭐ **Romanesque parish church**
Grossmünster, Zürich
p.63

⭐ **Historic library**
Stiftsbibliotek, St Gallen
p.72

⭐ **Tiny capital**
Vaduz, Liechtenstein
p.76

⭐ **Natural wonder**
Rhine Falls **p.79**

See map overleaf

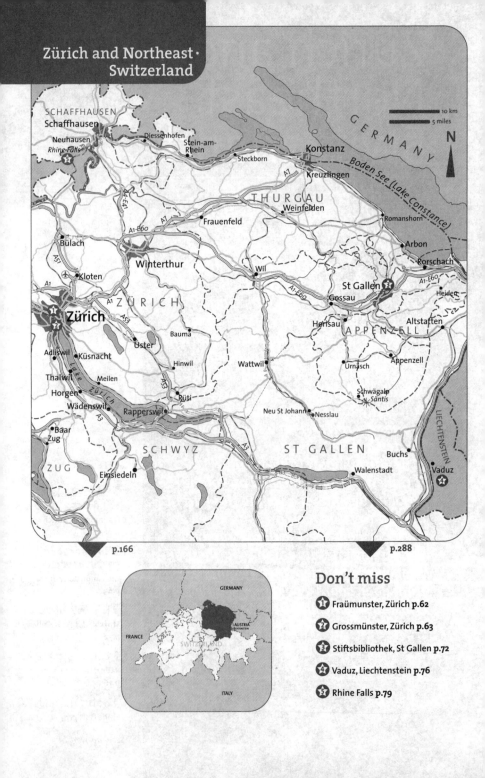

p.166

p.288

Don't miss

⓵ Fraümunster, Zürich **p.62**

⓶ Grossmünster, Zürich **p.63**

⓷ Stiftsbibliothek, St Gallen **p.72**

⓸ Vaduz, Liechtenstein **p.76**

⓹ Rhine Falls **p.79**

Zürich

Zürich used to have a reputation as a somewhat dull city, possibly because of its historical role as leader of the Reformation in Switzerland and its modern role as the country's financial capital. Present-day visitors will quickly realize, however, that this is no longer the case.

The city boasts a great geographical location. Situated in the centre-north of the country, at the far north end of the lake that shares its name and with snow-capped mountains looming in the east, scenically beautiful Zürich enjoys a fine climate for most of the year.

With a population approaching 400,000, it is also Switzerland's largest city. You might expect such a business-minded place to be constrained and bland, but culturally conscious Zürich is neither. It enjoys an international reputation as an art-dealing centre, with many notable auction houses based here. Museums, art galleries, theatres, music and clubs abound, along with an outdoor environment of pavement cafés and bars that make for a lively atmosphere. Shoppers will not be disappointed, either, with every world-famous brand on show along the one-and-a-quarter mile length of the Bahnhofstrasse, Switzerland's most famous street. The charming Old Town is home to a variety of art galleries, antique dealers and bookshops, not to mention any number of stylish boutiques in the area between the Bahnhofstrasse and the River Limmat. On the opposite side of the Limmat, the pedestrian area known as Dörfli offers an array of more shops, bars, nightclubs and discos. Take a look, too, under the train station at ShopVille-RailCity. Hotels are of the highest standard and the restaurants have a decidedly international flavour, though prices can be quite high.

Within more or less an hour of Zürich, by train, there are a handful of interesting places to explore. **Rapperswil** is the closest, and lunch on a lake steamer on the way back is a delightful experience. South of Rapperswil is the small town of **Einsiedeln**, which played an important part in Switzerland's history and is home to the Benedictine Abbey that is the most important place of Roman Catholic pilgrimage in Switzerland. **Schaffhausen**, an attractive place in itself, is enhanced by the nearby Rhine Falls (Rheinfall); and **Stein am Rhein**, a fascinating medieval city, is just a river cruise away when continuing on from Schaffhausen or a short train trip from Zürich. Slightly father away, but worth a visit for its famous library and cathedral, is St Gallen. Between **St Gallen** and Zürich is **Winterthur**. It is often overlooked by tourists but is worth a daytrip as it has several fascinating art museums. Finally, if you want to visit a different country you can go to **Vaduz** in Liechtenstein, which has several places of interest.

07 Zürich and Northeast Switzerland | Zürich

Getting to Zürich

By Air

Flights from Europe, North America (and many other countries worldwide) arrive at Zürich's **Kloten International Airport**, *www.flughafen-zuerich.ch*, which is 12km from the city centre.

Swiss Rail (SBB) trains, *www.sbb.ch/en/*, run from the airport rail station (underneath the airport) to the **Hauptbahnhof** every 10mins or so between around 6am and midnight. The journey takes just 10mins. A **taxi** to the city centre costs about CHF 60.

Many hotels operate their own **shuttle bus service** to and from the airport; check before you leave.

By Car

The A1 motorway runs in a northeasterly direction through Switzerland linking Zürich with Geneva, Lausanne and Bern to the southwest and Winterthur and St Gallen to the east. From Ticino, the A2 motorway runs through Bellinzona and up to Mt Pilatus, where it joins with the road north from the Bernese Oberland, then due north to Luzern where it splits for Basel or Zürich.

By Train

Eurostar, *www.eurostar.com*, runs from London (St Pancras International) to Paris (Gare du Nord), and then from Paris (Gare de Lyon) a high-speed TGV, *www.sncf.fr*, operates to Zürich, via Basel. Zürich is connected to every other major Swiss city, usually with a service every 30mins, and from Lugano hourly.

Getting around Zürich

By Public Transport

Public transport in and around Zürich, on any combination of trams, buses, cable cars, boats, the S-Bahn (a rapid suburban train) and some railways, is fast, clean and efficient and operated by **Zürcher Verkehrsverbund**, *www.zvv.ch*. **Tickets** must be purchased from ticket-vending machines, ticket offices or the tourist office before each trip and are available for single trips or, more advantageously, as an Unlimited Day Pass. The latter, for 2nd class, costs CHF 8 for Zones 1 and 2 in the city of Zürich.

By Car

Many **car hire companies** have branches in the city itself and at the airport. Companies include **Avis**, *www.avis.ch*, **Europcar**, *www.europcar.ch*, and **Hertz**, *www.hertz.ch*.

By Bicycle

From May to Oct over 200 **city bikes**, *www.zuerirollt.ch*, are available daily without any charge or reservation from: Globus City, 9am–9.30pm; Bürkliplatz, 9am–9.30pm; Oerlikon Station/Swissôtel, 10am–9.30pm and Bahnhof Enge, 10am–9.30pm. Bikes are available all year round at the Velogate (Swiss National Museum) and at the Bike Station South (Sihlpost). Take a valid form of ID and a deposit of CHF 20.

By Boat

Zürichsee Schiffahrtsgesellschaft, t 044 487 13 13, *www.zsg.ch*, offers a variety of **boat trips** on Lake Zürich throughout the year, but with a much expanded schedule April–Oct. Some of these are evening trips featuring music and dancing and even fondue cruises. However, your best bet may be a short round-trip lasting 1¼ hours and departing from Bürkiplatz (on the southwest side of where the Limmat meets the lake) – either via Thalwil or Küsnacht. The boats leave hourly and cost CHF 8.

History

Although the Romans built a customs post at Lindenhof as early as 15 BC, thereby founding *Turicum*, Zürich was first recorded as a town in official documents in AD 929. It subsequently acquired the status of Free Imperial Town in 1218. A little over a century later, in 1336, local artisans, organized in guilds and led by Rudolf Brun,

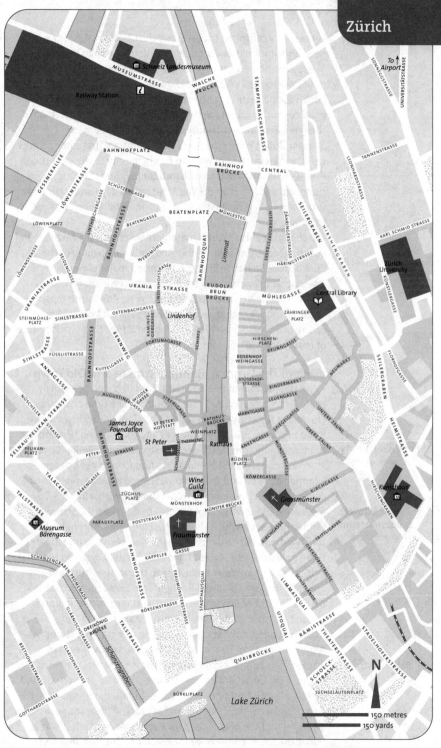

Railway Station

Schweiz Landesmuseum

MUSEUMSTRASSE
WALCHE BRÜCKE
STAMPFENBACHSTRASSE

To Airport
SONNEGGSTRASSE
UNIVERSITÄTSTRASSE

BAHNHOFPLATZ
BAHNHOF BRÜCKE
CENTRAL
TANNENSTRASSE

GESSNERALLEE
LÖWENSTRASSE
SCHÜTZENGASSE
BEATENPLATZ
MÜHLESTEG
LEONHARDSTRASSE
KARL SCHMID STRASSE

LÖWENPLATZ
LINDENHECKERGASSE
BEATENGASSE
NIEDERDORFSTRASSE
ZÄHRINGERSTRASSE
SEILERGRABEN
HIRSCHENGRABEN

LÖWENSTRASSE
BAHNHOFSTRASSE
WERDMÜHLE
BAHNHOFQUAI
Limmat
HÄRINGSTRASSE
Zürich University

SEIDENGASSE
URANIA STRASSE
LINDENHOFSTRASSE
RUDOLF BRUN BRÜCKE
MÜHLEGASSE
Central Library
KÜNSTLERGASSE

URANIASTRASSE
STEINMÜHLE-PLATZ
SIHLSTRASSE
OETENBACHGASSE
Lindenhof
ZÄHRINGER PLATZ

SIHLSTRASSE
FÜSSLISTRASSE
RENNWEG
KAMINFEGERGASSE
FORTUNAGASSE
SCHIFFE
HIRSCHEN-PLATZ
BRUNNGASSE
FLORHOFGASSE

ANNAGASSE
BAHNHOFSTRASSE
KUTTELGASSE
ROSENHOF
WEINGASSE
NEUMARKT
SEILERGRABEN

NÜSCHELER STRASSE
AUGUSTINER GASSE
WIDDER GASSE
STREHLGASSE
STÜSSIHOF-STRASSE
RINDERMARKT
HEIMSTRASSE

SELNAU-PELIKAN STRASSE
James Joyce Foundation
ST PETER HOFSTATT
RATHAUS-BRÜCKE
LEUENGASSE
MARKTGASSE
SPIEGELGASSE
UNTERE ZÄUNE

PELIKAN-PLATZ
St Peter
WEINPLATZ
THERMENG.
Rathaus
ANKENGASSE
OBERE ZÄUNE

PETER-
HOFSTRASSE
STRASSE
RÜDEN-PLATZ
MÜNSTERGASSE
Kunsthaus

TALACKER
BARENGASSE
ZÜGHUS-PLATZ
Wine Guild
RÖMERGASSE
Grossmünster
HIRSCHENGRABEN

TALSTRASSE
Museum Bärengasse
PARADEPLATZ
POSTSTRASSE
MÜNSTERHOF
MÜNSTER BRÜCKE
KIRCHGASSE
TRITTLIGASSE

BAHNHOFSTRASSE
Fraumünster
OBERDORFSTRASSE

SCHANZENGRABEN PROMENADE
KAPPELER GASSE
FRAUMÜNSTERSTRASSE
KIRCHGASSE
SCHIFFLANDE

GLARNISCHSTRASSE
DREIKÖNIG BRÜCKE
BÖRSENSTRASSE
STADTHAUSQUAI
LIMMATQUAI

BEETHOVENSTRASSE
CLARIDENSTRASSE
TALSTRASSE
Schanzengraben
UTOQUAI
RAMISTRASSE
THEATERSTRASSE
STADELHOFERSTRASSE

GOTTHARDSTRASSE
BÜRKLIPLATZ
QUAIBRÜCKE
SCHOECK STRASSE
SECHSELÄUTENPLATZ

Lake Zürich

N

150 metres
150 yards

successfully conspired to overthrow the city council, instituting a new constitution that, naturally, gave domination to the guilds. These days, however, things have changed. The guilds appear in public only once a year, on the third Monday in April, during the Zürich Spring Festival of *Sechseläuten*. Members don traditional guild costume and parade throughout the city before reaching their destination, Sechseläuten Square, in early evening.

In 1351, Zürich joined the Swiss Confederation. That same century saw the construction of walls to fortify the city centre. And strong they were, lasting well into the 19th century and standing, preserved and intact, in the Old Town to this day. During the early 16th century, in 1519, Huldrych Zwingli brought the Reformation to Zürich.

In the 19th century Zürich metamorphosed into the financial and economic centre of Switzerland. And with the opening of the Zürich Stock Exchange in 1877, it became a major player in international financial and trade markets as well. In fact, today, Zürich is home to what is considered the world's fourth most important stock exchange, is the world's largest gold trading centre and hosts a variety of thriving industries that provide a total of more than 350,000 jobs.

West of the Limmat: Bahnhofstrasse and Old Town

The **Hauptbahnhof** (main railway station) is a place virtually every visitor to Zürich will pass through at one time or another. Opened in 1872, this station superficially looks just like a station. But don't be deceived. Delve deeper and you will find beneath it a huge shopping complex of over 170 stores, **ShopVille-RailCity**. The station forecourt is the best place to find foreign newspapers.

ShopVille-RailCity
www.railcity.ch

Immediately behind the station it is impossible to miss the large, castle-like structure – dating from 1898 and with a tower replicating the town gate of Baden – that houses the **Schweiz Landesmuseum** (Swiss National Museum). Enter through a huge courtyard, passing cannons and a small cafeteria, to investigate three floors and a basement filled with exhibits, grouped together in tours taking you from prehistory to the 20th century and giving an interesting and innovative insight into Swiss cultural history. Once a year the courtyard becomes the stage for 'Live at Sunset' concerts featuring international music stars.

Schweiz Landesmuseum
Museumstrasse 2,
t 044 218 65 11,
www.landesmuseen.ch;
open Tues–Sun 10.30–5;
adm

Back outside, on the station's opposite side stands a statue of Alfred Escher (1819–82), founder of the Swiss railway system. Immediately behind him is **Bahnhofstrasse**, the most famous street in Switzerland. Along its 1¼-mile (2-km) length you will find an eclectic variety of fine stores, banks, hotels and restaurants; the cost of property here is astronomically high. A pleasant, seemingly incongruous little **park** hides a dark secret. At one time it was a public execution site – hence the reason no one was anxious to build on it. The statue in the park's centre is of **Jo Heinrich**

Bahnhofstrasse
www.bahnhofstrasse-zuerich.ch

Pestalozzi, who acted upon his opposition to private education by founding the city's public school system.

Take a look, now, at the small **fountain** at the end of the park alongside Bahnhofstrasse. Actually, as fountains go in Zürich – there are more than 1,200 of them in all shapes and sizes – this seems like nothing extraordinary. It is elegant, and interesting in that it was donated by the city of Paris to Zürich in 1870 to initiate the World Convention of Water Experts. The four nymphs – one set on each corner – personify simplicity, purity, sobriety and charity, and are meant to symbolize international cooperation. Don't be frightened to take a drink either, as the water flowing from the city's fountains is considered to be of better quality than that running to the taps of local residences.

If you are here on or around the hour, then make a point of looking above the door of the Kurz shop, diagonally across Bahnhofstrasse, where you will see a delightful musical clock featuring a parade of characters in Swiss national costumes.

The nearby **Brasserie Lipp** may look like an ordinary restaurant, but a real treat unfolds when you take the lift to the **Jules Verne Panorama Bar** (*see* p.68) on the 12th floor of this unusual, octagonal-shaped tower. Apart from the chance to have a drink and a rest, it offers a fantastic bird's-eye view of the city and a breathtaking panorama of the surrounding countryside.

Just behind here and to the south, **Kaminfegergasse** is an interesting, tiny, cobblestoned street. Lining the way are ancient houses, one of which dates from 1401 and is thought to be the oldest brick home in Zürich. Note, also, the pulleys in the gables that are ingeniously used, as in many houses in Amsterdam, to haul furniture and other unwieldy objects by crane to the upper floors.

Further on, and closer to the river, **Lindenhof** is an area set up for open-air chess, with game sets and seats around the edge of what is a popular little park. Although it may look insignificant, this has a story to tell – and the statue, dating from 1292, of a woman dressed in military uniform, gives a clue. On one occasion, the Hapsburgs were attacking the city from below, while the men of Zürich were away battling at Winterthur. The women of the city, determined to defend their homes, devised a clever plan that foiled the advancing troops. Dressed in military uniforms, they stood in lines along the walls of Lindenhof. The Habsburgs, convinced the city was formidably protected, retreated. A more peaceful place these days, Lindenhof affords wonderful views over the Limmat River, with the old town hall in the foreground and the two towers of the cathedral on the hill behind, and provides a delightful atmosphere in which people simply come to relax.

Leaving Lindenhof from its south side, you are confronted with quite an unusual perspective. Directly ahead, with one almost directly behind the other, are two contrasting spires, each adorned with a striking clock. The nearest, belonging to St Peterskirche (St Peter's Church) and looming at 28½ft (8.7m), boasts the largest clockface in Europe – beating Big Ben in London by an inch or so (just a few centimetres). The furthest embellishes the Fraumünster, home to Chagall's famous stained-glass windows (*see* p.63).

St Peterskirche
www.st-peter-zh.ch;
open Mon–Fri 8–6, Sat
10–4, Sun 11–5

St Peterskirche, the oldest of Zürich's medieval churches, was first mentioned in documents in 857. Although remnants of the four earlier constructions remain, the current structure dates from 1705–6 and was the first of the churches built after the Reformation in Zürich. In the tower, used as a fire watch as late as 1911, there are five bells, with the largest, an A-flat, weighing 6.1 tons (6,203kg).

Pay close attention now because, even though it's easy to miss, you need to descend down along narrow **Thermengasse**, the name of which offers a clue to its attraction. Metal grille steps offer a view of the ruins that lie beneath, and diagrams and other documentation verify that in Roman times this was a thermal spring. What you see is only a small part of what once was, and quite impressive it must have been.

Weinplatz, an attractive little square with a wonderfully ornate wrought-metal fountain, is situated right next to the Limmat River. It is also home to Zum Storchen, the hotel with the finest river views in Zürich. A footpath runs alongside it and the Limmat towards the next bridge, with a good view of the ancient town hall across the crystalline swift-flowing waters of the Limmat. South, near the next bridge, Münsterbrucke, is a uniquely elegant building with an ornate gold wrought-iron balcony. It becomes apparent just what a fine house this is when its main façade reveals itself in Münsterhof square. As previously explained, guilds have played an important part in Zürich's history, and the Wine Guild is one of the grandest of them all. Obviously not wishing to skimp on any luxury for themselves the members constructed this

Zunfthaus zur
Meisen
Münsterhof 20,
t 044 221 28 07,
www.landesmuseen.ch;
open Tues–Sun 10.30–5;
adm

guild house as their headquarters in 1750. It is now the **Zunfthaus zur Meisen**, a branch of the Swiss National Museum that houses an amazing collection of porcelain and glazed pottery, with notable examples from the Schooren factory near Zürich and Nyon. Note also the memorial in honour of Sir Winston Churchill (1874–1965), who made his famous 'Europe Arise' speech from here on 19 September 1946.

⭐ Fraumünster
Münsterhof 2,
t 044 211 41 00,
www.fraumuenster.ch;
open April–Oct 10–6;
Nov–Mar 10–4; closed
during church services
on Sun, usually 10–11

Churches abound in Zürich. There are over 100 in the city – 60 per cent Protestant and 30 per cent Catholic. Back on Münsterhof, the **Fraumünster** (Women's Cathedral) is easily identifiable by its elegant spire and four large clockfaces. It has a truly ancient history. Legend, of course, plays its part, but it is documented that, as far back as AD 853, the German King Ludwig donated an existing convent to his daughter, Hildegard. It was she who, soon after, commissioned the construction of a new church that has been perpetually enlarged, renovated or reconstructed over the ensuing centuries. As intriguing as this history is, it is not the primary reason people from around the world come to visit the Fraumünster. That honour goes to its innovatively interpretive stained-glass windows. The most famous of these are by the Russian emigré Marc Chagall (1887–1985), who was commissioned by the church in the 1960s. His five-part biblical stained-glass cycle was installed in the choir in 1970 and in the south transept in 1980. Not to be overlooked, either, is the work of the Swiss artist Augusto Giacometti (1877–1947), whose creation *Heavenly Paradise* was installed following the Second World War.

Zürich James Joyce Foundation
Augustinergasse 9,
t 044 211 83 01,
www.joyce
foundation.ch; open
Mon–Fri 10–5

James Joyce spent many creative years, and actually died, in Zürich and the **Zürich James Joyce Foundation**, very close to Lindenhof, was established in 1985 to keep the memory of his life and work alive.

East Side of the Limmat

🏛 **Grossmünster**
Zwingliplatz,
t 044 252 59 49,
www.kirche-ch; open
mid-Mar–Oct 9–6,
Nov–mid-Mar 10–5

Almost directly across from the Fraumünster, the twin round-topped towers (not the originals) of the **Grossmünster** dominate this area. Walking around the plaza to the main entrance, note on the exterior the representation of a horse and rider, and a figure of Charlemagne. The former, *c.* 1180, is considered the earliest portrayal of a horseman in the northern Alps. The latter is just a copy; exposure to weather was damaging the 15th-century original, which can now be seen in the Romanesque crypt.

According to a rather intricate legend, Charlemagne founded the Grossmünster. As the story goes, Feliz and Regula, city and cathedral patrons and members of the Christian Thebaic Legion that had been decimated in the Valais in the 3rd century, escaped to Zürich only to meet martyrs' deaths. Afterwards, they reportedly picked up their own decapitated heads and ascended to a location where they wished to be buried. Later during a hunting excursion, Charlemagne was pursuing a stag from Aachen, in northern Germany, to Zürich. There, his steed stumbled over the graves of Feliz and Regula, which Charlemagne then designated as the site of the Grossmünster.

Construction commenced on this Romanesque-type structure at the beginning of the 12th century, though it was not completed for another hundred years. The interior, with the exception of the stained-glass windows by Augusto Giacometti and the Bronze Doors by Otto Münch, is rather austere, but that is not without reason. This, the parish church of Zürich, was at the epicentre of the Swiss Reformation movement, led by Huldrych Zwingli (1484–1531) and Heinrich Bullinger (1504–75). One of the first initiatives of these leaders was to remove, in 1519, all artwork, altars and other physical embellishments – even the organ. It is Heinrich Bullinger, an elected pastor of the Grossmünster, who can be thanked for the Reformed Church seen today. In 1566, he wrote the Second Helvetic Confession that, even now, belongs to the Book of Confessions of the United Presbyterian Church in the USA.

Interestingly, Zwingli's and Bullinger's work managed to transcend pure theology – becoming the basis of Swiss democracy and social policies and instrumental in the economic and industrial growth of Zürich. Rather than a hierarchical organization, they envisioned the church as a meeting place for parishioners to worship as equals. This movement paved the way for national referenda that placed special emphasis on improving the lot of the weak and persecuted, and saw Zürich become a model system for providing for the poor. A new work ethic emphasized law and discipline both in public and personal spheres. And, as citizens were required to study the Bible in German, a majority of the population learned to read and write. This, in turn, contributed to industrial and economic growth in the city.

Kunsthaus
Heimplatz 1,
t 044 253 84 84,
www.kunsthaus.ch;
open Wed–Fri 10–8, Sat,
Sun, Tues 10–6; adm

Just a few blocks east is the **Kunsthaus** (Museum of Fine Arts), one of the most important art museums in Switzerland. Its wide and varied collection includes many Old Masters, Swiss art from the 19th and 20th centuries, a unique collection of Alberto Giacometti's work, the largest Munch collection outside Norway, some of Monet's French impressionistic art, Picassos and much, much more.

North from the Grossmünster runs Münstergasse, where you can leave thoughts of art and austerity behind and instead see just how cosmopolitan Zürich can be. This area is known as the Dörfli, Zürich's pedestrian zone. Among the trendy shops, art galleries and interesting restaurants, there are two places that merit special attention: the **Bodega Española** and **Conditorei Café Schober**, both described in 'Eating Out in Zurich' (*see* pp.68 and 69).

Back outside, and further down Münstergasse, a warrior stands at a safe distance – atop another fountain. This, the **Stüssihofstatt Fountain**, dates from 1574, although the original water receptacle was replaced in 1811. From here Niederdorfstrasse slopes gently down to Central, just across the Limmat from the Hauptbahnhof. In truth this is less salubrious, and expect it to get somewhat seedier along the way. A shop selling condoms, a Condomeria, indicates the presence of sex shows, and cheaper restaurants (sometimes not much more than shop fronts) and of course the irrepressible McDonald's predominate. The area is, however, by no means threatening. You may even find a craft market open near the Hotel Biban, and enjoy the entertainment of street artists along your way.

Dada Movement

In 1916 Dadaism was born at the **Cabaret Voltaire** (*www.cabaretvoltaire.ch*) in a house at Spiegelgasse 1. Its most important years were until 1922, and the movement involved visual arts, literature, poetry, art theory, theatre and even graphic design, all with a heavy anti-war influence. Now, 90 years on, the Cabaret Voltaire has been reinaugurated as a lively cultural centre dedicated to linking Dadaism and present-day social and cultural movements.

Kunsthalle Zürich
Limmatstrasse 270, t 044 272 15 15, www.kunsthallezurich.ch; open Tues, Wed, Fri 12–6, Thurs 12–8, Sat–Sun 11–5; adm, combined with the Migros Museum für Gegenwartskunst, free Thurs 5–8

Migros Museum für Gegenwartskunst
Limmatstrasse 270, t 044 277 20 50, www.migrosmuseum.ch; same opening hours and adm as Kunsthalle

Two Galleries Northwest of the Hauptbahnhof

If you are interested in modern art, take a walk along Limmatstrasse and you will find two interesting museums (plus other smaller galleries and a bookshop) housed in the converted Löwenbrau brewery.

At the **Kunsthalle Zürich** you will find contemporary art that will not yet have reached a wide audience. Generally, the work of only one artist – usually young – is displayed at a time.

The aim of the **Migros Museum für Gegenwartskunst** (Migros Museum of Contemporary Art) is to make international contemporary art available to as wide an audience as possible. The museum houses a permanent collection of 1,300 artworks by 700 artists and there is a rolling programme of temporary exhibitions.

Tourist Information and Services in Zürich

(i) Zürich >
Zürich Tourismus: ground-floor concourse, Hauptbahnhof, t 044 215 40 00, www.zuerich.com; open Nov–April Mon–Sat 8.30–7, Sun 9–6; May–Oct Mon–Sat 8–8.30, Sun 8.30–6.30; offers a hotel reservation service

ZürichCARD is available from the tourist office in the main station, at Zürich Airport and at some hotels. It is valid on all forms of transport, gives free admission to more than 40 museums, a complimentary welcome drink in 20 restaurants and a number of other discounts; CHF 19 for 24 hours or CHF 38 for 72-hours.

Guided Walk

Stroll Through The Old Town: this tour departs from the tourist office in the train station on Wed, Sat, Sun at 11am. It operates year-round. The commentary is in English and German, it takes 2 hours and the ticket costs CHF 20.

Internet Café

Internetcafé, Uraniastrasse 3, t 044 210 33 11, www.internetcafe.ch. Open Mon–Fri 7–11, Sat 8–11, Sun 10–10.

Lost Property and Police

Fundbüro Hauptbahnhof (Railway (SBB) Lost Property Office), the main station, t 0900 300 300, www.sbb.ch/fundservice, Mon–Fri 7–6.

Fundbüro der Stadt Zürich (Zürich City Lost and Found Office), Werdmühlestrasse 10, t 044 412 25 50, Mon–Fri 7.30–6.30.

Police Station, Bahnhofquai 3, t 044 216 671 11.

Market Days

Vegetable and Flower Market, Tues and Fri, Bürkiplatz, 6–11am.

Medical Services

Bellevue Apotheke, Theaterstrasse 14, t 044 266 62 22, www.bellevue-apotheke.com. A 24-hour pharmacy. **UniversitätsSpital Zürich** (University Hospital), Rämstrasse 100, t 044 255 21 11, www.usz.ch.

Exhibitions and Festivals in Zürich

Late Jan: Mercedes-CSI Zürich, www.mercedes-csi.ch, is a major international equestrian event.

Early Feb/late Mar: International Country Music Festival, which, lasting 6½ weeks, is the longest festival of its type in the world.

Late Feb/early Mar: Carnival.

Mid-April: Zürich *Sechseläuten*, the city's traditional spring festival.

Mid-June: Festival Tropical Caliente, *www.caliente.ch*, considered to be the largest Latin event in Switzerland and Europe.

Late June/mid-July: Zürich Festival, *www.zuercher-festspiele.ch*, with theatre, opera, music and other exhibitions.

1 Aug: Swiss National Day, celebrations and fireworks.

Late–end Aug: Zürich Theatre Spectacle, *www.theatrespektakel.ch*, international theatre festival.

Mid-Sept: *Knabenschiessen*, *www.knabenschiessen.ch*, Switzerland's largest fair where boys and girls aged 12 to 17 compete in a shooting competition, and the winners are crowned.

Late Sept/early Oct: Zürich Film Festival, *www.zurichfilmfestival.org*.

Shopping in Zürich

Undoubtedly, the best place to start shopping in Zürich is along Bahnhofstrasse, where you can find almost everything, from designer merchandise to souvenirs. It is well worth it, too, venturing off to explore the shops and boutiques in the pretty, old area between Bahnhofstrasse and the Limmat. The other side of Bahnhofstrasse is more modern, and you will find department stores and other larger shops.

ShopVille-RailCity, underneath the main railway station, *www.railcity.ch*, minimum opening hours Mon–Fri 9–9, Sat–Sun 9–8. Besides the airport, this is the only place in Zürich where you will find shops open on a Sunday; in fact the centre is open 365 days a year.

Meng Cutlery, *www.mengcutlery.ch*, has two shops close to Bahnhofstrasse. The one at Rennweg 31, **t** 044 211 18 48, has a fine collection of conventional (and unconventional) souvenirs, whilst the other at Poststrasse 4, **t** 044 211 23 67, has a wide range of knives, cutlery, etc.

Schweizer Heimatwerk, *www.heimatwerk.ch*, offers a good alternative to souvenirs – superb design in contemporary Swiss handicrafts in the form of household items, home furnishing accessories, jewellery, clothes and toys. Their shops are easily found as they are located at Rudolf Brun-Brücke, Bahnhofstrasse 2, Rennweg 14, the main hall of the Hauptbahnhof and at the airport in Transit Hall A behind passport control in the basement.

Drinks of the World, Halle Landesmuseum, ShopVille-RailCity, **t** 044 211 10 51, open daily 9–10, not only has the widest array of beers you can find anywhere, but it is the only place in Zürich where you can buy beer, wine and spirits to take away on a Sunday.

Confiserie Sprüngli, Paradeplatz, **t** 044 224 46 46, *www.confiserie-spruengli.ch*. This shop has been in business since 1836. One glance at the shop window will tell you instantly why – this is the famous address for exquisite Swiss chocolate, confectionery and cake specialities.

Where to Stay in Zürich

Luxury

*****ALDEN Hotel Splügenschloss, Splügenstrasse 2, **t** 044 289 99 99, *www.alden.ch*. This particularly gracious and charming hotel in a classic turn-of-the-century building is in a quiet suburb near the lake, but just a few minutes from the city centre. In 2004 it was completely refurbished and in the process the number of rooms was reduced to just 22. The rooms (including junior suites and suites) are not just huge, anywhere from 700–1,000sq ft (65–93sq m), but they are equipped to the very highest standards possible and have understated luxurious décor. Famous for its personal service and attention, the hotel has a delightful ambiance and a beautiful restaurant. In the summertime you can eat *al fresco* in an area in front of the hotel.

Expensive

****Schweizerhof Zürich, Bahnhofplatz 7, **t** 044 218 88 88, *www.hotelschweizerhof.com*. In a prime location directly across from the main railway station and on the corner of the famed Bahnhofstrasse. It offers 115 spacious rooms that all feature, amongst other facilities, an adjustable bed and tea/coffee kettle. Besides a welcome cocktail at check-in, expect a fabulous champagne breakfast buffet. The La Soupière restaurant features French cuisine and a particularly interesting wine list, while the Café Gourmet, with 20 seats and 10 stand-up places – and outside in the summertime – has an enticing champagne and caviar bar.

****Ambassador**, Falkenstrasse 6, t 044 258 98 98, *www.ambassador hotel.ch*. The location here is a little different, as it is tucked away behind the Opera House close to the lake. The 45 rooms are fair-sized and modern, with a safe for a laptop and modem connection (some rooms have an ISDN connection), as well as soundproof windows. There's a good bar, too.

Moderate–expensive

***Scheuble**, Mühlegasse 17, t 044 268 48 00, *www.scheuble.ch*. Behind an attractive 19th-century façade and the Florist Diel, is a hotel of some charm. In 1991 it was completely renovated by the architect Pia Schmid, who has brought a bright, modern ambiance with a blend of European and Asian accents to the 65 rooms. The location, too, is a real plus.

Moderate

***Hôtel du Theatre**, Seilergraben 69, t 044 267 26 70, *www.hotel-du-theatre.ch*. This once was an important German-speaking theatre in the 1950s. These days it is an interesting B&B hotel with 50 rooms innovatively designed, technically up-to-date and with soundproof windows. Forget bedtime reading, there are dozens of audio books awaiting your attention.

***Leoneck**, Leonhardstrasse 1, t 044 254 22 22, *www.leoneck.ch*. Less than a 6-min walk from the train station, at the tram stop 'Haldenegg', on lines 6, 7, 10 and 15. Its 65 very clean and comfortable rooms each have an often amusing Swiss ethno-style mural depicting a traditional Swiss scene behind the bed. Breakfast is in the highly whimsical Crazy Cow restaurant.

****Limmathof**, Limmatquai 142, t 044 267 60 40, *www.limmathof.com*. Centrally located directly across the Limmat River from the railway station. The comfortable, well-equipped rooms are within an historic house in the old part of town. It also has a vegetarian and a Swiss restaurant.

Lady's First, Mainaustrasse 24, t 044 380 80 10, *www.ladysfirst*. An unusual hotel in many respects; men are now allowed in, but not on the top two floors or in the spa. There are 28 high-ceilinged and parquet-floored modern and stylish rooms – as would be expected of those designed by Pia Schmid (*see* Hotel Scheuble) – in this 19th-century house. Take the No. 4 tram from the railway station, in the Tiefenbrunnen direction.

Zic Zac Rock-Hotel, Marktgasse 17, t 044 261 21 81, *www.ziczac.ch*. Every room here – and they come in varying sizes – is named after a pop star. It also offers 24-hour check-in and has two restaurants.

Moderate–inexpensive

*Martahaus–Garni**, Zähringerstrasse 36, t 044 251 45 50, *www.martahaus. ch*. Centrally located, this offers a wide variety of accommodation: single, double, treble or 4-bedded rooms, studios and even dormitories. To economize, choose rooms with toilet and shower on the floor.

Inexpensive

Villette, Kruggasse 4, t 044 251 23 35. Located in an old house in one of the narrow streets behind the Grossmünster and close to the Quai Brücke, its rooms are clean and comfortable. Continental breakfast included.

Youth Hostel Zürich, Mutscellenstrasse 114, t 043 399 78 00, *www.youth hostel.ch*. A combination of double/single with shower and toilet, 4-bedded rooms with shower and toilet and 4- and 5-bedded rooms with washbasin, as well as a recreation and TV room, washing and drying machines and an Internet corner. Take tram 4 from the railway station to the Morgental stop, then it's a short walk.

Hotel Biber–City Backpacker, Niederdorfstrasse 5, t 044 251 90 15, *www.city-backpacker.ch*. In the Old Town, this has kitchen and washing facilities, Internet station, a rooftop terrace and lockers, and offers dormitory accommodation.

Eating Out in Zürich

Very expensive

Haus zum Rüden, Limmatquai 42, t 044 261 95 66, *www.hauszum rueden.ch*. This building, beside the river, was first mentioned in 1295, and the first-floor restaurant has a genuine Gothic atmosphere. The classical Zürich specialities and the very fine wine list – try the unusual white Humagne du Valais – are equally impressive. The *menu gastronomique*, CHF 148pp without wine, is for those with fine palates and deep pockets. *Open Mon–Fri for lunch and dinner.*

Le Poisson, Claridenstrasse 30, t 044 286 22 22, *www.hotelglaernischhof.ch*. This award-winning restaurant is found in the Hotel Glärnischhof. Obviously, fish is the speciality, and it comes in many enticing combinations – including several dishes of gilt head bream, a local favourite. Leave room for the tasty, often alcohol-flavoured desserts, and from the smallish wine list select the rather unusual White Merlot. *Open Mon–Fri for dinner.*

Expensive

Le Dézaley, Restaurant Vaudois, Römergasse 7 + 9, t 044 251 61 29, *www.le-dezaley.ch*. This restaurant, under the shadow of the Grossmünster and in a 13th-century house, serves up a wide selection of traditional delights: Swiss cheese fondues, meat and Chinese fondues, sausages, *rösti* with liver, Zürich-style veal, local snails and crisp fried bread with all kinds of additions. *Closed Sun.*

Expensive/Moderate

Bodega Española, Münstergasse 15, t 044 251 23 10. In a circa 1874 building of much character, this is as good, and as authentic a Spanish restaurant as you will find. A formal restaurant is located upstairs, with a bodega-style bar on the ground floor, where mouthwatering tapas and robust wine are served at bench tables. *Open daily.*

Moderate

Turm, Tony Navarro Restaurant, Obere Zäune 19, t 044 262 52 00. The inside is nothing less than a tropical forest, enhanced with brightly covered chairs and tablecloths. Dishes are based on Mexican/Spanish cuisine – with a touch of Caribbean thrown in for good measure – and include such unusual, and debatable, delicacies as kangaroo and alligator fillets. *Open daily.*

 Raclette Stube >>

Raclette Stube, Zähringerstrasse 16, t 044 251 41 30, *www.raclette-stube.ch*. A small, typical Swiss restaurant of a style found more often in the countryside. Cheese specialities such as fondue and raclette, at reasonable prices, are the order of the day.

Restaurant Zeughauskeller, Bahnhofstrasse 28a, t 044 211 26 90, *www.zeughauskeller.ch*. Built in 1487 as the ancient arsenal of Zürich, this enormous restaurant, in which the original wooden beams and walls have been retained, along with everything from a modern cannon to bows and arrows, abounds with character. Enjoy hearty traditional Swiss dishes, many featuring pork and sausage, along with dessert specialities, served on huge bench tables.

Brasserie Federal, Bahnhof, t 044 217 15 15. Conveniently, this is in the main railway station, right next to the tourist office. The daily lunch menu is very reasonably priced, or you might want to select from over 100 Swiss beers whilst mulling over your tourist information.

Bars and Cafés in Zürich

Jules Verne Panorama Bar, Uraniastrasse 9, t 044 211 11 55 *www.brasserie-lipp.ch*. The entrance to this bar is through the Brasserie Lipp, where a lift will whisk you up to the 12th floor bar. Once there, treat yourself to one, or more, of an enticing selection of tapas and *pâtisseries*, and wash them down with champagne or a cocktail.

Restaurant Rheinfelder Bierhalle, Niederdorfstrasse 15, t 044 251 29 91. This is exactly what its name says it is – half restaurant, half beer hall – very informal, no privacy, but as cheap as you'll get. *Hauptbahnhof rösti, würste* and spaghetti Bolognese are among the dishes that feature on the menu.

Conditorei Café Schober, Napfgasse 4, t 044 251 80 60, *www.cafe-conditorei-schober.ch*. This should not be missed. It has the most tempting array of cakes, biscuits, chocolates and other goodies, along with all kinds of flavoured – including alcohol – teas, coffees and chocolates, juices and even aperitifs that you are ever likely to see. These can be taken in the lavishly decorated rooms or in a pleasant little outside patio.

Entertainment and Nightlife in Zürich

Zürich Opernhaus (Opera House), Falkenstrasse 1, t 044 268 64 00, *www.opernhaus.ch*. A gracious, Baroque-style building, where famous stars such as Cecilia Bartoli and Ruggero Raimondi perform.

The **Tonhalle**, Claridenstrasse 7, t 044 206 34, *www.tonhalle.ch*. Built in 1895; the present conductor of this world-famous orchestra is David Zinman.

Schauspielhaus, Schiffbaustrasse 6, t 044 265 58 58, *www.schauspielhaus.ch*. The city's largest theatre, and one of the most important theatres in the German-speaking world. Often features seasons with works of Chekhov, Ibsen and Frisch.

Hallenstadion, Wallisellenstrasse 45, t 044 316 77 77, *www.hellenstadion.ch*. This is Zürich's largest indoor arena and, as such, hosts a wide variety of

events from theatre productions to ice hockey games.

There is certainly no shortage of nightlife in Zürich. The club scene changes frequently as trends come and go, but up-to-date information is freely available in *City Guide Zürich*, *www.hellovisitors.com*, which has pages of current details. Similarly, *Zürich News*, *www.zuerich.ch*, a bi-weekly brochure, has more such information.

Moods, Schiffbaustrasse 6, t 044 276 80 80, *www.moods.ch*. The place for jazz enthusiasts. Located in Zürich's trendy new Zürich-West area, it's the prime location for jazz, funk, soul, etc.

Widder Bar, Widdergasse 6, t 044 224 25 26, *www.widderhotel.ch*. Where musicians and their fans from all over Europe have been gathering for decades. The bar's Spirits Library has 1,000 bottles including 500 spirits and 250 single-malt whiskies.

Nelson Pub, Beatengasse 11, t 044 212 60 16, *www.thenelsonpub.com*. A typical British pub and you can expect international beers and music here until 2am or 3am on weekdays and as late (or early) as 5am on Fri and Sat.

Abart, Manessastrasse 170, t 044 201 82 45, *www.abart.ch*. Fans of alternative and modern rock will like this place. It has Fri parties and discos on Sat that go on very late.

Rote Fabrik, Seestrasse 395, t 044 485 58 68, *www.rotefabrik.ch*. At Wollishofen out by Lake Zürich and there you can find everything from concerts, theatre, literature parties and films to good food and drink.

The gay and lesbian scene is quite open in Zürich. The *City Guide Zürich*, *www.hellovisitors.com*, has up-to-date information and the Zürich Tourist Office website, *www.zurichtourism.ch*, offers some relevant websites.

Labyrinth, Pfingstweidstrasse 70, *www.labyrinth.ch*. Has an open-ended time limit on Fri and Sat nights, and plays wild dance music.

East of Zürich

Winterthur

The Romans built a fort in Oberwinterthur, named *Vitudurum*, in the 1st century, but many more signs of life have been found from the early Middle Ages. However, it wasn't until 1180 that the Bishop of Constance gave the Counts of Kyburg authority to build a settlement in what is now the Old Town. The Kyburgers died out by 1264, and the Habsburgers took over and Winterthur received its town charter that year. In 1467 the Habsburgs ran into financial problems and subsequently pledged Winterthur to Zürich, and it remained subject to the larger city for the next 331 years. Although politically constrained, Winterthur began to flourish economically and from 1523 to 1525 the Reformation took hold in the town. The cultural life that it is famous for these days (it has 16 museums) began in the early 17th century with the founding of the Musikkollegium in 1629, and later, in 1798, it finally gained independence from Zürich. This, in addition to the introduction of freedom of trade in about 1830 and the opening of links to the rail network in 1857, set the foundations of economic prosperity. Industry, foreign trade, banking and insurance all developed in the city. In 1922 the suburbs of Winterthur were incorporated into the city, thus almost doubling the population. It is now Switzerland's sixth-largest city.

Winterthur's Museums

Sammlung Oskar Reinhart am Römerholz
Haldenstrasse 95, t 052 269 27 40, www.roemerholz.ch; open Tues, Thurs–Sun 10–5, Wed 10–8; adm

Sammlung Oskar Reinhart am Römerholz, located in a beautiful villa, is surrounded by an historic park that contains numerous sculptures. Within the villa you will find Reinhart's collection of Impressionist works from 19th-century French artists such as Renoir, Cézanne and Monet, along with Old Masters such as Rubens, Goya and Bruegel. (This museum was closed in December 2008 and is not due to reopen until sometime in mid-2010. In the meantime, these works have been incorporated into the Museum Oskar Reinhart am Stadtgarten, *see* below.)

Oskar Reinhart (1885–1965)

Oskar's father, Theodor Reinhart (1849–1919), ran the family firm, Volkart Brothers. It was one of the first companies in Switzerland (and indeed in the whole of Europe) to develop trading links with India. As the textile industry was traditionally powerful in Winterthur, it concentrated on cotton trade. As the elder Reinhart had a great interest in the arts, particularly sponsoring young Swiss and German artists, Oscar grew up with, and was intrigued by, this environment. Consequently in 1924, at the age of 39, he became a full-time art collector and in the same year bought the Villa am Römerholz. It was to be both a home and a museum for his ever-growing collection. Unusually, he was one of the few collectors to focus on 19th-century German artists. Being a benefactor at heart, in 1940 he donated his 18th–20th-century collection of German, Swiss and Austrian art to the city. Later, in 1958 before his death, the rest of his collection was donated to the Swiss nation.

Getting to and around Winterthur

By **car**, Winterthur is just 25mins northwest of Zürich on the A1 motorway. With the exception of St Gallen, roads from all the other main cities pass by Zürich on the way.

With the exception of St Gallen, which has direct services, **train** services from every other major city run through, or require you to change at, Zürich, from where Winterthur is just 20mins away.

If you are visiting the **Sammlung Oskar Reinhart am Römerholz**, which is a little way out of the city on a hilltop, take the **Museumsbus**, *www.stadtbus.winterthur.ch*, that departs from platform G at the main railway station. It runs Tues–Sun, and also stops at the **Museum Oskar Reinhart am Stadtgarden** and the **Kunstmuseum**. On Sun it additionally calls at the **Villa Flora** and the **Fotomuseum**.

Museum Oskar Reinhart am Stadtgarten
Stadthausstrasse 6,
t 052 267 51 72,
www.museumoskarreinhart.ch; open Tues 10–8,
Weds–Sun 10–5; adm

Museum Oskar Reinhart am Stadtgarten opened in 1951 and holds Oscar Reinhart's extensive collection of 18th–20th-century German, Swiss and Austrian art. The 19-century German works within the collection are considered to be the most important outside Germany.

Villa Flora
Tösstalstrasse 44,
t 052 212 99 66,
www.villaflora.ch; open Tues–Sat 2–5, Sun 11–3; adm

Villa Flora is another delightful villa surrounded by gardens and sculptures. It houses the collection of Hedy and Arthur Hahnloser, who spent the years 1907–30 focusing on a very select group of artists, particularly post-Impressionist painters. As a consequence, they developed an exceptional collection of Swiss and French art, including such famous names as Vallotton, Bonnard and Vuillard, as well as the Fauves and Matisse. There are also works by Giovanni Giacometti and Ferdinand Hodler, one of the best-known Swiss painters of the 19th century. The collection is displayed in changing exhibitions.

Kunstmuseum
Museumstrasse 52,
t 052 267 51 62,
www.kmw.ch; open Tues 10–8, Wed and Sun 10–5; adm

The **Kunstmuseum** (Museum of Art) is housed in two buildings, one old and the other relatively new. In the former you will find art from the late 19th century up to the Cubist period, while in the latter the range is from avant-garde works through to the present. The works are divided into self-contained galleries based around a particular theme.

Fotomuseum
Grüzenstrasse 44–5,
t 052 234 10 60; open Tues, Thurs–Sun 11–6, Wed 11–8; adm

The **Fotomuseum** (Museum of Photography) is unique in Switzerland and it shares its home with the Swiss Foundation of Photography. Its extensive collection, ranging from 19th- and 20th-century to contemporary works, is shown in ever-changing exhibitions.

Tourist Information and Services in Winterthur

(i) **Winterthur >**
Winterthur Tourismus: Hauptbahnhof, t 052 267 67 00, www.winterthur-tourismus.ch; open Mon–Fri 8.30–6.30, Sat 8.30–4

The Winterthur **Museum Pass** is available at the tourist office (Winterthur Tourismus) and at the museums. A one-day pass is CHF 20, two days CHF 30 (check before buying as some museums are excluded). It also allows use of the Museumsbus (*see* top of this page).

Where to Stay and Eat in Winterthur

***Sorell Hotel Krone**, Marktgasse 49, t 052 208 18 18, *www.krone winterthur.ch* (*expensive*). This boutique hotel has 40 recently refurbished modern and spacious rooms. The Bistro La Couronne offers creative cuisine classic dishes, enhanced by wine sold by the glass. Look for special venison dishes when in season.

St Gallen

St Gallen, the seventh-largest city in Switzerland, is a thoroughly charming town whose medieval centre co-exists in easy harmony with 21st-century demands.

According to legend, the town was founded in 612 by a roving Irish monk by the name of Gallo. He built a hermitage here that became the foundation for an abbey, the first stone buildings of which were erected in 719. Within this complex, art and culture thrived, and during the 9th and 10th centuries it was one of the foremost centres of learning in the Western world. The growing numbers of visitors attracted tradesmen, and in the mid-14th century a guild constitution gave power over the city to the six trade guilds and the association of powerful businessmen (Zum Notenstein). The manufacture of textiles has played an important role in the history of St Gallen since the Middle Ages, with linen production superseded by cotton and embroidery in the 18th century.

The Old Town

Stiftsbibliothek St Gallen

t 071 227 34 16, www.stiftsbibliothek.ch; open Mon–Sat 10–5, Sun 10–4; closed/ reduced opening hours on certain hols; adm; overslippers provided

The main attraction here is undoubtedly the world-famous **Stiftsbibliothek St Gallen** (Abbey Library of St Gallen). This is one of the oldest libraries in the world, and houses a collection of more than 100,000 books and manuscripts, some dating back to the 5th century. There are magnificent examples of handwritten books and a collection of 1,650 incunabula (books printed before 1500). The building was constructed in 1758, with a highly elaborate interior completed nearly a decade later in 1767, and it has a glorious elegance. Two tiers of incredible glassed-in bookcases stand beneath intricate ceiling frescoes depicting the first four Oecumenical Councils (Nicaea in 325, Constantinople in 381, Ephesus in 431 and Chalcedon in 451), between side lunettes portraying the Fathers of the Church; below is a lovely inlaid parquet floor. The abbey complex was added to the UNESCO world cultural treasures list in 1983, largely thanks to this extraordinary room.

Kathedrale

www.stifts bibliothek.ch; open 9–6 daily except when services are being held

Adjacent, the **Kathedrale** is dominated by two immense spires. It was constructed by Peter Thumb between 1755 and 1767 as a replacement for the previous medieval structures. The interior design was a collaborative effort by Josef Wannemacher, artist; the Gigel Brothers, stuccowork; and J. A. Feuchtmayer, wood-carving. An extensive restoration undertaken between 1961 and 1967 restored the building to its original condition, most notably

Getting to and around St Gallen

By **car**, motorways from Basel, Bern and Geneva converge at Baden and then the road continues on to Zürich, Winterthur and St Gallen. From Chur, Graubünden and Lichtenstein the motorway continues directly north to Lake Constance and then turns west to St Gallen.

From Zürich the quickest **train** services involve a change at either Winterthur or Schaffhausen. From Basel, services require a change at Zürich. From either Geneva or Bern the fastest services run through Zürich and on to St Gallen, other services require changes at Zürich.

There is a good local city **bus** network, but once you're in the city all of the places of interest are within reasonable walking distance.

Lapidarium
t 071 227 34 15 (recorded information on opening hours in German only); www.stiftsbibliothek.ch; open Mon–Sat 10–5, Sun 10–4; closed/reduced opening hours on certain hols and when cleaning/reorganization takes place; adm

St Laurenzen-Kirche
t 071 222 67 92; open winter Mon 9.30–11.30, 2–4, Tues–Sat 9.30–4; summer Mon 9.30–11.30, 2–4, Tues–Fri 9.30–6.30, Sat 9.30–4; adm for tower, by appointment only

uncovering the ceiling frescoes of the chancel and restoring that entire room to its original colours. By the cathedral west entrance is the **Lapidarium**, where there is a collection of valuable building stones from the 8th to 17th centuries.

Just north is the **St Laurenzen-Kirche** (Church of St Laurence). The first building on this site was a tiny cemetery chapel erected around AD 850, replaced by a larger one dedicated to St Laurence in the 11th century. It is widely held that it was associated in some way with the monastery. In the 13th century it became the parish church, giving the people who worshipped there some degree of autonomy from the monastery. The fire of 1314 destroyed the church and it was a full century later, in 1413, that work commenced on a new Gothic-style building. During the Reformation, in 1527, Holy Communion was celebrated in St Laurence's according to Protestant rites, and it emerged as the town's Protestant church. The church underwent significant rebuilding from 1850–54.

The narrow streets and alleys of the Old Town to the north, east and west of here remain essentially the same today as when the street plan was laid out following the Great Fire of 1418. Besides being a shopping area these days, the Old Town is famous for beautiful old houses, particularly their extended upper level windows, called oriels, of which over 100 have been preserved. They were once considered an indication of the wealth of the owner; the affluent cloth merchants would compete among themselves to design the most ornamental and intricate *beau idéal*. Two of the more notable examples along Multergasse are found upon the

1. Stock-biezlie

One of the pleasures of St Gallen is a visit to one of the '*1. Stock-biezlie*'. These quaint first-storey taverns serve tasty local specialities such as St Gallen sausage – made using a singular recipe that dates from 1438 – and *Biber*, a spicy honey cake filled with marzipan. The perfect accompaniment is a glass or two of Rheintaler wine.

Gothic edifice of the Zum Schiff (the Ship), on which the oriel dates from around 1600, and upon the Zum Rebstock (the Vine), a structure first mentioned in 1422, renovated in 1793 and embellished with a wooden oriel from 1783. Gallusstrasse and Gallusplatz, west of the cathedral, also have fine examples.

Around the periphery of the Old Town are some other interesting places. Starting clockwise to the north, the former **St Katharinen-Kloster** (Convent of St Catherine) in Katharinengasse was founded in 1228, but closed three centuries later and is now used as a lending library for toys. Pride of place here belongs to the calm Gothic cloister. South of that, the **Waaghus am Bohl** or **Kaufhaus**, adorned by an intricate clock, is where merchants took their goods to be weighed from the Middle Ages to the 19th century. Further around, close to the cathedral, the **Karlstor** (Karl's Gate) originates from 1570 and is the only fully preserved gate of the former city walls; it was named in honour of the first person to pass through it, Cardinal Karl Borromäus of Milan.

West of the Old Town

To the west towards the train station is **Broderbrunnen**, an intricately embellished water fountain at the junction of St Leonhard-Strasse and Oberer Graben. Further down Leonhard-Strasse is a striking Art Nouveau building that now houses the Austrian consulate. Surprisingly, this eccentric building is not alone in St Gallen: these early 20th-century structures are attributable to the wealth generated by the lucrative textile industry. Appropriately, the **Textilmuseum** (Textile Museum) is just around the corner, and displays historical embroidery from the 14th to 20th centuries and European lace from the 16th to 20th centuries.

Textilmuseum
Vadianstrasse 2,
t 071 222 17 44,
www.textilmuseum.ch;
open Mon–Sun 10–5;
adm

One other unusual attraction in this area is the **Stadtlounge** (City Lounge), opened in 2005, which has transformed the Bleicheli area, St Gallen's financial district. A local bank hosted a design competition to create a 'public living room' in the centre of the district. The winners, artists Pipilotti Rist and Carlos Martinez, came up with the innovative idea of covering the area in a bright red rubber 'carpet'. The carpet covers the pavements, street furniture and even a car. Roads in the area are covered in red asphalt. At night the district is lit by UFO-like hanging lamps. The area is intended to encourage people to congregate, chat and relax.

Stadtlounge
www.stadtlounge.ch

North of the Old Town

To the north of the Old Town, and suitably on Museumstrasse, is a group of other museums such as the **Naturmuseum** (Natural

Naturmuseum
Museumstrasse 32,
t 071 242 06 70,
www.naturmuseumsg.c
h; open Tues–Sun 10–5,
Wed till 8; adm

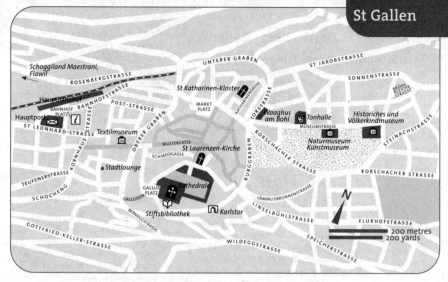

Historiches und Völkerkindmuseum
*Museumstrasse 50,
t 071 242 06 42,
www.hmsg.ch; open
Tues–Sun 10–5; adm*

Kunstmuseum
*Museumstrasse 32,
t 071 242 06 71,
www.kunstmuseumsg.ch;
open Tues–Sun 10–5, Wed
until 8; closed Mon and
certain hols; adm*

History Museum), the **Historiches und Völkerkindmuseum** (History and Folklore Museum) and **Kirchhofer House** (by appointment only) with Palaeolithic discoveries and the silver collection of Dr Giovanni Züst. On this street, too, is the **Kunstmuseum** (Museum of Fine Arts), one of the finest examples of 19th-century classical architecture in Switzerland. Pride of place belongs to works by Anton Graff, Carl Spitweg and Ferdinand Georg Waldmüller, along with fine examples of Bücklin, Feuerbach and Marées and their German Idealism work; modern art features, too, with some Klees and Picassos amongst others, and even work by Jean Tinguely (*see* p.104). The famous **Tonhalle** concert hall and puppet theatre are along here, too.

A Short Trip from St Gallen

Schoggiland Maestrani
*Toggenburgerstrasse 41,
Flawil,
t 071 228 38 88,
www.schoggi-land.ch;
open Mon–Fri 12 and 2–6,
Sat 9–12; guided tours
every Wed 2pm, and Thurs
2pm on certain days
during hols; adm*

Schoggiland Maestrani, a chocolate factory, is found just to the west of St Gallen in Flawil. Here you will discover the secret of how chocolate is made and what makes Swiss chocolate so different. You can watch the chocolate being made from the visitors' gallery and video terminals inform you about the company's history and how the chocolate is manufactured. The production machinery is not usually in operation on a Saturday, but the factory shop (including the highlight of the trip – free tastings) and visitors' gallery are open.

(i) **St Gallen >**
St Gallen-
Bodensee Tourismus:
Bahnhofplatz 1a,
t 071 227 37 37,
www.st.gallen-
bodensee.ch; open
Mon–Fri 9–6, Sat 9–12

Festival in St Gallen

Open Air St Gallen, *www.openairsg.ch*, has been a tradition since 1977. Held just outside the city in the picturesque Sitter River loop, this three-day event plays host to some of the world's best rock and contemporary music artists. The event takes place on the last weekend in June.

Where to Stay in St Gallen

****Einstein**, Berneggstrasse 2, **t** 071 227 55 55, *www.einstein.ch* (*expensive*). Close to the abbey, this classy hotel is also known as the 'Little Grand Hotel'. All its 113 rooms and suites are quiet, modern and very comfortable. It also has a restaurant with panoramic views over the abbey district and a bar that offers light meals.

***Gallo Garni**, St Jakobstrasse 62, **t** 071 242 71 71, *www.hotel-gallo.ch* (*moderate*). Easily recognizable by its second-floor oriel, this is a refined and stylish hotel situated close to the exhibition grounds, theatre and

concert hall and near the city centre. Affiliated with it is an Italian restaurant named, appropriately enough, Galletto.

***Boutique Hotel Jägerhof**, Brühlbleichestrasse 11, **t** 071 245 50 22, *www.jaegerhof.ch*, (*moderate*). Located in a gracious corner house, this has 41 interesting rooms, along with the first fully organic restaurant in Switzerland, and the biggest wine list in the region.

Eating Out in St Gallen

Bäumli, Schmeidgasse 18, **t** 071 222 11 74, *www.weinstube-baeumli.ch* (*moderate*). With its vaulted Gothic ceiling this tavern is a typical example of a 1. *Stock-biezlie* and it serves all of the dishes you'd expect.

Hörnli, Marktplatz 5, **t** 071 222 66 86, *www.hoernli.ch* (*moderate*). This is another 1. *Stock-biezlie*. It oozes atmosphere as mentions of this tavern have been traced back as far as 1720 and the ground floor has been used as a warehouse and stables. It offers 10 beers on tap and has a delightful garden restaurant.

 Vaduz

Vaduz, Liechtenstein

The city of Vaduz, with a population of around 5,000, is the capital of Liechtenstein, a tiny landlocked country in the centre of Europe between Austria and Switzerland. It is the fourth smallest country in Europe with a land area of just 61¾sq miles (16,006 hectares) and a population of a mere 34,500.

History

Permanently inhabited since 3000 BC, Liechtenstein was colonized by the Celts and later, around 800 BC, by the Rhaetians. The Romans conquered in 15 BC but the 5th century saw a mass migration of Germanic peoples from the north who forced the Romans out. Centuries later the area came under the rule of a German dukedom, becoming part of the country of Lower Rhaetia.

Historically Liechtenstein was divided into two parts: the Lordship of Schellenberg and the County of Vaduz, each owned over the years by various dynasties of counts. Prince Johann Adam Andreas of Liechtenstein's purchase of first Schellenberg in 1699 and subsequently Vaduz in 1712 earned him a seat in the Diet of the

Getting to and around Vaduz

By far the easiest way to reach Vaduz from all destinations in eastern Switzerland is by **car** on the A13 motorway from Zürich and on to Sargans, before turning north to Vaduz.

Trains do not operate from Switzerland to Liechtenstein. From Basel and Zürich it's necessary to change at Sargans for a **bus** connection to Vaduz. From Geneva and Bern change at Zürich before connecting with the bus at Sargans. From Graubünden, trains run from St Moritz to Chur and on to Sargans, for the bus connection.

With the exception of the **Prince of Liechtenstein's Court Winery** (take the no. 12 bus), all other places of interest are grouped together in the centre of town, so you can get around on foot.

Princes, which was under the dominion of the German Empire. In 1719 Kaiser Karl VI decreed that Schellenberg and Vaduz be elevated to the status of the Imperial Principality of Liechtenstein. It has the distinction of being the only country in the world to still carry the name of its original dynasty.

First a part of Napoleon's Rhine Confederacy and then of the German confederation, Liechtenstein has been a fully sovereign, neutral country since 1866 when the latter was dissolved. Since 1924 it has maintained a customs treaty with Switzerland that, effectively, has formed a common economic region between the two small countries in which Swiss customs officers patrol the border with Austria and the Swiss franc (CHF) is the legal currency.

Liechtenstein is 'a constitutional hereditary monarchy upon a democratic and parliamentary basis'. The prince, as head of state, represents Liechtenstein in its relationships with other countries, whilst the rights and interests of the citizens are protected by a parliament – the Landtag. The first prince to make his permanent residence in Liechtenstein, rather than Vienna, was Franz-Josef II, who reigned from 1938 until his death in 1989. He was succeeded by his oldest son, Prince Hans-Adam II, the reigning monarch.

High German is taught in the schools and used as the official language, but the majority of the natives speak a dialect similar to Swiss German – a derivative that is difficult even for other German-speaking peoples to understand.

Around the Town

Physically, Vaduz is dominated by the very grand castle that is home to the prince (not open to the public). Best guess is that the original, which was destroyed by troops of the Swiss Confederacy during the Swabian War of 1499, was constructed in the Middle Ages. The present structure dates from the 16th and 17th centuries.

Kunstmuseum
Städtle 32,
t 423 235 03 00,
www.kunstmuseum.li;
open Tues–Sun 10–5,
Thurs until 8; adm

The most important attraction in Vaduz is the **Kunstmuseum** (Museum of Fine Arts). The building itself, inaugurated in 2000, is an eye-catching cube of anthracite-coloured basalt rock that is stunning enough, but it is actually overshadowed by the exhibits based on the world-famous collections of the prince of Liechtenstein. Rembrandt's *Amor* and Rubens' *Venus* are the highlights of the Old Masters, and they sit next to important works from modern and contemporary art.

Postmuseum
Städtle 37 (in the same building as the tourist office), t 423 239 68 46, www.landesmuseum.li/ d/postmuseum.asp; open daily 10–12 and 1–5

Philately has always been important here, and the **Postmuseum** (Postage Stamp Museum) is very popular. Established in 1930, it houses a large collection of stamps issued by Liechtenstein from 1912 onwards, and of swapped stamps from other countries in the International Philatelic Society that date from 1921 onwards. There are numerous other exhibits of items relevant to the design and printing of stamps and the Liechtenstein postal service.

Another local tradition is detailed at the **FIS Ski-Museum**. Founded by former ski racer and expert Noldi Beck, its exhibits trace the evolution of skiing from its inception as a necessity for farmers and hunters to what is today almost exclusively a leisure pursuit.

FIS Ski-Museum
Fabrikstrasse 5, t 423 232 15 02, www.skimuseum.li; open Mon–Fri 2–6; adm

Hofkellerie des Fürsten von Liechtenstein
Fürstliche Domäne, Feldstrasse 4, t 423 232 10 18; www.hofkellerei.li; open Mon–Fri 8–12 and 1.30–6, Sat 9–1

The prince's presence here shows itself in some unexpected ways, and a visit to the **Hofkellerie des Fürsten von Liechtenstein** (Prince of Liechtenstein's Court Winery), just a short distance from the centre of Vaduz, is a must. Although covering less than 10 acres (4 hectares), Liechtenstein's wine-making tradition has a long and distinguished history supported by naturally conducive conditions – ideal southwest-orientated hillsides, calcareous soil and a climate that gives out about 1,500 hours of annual sunshine. The most famous of the wines are the dry reds of Süssdruck and Beerli, which can be tasted, along with vintages from the other winery at Wilfersdorf, and bought here.

Tourist Information in Vaduz

ⓘ **Vaduz >**
Liechtenstein Tourismus: Städtle 37, t 423 239 63 00, www.tourismus.li; open daily 9–5

The tourist office is also home to the **Liechtenstein Center**. It gives you the unique opportunity to get a comprehensive picture of the diversity of this small country using state-of-the-art multimedia technology and by watching fascinating film footage. You can also purchase unique Liechtenstein stamps and souvenirs in the shop.

If you wish to have your passport stamped as a memento of your visit, the tourist office staff will oblige for only CHF 3, with the official Fürstentum Lietchtenstein stamp.

Shopping in Vaduz

Thönys Schuhgeschäft, Städtle 17, t 423 232 23 18. The best place to buy Swiss Army knives, or any other souvenir.

Where to Stay and Eat in Vaduz

*****Park-Hotel Sonnenhof**, Mareestrasse 29, t 423 239 02 02, www.sonnenhof.li (*luxury*). A very comfortable hotel just a short distance from Vaduz. Set in a park, it offers a traditional style, modern facilities, pool and health club, and views of the Rhine and Alps. It also has an excellent restaurant.

***Le Real**, Städtle 21, t 423 232 22 22, www.hotel-real.li (*moderate*). A small hotel, just 13 rooms and suites, extremely comfortable and centrally located on the main pedestrian-only street in Vaduz.

North of Zürich

⭐ Rhine Falls
Schaffhausen and the Rhine Falls

Schaffhausen owes its existence to the Rhine Falls (Rheinfall), the largest in Europe. These rapids, formerly known as the Upper and Lower Laufen, interrupted the transport of goods by water so that all commodities not sold locally had to be moved by horse-drawn carriages around the falls.

History

Count Eberhard III of Nellenburg, anticipating the importance of this site to river merchants of the Rhine, Danube and Aare, founded a town here. His cousin, Heinrich III, who was the German emperor, granted Eberhard the right to mint coins for the new town, Scafusun, in 1045. Four years later, Eberhard founded the All Saints Abbey. And in 1080 Eberhard's son, Burkhart, gifted the town to the abbey. The needs of the abbey soon outgrew its structure, however, and, in 1104, the Bishop of Constance inaugurated a much larger replacement, which stands today as a magnificent example of the Romanesque style of architecture.

The early 16th century brought the Reformation. In turn, the religious wars that ensued between 1564 and 1585 brought the need for improved fortifications – hence the construction of the Munot. Schaffhausen enjoyed the fruits of prosperity for two centuries longer, especially during the 18th century when a flurry of construction saw, among other things, approximately 150 beautiful bay windows (oriels) added to its houses. Gradually, though, changes in the customs association, the discovery of new salt deposits in Schweizerhalle and, perhaps more importantly, the coming of the railways, altered the economic balance.

All was not lost, however. In 1866, Heinrich Moser constructed a large dam across the Rhine, and the power generated from its hydroelectric works provided Schaffhausen with the spark it needed to play a prominent role in the Industrial Revolution. Unfortunately this attracted the attention of the Allied Forces during the Second World War and Schaffhausen was bombed by the American air force on 1 April 1944.

Today, this town of just over 34,000 people has the ambiance of one that time has passed by. On nearly every street, all of which are dominated by the massive Munot fortress towering above, you will find picture-perfect houses with elaborately decorated, painted and sculptured façades. Squares, large and small, are graced by fountains and guarded by statues of the likes of William Tell. Few will know, also, that this northwestern corner of Switzerland is an important wine-growing region.

Getting to and around Schaffhausen

By **boat**, you can travel from Stein am Rhein on a **Schweizerische Schiffahrtsgesellschaft Untersee und Rhein** service, t 052 634 08 88, *www.urh.ch*.

If travelling by **car**, with the exception of St Gallen, which is connected via Winterthur, all other motorway links run via Zürich. From Basel it's possible to take a non-motorway route via Tiengen, Germany.

From Zürich there are direct **train** services, or those with changes at Winterthur. From Basel there are services on **SBB** via Zürich or more complicated routes from the German **Badischer** station. From either Geneva or Bern services run via Zürich. From St Gallen it is much more complicated: some services require changes at Weinfelden and Winterthur, another a change at Romanshorn and continuing via Stein am Rhein, and a very roundabout one changes at Kreuzilingen, Konstanz and Singen.

Once you are in the town everything is within **walking** distance.

Schaffhausen

Münster zu Allerheiligen
t 052 624 39 71;
open daily 8–6

The **Münster zu Allerheiligen** (Cathedral of All Saints), originally founded by Eberhard von Nellenburg in 1049, and rebuilt shortly afterwards, is one of the finest examples of pure Romanesque architecture in Switzerland. The tower, constructed around 1200, is considered one of the most beautiful in the country, and Count Eberhard is interred in the crypt. The aura of tranquillity extends itself into the adjoining cloister and herb garden. The former, part 12th-century Romanesque and part 13th-century Gothic, is the largest in the country. It includes a delightful garden and the Junkernfriedhof (Noblemen's Cemetery), in which civic dignitaries and other important townspeople were laid to rest between 1582 and 1874.

Museum zu Allerheiligen
Baumgartenstrasse 6,
t 052 633 07 77,
www.allerheiligen.ch;
open Tues–Sun 11–5;
adm

There are two museums of some interest next to the cathedral. The **Museum zu Allerheiligen** (Museum of All Saints) is in an attractive old building and has a mixed bag of exhibits. The **Hallen für Neue Kunst** (Halls of Modern Art) is located in an old worsted yarn factory and hosts large-scale installations by a number of contemporary artists.

Hallen für Neue Kunst
Baumgartenstrasse 23,
t 052 625 25 15,
www.modern-art.ch;
open Sat 3–5, Sun 11–7,
otherwise by
appointment; adm

High to the east, the imposing **Munot**, with vineyards around it, is the symbol of Schaffhausen. This highly unusual defensive battlement was constructed between 1564 and 1585 in a prominent defensive position with views over the town, the Rhine and the surrounding countryside. It has a unique circular keep that is protected by thick walls, and a ceiling supported by round, very thick columns and arches. The watchman still resides in the solitary tower and every evening at 9pm he rings a bell that, in days gone by, was the signal to close the town gates and public houses.

Munot
www.munot.ch; open
May–Sept 8–8;
Oct–April 9–5

The **Fronwagplatz** is the traditional marketplace, and the home of the Fronwagturm tower, adorned with an astronomical clock that dates from 1564 and shows no less than ten different features.

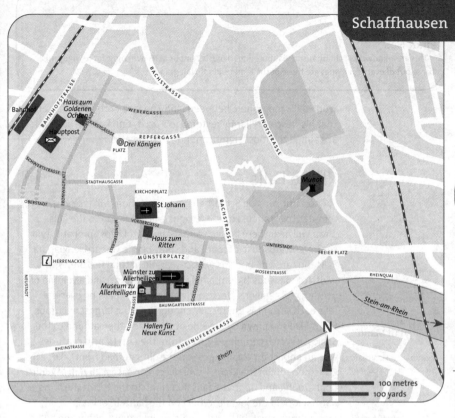

Colourful water fountains adorn the Old Town, and nearby is the **Mohrenbrunnen** (Moor's Fountain) that dates from 1535 and is named after Kaspar, the youngest of the Three Holy Kings. Another fine example of this genre, with an octagonal pool and dating from 1632 (replacing the 1522 original), is the **Tellenbrunnen** (William Tell Fountain) to the east.

Beautiful houses are one of the features of Schaffhausen, and just north of Fronwagplatz, at Vorstadt 17, the **Haus zum Goldenen Ochsen** (House of the Golden Ox), which prior to 1608 was an inn, is one of the grandest. Notable among its features are a late Gothic façade decorated with frescoes showing a golden ox and symbols from Babylonian and ancient Greek history. At Platz 7, just to the east, the house of the **Drei Königen** (Three Kings) dates from 1746 and, in addition to its rococo façade, is known for the statues of the Three Kings that sit above the second-floor windows. Just to the south, near the corner of Vordergasse and Münstergasse, the **Haus zum Ritter** (Knight's House) is considered the most beautiful in town. Knight Hans von Waldkirch rebuilt it in 1566, commissioning local artist Tobias Stimmer to decorate the exterior. Stimmer

Pinot Noir
This area, known as Schaffhausen Blauburgunderland, is famous in its own right for its vineyards. Three out of every four vines are those of the famous Pinot Noir grape.

worked his magic here between 1568 and 1570 with such mastery that his fresco, brilliantly restored in 1943 by Carl Roesch, has been acclaimed the most significant north of the Alps.

Rhine Falls

A no. 1 **bus**, outside Schaffhausen train station, will take you in 15 minutes to Neuhausen, where signs will direct you to the falls.

You will hear them before you see them and, most probably, will see an upwards rush of foam and spray before you arrive. Niagara Falls they are not; but this 17,000-year-old natural feature, with a width of 164 yards (150m), a height of 75½ft (23m) and a volume of over 153,978.5 gallons (700,000 litres) of water passing over the falls each second, is impressive enough, and the largest in Europe. Steps lead you down by the side of them, and then around to the Schlössli Wörth complex – which from the 12th to 19th centuries was an important trading post on the old salt road from Lake Constance down the Rhine – where you can take a **Rhyfall Mändli** boat around and up to the falls and climb to the top of the famous Känzeli rock in the middle. Whilst on the Känzeli rock it is fascinating to watch the Arlette fish vainly trying, again and again, to jump over the falls on their way upriver. Also from here, **Schiff** boats embark on longer cruises down the Rhine. On 1 August, Swiss National Day, a glorious fireworks display explosively adds a rainbow of illumination to this already magnificent sight.

Rhyfall Mändli
*t 052 672 48 11,
www.maendli.ch; open
April–Oct 11–5; May and
Sept 10–6; July–Aug
9.30–6.30*

Schiff boats
*t 052 659 69 00,
www.schiffmaendli.ch;
open Mar–June;
Sept–Oct weekends;
July–Aug daily*

ⓘ **Schaffhausen >**
*Schaffhauserland
Tourismus:
Herrenacker 15,
t 052 632 40 20,
www.schaffhauser
land.ch; open June–Sept
Mon–Fri 9.30–6, Sat
9.30–4, Sun (May–Aug)
9.30–2; Oct–May
Mon–Fri 9.30–5, Sat
9.30–2*

Tourist Information and Services in Schaffhausen

Guided Walk

Guided **old town** strolls, organized by Schaffhauserland Tourismus, take place May–mid-Oct on Tues at 10am and Sat at 2pm. The tour takes 1¼ hours and costs CHF 14.

Shopping in Schaffhausen

Grieshaber, Vordergasse 84, **t** 052 624 77 31. Has a deer's head as a symbol, and one is on display in this shop that has a wide range of Victorinox products and other souvenirs.

Where to Stay in Schaffhausen

*****Rheinhotel Fischerzunft**, Rheinquai 8, **t** 052 632 05 05, *www.fischerzunft.ch (expensive)*. Standing within a few feet of the Rhine, this 19th-century building is home to just 10 comfortable rooms, each appointed to the highest standards and decorated in European style with Asiatic influences. Added to this is the chance to experience owner/chef André Jaeger's astounding culinary creations (*see* below).

(i) **Rhine Falls >>**
Info-Shop Rheinfall:
Rhenfallquai,
t 052 670 02 37,
www.schaffhauserland.
ch; open Nov–Mar daily
10–4; April–May, Oct
9.30–5; June–Sept 9–6

(★) **Rheinhotel**
Fischerzunft >

***Zunfthaus zum Rüden**, Oberstadt 20, **t** 052 632 36 36, *www.rueden.ch* (*moderate*). Built in the 14th and 15th centuries, this old Guildhall is located just a couple of minutes from the train station. Its 30 rooms and public areas combine historical ambience with 21st-century convenience.

Eating Out

Schaffhausen

Rheinhotel Fischerzunft, Rheinquai 8, **t** 052 632 05 05, *www.fischerzunft.ch* (*very expensive*). A unique restaurant and dining experience. André Jaeger, the owner/chef and president of Les Grandes Tables de Suisse (*www.grandestables.ch*), has combined the best of oriental and French cuisine to create dishes that are not only delectable to the palate, but beautiful to the eye. The dining room has wooden beams, antiques and even a modern art collection. Its lovely tables, set to perfection right down to the fine crystal, are a fitting compliment to the unique dishes.

Güterhof, Freier Platz 10, **t** 052 630 40 40, *www.gueterhof.ch* (*moderate*). A restaurant with a delightful location on the banks of the Rhine, it has a beautiful terrace from which you can admire the view. It's an interesting combination of a restaurant with a gastronomic menu, a café, a sushi bar and a bar/lounge. It also offers a takeaway service.

Rhine Falls

Schlössli Wörth, Rhenfallquai, **t** 052 672 24 21, *www.schloessliwoerth.ch* (*expensive*). Located in the old fort, this is a charming restaurant with huge picture windows overlooking the falls themselves. Besides a fine regular menu, there are also daily specials.

Stein am Rhein

Stein am Rhein is located at a strategic spot where the Rhine leaves the Untersee – one of the three sections of Lake Constance (Bodensee). Its name means 'Stone on the Rhine'. The Romans built the first bridge over the river here, and a Benedictine monastery has been at Stein since the 14th and 15th centuries. Its medieval connections, however, are its claim to fame, with a fantastic array of wooden-beamed houses that are beautifully and extensively decorated with intricate frescoes and extended bay windows (oriels). It is regarded as Switzerland's best-preserved small medieval town, which means that its small population of 3,000 can be overwhelmed with tourists in the summer season.

The Old Town

Rathausplatz is both the social centre and the main attraction of the town. The *rathaus* (town hall) was built between 1539 and 1542, although it has been renovated twice since. The houses around the square, and elsewhere, have the most ornate decorations you are ever likely to see. Originally, the wealthy residents decided that, as testimony to their affluence, they would decorate the exteriors of their mansions with the most detailed frescoes. Many of these were painted between 1520 and 1525 by the German Thomas Schmede. The town is now reputed to have the world's largest

Getting to and around Stein am Rhein

Stein am Rhein can be reached by **boat** from Schaffhausen on a **Schweizerische Schiffahrtsgesellschaft Untersee und Rhein** service, **t** 052 634 08 88, *www.urh.ch*.

By **car**, Stein am Rhein sits on the main road running along the south bank of the Rhine and on to Lake Constance. From Geneva, Bern and Basel the motorway connects with Zürich and then continues north via Winterthur to Schaffhausen, where you turn east on the road to Stein am Rhein. From Basel it's possible to take a non-motorway route via Tiengen, Germany and Schaffhausen. From St Gallen the motorway connects to Schaffhausen, via Winterthur, where you turn east on the road to Stein am Rhein.

From Zürich the quickest **train** services involve a change at either Winterthur or Schaffhausen. From Basel there are services on **SBB** with changes at Zürich and Winterthur, or more complicated, but slightly faster services from the German **Badischer** station with stops at Erzingen and Schaffhausen. From either Geneva or Bern services run via Zürich. From St Gallen you have to change at Romanshorn before continuing to Stein am Rhein.

It's a very small town, so once you're there you can **walk** to every place of interest.

concentration of frescoes, and modern-day owners are legally obliged to maintain them in good condition. The small bay windows (oriels) had their practical use, as residents could see what was happening below without being noticed themselves. Worth seeking out are the **Weisser Adler** (White Eagle), the **Vordere Krone** (Fore Crown) and the **Roter Ochsen** (Red Ox) houses.

Klostermuseum St Georgen
t 052 741 21 42; open April–Oct daily 10–5; adm

Don't miss the 1,000-year-old **Klostermuseum St Georgen** (St George Cloister) standing next to the river. The frescoes and paintings include one of St George slaying the dragon, and there are wonderfully intricate wooden-beamed ceilings. In the outbuildings is a huge wooden wine press.

Museum Lindwurm
Understadt 18, t 052 741 25 12, www.museum-lindwurm.ch; open Mar–Oct Mon, Wed–Sun 10–5; adm

The **Museum Lindwurm** is housed in the most delightful blue-and white-painted mansion with, uniquely in Stein, an Empire façade dating from 1819. Actually, the oldest part of the museum dates back to 1279 and the building carried this name as early as 1495, although it was considerably expanded in the 16th century. The urban way of life and agriculture have always been closely intertwined here, and inside you will see how affluent citizens of the middle 1800s lived.

Schloss Hohenklingen
Hansjörg Zaugg, t 052 741 21 37; www.burghohen klingen.ch; open Tues–Sun 10am–11pm

Above the Town

Schloss Hohenklingen (Hohenklingen Castle) dates from the 13th century and overlooks Stein from a height of 630ft (192m). It is one of the best preserved castles in the region and it can be visited with no admission fee. It has a highly rated restaurant.

ⓘ **Stein am Rhein ›**
Tourismus Stein am Rhein: Oberstadt 3, t 052 742 20 90; www.steinamrhein.ch; open Mon–Fri 9.30–12, and 1.30–5; May–Sept Sat–Sun 9.30–12 and 1.30–4

Where to Stay and Eat in Stein am Rhein

***Adler**, Rathausplatz 2, **t** 052 742 61 61, *www.adlersteinamrhein.ch* (*moderate*). In the town hall square and with a beautiful Carigiet façade; two singles, nine doubles, two triples and two junior suites on offer, and also an apartment with two bedrooms. Nice public areas, and a restaurant serving local and French cuisine.

South of Zürich

Rapperswil

Rapperswil is a charming small town with just 7,400 inhabitants, situated some 30 miles (50km) east of Zürich at the other end of Lake Zürich. What there is to see is mostly found on the hill up by the castle, although the lower town is particularly well preserved. It will not take long to look around – the attractions have quite odd opening hours – and it's best to visit between April and September. If coming from Zürich, make an early start and then take a leisurely lunch on a lake steamer back to the city.

History

The first recorded document relative to this area dates back to 1229. At that time Rapperswil was settled by people who moved across from the other side of the lake. Very shortly after, in 1233, an earldom was awarded to the first lords, though the dynasty lasted only another 60 years. During the next century, in 1350, Rudolf Brun, burgermeister of Zürich, and his forces took over the town. It was subsequently taken over by the Habsburgs of Austria four years later. In 1415, officials granted permission for Rapperswil to hold a market, a tradition that still continues to this day. The city joined the Swiss Confederation in 1458.

In 1656, although its freedom was threatened, it withstood a siege by the forces of Zürich. During the French Revolution in 1798 it was separated from nearby Jona and incorporated into the then canton of Linth. However, in 1803 when the current political districts were established, it was incorporated into the newly formed canton of St Gallen. Later that century, between 1830 and 1836, the town walls were demolished, and this is how you will find it today – an open town.

By the Lake and the Lower Town

The most important sights in Rapperswil are on the top of the hill that dominates the town. However, as most people arrive either by train or by lake steamer, the appropriate place to start is at the tourist office, before strolling north through the lower town to the elaborate steps that lead up to the castle.

Circus Museum
*Fischmarktplatz 1,
t 055 220 57 57; open
daily April–June 10–6;
July–Aug 10–7; Sept–Oct
10–6; Nov–Mar 1–5;
adm*

First, take a look at the **Circus Museum**, in the same building as the tourist office. Rapperswil has a close connection with the most famous Swiss circus, Knie, who have made the town their winter headquarters since 1919. In here you will find memorabilia, models, etc.

Getting to Rapperswil

The most pleasant and relaxing way to travel is to take a **Zürichsee Schiffahrtsgesellschaft lake steamer**, **t** 044 487 13 13, *www.zsg.ch*. Sailing time from Zürich is about 1¼ hours – consider having lunch on board.

By **car**, from Zürich either take the motorway to the west/south of Lake Zürich then exit and take the bridge across the lake to Rapperswil or follow the road from Zürich on the east/north side of the lake directly to Rapperswil.

Trains from Zürich to Rapperswil take just 36 minutes.

Once you are in the town, all of the sights are within **walking** distance.

Up to the Castle

Just north of the Fischmarktplatz is the *rathaus* (town hall) that was first mentioned in 1429, and past that is the sloping **Hauptplatz**. The street pattern in this area was, in large part, laid out in the 13th century. The original houses were constructed of wood, but, age having taken its toll, these were replaced by stone homes over the course of the 16th and 17th centuries. The architectural harmony you see today is certainly not an accident as construction, renovation and maintenance of all buildings are subject to strict local regulations. This part of town, the social centre of Rapperswil, is also the access point to the castle, by way of an impressive double stairway, easily recognizable by the elegant water fountain set between the flights at its base.

Believed to date from the early 13th century, this formidable **schloss** (castle) sits at the highest point of a narrow promontory, the **Lindenhof**. Just outside the castle entrance is the Liberty of Poland column, topped by an eagle, with the words MAGNA RES LIBERTAS (Freedom Above All) inscribed on it, erected in 1868. Inside, the **Polenmuseum** (Polish Museum), founded by Polish exiles and their Swiss friends, presents a wide-ranging array of exhibits. Don't leave the castle before climbing the **Gügeler tower**, which offers magnificent views of the lake and the mountains to the east.

Polenmuseum
*t 055 210 18 62;
www.muzeum-
polskie.org; open Mar,
Nov–Dec Sat–Sun 1–5;
April–Oct daily 1–5;
Jan–Feb by
appointment only*

Immediately to the east of the castle is another domineering structure, the **Catholic church of St Johann** with its Renaissance altars and rich treasures. The first church on this site, built in 1253, succumbed to fire in 1882; this new one was consecrated shortly after, in 1885. Be sure to investigate, also, the **Liebfrauenkapelle** (Cemetery Chapel) just behind the church. It dates from 1489 and has a beautiful wooden ceiling. The cemetery itself, on a lower level, has rather strange metal headstones on many graves.

Stadtmuseum
*Herrenberg 40,
t 055 210 43 76,
www.ogrj.ch; open
April–Oct Tues–Sat 1–4,
Sun 11–4; adm*

Not very far away, again eastwards, is the Stadtmuseum (Museum of Local History), where there are some interesting exhibits, including a model of the town as it appeared around 1800.

Along the Promontory, Back to the Lake

Back to the west, follow the Lindenhof along the promontory. From this vantage point, the views are spectacular: the vast expanses of Lake Zürich unfold on either side and the Alps rise majestically in the distance. It also offers the finest perspective of the **wooden bridge** built in 2001, the longest in Switzerland at 920 yards (841m), connecting Rapperswil to Hurden on the other side of the lake. On the slopes to the north is a **deer park** that was established in 1871 and is home to between 10 and 15 fallow deer.

To the south are the expansive **Rosengärten** (Rose Gardens) where, between June and October, 6,000 rose bushes – of 180 varieties – bathe the horizon in a breathtaking display of kaleidoscopic blooms. This attraction also has a distinctive connection to the town; upon Rapperswil's coat-of-arms you will find two rose blossoms.

The **Capuchin monastery**, built around 1606, and other fortifications occupy the western tip of the promontory, and steep steps that run between the monastery and the Rose Gardens descend back to the lakeside.

Tourist Information and Services in Rapperswil

ⓘ **Rapperswil >**
Rapperswil Jona Tourismus: Fischmarktplatz 1, t 055 220 57 57, www.rapperswil.ch; open April–Jun, Sep–Oct daily 10–6; Jul–Aug daily 10–7, Nov–Mar daily 1–5

Market Days

Rapperswiler market (fresh goods, flowers, spices and pastries): Fri morning Mar–Dec.

Where to Stay in Rapperswil

****Schwanen, Seequai 1, t 055 220 85 00, *www.schwanen.ch* (*expensive*). This has the best location in Rapperswil on the lakeshore promenade. Some of its modern rooms have balconies overlooking the lake. Also a fine restaurant (*see* below), brasserie and live music at the bar.

***Hirschen, Fischmarktplatz 7, t 055 220 61 80, *www.hirschen-rapperswil.ch* (*moderate*). In a traditional 400-year-old building on the main square, this small hotel has much charm. All of the rooms have different décor and some have four-poster beds.

Eating Out in Rapperswil

Le Jardin, Seequai 1, t 055 220 85 00, *www.schwanen.ch* (*expensive*). This is the best restaurant in the Hotel Schwanen. Whether you choose to eat in the highly classical dining room or on the outdoor terrace overlooking the lakeshore promenade, you are assured of fine service and gastronomic delights.

San Marco, Marktgasse 21, t 055 211 22 24, *www.san-marco-rappi.ch* (*moderate*). A restaurant and pizzeria, offering 23 different pizzas and an equally wide range of *antipasti* and pasta dishes along with a nice wine list and drink selection.

Café Rosenstädter, Fischmarktplat 4, t 055 210 16 43, *www.rosenstaedter.ch* (*inexpensive*). You can sit outside on this fine square; besides an interesting menu the speciality here is a large range of Appenzeller beers.

Getting to and around Einsiedeln

By **car**, Einsiedeln is situated halfway between Schwyz and Rapperswil off the main road to the east. From Zürich take the motorway south of the lake to the Rapperswil exit, then go south to Einsiedeln.
Trains run from Zürich via Wädensil or Pfäffikon.
Once in the town, the abbey is within easy **walking** distance.

Einsiedeln

Einsiedeln is a small town with a population of around 14,000. It is situated between lakes Luzern and Zürich, about midway between Schwyz and Rapperswil. (It is actually in Central Switzerland, but has been included in this chapter because transportation is easier from Zürich.) Although Paracelsus, a medieval doctor and alchemist who is credited with giving zinc its name, was born here, it is a Benedictine monk who brought the town international fame.

Kloster Einsiedeln
t 055 418 61 11,
www.kloster-
einsiedeln.ch; open daily
5.30am–8.30pm

It was when the Benedictine monk, Meinrad, found his way from the Lake Constance area to become a hermit in this region, with his statue of the Virgin Mary, in 835 that the origins of the **Kloster Einsiedeln** started. Others soon followed, including Bishop Benno from Metz, France, but it took the priest and canon of the cathedral of Strasbourg, Eberhard, to organize them into a monastic community in 934, and a monastery followed later that year. This, in turn, attracted such figures as Blessed Abbot Gregory of England in 996 and St Wolfgang, who became the Bishop of Ratisbonne. Soon, it gained the support of bishops, nobility and royalty, and became the main spiritual and cultural centre for the Germanic region from Bavaria to Upper Italy.

Conflicts often arose between Einsiedeln and Schwyz, and it wasn't until the mid-14th century that boundaries were defined. During the 14th century the pilgrimage here took hold and after the troubles of the Reform era the Baroque period brought with it a time of prosperity. Construction began on the symmetrically shaped monastery in the early 18th century. By the 19th century the abbey had become the centre of Swiss Catholic piety.

These days, the abbey is considered one of the most important places of Roman Catholic pilgrimage in Europe, and the most important dedicated to the Virgin Mary in Switzerland.

(i) **Einsiedeln >**
Einsiedeln Tourismus:
Hauptstrasse 85,
t 055 418 44 88,
www.einsiedeln.ch;
open Mon–Fri 9–5, Sat
9–4; Sun April–Nov
10–1, Dec–Mar 9–12

Where to Stay and Eat in Einsiedeln

***Hotel Linde, Schmiedenstrasse 28, t 055 418 48 48, *www.linde-einsiedeln.ch* (*moderate*). Located in a traditional building in the centre of town. Its 17 rooms are pleasant, elegantly furnished and most fairly large. The restaurant here has 14 Gault-Millau points and offers a range of menus including a seasonal wild menu, a vegetarian menu and a wide à la carte choice.

Basel and Northwest Switzerland

Basel is a major city where three countries – Switzerland, France and Germany – meet at the fast-flowing Rhine before it makes its sharp turn north through Germany. As the region sweeps southwesterly down to La Chaux-de-Fonds/Le Locle it passes through a mountainous region, the Jura, that though far from dramatic by Swiss standards is rarely less than attractive.

One of the things that makes this north-west region different from the rest of the country is the interconnecting rivers and lakes on its eastern border. It's possible to cruise from one town to another, which is a particularly pleasant way to appreciate the region.

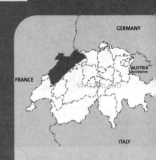

08

Don't miss

⭐ **Tall spires beckon**
Münster, Basel **p.99**

⭐ **Unique river crossing**
Ferryboats, Basel **p.99**

⭐ **Ready for battle**
Altes Zeughaus, Solothurn **p.110**

⭐ **Up on the hill**
Église Collégiale and Château, Neuchâtel **p.116**

⭐ **Watch time pass**
Musée International d'Horlogerie, La Chaux-de-Fonds **p.123**

See map overleaf

Don't miss

⭐ Münster, Basel **p.99**

⭐ Ferryboats, Basel **p.99**

⭐ Altes Zeughaus, Solothurn **p.110**

⭐ Église Collégiale and Château, Neuchâtel **p.116**

⭐ Musée International d'Horlogerie, La Chaux-de-Fonds **p.123**

Getting to Northwest Switzerland

By Air

See 'Getting to Basel, By Air', p.92.

By Car

The main road connection through this region runs from Basel and Zürich to Solothurn and Biel/Bienne and on to Neuchâtel from where it continues south to Lausanne and Geneva. Bern is also connected by motorway to Solothurn and Basel, but although it's by far the closest of the major cities to Neuchâtel, the motorway only currently runs halfway and it's necessary to take a non-motorway road the rest of the way.

By Train

There are fast train connections from Basel, Bern, Zürich and Geneva to all of the main destinations detailed in this chapter.

Basel

Basel's strategic location, in the centre of Europe and at the point where the mighty **River Rhine** takes a dramatic ninety-degree turn to the north, ensured from the outset that this city would play a significant role in the history of Europe and, indeed, the world.

History

Although the origins of the city can be traced back to Celtic times, it was in 44 BC that the Roman general, Lucius Munatius Plancus, founded the settlement of *Augusta Raurica* (Augst). And it was in AD 374 that the name of *Basilea* was first documented, during a visit by Emperor Valentinian I to the city. In the 7th century, the Bishop's seat was transferred from Augst to Basel. Three hundred years later Basel was overrun and destroyed by Hungarians, who then destroyed the settlement. In 1006, the civil power of the Bishop was established by decree of Emperor Henry II who, thirteen years later, inaugurated the Münster (cathedral). The same century saw the first fortifications of the city that, in 1185, was burned down by a great fire. Early the next century, in 1226, the city's recovery continued as Bishop Henry of Thun organized the construction of the first bridge across the Rhine. The 14th century wasn't so kind to Basel. During the period around 1340 the 'Black Death' plague raged throughout the city and, just sixteen years later, most of the city was destroyed by the earthquake of 18 October 1356. During the reconstruction, the second town wall was completed; parts of this and some of the gates are preserved to this day. Yet another fire struck Basel in 1417, and in 1444 the city once again felt the scourge of war when the Battle of St Jacob, between the Swiss Confederates and French Dauphin and his allies, took place close to Basel.

It was Basel's geographic position that encouraged leaders of the Church to hold their council in the city between 1431 and 1448, during which Amadeus VIII of Savoy was elected Pope (taking the

Getting to Basel

By Air

Basel's EuroAirport, actually in Mulhouse, France, t 061 325 31 11 (from Switzerland), *www.euroairport.com*, receives flights from the UK operated by easyjet, Ryanair and Swiss, as well as from other European countries, and internal flights from other cities in Switzerland. From the airport the no. 50 **bus** runs four times an hour to the **SBB Swiss/SNCF French** railway station in Basel, a journey of about 15 minutes. **Taxis** cost approximately CHF 40 into Basel city centre.

By Train

The **Eurostar**, *www.eurostar.com*, runs from London (St Pancras International) to Paris (Gare du Nord) and then from Paris (Gare de Lyon) a high-speed **TGV**, *www.sncf.fr*, operates to Basel, French station. Basel has two main railway stations: the **SBB Swiss/SNCF French** (the two parts of this station are separated by immigration and customs facilities); and **DB Badischer**, the German one, which although it is in Basel is actually German national territory. Trains arriving from other Swiss destinations arrive at the SBB Swiss station, those arriving from France use the SNCF French station and those from Germany arrive at the DB Badischer station.

By Car

From other Swiss destinations traffic takes the Basel City exit off the A2 motorway. From France traffic enters Basel at the Basel/St Louis customs point on the A35 motorway. From Germany traffic enters Basel at the Basel/Weil customs point on the A5/E35 motorway.

Getting around Basel

Public transport in and around Basel is fast, clean and efficient (*www.bvb-basel.ch*). **Trams** are the best way of getting around and most visitors will find the no. 8 service very useful: it runs from the SBB Swiss railway station down to Barfüsserplatz, Marktplatz and across the Middle Bridge.`
Tickets must be purchased from ticket-vending machines, ticket offices or the tourist office prior to each trip and are available for a singe trip or, more advantageously, for an **Unlimited Day Pass**. The latter, for second class, costs CHF 7.40 for the City of Basel and CHF 23.40 for the expanded metropolitan traffic area.

By Car

There are **car hire companies** in the Swiss sector of the EuroAirport, terminal building, Hall 4, Level 2. Companies include **Avis**, t 061 325 28 40, *www.avis.ch*; **Hertz**, t 061 325 27 80, *www.hertz.ch*; and **Sixt**, t 061 325 15 40/41, *www.sixt.ch*.

By Bicycle

Bicycles can be hired from **Vélo**, Centralbahnplatz, t 061 272 09 10, *www.veloparking.ch*. This is an underground cycle park at the SBB Swiss station.

By Boat

See box on p.100.

name Felix V), an event that would have far-reaching cultural and intellectual consequences. Aaneas Silvius Piccolomini, later to become Pope Pius II, familiar with the city from his attendance at the Ecumenical Council, the last Church Council of the Middle Ages, thereafter founded the University of Basel, which was the first university of the Swiss Confederation. Basel, in turn, became an educational base and a centre for humanism and the arts. Many great scholars such as Erasmus of Rotterdam (who published the first edition of the New Testament in the original Greek text in

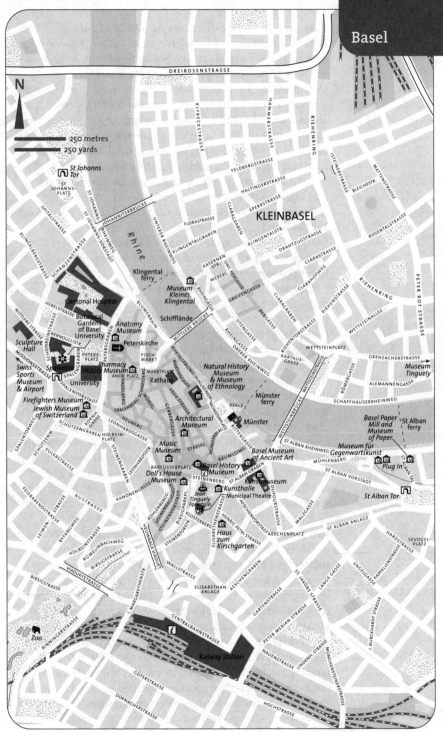

N

250 metres
250 yards

DREIROSENSTRASSE

KLYBECKSTRASSE

HAMMERSTRASSE

RIEHENRING

ISTEINERSTRASSE

MAITTENSTRASSE

BLEICHESTR.

St Johanns
Tor

ST
JOHANNS-
PLATZ

SPITALSTRASSE

ST JOHANNS-VORSTADT

JOHANNITERBRÜCKE

FELDBERGSTRASSE

HALTINGERSTRASSE

SPERRSTRASSE

CLARAGRABEN

KLEINBASEL

ROSENTALSTRASSE

KLINGELBERGSTRASSE

SCHANZENSTRASSE

ST JOHANNS-RHEINWEG

Rhine

UNTERER RHEINWEG

FLORASTRASSE

KLINGENTALGRABEN

KLINGENTAL

DRÄHTZUGSTRASSE

CLARASTRASSE

CLARAHOFWEG

RIEHENRING

PETER ROT STRASSE

Klingental
ferry

KASERNEN
STR.

UNT. REBGASSE

WEBERG.

GREIFENGASSE

REBGASSE

CLARAGRABEN

RIEHENTORSTRASSE

WETTSTEINALLEE

Cantonal Hospital

HEBELSTRASSE

SCHÖNBEINSTRASSE

BERNOULLISTR.

MITTLERE STRASSE

Museum
Kleines
Klingental

RHEINGASSE

UTENGASSE

OBERER RHEINWEG

WETTSTEINPLATZ

GRENZACHERSTRASSE

Museum
Tinguely

Schifflände

RHEINSPRUNG

RHEINGASSE

AUGUSTINERGASSE

KARTAUS-
GASSE

RÖMERGASSE

ALEMANNENGASSE

Sculpture
Hall

Botanical
Gardens
of Basel
University

Anatomy
Museum

Peterskirche

Natural History
Museum
& Museum of
Ethnology

Münster
ferry

WETTSTEINBRÜCKE

SCHAFFHAUSERRHEINWEG

Swiss
Sports
Museum
& Airport

MISSIONSSTRASSE

SCHÖNBEINSTRASSE

PETERSGRABEN

PETERS-
PLATZ

FISCH-
MARKT

Pharmacy
Museum

Spalentor

University

SPALENVORSTADT

Firefighters Museum

Jewish Museum
of Switzerland

NADELBERG

Rathaus

MARKTPLATZ

ANDR. PLATZ

FREIE STRASSE

PFALZ

Münster

MÜNSTERBERG

RITTERGASSE

Basel Paper
Mill and
Museum
of Paper

ST ALBAN RHEINWEG

St Alban
ferry

MÜHLENBERG

Museum für
Gegenwartskunst

ST ALBAN VORSTADT

Plug In

ST ALBAN TAL

SPALENVORSTADT

KOHLE

LEONHARDSGRABEN

HEUBERG

Architectural
Museum

MÜNSTERPLATZ

BÄUMLEING.

ST ALBAN GRABEN

MÜHLENBERG

SPALENTORWEG

SCHÜTZENGRABEN

HOLBEIN-
PLATZ

LEONHARDSGASSE

STEINGRABEN

Music
Museum

STREITG.

Basel Museum
of Ancient Art

ST ALBAN VORSTADT

St Alban
Tor

EULERSTRASSE

SCHÜTZEN-
MATTSTR.

KANONENGASSE

BARFÜSSERPLATZ

STEINENBERG

Basel History
Museum

Kunstmuseum

Kunsthalle

DUFOURSTRASSE

FEIERABENDSTRASSE

AUSTRASSE

Doll's House
Museum

Jean
Tinguely
Fountain

Municipal Theatre

AESCHENVORSTADT

MALZGASSE

ST ALBAN ANLAGE

HARDSTRASSE

SEVOGEL-
PLATZ

LEIMEN-
STRASSE

BYFANGWEG

KOHLENBERG

STEINENVORSTADT

BIRSIG-VORSTADT

ELISABETHENSTRASSE

HENRIC PETRI STRASSE

Haus
zum
Kirschgarten

AESCHENPLATZ

ST ALBAN ANLAGE

HOLBEINSTRASSE

RÜMELINBACHWEG

BIRSIGSTRASSE

VIADUKTSTRASSE

HEUWAAGE VIADUKT

STEINENTORSTR.

KLOSTERBERG

WALLSTRASSE

ELISABETHAN
ANLAGE

AESCHENGRABEN

GARTENSTRASSE

ST JAKOBS STRASSE

LANGE GASSE

ENGELGASSE

KAPPELENSTRASSE

Zoo

BINNINGERSTRASSE

I. MARGARETHENSTR.

CENTRALBAHNSTRASSE

Railway Station

PETER MERIAN STRASSE

LINDENH. STRASSE

MÜNCHENSTEINERSTRASSE

J. BURCKHARDT STRASSE

GÜTERSTRASSE

DORNACHERSTRASSE

NAUENSTRASSE

HOCHSTRASSE

1416), the physician Paracelsus, mathematicians Euler and Bernoullis, philosopher Friedrich Nietzsche and the historian Jakob Burckhardt were attracted to the city. Trade, naturally, blossomed and in 1471 Basel obtained permission to hold two fairs annually. Monuments to the resulting wealth are still visible in the array of elaborate medieval buildings, most notably the highly decorative and very unusual *rathaus* (town hall), which dates from 1504; the equally impressive, but rather more austere, Romanesque/Gothic cathedral; and the imposing Spalentor, which dates from when Basel was last walled in during the 14th century.

In 1501, Basel was accepted into the Swiss Confederation, and 1529 saw the Reformation accepted by the city. Since 1833 the canton of Basel has been divided into two half cantons, Basel Town and Basel Country. Travel between the city and other parts of Switzerland was made considerably easier when the first railway reached the city in 1844, and maritime connections were enhanced by the opening of the port of Basel in 1906.

Today Basel (Bâle in French, Basiliea in Italian, and often anglicized to Basle), Switzerland's second largest city, is a lively and progressive place with a population of some 200,000. Situated at the border of three countries – France, Germany and Switzerland – it is home port to more than 500 river-going vessels, serves as one of Europe's largest railroad junctions and is recognized as a great financial and industrial centre. It is also headquarters to some of the world's major pharmaceutical companies and is the base for the Bank of International Settlements (BIZ), where representatives of all industrialized countries routinely meet to discuss the world economy. The Church Council held five centuries ago was only the start of Basel's vocation as a centre for worldwide conventions and trade fairs. In 1917, the first Swiss Industries Fair took place here, and it is now the largest fair and congress organizer in the country, responsible, in its own right, for over one million visitors to the city.

Art and culture also play a major role in the life of Basel. Approximately 30 museums, ranging from the more traditional and world-renowned Kunstmuseum (Fine Arts Museum) to the less conventional Basler Papiermühle (Paper Mill and Museum), not to mention numerous other galleries, concert halls and theatres, call the city their home. The most popular cultural event, however, is the colourful and wild **Basel *Fasnacht*** carnival. The festivities begin in January with the appearance of three mythological figures who appear to chase winter away. The Monday after Ash Wednesday, at the unearthly hour of 4am, the Carnival breaks loose with a morning parade. What follows are three days of unbroken revelry complete with traditional feasts and a procession of elaborate floats, brass bands and a motley collection of followers in outrageous costumes that have to be seen to be believed.

A Fountain Tale

For over 600 years, from the mid-13th century until the first pumped water supply to Basel's municipal buildings in 1866, the city's demand for water was met by its fountains. Today, although having long lost their original function, they are still operated by the *Industrielle Werke Basel* and much loved by children who use them as paddling pools in the warm summer months.

In the summer of 2008 it was one of the host cities for the European Football Championships.

Basel is an absolutely charming place to visit. The medieval Old Town, more than 150 water fountains, the attractions of the Rhine and the progressiveness of its people create a truly unique and enticing atmosphere.

The Old Town: Between Mittlere Brücke, Marktplatz and the Münster

For the sake of convenience, this itinerary follows a roughly anti-clockwise direction from the bridge.

The Schifflände boat landing and an equestrian statue of Karl Burckhardt (1878–1923) are situated near the famous **Mittlere Brücke** (Middle Bridge). The first bridge was built here in 1226 by the bishop-prince Heinrich von Thun to cross the mighty perpetually rushing waters of the Rhine that are 870ft (265m) wide here. To protect the bridge, von Thun established the fortified town of Kleinbasel on the north bank of the river. Later, in 1392, the city parliament of Grossbasel, on the south side, bought Kleinbasel from Bishop Friedrich von Blankenheim for an astounding price of 29,800 guilders, thus joining the two cities. The bridge had its more sinister uses, too, as in the Middle Ages women accused of infidelity or infanticide were bound and thrown into the Rhine; for the lucky ones, it was taken as a sign of their innocence if the swift currents deposited them on the riverbanks. In the middle of the bridge there was a chapel where merchants and seamen could offer up prayers; the **Käppelijoch** you see today is just a replica. Tradition says, though, that walking around it three times will cure a toothache! A fortified gate once protected the Grossbasel end of the bridge, and in 1640 a strange mechanical head, the **Lällekönig** (*lälli* being the Basel word for tongue) was mounted on the Rhine façade. It came across its name because the copper-beaten head, adorned with a many-pointed crown, was connected to a clockwork mechanism that made the figure roll its eyes and stick out a long, red tongue towards the Kleinbasel side of the city. Again, what you see today – on the façade of the Churrasco restaurant – is a replica; the original is in the Historiches Museum Basel (Basel History Museum) (*see* p.97).

Just south is the traffic circle of **Fischmarkt**, and this is dominated by what was originally a late Gothic 36ft (11m) fountain, dating from the late 14th century and created by the master stonemason Parler. Richly decorated, either with paintings or gilt, the three principal figures are the Virgin Mary with child and sceptre, the Apostle Peter with a key and John the Evangelist grasping a chalice and a book. There are numerous smaller angels, holding either musical instruments or the Basel coat-of-arms, with more saints on the baldachin; on the finial, at the very top, stands another angel clasping a palm leaf. Again, the original is in the Historiches Museum Basel (see p.97); this is just an early 20th-century copy.

The Rhine and its tributaries were rich in fish, and this played an important role in most people's diets in the Middle Ages, especially during Lent. On market days, fish merchants would keep their wares fresh by placing baskets of live 'green' fish in the basin of the fountain.

Immediately behind are a series of steep steps whose walls are covered with the unfortunately all-too-common scourge of graffiti. These lead up to an area near the botanical gardens (see p.102).

Pharmazie-Historisches Museum der Universität Basel
Totengässlein 3, t 061 264 91 11, www.pharmazie museum.ch; open Tues–Fri 10–6, Sat 10–5; adm

To the southwest of Fischmarkt is the **Pharmazie-Historisches Museum der Universität Basel** (Pharmacy History Museum of Basel University). Here, around old buildings in a neat courtyard, is one of the world's largest museums of this type, including apothecary shops and an historic drugstore – Herbarium – in a former pharmacy.

Marktplatz, next door, is not just, as the name implies, the past and present site of Basel's daily open-air market. It is also home to the city's magnificent *rathaus* (town hall). In 1501, it was the influence of the craftsmen, who organized themselves into 15 guilds, which persuaded the city of Basel to join the Swiss Confederation. To celebrate this, in the early 16th century a new, red town hall was built with a frescoed façade, although it has been recently renovated. It dominates the square, as does its impressive tower, added retroactively early in the 20th century, and both are roofed with the colourful tiles so popular in Basel. Look, also, for the coats-of-arms of the 12 cantons that formed the Swiss Confederation in 1501 on the battlements. On the right-hand side of the central arcade is an unusual plaque: the **Birsigmarke** (Birsig Mark) indicates the levels the Birsig river flooded to in 1529 and

Walks from Marktplatz

Basel makes extreme efforts to assist its visitors. You will find evidence of this on the side of the plaza opposite the town hall, where the authorities have erected a metal signpost directing you to five different walks around the city. These all begin here, last between 30 and 90 minutes, and are named after a prominent personality of Basel – Erasmus, Thomas Platter, Jakob Burckhardt, Paracelsus and Hans Holbein. To keep you on course, signs are posted along each route displaying a portrait of the respective person. An information brochure to accompany the walks is available from the tourist office.

1530. These days it is home to the government of the canton of Basel City.

Freie Strasse, running southeast from Marktplatz, is the main shopping street these days, lined with buildings of differing architectural styles. In the 3rd and 4th centuries it was a main Roman military and trade route, and became a main city thoroughfare in the Middle Ages; in the 19th century many ancient guild houses along here were demolished, and replaced by buildings of the Historicist and Jugendstil style. Look, especially, across from the post office at the blue and white façade of the **Haus zum Schlüssel**, the only guild house to retain its original character. This belonged to the **Zunft der Kaufleute** (Merchant's Guild), the most important of the four senior guilds and consequently known as the Schlüsselzunft (Key Guild). The impressive **post office**, dating from 1853, replaced the city merchants' hall of 1376–8.

Barfüsserplatz, just to the south, is another important and busy square – a transport hub with an important and always busy tram station. There are some old houses here, dating from the late 17th century, and some good restaurants both here and in the **Stadt Casino** just across the road – which is also home to the tourist office.

Incidentally, the name Barfüsser originates from the bare-footed Franciscan monks who once occupied the imposing, sharply sloping-roofed church. If you take a moment to look around the back you will discover, under a wooden protective roof, carved sandstone exhibits with coats-of-arms, house signs, inscriptions and border stones moved from their original locations. Constructed in the mid-13th century, the **Barfüsserkirche** – a major example of mendicant religious orders north of the Alps – now

Historiches Museum Basel
*Steinenberg 4,
t 061 205 86 00,
www.hmb.ch; open
Tues–Sun 10–5; adm*

functions as the **Historiches Museum Basel** (Basel History Museum), considered the most important cultural museum on the Upper Rhine. Notable exhibits include the Amerbach Cabinet, the Basel cathedral treasury containing unique examples of medieval goldsmith's art, Basel's *Dance of Death*, Gothic tapestry carpets and late Gothic and Renaissance glass painting, ecclesiastical art and furniture. Barfüsserplatz was also once used as a cattle market, thus its dialect name **Seibi** (Swine Square).

Architektur-museum
*Steinenberg 7,
t 061 261 14 13,
www.sam-basel.org;
open Mon, Tues, Thurs
11–6, Wed 11–8.30,
Sat–Sun 11–5; adm,
combined with
Kunsthalle*

Other museums around Barfüsserplatz include, just north, the **Architekturmuseum** (Architectural Museum). Suitably, this is housed on four floors of the most unusual example of 1950s architecture in Basel. Founded in 1984, the museum has an exhibition programme centred around three principles: Swiss architecture of the classical modern period; contemporary architecture in the international field; and various themes from the architectural periphery.

Just to the south, and in a renowned building on Barfüsserplatz that has been remodelled and has disabled access, is Europe's largest **Puppenhausmuseum** (Doll's House Museum). On four floors, each one with a modern interactive information system, there are over 6,000 exhibits including teddy bears, dolls, doll's houses, carousels and many more items that will take you back to your, or your children's, childhood.

Puppenhausmuseum
Steinenvorstadt 1,
t 061 225 95 95,
www.puppenhaus
museum.ch; open daily
10–6; adm

To the west, now, and along Steinenberg, on the right a combination of different level squares, just outside the Municipal Theatre, provide a popular gathering place for young and old alike. The favourite attraction by far, though, and set in the midst of a large water basin that used to be the stage of the old City Theatre, is the highly imaginative **Tinguelybrunnen** (Jean Tinguely Fountain). A native of Basel, Tinguely (1925–91) had, to understate the obvious, quite a creative mind. Any attempt to describe this unbelievably outlandish fountain, opened in 1977, would never do it justice. Suffice it to say that the numerous components are made from parts of old machines, etc. connected by other pieces of metal, and you never know where to look next for the fine sprays of water they emit. The best comparison that might be made is with the wondrous inventions of Salvador Dalí, an analogy that will be reinforced if you are curious enough to visit the Museum Tinguely (*see* p.104).

At the eastern end of the street is an interesting art museum, the **Kunsthalle Basel**. It held its first exhibition in 1872 and since then has put on numerous important modern art exhibitions.

Kunsthalle Basel
Steinenberg 7,
t 061 206 99 00,
www.kunsthallebasel.
ch; open Tues, Wed, Fri
11–6, Thurs 11–8.30, Sat,
Sun 11–5; adm,
combined with
Architectural Museum

You can find more art, albeit in two differing forms, just to the northeast on St Alban-Graben. Housed in two classical town houses is the unusual **Antikenmuseum Basel** (Basel Museum of Ancient Art). Opened in 1966, it is the only one of its kind in Switzerland solely devoted to the ancient civilizations of the Mediterranean area. Ranging from the 4th millennium BC to the 7th century AD, the permanent exhibition displays ancient art from the Egyptian, Greek, Etruscan and Roman cultures, as well as some examples from the Ancient Near East and Cyprus.

Antikenmuseum Basel
St Alban-Graben 5,
t 061 201 12 12,
www.antikenmuseum
basel.ch; open Tues–Sun
10–5, Wed to 8; adm

On the other side of the street is the **Kunstmuseum** (Fine Arts Museum). In fact, the **Öffentliche Kunstammlung Basel** (Basel Public Art Collection) has three sections: the Kunstmuseum and the Kupferstichkabinett (**Copper Etchings Gallery**), housed in this building, and the Museum für Gegenwartskunst (*see* p.104), to the east by the Rhine. Opened in 1661, the highly regarded Kunstmuseum was not only the first museum open to the public in Basel, but claims to be the world's first public art collection. Its main specialities are paintings and drawings of the Upper Rhine region and the Netherlands between 1400 and 1600, and 19th- and 20th-century art. Not only does it have the world's largest

Kunstmuseum
St. Alban-Graben 16,
t 061 206 62 62,
www.kunstmuseum
basel.ch; opening hours
as Kunsthalle; adm, free
first Sun of month

collection by the Holbein family, but its Renaissance collections include important works by Witz, Schongauer, Cranach the Elder, Grünewald and others. More up-to-date works by Arnold Böcklin, the Basel artist, feature in the 19th-century collection. Cubism works by Picasso, Braque and Léger, and German Abstract and American art since 1950 form part of the impressive collection of 20th-century paintings.

⭐ **Münster**
www.muenster basel.ch; open Easter Sat–15 Oct Mon–Fri 10–5, Sat 10–12 and 2–4, Sun and hols 1–5; 16 Oct –Good Friday Mon–Sat 11–4, Sun and hols 2–6; adm, tower visit

Due north, the tall spires and coloured tiled roof of the **Münster** (Cathedral) beckon. This area of Basel has been inhabited for 2,000 years, and a variety of churches and cathedrals have existed on this site. The first recorded one dates back to the Carolingian period, but it was destroyed in 917 at the hands of the Hungarians. It is recorded that, in 1019, a cathedral was consecrated here in the presence of Emperor Henry II, heir of the last Burgundian king. Construction of the present structure was begun at the end of the 12th century, in the late Romanesque style. But by the time it had been completed, it had gained Gothic additions – and, of course, it has seen many more additions and renovations throughout the centuries.

Turning to the façade of the Münster, the 221ft (67.3m) Georgturm (George Tower) was rebuilt in the Gothic style after the 1356 earthquake, except for three yellow sandstone levels that date from the 11th century. It was named after the prominent equestrian statue of St George slaying a dragon, dating from 1372. Other ornamentation includes, on the Martinsturm (Martins Tower), an equestrian statue of St Martin in the act of sharing his cloak.

Still outside, the small Gothic **cloister** on the Rhine side of the Great Hall dates from 1467–87 and is worth investigating. And don't overlook the small garden where, incongruously, modern sculptures stand in restless harmony with the ancient gravestones and sepulchres. Look at the back of the cathedral, too, where you will find the **Pfalz**. The word derives from 'palatium' meaning palace, and is so-called because the bishop's residence was very close by. This little square directly overlooks the Rhine, and steep steps lead down to the **Münsterfähre ferry** (*see* box, p.100).

⛴ **Ferryboats**

From the river and opposite bank, Basel can be seen from a different perspective. The opposite bank is delightful, with tall houses, no two the same, adorning the tree-lined river front and embellished by all manner of flowers and plants sprouting from their window boxes. Cafés, too, add to the atmosphere. In the warm summer months you will come across the sight of sunbathers completely covering the gently sloping quayside. In the direct background are the beginnings of the Black Forest of southern Germany, and towards the west are the French Vosges mountains.

The Rhine Ferryboats

Since the late 19th century, the cheapest and most efficient way of crossing the Rhine has been by way of one of four ferryboats, and these are quite unusual. Small, wooden and only half covered, they would have no hope whatsoever of succeeding against the swift-flowing currents under their power alone. To solve the problem, therefore, a strong cable was stretched from bank to bank, with a much smaller one attached from that to the ferry itself. The undertow keeps the smaller cable stretched to its limit, and it is this that determines the position of the landing pier. Watch closely and you will notice how the ferryman skilfully holds the boat to the pier solely by the pressure of his wooden pole. These boats are quite an experience, as well as an unparalleled opportunity to see a parade of diverse vessels on the river.

The price is just CHF 1.60. The 'LEU' crossing to the cathedral is the most popular for visitors (*www.faehri.ch*).

Back outside the cathedral, take a look at the tracery in the round window of the south transept that depicts a Star of David, an ancient symbol for the intermingling of the visible (material) and the invisible (spiritual) worlds. The grand door, Galluspforte (Gallus Gate), of the northern portal dates from the late 12th century and is named after the nearest altar; on it are splendid depictions of the *Last Judgement*.

The comparatively plain interior is highlighted by stained-glass windows, a simple altar, elaborately carved choir stalls and, particularly, a dragon sculpted into the floor of the nave that is thought to date from around 1170. The ambitious and energetic may want to consider climbing the more than 200 steps to the top of the St George Tower. The reward is a splendid panoramic view over the city.

Just to the east of the cathedral, along Rittergasse, is a charming house and garden protected by beautifully crafted wrought-iron railings. Almost directly across from the larger house is the small **Archäologischen Park** (Archaeological Park), which has illuminated panels set in the ground revealing ancient walls, and even some bones, encased in glass to protect them from the elements. This is a reminder that, over 2,000 years ago, the Celts from the Rauriker tribe settled here.

The forecourt of the cathedral was at one time gated in and this space, **Münsterplatz**, is now rather charming. As well as *boules* courts, there is the notable **Pisonibrunnen** (**Pisoni Fountain**), sitting under horse chestnut trees. Created in 1784 by Paolo Antonio Pisoni, it is considered a particularly attractive example, not just in Switzerland, but also in southern Germany, of a so-called Zopfbrunnen (Braid Fountain). This motif was popular during the transition from rococo to classicism during the Age of Enlightenment. Ceremonial processions, festivals, tournaments and parades of royal and imperial visitors were held here, as well as markets. And many of the buildings around the square were built in the late Gothic style for senior clerics. After the reformation, however, in 1529, the bishop and his acolytes were forced to leave and the mansions were left empty. Quickly, though, wealthy merchants saw the opportunity to buy them up and, usually, altered them to late Baroque and classical styles during the 18th century. A perfect example is the large **Rollerhof**, which was altered in 1758 by the silk ribbon merchant Martin Bachofen and today plays host to a restaurant on its ground floor.

Museum der Kulturen
*Münsterplatz 20,
t 061 266 56 00,
www.mkb.ch; open
Tues–Sun 10–5*

Next door to the Rollerhof is the entrance to the **Museum der Kulturen** (Museum of Ethnology). Exhibits of European and non-European culture, such as the cult house of the Abelam of Papua New Guinea, wooden copies of two Mayan temples and ghost masks from Cameroon, feature in Switzerland's largest such museum.

Back to the northwest of the cathedral, in **Augustinergasse**, you will come to the **Augustinerbrunnen** (Augustiner Fountain), which has a basilisk (*see* box below) sitting atop a column, dating from 1530, grasping in its talons the Basel coat-of-arms.

Almost across from it is an interesting building, built in 1844–49 by Melchior Berri (1801–54) to replace the Augustinian Monastery with a multipurpose building that was to become one of the earliest museum buildings in Switzerland. A figurative frieze by the sculptor Johann Jakob Oechslin adorns the façade, as does the basilea, embodying the city of Basel – holding the coat-of-arms and a cornucopia, and wearing a crown. The **Naturhistorischen Museum Basel** (National History Museum) is housed in this building, where you can see animals through the millennia and around the world.

Naturhistorischen Museum Basel
*Augustinergasse 2,
t 061 266 55 00,
www.nmb.bs.ch; open
Tues–Sun 10–5; adm*

Along the opposite side of Augustinergasse, which changes its name to **Rheinsprung** as it goes down the hill, nicely restored private Gothic and Baroque houses have a unique view directly over the Rhine. Rheinsprung is a particularly historic street. On the Rhine side stands the college building of the Old University that opened in 1460 and is the oldest in Switzerland. The Haus zum Kranichstreit, with a Gothic window and decorated, as was common in the Renaissance era, with shell patterns, dates from 1563. Much more modern is the mural on the windowless extension. Created by Samuel Buri in 1935, the **Gänseliesel** shows, behind scaffolding that the painter 'used' to execute it, a goose maiden.

Nearby are two late Baroque houses – dating from the 1760s – built for brothers and replacing earlier Gothic residences on

08 | Basel and Northwest Switzerland | Basel

Basel Basilisks
Omnipresent in Basel, basilisks have over the centuries been depicted in a variety of different forms of mythical beasts, and since the first half of the 15th century have featured on Basel's coat-of-arms. A competition was held in 1884 for the design of cast-iron basilisk fountains, and today there are about 30 green basilisk fountains throughout the city.

Augustinergasse. Lukas and Jakob Sarasin were very affluent silk merchants and their houses, the Blaue and Weisse (Blue and White), with large courtyards to their rear, are named after their coloured plaster. Today they are the seat of the Justice Department. Take a look at the pale stone in the cobbled street in front of the White House, as it gave rise to a Basel legend. Supposedly, in November 1797 the Guild Director Ochs took a stroll along Rheinsprung, as far as this stone, with Napoleon.

West of the Old Town

The area here is quite high above the Old Town, and is best reached on foot either by the steps next to the Fischmarkt or by leaving Barfüsserplatz by way of the steep hill to the more even street of LeonhardsGraben.

The most important attraction up here is one of Basel's splendours from the past. Dating from the 14th century, when the city was last walled in, the **Spalentor** gate was reinforced a century later and is magnificent indeed. Twin turrets, joined by fortifications topped by another colourful tiled tower, protect a portcullis and an obviously ancient wooden gate. There is also the obligatory moat.

Immediately to its north, even non-gardeners will be impressed with the **Botanischer Garten der Universität Basel**, but green-fingered visitors will be positively envious. The gardens themselves, the oldest in northern Europe, originally founded in 1589 and here since 1898, are pleasing enough, but the huge glass houses – often with a central pond, and home to tremendous cacti and a variety of other flora (more than 8,000 species) as well as tropical birds, butterflies and frogs – are an absolute delight.

This area is not short of museums, either, with three to both the north and southeast of Spalentor. Starting with the north, the one farthest away is the **Anatomisches Museum** (Anatomy Museum). If body parts are your thing, this is your place. The museum shows many dissections of human body parts, organs and tissues, explains pre-natal development of the body and exhibits an immense number of important specimens. It also has the oldest preserved skeleton in existence, that of Jacob Karrer dating from 1543.

The two museums closest to Spalentor are in adjacent streets. The **Skulpturhalle** (Sculpture Hall) has one of the largest collections of ancient sculptures including, uniquely, a reconstruction of Athens' Parthenon. The other is the **Schweizer Sportmuseum** (Swiss Sports Museum), with a cross-section of sports and games covering three centuries.

Botanischer Garten der Universität Basel
Schönbeinstrasse 6,
t 061 267 35 19,
www.unibas.ch/bot
garten; open April–Oct
daily 8–6; Nov–Mar
8–5; greenhouses 9–5

Anatomisches Museum
Pestalozzistrasse 20,
t 061 267 35 35,
www.unibas.ch/
anatomie/museum;
open Mon–Fri 2–5, Sun
10–4; adm

Skulpturhalle
Mittlere Strasse 17,
t 061 261 52 45,
www.skulpturhalle.ch;
open Tues–Fri 10–5,
Sat–Sun 11–5; adm

Schweizer Sportmuseum
Missionsstrasse 28,
t 061 261 12 21,
www.sportmuseum.ch;
open Sun–Fri 10–12 and
2–5, closed Sat

Now heading southeast, back towards Barfüsserplatz, there are two museums just around the corner from each other. The one on the busiest street, the **Schweizerisches Feuerwehrmuseum** (Firefighters' Museum), will only appeal to a few. However, of more interest culturally but with equally strange opening hours is the **Jüdisches Museum der Schweiz** (Jewish Museum of Switzerland). There are tombstones from the Middle Ages, Hebrew prints and documents relating to Jewish history in Basel and to Judaism generally, as well as exhibits detailing day-to-day aspects of Jewish life.

The last museum up here has many interesting aspects. The **Musikmuseum** (Music Museum) has sections dating back to around 1070, when it was a monastery for Augustine canons. Later, it was given the name of Lohnhof after the employers Lohnherren, who worked here after 1669. From 1835 to 1995 it served as a prison, and 24 of the cells on three floors are now exhibition cabinets. On the ground floor you will see instruments in their musical and social context in a 'Music in Basel' exhibition; the first floor concentrates on concerto, chorale and dance instruments, whilst on the upper floor are those involved in parades, celebrations and signals.

Schweizerisches Feuerwehrmuseum
Spalenvorstadt 11,
t 061 268 14 00,
www.rettung-bs.ch;
open Sun 2–5

Jüdisches Museum der Schweiz
Kornhausgasse 8,
t 061 261 95 14,
www.juedisches-museum.ch; open Mon and Wed 2–5, Sun 11–5

Musikmuseum
Im Lohnhof 9,
t 061 205 86 00,
www.hmb.ch; open Wed–Sat 2–6, Sun 11–5;
adm

South and East of the Old Town

The **Haus zum Kirschgarten** is a magnificent mansion that was built between 1775 and 1780 as a home and office for a Basel silk ribbon manufacturer. The two floors of historical rooms depict the culture of the 18th and 19th centuries; this is one of Switzerland's most important such museums. Look especially for the Pauls-Eisenbeiss Foundation's porcelain collection, as well as the Nathan-Rupp and Dr Eugen Gschwind watch and clock collections.

Three more very diverse and eclectic museums are grouped together close to the river, near the St Alban ferry. The closest to it is the very interesting **Basler Papiermühle** (Basel Paper Mill and Museum of Paper). During the 12th century the Cluniac monastery of St Alban built a canal to provide waterpower by means of waterwheels for 12 mills. Later, during the Middle Ages, 10 of these were converted to paper mills, and for no less than 446 years – until 1924 – paper was still produced in two of them. Since 1980 a museum has been housed in the Stegreif and Gallician mills; in 1983 it was recognized by the government as a rehabilitation centre for the employment of disabled people and it became the Swiss Paper Museum two years later. The affluence that this business produced for the Gallician family can be clearly seen on the first two floors, but this really is a working museum focusing on paper, writing and printing. So much so, you can even try your hand working the old, but still functioning, machines and other equipment.

Haus zum Kirschgarten
Elisabethenstrasse 27–29, t 061 205 86 78,
www.hmb.ch; open Tues–Fri and Sun 10–5, Sat 1–5; adm

Basel Papiermühle
St Alban-Tal 37,
t 061 225 90 90,
www.papiermuseum.ch;
open Tues–Sun 2–5;
adm

Plug In
St Alban-Rheinweg
64, t 061 283 60 50,
www.iplugin.org; open
Wed–Sat 2–6

Museum für
Gegenwartskunst
St Alban-Rheinweg
60, t 061 206 62 62,
www.mgkbasel.ch; open
Tues–Sun 10–5; adm
combined with
Kunstmuseum

A little west is a most unusual museum, the **Plug In**, which invites you into its public living room to see how there can be artistic interaction with new media. Next door is the third part of the Öffentliche Kunstammlung Basel (Public Art Collection; *see* p.98), the **Museum für Gegenwartskunst**. This displays work from the 1960s to the present day: minimal and conceptual art to the German Neuen Wilden (New Wild Ones) and neo-Expressionist painters. It is housed in a 19th-century factory building that has been converted specifically to combine, harmoniously, the old structure with modern art.

The North Side of the Rhine

Museum Kleines
Klingental
Unterer Rheinweg 26,
t 061 303 00 82,
www.mkk.ch; open
Wed–Sat 2–5, Sun 10–5

Another museum is easily reached as it is just north of the Middle Bridge. Located in the former Klingental Dominican Convent, the **Museum Kleines Klingental** features original medieval sculptures from Basel Münster. Go, also, to see a 17th-century model of the city and an exhibition devoted to the history of the convent.

Museum Tinguely
Paul Sacher-Anlage 1,
t 061 681 93 20,
www.tinguely.ch; open
Tues–Sun 11–7; adm

Unfortunately, the best museum, and greatest attraction, this side of the Rhine is rather less accessible as it is far to the east by the river and almost next to the railway bridge over it. It's too far to walk, so hop on either a no. 31 or 36 bus, and get off when you see a large, square building whose exterior walls are different from each other – a feature added by the Ticino architect Mario Botta (*see* p.271) to establish a differing spatial relationship to the surroundings. The extraordinary **Museum Tinguely** is dedicated to the life and amazingly intricate post-war kinetic art of Jean Tinguely (1925–91). Growing up in Basel, he tinkered with experiments making constructions that moved and made noises. Moving to Paris in 1953, he created unique artistic machines using randomly driven mechanical movement with optical-spatial and acoustic changeability components. They were later to become known as *Méta-mécaniques*, and four years later he evolved into *Méta-Matics* – machines that a user can operate to create abstract works of art.

In 1960 his sensational 'Homage to New York' was placed in the gardens of the Museum of Modern Art in that city. Always innovating, he decided to paint everything black in 1963, and then started using ball bearings to create shaking, circling and rotating movements in *Bascule* and *Eos* sculptures. Following up earlier ideas, he then delved into the idea of large sound-mixing machines that came to be known as *Méta-Harmonies*. Towards the end of his life, in 1987, he created the *Grosse Méta Maxi-Maxi Utopia*, his vision of a walk-in, poetically utopian dream world made from everyday, but widely diverse, materials. The interior is as creative as the exterior, and within large open-plan galleries you will find examples of all of his ultra-imaginative work.

Greater Basel

North of the Rhine

Fondation Beyeler
Baselstrasse 101,
t 061 645 97 00,
www.beyeler.com; open
daily 10–6, Wed till 8;
adm

The **Fondation Beyeler**, surrounded by a 19th-century English landscape garden, is situated in the northwest suburb of Riehen and can be reached by a no. 6 tram from the city centre to Riehen Dorf. For a period of 50 years Hildy and Ernst Beyeler built up a particularly fine collection of 20th-century modern masters whilst working as gallery owners. Transferred to a foundation in 1982, it was first shown as a full collection in Madrid's Centro de Arte Reina Sofia in 1989. The Genovese architect Renzo Piano specifically designed this building for the requirements of this art form, and the current 200 works are by such artists as Cézanne, Van Gogh, Monet, Picasso, Bacon and Warhol, along with a small selection of tribal art from Africa, Oceania and Alaska.

Vitra Design Museum
Charles-Eames-Strasse 1,
t (49) 7621 702 32 00,
www.design-museum.de; open
Mon–Sun 10–6, Wed till 8; adm; bring your passport

Another place that is well worth the effort to get to (take a no. 55 bus from Basel Claraplatz) is the **Vitra Design Museum** in Germany. Itself housed in a spectacular building designed by the American Frank O. Gehry, this is one of the world's leading industrial furniture design and architecture museums. As well as ever-changing exhibitions it offers, daily at 11am, 1pm and 3pm, architectural tours of nearby buildings such as the Conference Pavilion and Fire Station, both dating from 1993. These take place even when the museum itself is closed to prepare for new exhibitions.

Dreiländereck (Three Countries Corner)

Verkehrsdreh-scheibe
Westquaistrasse 2,
t 061 631 42 61,
www.verkehrsdreh-scheibe.ch; open
Mar–Nov Tues–Sun 10–5; Dec–Feb Tues, Sat, Sun 10–5; adm

This is an interesting diversion from the history and culture of the city centre. Cross the Mittlere Brücke (Middle Bridge) and continue straight to the junction of Greifengasse and Rebgasse to take a no. 14 tram to the end of the line. Alighting, follow the signs directing you towards your destination, Dreiländereck (Three Countries Corner). This journey winds you through the docks, passing the **Verkehrsdrehscheibe** (Shipping Museum). It's a small museum with many models of ships, etc. Within a short distance you will reach the banks of the Rhine and a riverside walk that snakes around to the right. Small marinas are on one side, docks on the other and, across the Rhine, it will be immediately apparent from the architectural styles where Switzerland and France meet. After a few hundred yards the land narrows dramatically to a point, and you come to the **Dreiländereck** itself, with Germany and its rolling hills forming a backdrop straight ahead. Of course, some entrepreneur could not resist the temptation to open the futuristic Dreiländereck bar/restaurant here.

(i) **Basel >**

*Basel Tourismus: Stadt-Casino at Barfüsserplatz, Steinenberg 14, **t** 061 268 68 68, www.basel.com; open Mon–Fri 8.30–6.30, Sat 9–5, Sun and hols 10–4*

Tourist & Hotel Information Office: Swiss SBB Bahnhof; open Mon–Fri 8.30–6.30, Sat 9–5, Sun and hols 9–4

Tourist Information and Services in Basel

The **Weekend-Break**, run by Basel Tourismus, is valid Fri–Mon – all week long during July, Aug and Dec – for a maximum of three nights, for selected hotels. The rates range from CHF 79 per person in a double room and CHF 106 in a single room for a 2-star hotel to CHF 139 per person in a double room and CHF 214 in a single room for a 5-star hotel. This includes breakfast, **Mobility Ticket** for use during your stay (*see* below) and taxes, except for a CHF 3.20 per person city guest tax.

BaselCard gives free admission to 25 museums, a free city sightseeing tour, free ferryboat rides and reductions for theatre and musical tickets, restaurants and some shops. It is available for periods of 24 hours at CHF 20, 48 hours at CHF 27 and 72 hours at CHF 35. It can be purchased in some hotels or from Basel Tourismus.

Mobility Ticket – Basel grants its guests a special treat as everyone who spends a night at a city hotel automatically receives a Mobility Ticket allowing free use of public transport for the duration of their stay.

Disabled Travellers

A city map for **wheelchair** users showing accessible buildings, public WCs, car parks for disabled people and useful telephone numbers is available from the tourist office.

Transport for disabled people is available but must be ordered 24-hours in advance: **IVB, t** 061 426 98 00 or **22er-Taxi, t** 061 271 22 22.

Lost Property

City and BVB, St Johanns-Vorstadt 51, **t** 061 267 70 34.
Bahnhof SBB, t 0512 29 24 67.

Market Days

Fruit and vegetables, Marktplatz, Tues, Thurs and Sat 6–1.30 and Mon, Wed and Fri 6am–7pm.
Flea Market, Petersplatz and Kserne, Sat 7.30–4; Barfüsserplatz, every second and fourth Wed 7–7.

Medical Emergencies

Dentist, doctor and pharmacy, t 061 261 15 15.

Guided Tours

A **walking tour** through the old city is conducted by Basel Tourismus. It departs from the Welcome Desk at Barfüsserplatz 1 May to mid-Oct daily at 2.30pm and at other times of the year on Sat at 2.30pm. It takes two hours and a ticket costs CHF 15. Tickets are available from Basel Tourismus offices.

Panoramic tour by tram every Sun at 10.30am. A vintage streetcar departs from the SBB railway station tram stop on a one-hour guided roundtrip tour of Basel. Another tour leaves at 11.30am, but reservations are required for this. Tickets, costing CHF 20, can be bought in front of the Hotel Euler for the earlier tour, or at the Basel Tourismus Welcome Desk at Barfüsserplatz for the 11:30am trip.

Festivals in Basel

Late Jan: **Vogel Gryff** – a local custom that is Kleinbasel's major festival.
Feb: *Fasnacht* – begins after Ash Wednesday and is the most famous carnival in Switzerland.
May: **Basel Summer Festival.**
Aug: **Theatre Festival Basel,** *www.theatrefestival.ch.*
Sept: *Basler Begge Brotmärt* – about 35 Basel bakers sell over 150 types of bread at Barfüsserplatz on a Tues in mid-month.

Oct/Nov: Swiss Indoors, *www.davidoff swissindoors.ch*. The largest international tennis tournament in Switzerland.

Late Oct to mid-Nov: Basler *Herbstmesse* – autumn fair.

End Nov to before Christmas: *Weihnachtsmarkt* (Christmas market) – 150 stalls at Barfüsserplatz selling all kinds of goodies.

New Year's Eve: Silvester – a New Year celebration starting at Münsterplatz at 11.30pm.

Shopping in Basel

As might be expected of the country's second-largest city, the shopping experience ranges from large department stores and designer boutiques to local shops, and just about everything in between. The Basel Tourismus website has links to all the important and interesting stores in the city. What's more, with shoppers in mind, it has a **Shopping Weekend** package, which offers preferential room rates and also includes a CHF 50 voucher that is valid in numerous shops in the city.

Where to Stay in Basel

Luxury
*****Les Trois Rois, Blumenrain 8, **t** 061 260 50 50, *www.lestroisrois.com*. Considered the oldest hotel in Europe, its name 'Three Kings' dates from 1032, when a royal delegation met here to settle questions over the succession of the royal line among three kings. The hotel has played host to all manner of kings and royalty, entertainers, politicians and artists, from Bonaparte to Picasso. It sits on a fantastic riverside site, very near to the city centre and the Middle Bridge. Some of the rooms and suites directly overlook the Rhine. First-class service, an elegantly traditional ambience and all modern comforts. One of the most renowned hotels in Switzerland.

Expensive

Merian am Rhein >

****Merian am Rhein, Rheingasse 2, **t** 061 685 11 11, *www.hotelmerian basel.ch*. Has a privileged riverside location on the north bank of the Rhine. The rooms are modern and spacious, with some having small balconies that overlook the river. The excellent restaurant and riverside terraces, its central location and pleasing décor and ambience make this hotel excellent value for money.

****St Gotthard, Centralbahnstrasse 13, **t** 061 225 13 13, *www.st-gotthard.ch*. Opposite the Central Station and originally built in 1882. Owned ever since by the Geyer family, all of the 94 rooms are of a very high standard. This is an attractive boutique-style hotel, but it's a little way from many of the attractions.

****Der Teufelhof, Leonhardsgraben 47–49, **t** 061 261 10 10, *www. teufelhof.com*. Calling itself a 'Culture and Guest House' this, the most eclectic hotel in Basel, offers a tempting combination of art, haute cuisine and even theatre. The Art Hotel, featuring eight rooms and a suite – TVs available on request – was created in July/Aug 2002 with a dream theme. Three designers, one Swiss and two Italians, have designed the 20 rooms, 3 suites and a junior suite in the Gallery Hotel. There are also superb restaurants (*see* p.108) and, of course, theatres.

Moderate
***Rheinfelderhof, Hammerstrasse 61, **t** 061 699 11 11, *www.rheinfelderhof.ch*. This occupies an impressive corner site on the north side of the Rhine, and is an amalgamation of a beer hall and another hotel. There are 35 modern and spacious rooms, some of which have views across the river to the cathedral.

***Basilisk, Klingentalstrasse 1, **t** 061 686 96 66, *www.hotel-basilisk.ch*. On the north side of the Rhine, near the old Klingental Monastery and the Exhibition Centre, this has quite large modern rooms that were designed according to feng shui theory, as well as a restaurant with garden terrace.

Rochat, Petersgraben 23, **t 061261 81 40, *www.hotelrochat.ch*. A neo-classical 1899 building in a quiet location not too far from the Botanic Gardens. Its 50 rooms – non-smoking and air-conditioned on request, as well as some for five people – have modern, unfussy décor, an Internet connection and a safe. It also has an alcohol-free and non-smoking restaurant.

Inexpensive

Stadthof, Gerbergasse 84, t 061 261 87 1, *www.stadthof.ch*. Located just off Barfüsserplatz, this small nine-room hotel was first recorded in 1295. The restaurant's clay-baked fish dish is famous, its pizzeria was the city's first and their Brötli-Bar is well-known for its healthy fast food.

Bed & Breakfast Agency, Sonnenweg 3, t 061 702 21 51, *www.bbbasel.ch*. This agency has contacts with more than 170 places to stay, some providing meals or cooking facilities.

Juegendherberge Basel, St Alban-Kirchrain 10, t 061 272 05 72, *www.youthhostel.ch/basel*. Located in a long, strange, ochre-coloured building, there are the normal range of rooms and facilities, all simple, basic and clean, and rates are inclusive of breakfast and sheets.

Basel Back Pack, Dornacherstrasse 192, t 061 333 00 37, *www.baselbackpack.ch*. Not central as it is some blocks south of the Central Station. A real mix of accommodation: double beds, three beds and five dorms, along with house bar and lounge, shop corner, community kitchen and dining area.

Eating Out in Basel

(★) **Bruderholz >**

Bruderholz, Bruderholzallee 42, t 061 361 82 22, *www.stucki-bruderholz.ch* (*very expensive*). With two Michelin stars, the Bruderholz is situated above the city and ranks equally high above most other restaurants in Basel. Set in an elegant mansion with lovely gardens and classical salons, the gourmet creations of French cuisine are presented in such an elegant manner that they are nearly too beautiful to be eaten. Indulge yourself, though, in a culinary delight that will long be remembered.

Cheval Blanc, Blumenrain 8, t 061 260 50 50, *www.lestroisrois.com* (*very expensive*). Located within the Hotel Les Tres Rois (*see* p.107), this luxurious riverside restaurant has two Michelin stars. You can expect delicious Mediterranean-style creations by famed chef Peter Knogl, accompanied by wine from a list of select vintages including, naturally, those of Château Cheval Blanc.

Bel Etage, Leonhardsgraben 49, t 061 261 10 10, *www.teufelhof.com* (*very expensive–expensive*). The gourmet restaurant of the Hotel Teufelhof (*see* p.107), with one Michelin star. Like the hotel itself, it is self-indulgent in both art and cuisine with new, market-fresh dishes daily. The wine list contains more than 450 selections, some of which are particularly rare.

Café Spitz, Rheingasse, 2, t 061 685 11 11, *www.hotelmerianbasel.ch* (*very expensive–expensive*). Known as the fish restaurant, and with good reason as it is, undoubtedly, the finest of its genre in Basel, having won the Goldener Fisch award. Sitting on the terrace with a 'postcard' view of the Rhine and Münster, the only problem is what to select as the menu is full of innovative dishes featuring many different species. Unexpectedly, come October there is also a very full and special game menu.

Safran Zunft, Gerbergasse 11, t 061 269 94 94, *www.safran-zunft.ch* (*expensive*). This spice guild was first mentioned in the 14th century. The original building was demolished and this replacement dates from 1902. A favourite at *Fasnacht* time, it specializes in typical Swiss cuisine and has a worldwide wine list. Famous for its Fondue Bacchus where you cook tender, thinly sliced pieces of veal in a heated, spicy rosé wine broth. Awarded winner of the Historical Restaurant of the Year 2008.

Brasserie zum Braunen Mutz, Barfüsserplatz 10, t 061 261 33 69, *www.brauner-mutz-basel.ch* (*moderate*). Basel's only real traditional beer hall – and delightful it is too – offering authentic dishes such as veal sausages and *sauerkraut*.

Hasenburg (Château Lapin), Schneidergasse 20, t 061 261 32 58 (*moderate–inexpensive*). Behind Marktplatz, this quaint typical pub is very popular during *Fasnacht*. It has a varied menu and a reasonable set meal, with a nice *rösti*.

Entertainment and Nightlife in Basel

Bird's Eye Jazz Club, Kohlenberg 20, t 061 263 33 41, *www.birdseye.ch*. Music lovers should head here.

Caram Bar, St Johanns-Vorstadt 13, t 061 382 47 07. Housed in a former bowling alley and featuring a variety of music styles.

Basel is not short on dance clubs and discos.

Mayday Dance Club, Steinenvorstadt 55, t 061 281 88 55. Offers a variety of music and is a favourite of trendy clubbers. *Open Thurs, Fri and Sat.*

Mad Max, Steinentorstrasse 35, t 061 281 88 55. Has a futuristic design and, with two floors and five bars, is Basel's largest club. You have to be smartly dressed and over 28 to gain entry. *Open Fri and Sat.*

Route 66, Freie Strasse 52 (in the passage), t 061 261 79 75, *www.club-route66.ch*. Caters to a mixed bunch and has an American focus.

Solothurn

The name Solothurn (Soleure in French) derives from its Celtic heritage, Saloduron – meaning the 'Stronghold of the Salos'. The Romans established a fortress here around AD 370, the remains of which are still visible today. At the northern corner of the Burgundian kingdom, Solothurn flourished in the 10th century. In 1481, it became the 11th canton to join the Swiss Confederation. Consequently, the number 11 has great significance here and, in fact, is referred to as the 'Holy Solothurn number 11'. Many things here are found in multiples of eleven

The town's greatest days were between 1530 and 1792. Affluent merchants brought fame and prosperity and, in turn, ambassadors were sent by the French kings – hence the sobriquet 'Ambassadorial Town'. These entrepreneurs built luxurious mansions, many of which can be seen today, harmoniously combining French charm, Italian splendour and German Swiss stability. Quite rightly, Solothurn has acquired the reputation of being Switzerland's best-preserved Baroque town.

Once a year, at carnival time, the town goes wild as citizens, disguised by weird and wonderful masks, parade through the streets to celebrate *Chesslete*. During this period, when life is turned upside down, the town is re-christened Honolulu. And as incongruous as this may appear, it has its logic. Honolulu is directly opposite Solothurn – on the other side of the world.

Around the Town

Kathedrale St Ursen
open 6–12 and 2–7

The most dominant structure in Solothurn, approached up a sweeping stone stairway of 11 steps, is the **Kathedrale St Ursen**, which towers above every other building. The inside, somewhat austere, as is the norm for Swiss cathedrals, has 11 bells and 11 altars. Made from greyish/white Solothurn stone, its tower is 216½ft (66m) tall.

Getting to and around Solothurn

By **train**, you can travel from Basel, via Olten; from Bern direct on the regional train, or via Biel/Bienne on the main line. From Zürich the journey is either direct or with a change at Olten; from Geneva it is direct on the mainline to Zürich.

Solothurn is easily reached by **car** from Basel in the north, Bern to the south, Zürich from the west and Biel/Bienne from the east.

The **Waldegg Castle** and **Blumenstein Museum** can both be reached on the no. **4 bus**. Otherwise you can **walk** to the rest of the sights.

Just outside, to the east, stands the **Baseltor** (Basel Gate). From the outside it is impressive and has a central tower, with a portcullis, which is dominated by the figure of a knight.

To the north of the cathedral lie two interesting museums, a collection of churches and the impressive round **Riedholz Turm** (Riedholz Tower) – one of 11 in Solothurn – that reinforces one of the corner fortifications of the old walls.

First, check out the old Arsenal's massive façade that is dominated by a steeply sloping roof, which tapers the levels above the third floor. Two great wooden doors guard the ground floor level. Formidable it looks, and formidable it was meant to be. In the old days of the Swiss Confederation, power in a city-state was symbolized by two buildings: the Arsenal, of which this is a perfect example, and the *rathaus* (town hall) – just around the corner – that here has an elaborate and ornate façade and was constructed between 1476 and 1711. Although an earlier armoury was located on this site in the mid-15th century, this one, unlike others of its genre, was built solely for military purposes between 1609 and 1614. It is now designated an ancient monument of Switzerland and, appropriately, houses the **Altes Zeughaus** (Old Arsenal Museum), one of the more fascinating museums in Switzerland. In addition to a vast collection of weapons (one of Europe's largest), the six floors contain an array of fascinating military exhibits, including, but not limited to, uniforms, drums, swords, huge muskets, cannons and even an armoured personnel carrier. The Armour Room, where over 400 suits of armour are lined up in battle order beneath a beautiful wooden beamed ceiling, is the most impressive.

Further north, just outside the old walls, is the traditional façade of the **Kunstmuseum** (Fine Arts Museum). Several statues of nude women adorn the park in front of it; once inside, look for a fine collection of post-1850 Swiss art represented by the likes of Hodler, Giacometti, Berger and Gubler as well as some Solothurn-born artists. A small collection of Old Masters includes the Solothurn *Madonna* painted in 1522 by Hans Holbein the Younger.

🌟 **Altes Zeughaus**
*Zeughausplatz 1,
t 032 623 35 28,
www.altes-
zeughaus.ch; open
May–Oct Tues–Sun
10–12 and 2–5;
Nov–April Tues–Fri 2–5,
Sat–Sun 10–12 and
2–5; adm*

Kunstmuseum
*Werkhofstrasse 30,
t 032 624 40 00,
www.kunstmuseum-
so.ch; open Tues–Fri
11–5, Sat–Sun 10–5*

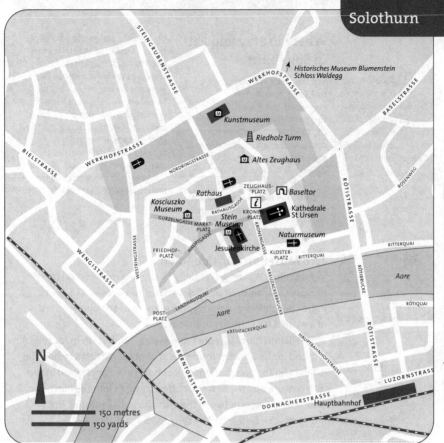

Naturmuseum
Klosterplatz 2,
t 032 622 70 21,
www.naturmuseum-
so.ch; open Tues–Sat
2–5, Sun 10–5

Kosciuszko Museum
Gurzelngasse 12,
t 032 622 80 53; open
May–Oct Sat–Sun 2–4

Stein Museum
Hauptgasse 60 – by
the Jesuit Church,
t 032 621 00 53,
www.steinmuseum.ch;
open May–Oct Tues–Sat
2–5, Sun 10–5

Another museum, the **Naturmuseum** (Natural History Museum), is just south of the cathedral. This, one of the most modern of its kind in Switzerland, operates under the theory that visitors should not just see, but touch also.

To the west of the cathedral is the hugely ornamental Baroque Jesuit Church, and just past this is **Marktplatz**, the social hub of Solothurn. Standing sentry is a colossal clock tower, inhabited by enchanting animated figures designed to lie dormant until the toll of the hour brings them magically to life. There is also another colourful water fountain topped by a well-armed bearded knight – and yes, you've guessed it, one of 11 in Solothurn. If you are visiting on a Wednesday or a Saturday, you will find the streets around here lined with a colourful display of fresh produce.

Two other museums in town are the **Kosciuszko Museum**, which honours the Polish freedom fighter and hero Tadeusz Kosciuszko; and the **Stein Museum** (Stone Museum), with a collection of religious stonework.

Where to Stay and Eat in Solothurn

ⓘ **Solothurn >**
Region Solothurn
Tourismus: Hauptgasse
69, t 032 626 46 46,
www.solothurn-city.ch;
open Mon–Fri
8.30–12.30 and 1.30– 6,
Sat 9–12

****Die Krone**, Hauptgasse 64, t 032 626 44 44, *www.diekrone.ch* (*moderate*). This is a delightful traditional hotel in the centre of the Old Town directly opposite the cathedral. It offers comfortable, well-equipped rooms, each with its own individual character, with charming public areas and a fine restaurant.

****Zunfthaus zu Wirthen**, Hauptgasse 41, t 032 626 28 48, *www.wirthen.ch*, (*moderate*). Located just across from the clock tower by Marktplatz, this hotel has a traditional Solothurn façade. Its 16 rooms are of varying sizes and are bright, open and nicely furnished. The restaurant has a wonderful wood-lined dining room and also an outdoor terrace sheltered by the arcade of the traditional façade. Besides daily specials, the menu features many local Solothurn dishes such as perch, fera and trout, and many variations of veal.

Schloss Waldegg
t 032 624 49 49,
www.schloss-
waldegg.ch; open
Mar–Oct Tues, Wed,
Thurs and Sat 2–5, Sun
10–5; Nov–Dec Sun
10–5; adm

Historisches
Museum
Blumenstein
Blumensteinweg 12,
t 032 622 54 70,
www.museumblumenst
ein.ch; open Tues–Sat
2–5, Sun 10–5

Two Museums Outside Town

The **Schloss Waldegg** (Waldegg Castle) is a marvellous late 17th-century château. Built by Johann Viktor von Besenval (1638–1713), a mayor of Solothurn, it gives you a glimpse of the opulent lifestyle of a man of his standing in that era.

The **Historisches Museum Blumenstein** (Blumenstein Museum) is found in the summer residence of another patrician family. The exhibits on the ground floor reflect how such people lived in the 18th century, and the first floor offers insights into the lifestyle of Solothurn citizens between the 17th and 20th centuries. Both museums can be reached by the no. 4 bus.

Neuchâtel

Neuchâtel is located on the western side of the lake of the same name, and is in the western, French-speaking part of Switzerland. Close to the French border, it looks to the nearby Jura mountains on one side, and the lake and the peaks of the Bernese Oberland in the distance on the other.

For a fairly small city – it has a population of approximately 35,500 – it has a long and interesting history, much of which centres around the **Old Town** and, particularly, the Église Collégiale and the château. It is low on museums, but the one for art and history is worth a close look. And there are opportunities for boat trips out on the lake, as well as the funicular to Chaumont that offers spectacular views.

Although perhaps not the best place for shopping or nightlife, Neuchâtel does possess some very fine restaurants, and one unique hotel.

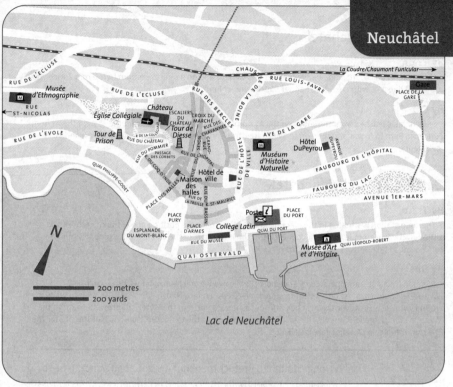

History

In the 10th century a fortified township, of which the Prison and Diesse Tower remain as evidence today, was built in Neuchâtel, as was a new castle – from which the name Neuchâtel originated. This was constructed on the instigation of Rudolph III of Burgundy and presented in 1011 to his wife, Irmengarde.

At the beginning of the 12th century the first Counts of Neuchâtel were titled and, in 1214, granted the city burghers their first charter. It was during this era, also, that the Romanesque wing of the present castle and Romanesque apse and apsidioles of the Église Collégiale were constructed. The cenotaph of the Counts of Neuchâtel, dated 1373 and considered a masterpiece of medieval sculpture, can still be admired in the church.

From 1512 to 1529 the territory was occupied, for strategic reasons, by the Swiss cantons, and in 1530 Neuchâtel adopted the Reformation. Henry II of Orléans-Longueville became the first Prince of Neuchâtel at the beginning of the 17th century. In 1707 Mary of Orléans died without leaving an heir, and the citizens chose her successor from among 15 claimants. It appears they were selective, too, wanting their new leader to be Protestant and

Getting to Neuchâtel

By Train

Neuchâtel is on the mainline between Basel and Geneva and on a direct line from Bern. From Zürich you can travel direct or with changes at either Biel/Bienne or Bern.

By Car

Neuchâtel is reached from the south on the A1 from Geneva and Lausanne; from the east on the A1 from Zürich via Bern to Morat and then on to Neuchâtel; and from Basel in the north via Solothurn and Biel/Bienne.

Getting around Neuchâtel

By Train

The train station is situated in the place de la Gare, in an elevated position above the city proper, and although the **Fun'ambule funicular** connects it to the lower part of the Old Town it is probably more convenient to take a no. 7 or 9 **bus** to the place Pury.

By Bus

Buses in Neuchâtel are operated by **Transports Publics du Littoral Neuchatelois, t** 032 720 06 58, *www.tnneuchatel.ch*. Most buses start or stop at place Pury. In fact, Neuchâtel is small enough to **walk** around with ease. However, the no. 1 bus is useful as it goes north to the Hôtel Palafitte and south to the Musée d'Ethnographie. Similarly, the no. 7 bus drops you off at the La Coudre stop, north of the city, for the Chaumont funicular. A single fare is CHF 1.60.

strong enough to protect them but distant enough not to be too meddlesome. Eventually, they settled on Frederick I, King of Prussia, whose entitlement originated through the Houses of Chalon-Orange and Nassau.

The 18th century saw the emergence of industry – especially watchmaking, the manufacture of printed fabrics and lace, commerce, banking and agriculture. The tide of affluence that ensued brought with it many fine houses, most constructed of local yellow stone.

The Napoleonic era brought more changes. The defeated King of Prussia exchanged Neuchâtel for Hanover, and Napoleon elevated his favourite Marshal, Berthier, to the rank of Prince of Neuchâtel – a place he never actually visited. Napoleon's demise allowed the then King of Prussia, Frederick-William III, to retain control of Hanover and reassert his rights to Neuchâtel. Being too distant from his territory, however, he encouraged its incorporation into the Swiss political system. Accordingly, on 12 September 1814, the Principality of Neuchâtel was admitted to the Swiss Confederation as the 21st canton. The paradox of a principality within the confederation was short lived, though, as the French Revolution encouraged the citizens of Neuchâtel to follow suit. Fortunately this revolution was bloodless, and Neuchâtel was proclaimed a republic on 1 March 1848.

The Old Town

The **tourist office** is just on the edge of the Old Town and is housed in the **post office**, at the place du Port, a very impressive building with the names of the countries of the world sculpted around the top.

Just west on the rue de l'Hotel de Ville is the equally impressive *hôtel de ville* (town hall), which dates from 1784–90; note the two tympanums and the handsome, classical columns. On the east side, Minerva and Liberty are depicted either side of a shield decorated with the city's coat-of-arms, and the opposite side has another shield symbolizing Trade and Abundance, protected on either side by two winged and cloud-borne figures. Inside, on the ground floor, there is a model of 18th-century Neuchâtel. Just across the road there is a very large ornamental Louis XVI-style fountain.

The Old Town is to the south, and one of its features are the fountains, similar to those found in Bern and other parts of Switzerland, with their columns topped by brightly coloured statues. The **Fontaine de la Justice** (Justice Fountain) is the closest of them, at the junction of rue de l'Hôpital and Grand-Rue; this was carved by Laurent Perroud between 1545 and 1547. It has an octagonal basin and the statue is that of Justice, surrounded by figures representing a pope, a magistrate, an emperor and a sultan that, in earlier eras, represented various forms of government. Just a block or so further south is the **Croix du Marché** (Market Crossing), the most ancient square of the town, where the surrounding 18th-century façades provide a suitable backdrop for the oldest fountain outside the old Neuchâtel town walls. It started life as a watering spot for cattle, but the **Fontaine du Banneret** (Banneret Fountain) was enlarged and in 1581 Laurent Perroud created the figure of the standard bearer that gives it its name. The adjacent Hôtel du Banneret, built in 1609, is considered the finest example of late Renaissance architecture in the region, and has been perfectly conserved. Just to the west, check out the Baroque façade of the Montmollin House at rue des Moulins, and look carefully to the east for the small **passage des Corbets** to spot a very unusual Renaissance spiral staircase.

Up the Hill to the Château and Church

Neuchâtel's main attractions sit at the top of a steep hill, and a little way up it the **Fontaine du Griffon** (Griffon Fountain), just past the Tour de Diesse, is a suitable place to stop and decide which route to take to them. Actually, until the Reformation in 1530, there used to be a statue of Neuchâtel's patron saint, William, here. The fountain you see today was enlarged in 1664 and on public holidays wine, rather than the usual water, flowed through it. To the south, take note of some fine 18th-century houses in the **rue du Pommier**, which replaced others burnt down in the fire of 1714.

The quick way up to the castle and church is by way of the escaliers du Château, but these are extremely steep and are perhaps better left for the descent. Better, by far, to follow the rue du Château and rue de la Collégiale up to the ramparts and then around to the church itself. Along the way, take time to look at the **Tour de Prison** (Prison Tower). This has the distinction of being the most ancient building in Neuchâtel, and it is fascinating to note how easily discernible layers chronicle its constructive history: a white limestone base that dates from Roman times is topped by uncut blocks of granite from around the beginning of the 11th century and finished off by medium-sized white limestone and yellow stone added by 11th- and 12th-century builders. The entire tower was renovated in 1803. There are models of Neuchâtel as it appeared during the 15th and 18th centuries inside, and the top level affords splendid views of the neighbouring district, lake and the peaks of the Bernese Oberland in the distance.

Tour de Prison
open April–Sept 8–6; adm with CHF 2 coin through an automatic turnstile

✪ **Église Collégiale and Château**

Église Collégiale

There is little documentation regarding the early history of the Église Collégiale, but it is known that the building was begun prior to 1185 in the Romanesque style, and was influenced by Basel's cathedral and the Grossmünster in Zürich. A now obliterated inscription on the southern portal identified the founders as Ulrich II of Neuchâtel and his wife Bertha. It was consecrated on 8 November 1276, a date that probably marks the completion of the western, largely Gothic end. Renovations followed in 1360, 1372 and 1428; in 1530 during the Reformation, Neuchâtel soldiers returning from Geneva stripped the interior of altars and decorative additions. Major alterations were made to the exterior during a general renovation in the mid-19th century, including the destruction of the original church tower in favour of a stone spire. A copy of that tower was grafted on to the northern side of the building, leaving the southern steeple as the only original on the structure.

Inside, **stained-glass windows** by Clément Heaton were added to the choir in 1905. The wonderful rose window and others on the southern side representing the *Announcement of the Shepherds*, the seal of the Reformer Guillame Farel and the apostles and their symbols are by Theodor Delachaux and were installed between 1930 and 1947. The windows on the north and west, of the prophets and Moses and John the Baptist respectively, are creations of Marcel Poncet in 1951. Take a look at the capitals, decorated with

Daniel in the lion's den, palmettes, heads of wildcats and even musician eagles and monkeys.

Notwithstanding this, pride of place undoubtedly lies with the gloriously sculpted **cenotaph of the Counts of Neuchâtel**, considered one of the most remarkable works of art from the Middle Ages and the most important north of the Alps. It was begun on the order of Louis of Neuchâtel in 1372, and consists of no less than 15 carved, painted and almost life-size statues. During the Reformation the governor prevented its desecration and between 1678 and 1840 it was actually hidden behind planks before the broken parts were reconstituted and repainted. In fact, what you see today is an amalgamation from different ages: the knights and their ladies at the entrance of the arcades are from the 14th century; the images of Jean and Conrad de Fribourg were created between 1425 and 1458 by Master Matthäus Ensinger; an unpainted Count is thought to be Rodolphe de Hochberg who died in 1487; and the gables topping the cenotaph are clearly from the 15th century.

On the exterior, facing the castle two smaller apses standing either side of a larger one are Norman. Of the small open *cloître* (cloister), only the Romanesque arcades built on to the north wall of the church are original; the rest was renovated in neo-Gothic style in 1875.

The Château

Château
t 032 889 40 03; free guided tours, with commentary in English, French and German, start from the entrance at door number one, April–Sept Mon–Fri 10, 11, 12, 2, 3 and 4, Sat 10, 11, 2, 3 and 4, Sun and public holidays 2, 3 and 4

Construction of the imposing château was begun near the end of the 12th century. It was enlarged in several stages over the next three centuries, and renovated extensively following the city-wide fire of 1450. Initially serving as the principal dwelling for the first Lords of Neuchâtel, it became, after 1405, a residence for the governors and a series of councillors. From 1848 to the present it has housed important government offices and it is, in fact, the oldest building in Switzerland that has been in continuous use. In short, in one form or another, the regional authority has made its home in the castle for the past 800 years. The structure is divided into three main sections: the **Romanesque tower**, the **Main Gate** and the **southern Gallery**. The highly ornamental Romanesque section, the oldest part of the château dating back to the 12th century, has an interesting carriage gateway that gave access to the wine cellars – the principal source of income of the counts. The southern Gallery was built in 1488, and has as its main focal point a wall upon which are emblazoned the coats-of-arms of the first 13 Swiss cantons. Philippe de Hochberg commissioned the construction of the twin-towered Main Gate in 1496–98 as a permanent reminder of his service to the French kings.

Inside there are many notable rooms. The **Antechamber of the Grand Council Hall** has a Robert Flemier painting of *The Blessing of the Plough*. The **Grand Council Hall** itself, built in 1875 over the stables, is where the canton parliament meets. The **Grotto** was originally a stone barrel vault where the Neuchâtel archives were kept, but in 1649 it was ornamented with marble panels painted in grisaille and with the coat-of-arms of Henry II of Orléans-Longueville. The wonderfully wooden-beamed **Knights' Room**, the castle's largest, was once just a cellar before becoming an arsenal; it is now beautifully restored and contains a very large painting by Jules Girardet depicting a battle in front of the Thielle Bridge. The **Department of Agriculture's Vestibule** is noted for its rafters, portraits of magistrates and Marcel Mathy's *Woman with Necklace* sculpture. The parquet-floored – note the tiles evoking the ruling families in the corner – and wooden-beamed **Marie of Savoy Room** is very distinguished, and named after the daughter of the Count of Savoy and niece of King Louis XI of France who married Philip of Hochberg in 1478. It is dominated by a huge yellow stone fireplace, where painted above it two angels support the Count of Neuchâtel's coat-of-arms. A corridor above the Marie of Savoy Room has notable wall drawings featuring coats-of-arms of some 17th-century Neuchâtel governors and the Gallandre family, and a red-chalked image of a mustachioed soldier. Built by, and named after himself, the **Philippe de Hochberg Gallery** dates from 1488; it was enlarged in 1836 and 12 years later when the republic was founded in 1848 members of the former State Council were imprisoned here. The **State Council Room** on the upper floor of the Romanesque wing was once Count Philippe's bedroom, but since 1848 it is where the five members and the chancellor of the Neuchâtel government convene for deliberations. The wooden ceilings of the **Antechamber of State Council** are particularly decorative and feature the coats-of-arms of Philippe de Hochberg and Marie of Savoy. The **State Room**, seat of the State Court, has a décor that has more or less remained the same since 1691; armorial shields of the rulers and governors of Neuchâtel cover the walls. Look, also, for the handsome Josué Robert clock that dates from 1732. Originally built of wood in the 15th century, the **Castle Chapel** was reconstructed with a stone barrel roof in the 18th century. It is somewhat incongruous that this, with its original Gothic window, is now used as a library.

Before leaving this area, take a walk around the battlements and admire these wonderful buildings from quite a different perspective.

Back to the Lower Old Town

Three more places are worth seeing back in the lower area of the Old Town. The **rue du Seyon** is an important shopping street, with water channels down one side; in times gone by the Seyon River used to flow through here. At its western end is the **place Pury** where you will find a statue of David de Pury, a major benefactor to Neuchâtel who was responsible for several buildings that are a part of the town's heritage. It is also a major open-air bus terminal. Finally, just south, there is the **place des Halles** surrounded by a wealth of 18th-century buildings. The most notable one is now a restaurant, but it was originally constructed from 1569 to 1575 – with much Renaissance decoration – by Laurent Perroud for use as a *maison des halles* (covered market).

Along the Lakeside – South to North

A foot tunnel leads from place Pury to the very pretty **esplanade du Mont-Blanc** and gardens where you will find, just south of the impressive Beau-Rivage Hotel, several statues of international artists like Vasarely and Arp.

The **Collège Latin**, a pleasing Empire-style building, is just north on the **quai Ostervald**, and this is now the library which houses important manuscripts by Jean-Jacques Rousseau and other valuable collections.

The very picturesque **port de la Ville** is the departure point for cruises on the lake, and also a wonderful place just to pass the time of day. Yachts bob gently at their moorings, and swans and ducks glide effortlessly over the waters or waddle around the promenade begging for lunch. With the Alps glistening in the distance it is an idyllic sight.

Lake voyages
Société de Navigation sur les Lacs de Neuchâtel et Morat, **t** *032 729 96 00, www.navig.ch*

There are actually three interconnected lakes. The Lac de Neuchâtel, the greatest of them, is in fact also the largest lake located entirely in Switzerland; Lac de Bienne (Bielersee in German) to the north is much smaller; and Lac de Morat (Murtensee in German) to the east is smaller again. Any number of **lake voyages** may be made, taking in any combination of the lakes, or just the Lac de Neuchâtel itself. The choice is yours, and the only parameters time and preference.

Musée d'Art et d'Histoire
esplanade Léopold-Robert 1, **t** *032 717 79 20, www.mahm.ch; open Tues–Sun 10–6; adm, Wed free; every Tues 12.15–1.15 lectures, guided visits and concerts (in French), CHF 4, includes adm to museum*

Immediately north is the home of the **Musée d'Art et d'Histoire** (Museum of Art and History). The exhibits here, in 20 permanent and temporary rooms, are both varied and interesting, ranging from paintings – such as the huge one of *Christ Rising to the Heavens* which dominates the lobby – to carriages, household wares and furniture. The main attractions, however, are three 18th-century androids invented by the creative mind of Jaquet-Droz. To see the automatons in action you will either have to time it right (the first Sunday of each month at 2pm, 3pm and 4pm) or, by special and prior arrangement, pay for a private showing.

Take a short stroll down the promenade, quai Léopold-Robert, north from the museum, to admire an array of impressively beautiful houses.

Just North of the Old Town

There are three places worth investigating in this area. The one closest to the Old Town is the **Muséum d'Histoire Naturelle** (Natural History Museum). Modern artwork and sculptures adorn the sandstone façade, and inside you will find a fascinating array of Swiss mammals and birds presented in their natural environment, with a slide show with sound effects for the birds. Look, too, for the giant fossils.

Muséum d'Histoire Naturelle
rue des Terreaux 14,
t 032 717 79 60,
www.museum-neuchatel.ch; open
Tues–Sun 10–6; adm,
Wed free

Immediately north, a few blocks away, is the most magnificent, and one of the most historic, mansions in Neuchâtel. Set in French-style formal gardens that slope down westwards towards the lake – which at one time actually reached this far inland – is the grand Louis XVI-style **Hôtel DuPeyrou**. This was built for Pierre-Alexandre DuPeyrou by the Bernese, but Paris-trained, architect Erasmus Ritter between 1765 and 1770. DuPeyrou's close friend was Jean-Jacques Rousseau, and after the latter's death he had the first complete edition of his work published in Geneva in 1788. Two years later, in 1790, he had the second part of those same *Confessions* published in Neuchâtel itself. When DuPeyrou died in 1794 he bequeathed a grand collection of Rousseau's manuscripts to the town library. The 19th century saw the mansion change hands frequently: in 1799 it was sold to Frédéric de Pourtalès, and the state purchased it 14 years later as the home for its new ruler, Marshal Berthier. Three years later it changed hands again and finally, in 1858, the town of Neuchâtel bought it. These days it is leased from the city by an Australian chef and his wife, who run a stylish restaurant on the lower floors under the name Hôtel DuPeyrou (*see* p.122).

There is another very good reason for visiting the Hôtel DuPeyrou, and that is in an inconspicuous part of the courtyard, behind the building. It is quite common for Swiss cities to own their own vineyards, and then lease the rights to produce wines under the city's own name (or even produce their own). So, it is here that you will find the **Caves de la Ville de Neuchâtel**. Its wines have won many prizes and are very good indeed, especially the Pinot Gris and Chardonnay. Taste a few and take a couple of bottles of your favourites home – remember that as about 95 per cent of all wines produced in Switzerland are consumed there, it's not easy

Caves de la Ville de Neuchâtel
avenue DuPeyrou 5,
t 032 717 76 95,
www.cavevillentel.ch

or cheap to get any at home. If you are lucky, you may be shown the original cellars of the mansion.

South of the Old Town

Musée
d'Ethnographie
rue Saint-Nicolas 4,
t 032 718 19 60,
www.men.ch; open
Tues–Sun 10–5; adm

The **Musée d'Ethnographie** (Museum of Ethnography) features interesting permanent exhibitions of ancient Egypt and the Himalayas, particularly Bhutan and Tibet; General Charles Daniel de Meuron's 18th-century natural history room; and a 21st-century curiosity room.

Outside Town

La Coudre/
Chaumont
Funicular
t 032 720 06 00,
www.tnneuchatel.ch;
fare CHF 9.20 return

Take the no. 7 bus from place Pury to the La Coudre stop and then transfer to the **La Coudre/Chaumont Funicular**. Opened in 1910, this takes just 13 minutes to transport you from an altitude of 1,696ft (517m) to 3,566ft (1,087m) over a distance of 1⅓miles (2,097.5m) at a speed of 9¾ft (3m) per second. This is the only panoramic funicular in the Jura region and from the curious tower at the summit there are unparalleled views over three lakes, the smaller mountains to the west and the peaks of the Bernese Oberland eastwards.

Tourist Information and Services in Neuchâtel

ⓘ Neuchâtel ›
Tourisme
Neuchâtelois:
Hôtel des Postes,
t 032 889 68 90,
www.neuchateltouris
me.ch; open July–Aug
Mon–Fri 9–6.30, Sat
9–4, Sun 10–4; rest of
year Mon–Fri 9–12 and
1.30–5.30, Sat 9–12

Train Tour

Train touristique de Neuchâtel (Neuchâtel tourist train) operates daily from May to Oct, with commentaries in French, German and English. It takes you on a 45-minute trip through the Old Town, with a stop at the castle; tickets costs CHF 7.

Market Days

General market, Tues, Thurs and Sat mornings at place des Halles.

Where to Stay in Neuchâtel

★ Palafitte ›

*****Palafitte, rte des Gouttes d'Or 2, t 032 723 02 02, www.palafitte.ch (luxury). Behind a bland exterior some distance north of town, you will find an extraordinarily unusual hotel. In the lobby you will be fingerprinted, and your finger then becomes the key to your room. A golf cart parked in the lobby will take you there. All the 40 junior suites are in the form of chalets, and you can select one on stilts directly over the lake itself. Inside, you are met by not just luxury, but a degree of sophistication that almost makes the term high-tech redundant. Expect a plasma TV, home video surround system and an individual 'SIM-pad' remote control for all in-room devices. The screens behind the bed part to reveal a stunning Jacuzzi right behind in the bathroom, and on your private deck a ladder leads directly down into the lake – making it your private pool. All in all, the most unique hotel in Switzerland.

***La Maison du Prussien, Gor du Vauseyon, t 032 730 54 54, www.hotel-prussien.ch (moderate). Situated a little south of town (take a no. 1 bus to the Beauregard stop), this distinguished building used to be an 18th-century brewery. It has just 10 rooms, but they are spacious and quite special, with wooden-beamed ceilings and fireplaces.

Hôtel du Marché, place des Halles 4, t 032 723 23 30, www.hoteldu marche.ch (inexpensive). Right in the centre of the Old Town, this is a small hotel with just 10 rooms (none en suite), either single, double or for three, that are clean and simply furnished.

Eating Out in Neuchâtel

Le Colvert, rte des Gouttes d'Or 2, t 032 723 02 02, *www.palafitte.ch* (*very expensive*). This is the gourmet restaurant of the Hôtel Palafitte, which more than matches the standards of the hotel itself. Directly overlooking the lake, it has a terrace for the warmer months. The *À La Découverte* menu is a six-course feast for CHF 120, whilst the *Au Plaisir* menu may be better for those with lighter appetites with just four courses and costing CHF 80 (CHF 62 without the appetizer). Or choose one of the delicious dishes from the main menu.

Hôtel Dupeyrou, avenue DuPeyrou 1, t 032 725 11 83, *www.dupeyrou.ch* (*very expensive*). Located in what is Neuchâtel's most imposing and historic building (*see* p.120), the elegant restaurant here is run by Australian chef Craig Penlington-Montadon and his Neuchâteloise wife, Françoise. The speciality is fish and other seafood, fresh from the market, used to create original and elaborate creations. Eat out on the terrace in good weather.

Brasserie du Jura, rue de la Treille 7, t 032 725 14 10 (*moderate–inexpensive*). Just off the place Pury, this has plenty of ambience and is an authentic Neuchâteloise brasserie. One of the specialities here is the local tripe and, of course, fondue features on the menu.

La Chaux-de-Fonds and Le Locle

La Chaux-de-Fonds is located close to the French border at an altitude of 3,280ft (1,000m) and, with a population of around 40,000, is the third-largest city in French-speaking Switzerland, after Geneva and Lausanne. Besides its cultural attractions this lovely mountainous region is also a popular place for outdoor sports and activities in all seasons – hiking, mountain-biking, cycling and cross-country skiing are all on the agenda here.

History

Although La Chaux-de-Fonds was first inhabited some 10,000 years ago, it wasn't until the 14th century that this forested area was colonized from the south. Unfortunately, because it is covered with porous sandstone the land suffered from a lack of water, and farming was problematic.

Because of this the local citizens turned their hands to other things and by the 17th century La Chaux-de-Fonds was already known for its watchmaking. In the following century it became a prominent industry, with artisans such as Pierre Lacquet-Droz being the most famous of his era.

A fire devastated the city in 1794, but this eventually had its beneficial effects as, in 1835, Charles-Henri Junod created the new

Getting to and around La Chaux-de-Fonds and Le Locle

By **train** from Neuchâtel there is a regional line to La Chaux-de-Fonds (30min journey) and on to Le Locle; from Geneva it is necessary to change at Neuchâtel; from Bern change at Biel/Bienne. Travel from Basel involves a train-bus-train connection, or changes at Biel/Bienne and possibly Olten are necessary.

By **car**, the simplest way is on the J20 from Neuchâtel, through the Vue-des-Alpes tunnel. It's a journey time of around 15mins.

Bus nos 60/61 operates between La Chaux-de-Fonds and Le Locle.

Once in the city the most effective way to get around is on **foot**.

city plan based on a gridlike pattern more familiar in America than Europe. Later, the Jugendstil (more well known by its French name, Art Nouveau) style of architecture – known as Style-Sapin locally – became popular, so much so that it is considered the most important city in Switzerland for this particular style.

Surprisingly for such a small city, it is the birthplace of famous personalities such as Charles Edouard Jeanneret-Gris, better known as the architect Le Corbusier (1887–1965). Le Corbusier started his work in La Chaux-de-Fonds; the **Villa Jeanneret-Perret**, better known as the **Maison Blanche**, which he built for his parents, is the best known of his early examples. Louis Chevrolet (1878–1941), founder of the famous car manufacturing company, was also born here. He emigrated to Canada in 1900 before moving to the USA the following year. Although the company is now owned by General Motors, it still carries his name to this day.

Timekeeping Museums

Horology, though, is what La Chaux-de-Fonds and its near neighbour Le Locle (just a few kilometres away) are really famous for. The two cities combined became the tenth Swiss site to be acclaimed with World Heritage status.

The **Musée International d'Horlogerie** (International Museum of Horology) in La Chaux-de-Fonds was originally funded by the Gallet family in 1899. These days it is owned by the city and is considered one of the most important places dedicated to horology in the world. It has an unparalleled display of clocks and watches, which shows the developments in technology over the centuries.

The **Musée d' Horlogerie du Locle** (Le Locle Museum of Horology) is housed in an immaculate Louis XVI-style castle in La Locle dating from the late 18th century, and offers a wide variety of permanent exhibitions.

✪ **Musée International d'Horlogerie**
rue des Musées 29,
t 32 967 68 61,
www.mih.ch; open
Tues–Sun 10–5; adm

Musée d'Horlogerie du Locle
Châteaux des Monts,
rte des Monts 65,
t 32 931 16 80,
www.mhl-monts.ch;
open May–Oct
Tues–Sun 10–5;
Nov–April Tues–Sun
2–5; adm

ⓘ La Chaux-de-Fonds >

Tourisme Neuchâtelois-Montagnes: Espacité 1, t 32 889 68 95, www.neuchatel tourisme.ch; open July–Aug Mon–Fri 9–12.15 and 1.45–6.30, Sat 10–4; Sept–June Mon–Fri 9–12 and 1.30–5.30, Sat 9–12

ⓘ Le Locle

Tourisme Neuchâtelois-Montagnes: Le Col 23, t 32 889 68 92, www.neuchatel tourisme.ch; open May–Oct Tues–Fri 9–12 and 1–5, Sat 10–12 and 1–5; Nov–April Tues–Fri 9–12 and 1.30–5, Sat 1.30–5.30; closed throughout year Sun and Mon

Events in La Chaux-de-Fonds

Sept: Louis Chevrolet Event – a vintage car memorial rally from La Chaux-de-Fonds to Beaune, France.

Oct: Swiss Watch Exchange – a gathering for expert watch collectors.

Where to Stay and Eat in La Chaux-de-Fonds

****Grand Hôtel Les Endroits, Boulevard des Endroits 94–96, t 32 925 02 50, *www.hotel-les-endroits.ch* (*expensive*). Located in a charming, modern building, this hotel has 42 bedrooms with all the facilities you'd expect from a 4-star establishment. The owners are chefs, as it started as a restaurant, and serve a wide range of regional dishes as well as new creations.

Bern and the Bernese Oberland

This is a region that definitely has a split personality. Bern, the capital, has a charming medieval centre while the dramatic heights of the region are further south.

The high peaks of the Bernese Oberland are not that far away and getting to them and around them is a delight. Initially, the journey south from Bern to Thun is non-descript. But, once the castle comes into view, closely followed by Lake Thun, the true beauty of this area begins to be revealed. As the lake winds south and then east, the hills become small mountains and they, in turn, are overshadowed by massive snow-capped peaks.

Interlaken is the gateway to the high mountains of the south, and soon the road splits, leading into two magnificent valleys that are connected to each other by an array of mountain transportation.

09

Don't miss

⭐ **Step back in time**
Old Town, Bern **p.130**

⭐ **Trip of a lifetime**
Jungfraujoch **p.152**

⭐ **Feat of nature**
Trümmelbach Falls **p.157**

⭐ **Wondrous alpine vistas**
Schilthorn **p.157**

⭐ **Huff and puff up a mountain**
Brienz Rothorn Bahn **p.160**

See map overleaf

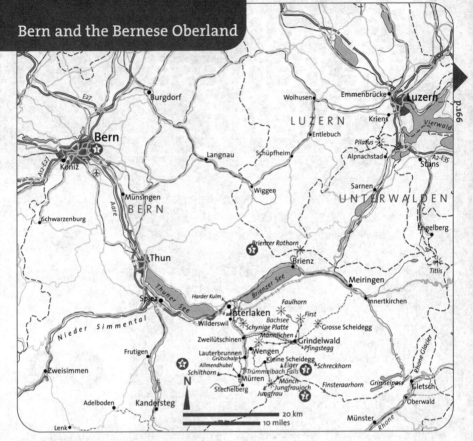

Don't miss

1 Bern Old Town **p.130**

2 Jungfraujoch **p.152**

3 Trümmelbach Falls **p.157**

4 Schilthorn **p.157**

5 Brienz Rothorn Bahn **p.160**

Getting to Bern

By Air

Bern-Belp Airport, **t** 31 960 21 11, *www.alpar.ch*, has a very limited number of international flights; there is a flight from Southampton with **Flybe** during the winter months. It has an internal flight to Lugano. The nearest airports are Zürich, Basel and Geneva, respectively 1hr 9mins, 1hr 7mins and 1hr 45 mins away by train.

An **airport shuttle bus** runs to the train station.

By Car

Bern is connected to the national motorway network with easy routes from Basel, Geneva and Zürich. The fastest way from the Valais is through the Lötschberg tunnel, putting the car on the car/rail link.

By Train

There are fast, direct services from Basel, Geneva via Lausanne, Zürich and eastern Switzerland and Brig through the Lötschberg tunnel. Bern also has fast international connections; it is the only European capital to be served by the high-speed French **TGV**, German **ICE** and Italian **Cisalpino** trains.

Getting around Bern

Public transport in and around Bern, on a combination of **trams**, **buses** and **trains**, is fast, clean and efficient. However, most visitors will only need to consider the no. 12 that runs past the Bahnhof all the way down the centre of the Old Town to the Bear Park, with some running all the way out to the Zentrum Paul Klee. **Tickets** must be purchased from ticket vending machines, ticket offices, hotels or the tourist office before each trip and are available for single trips or, more advantageously, as an **Unlimited Day Pass**.

By Car

Car hire is available from a number of companies including **Avis**, Wabernstrasse 41, **t** 031 378 15 15, *www.avis.ch*; **Europcar**, Laupenstrasse 22, **t** 031 381 75 75, *www.europcar.ch*; and **Hertz**, Casinoplatz, **t** 031 318 21 60, *www.hertz.ch*. Note that you can access hotels, but central Bern is largely closed to through traffic.

By Bicycle

Bicycles can be hired May–Oct from **Bern Rollt**, **t** 079 277 28 57, *www.bernrollt.ch*. The first four hours are free (need to pay a deposit), payable after that. Bicycles can also be hired from the railway station. **Bern Toursimus** (*see* p.136) has information about cycling trails and tours.

Bern

Bern, or Berne in French, is the administrative capital of Switzerland and has a dramatic location on an elevated promontory surrounded by the River Aare. Running on a west to east axis, it offers (weather permitting) spectacular views of the Bernese Oberland, and specifically the peaks of the Eiger, Mönch and Jungfrau, dominating the southwestern horizon.

History and fate have combined, equally spectacularly, to leave the city a special heritage. With its attractive sandstone buildings, colourful and historic water fountains, intricate towers and an extensive labyrinth of arcades (3¾ miles/6km of them) lining the long and comparatively narrow streets, its appearance has remained unchanged for many centuries. As a consequence, Bern's Old Town is actually one of the finest examples of medieval civic architecture in Europe and, as such, has been placed on the

UNESCO list of World Heritage Sites. It's impossible not to mention, either, the BärenPark (Bear Park); Bern was named after a bear, and this symbol of the city has been here since 1480.

The population of Bern only totals around 135,000, but it has all the attributes of a much larger city. Museums are plentiful; one of them has the world's largest collection of work by a single artist of world renown (Paul Klee), whilst another shows how Einstein lived here while he was developing his theory of relativity. Even Tobler created the world-famous Toblerone chocolate here. There are interesting theatres, even one as part of a hotel, and the nightlife is vibrant. Hotels are plentiful, although in general they lack the character found in other cities, but that is not reflected in the diverse and interesting restaurant scene. Shoppers will be delighted with Bern, especially as many of the shops are found under those famous arcades. On Tuesdays and Saturdays there are very lively and colourful fresh vegetable, fruit and flower markets in the city centre.

History

Drawn by Bern's strategic location, on a long promontory surrounded by the River Aare, Berchtold V, Duke of Zähringen, founded the first settlement here in 1191. Emperor Lothar III of Upper Burgundy had bestowed this title upon Berchtold, and Bern subsequently became a part of that region. Tradition has it that Bern came by its name in a curious manner. The surrounding areas were covered with forest and the Duke, reportedly, determined to name his new town after the first animal he killed while hunting there. This happened to be a bear, the German name for which is *bär*. The legend is somewhat corroborated by the local dialect pronunciation of Bern – *Bärn*. In 1224 the oldest version of the city's well-known coat-of-arms, featuring a bear and the name 'ob Berne', first appeared. And high on the list of the city's main tourist attractions is the new BärenPark (Bear Park) opened in October 2009 (*see* p.132). Formerly the bears lived in pits (which the public can still view). The bears, known affectionately as Mutze by the local population, have been living in the city since 1480.

Berchtold entrusted the construction of the city to Cuno of Bubenberg. Among his achievements was the clearing of the surrounding oak forests, the wood from which was used to construct houses. Around the initial settlement, situated at the end of the promontory, Cuno built a first city wall that was dominated in the centre by a huge clock tower. This also served as the main gate, giving access to and from the city. Bern was expanded in the 13th century when, under the protectorate of Count Peter of Savoy, the walls were extended westwards along the promontory. The main gateway then became the *käfigturm*

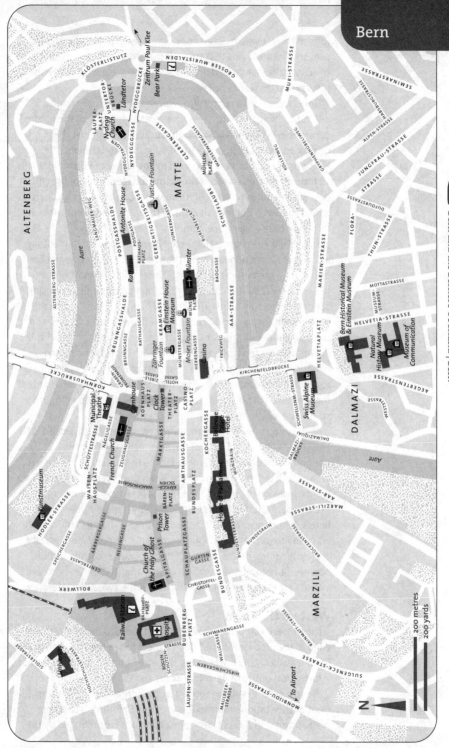

ALTENBERG

KLÖSTERLISTUTZ

GROSSER MURISTALDEN

Zentrum Paul Klee

Bear Park

Läuterplatz

Nydegg Untertor-Brücke

Nydegg Church

Läntdetor

MURI-STRASSE

SEMINARSTRASSE

HABSBURGSTRASSE

Aare

ALTENBERG-STRASSE

LANDMAUER-WEG

Antonite House

POSTGASSHALDE

POSTGASSE

Justice Fountain

NYDEGGGASSE

GERBERNGASSE

MATTE

MÜHLEN-PLATZ

WASSERWERKGASSE

GRYPHENHÜBELIWEG

ALPEN-STRASSE

JUNGFRAU-STRASSE

DUFOURSTRASSE

FLORA-STRASSE

THUN-STRASSE

Rathaus

RATHAUS-PLATZ

GERECHTIGKEITSGASSE

Münster

BADGASSE

JUNKERNGASSE

SCHIFFLAUBE

BUDENBERG

MARIEN-STRASSE

MOTTASTRASSE

BRUNNGASSHALDE

BRUNNGASSE

RATHAUSGASSE

KRAMGASSE

Einstein House Museum

MÜNSTER-PLATZ

Moses Fountain

HERRENGASSE

AAR-STRASSE

FRICKWEG

Bern Historical Museum & Einstein Museum

HELVETIA-STRASSE

Natural History Museum

Museum of Communication

DALMAZI

GRABEN

KORNHAUSBRÜCKE

Zähringer Fountain

MÜNSTERGASSE

Casino

HELVETIAPLATZ

AEGERTENSTRASSE

MUSEUM-STRASSE

WILERSTRASSE

Aare

Kornhouse

KORNHAUS-PLATZ

Clock Tower

HOTEL-ZIBELE-GASSE

THEATER-PLATZ

CASINO-PLATZ

KIRCHENFELDBRÜCKE

SCHWELLENMA-STRASSE

Swiss Alpine Museum

DALMAZIQUAI

DALMAZI-BRÜCKE

Aare

AAR-STRASSE

Municipal Theatre

SCHÜTTESTRASSE

NÄGELIGASSE

French Church

ZEUGHAUSGASSE

MARKTGASSE

Bellevue Palace Hotel

MÜNZRAIN

MARZILI

Kunstmuseum

HODLER-STRASSE

WAISENHAUSPLATZ

WACHHAUSGASSE

AMTHAUSGASSE

KOCHERGASSE

House of Parliament

BUNDESTERRASSE

BUNDESRAIN

MARZILISTRASSE

AAR-STRASSE

BRÜCKENSTRASSE

SPEICHERGASSE

RARBERGERGASSE

NEUENGASSE

Church of the Holy Ghost

Prison Tower

SPITALGASSE

KÄFIGASSCHEN

BÄRENPLATZ

SCHAUPLATZGASSE

BUNDESPLATZ

GURTEN-GASSE

CHRISTOFFEL-GASSE

BUNDESGASSE

SULGENECK-STRASSE

RAINMATT-STRASSE

HOCHSCHULWEG

GENFERGASSE

BOLLWERK

Railway Station

BAHNHOF-PLATZ

Hospital

BUBENBERG-STRASSE

BUBENBERG-PLATZ

SCHWANENGASSE

LAUPEN-STRASSE

HIRSCHENGRABEN

MAULBEER-STRASSE

MONBIJOU-STRASSE

To Airport

University

SIDLERSTRASSE

BOGEN-SCHÜTZEN-STRASSE

WALLGASSE

SCHWARZTORSTRASSE

200 metres

200 yards

N

(prison tower), which was subsequently reconstructed in the 17th century. The additions that took place during the 14th century saw the city walls, dismantled only 100 years ago, reaching where the railway station stands today.

Times were not all peaceful, however, and Bern often had to defend itself against attackers. The most significant of the battles occurred in 1339 when Bern fought successfully against the combined troops of the nobility of Burgundy and the city of Fribourg, which had been founded by the father of Berchtold V. This victory not only guaranteed the future independence of the city, but initiated an expansion of its powers. Soon after, in 1353, Bern joined the Swiss Confederation, and the succeeding centuries saw its power base widen considerably.

An unwelcome change that befell Bern, this one fundamentally altering the city's appearance, occurred in 1405. In that year a fire destroyed a great number of the timber buildings. Most of the houses were rebuilt on their original foundations, this time using sandstone from local quarries instead of wood. Many of these were rebuilt for a second time in the 16th and 17th centuries, and the consequent harmony of appearance and elaborate detail still delight visitors today. Also, in the mid-16th century the famous historic fountains that adorn the streets of Bern were built, mostly to replace the wooden ones of earlier centuries. These are guarded, more often than not, by an elaborate and vividly coloured figure standing proudly atop a column.

Between 1536 and 1798 Bern gained, mostly at the expense of the House of Savoy, large tracts of territory along Lake Geneva. And it is mainly because of these Bernese efforts that much of the French area of Switzerland is a part of the Swiss Confederation today. The French invasion of 1798, and the new Switzerland that emerged like a phoenix in 1815 from the ruins left by Napoleon, destroyed Bern's dominance. It was forced to cede nearly half its land, which was used to form the new cantons of Aargau and Waadt. The city even lost control of the canton of Bern. By way of compensation, however, it became the cantonal capital and, in 1848, was chosen by the first Swiss Parliament as capital of the Swiss Confederation.

Western Old Town

🌟 Old Town

The modern **Hauptbahnhof** (railway station) marks the western edge of the promontory, but don't expect to see the trains; they are hidden away on the lower levels. It is also home to the main tourist information centre of **Bern Tourismus** and the starting point for some interesting walking tours that they organize (*see* p.137). In front of the station's main exit is the busy Bahnhofplatz, where many trams and buses start from, and which is dominated by the impressive **Heiliggeistkirche** (Church of the Holy Ghost). This Protestant church was built between 1726 and 1729 in the Swiss-Baroque style.

A few minutes' walk northeast of the station takes you to the

Kunstmuseum

Hodlerstrasse 8–12,
t 31 328 09 44,
www.kunstmuseum
bern; open Tues 10–9,
Wed –Sun 10 –5; adm

Kunstmuseum (Fine Arts Museum). The classical-style building, enhanced by statues and engravings, includes amongst its exhibits some 3,000 paintings and sculptures and nearly 55,000 drawings, with art from the Italian trecento by Duccio and Fra Angelico; Swiss art from the 15th century including the work of Niklaus Manuel, Albert Anker, Ferdianad Hodler and Cuno Amiet; and international art from the 19th and 20th centuries. In the latter category are works by Wassily Kandinsy, Pablo Picasso and Salvador Dalí. Adolf Wölfi (1864–1930), the writer, poet, draughtsman and composer, is another native Swiss whose work is on display here. This, though, is in the form of texts, drawings, collages and musical compositions that together form a 25,000-page illustrated narrative of his childhood and mythological future.

A left out of the museum will bring you to **Waisenhausplatz** and an attractive old house. Constructed between 1782 and 1786, this once served as the **Knabenwaisenhaus** (Boy's Orphanage) but, since 1941, it has housed the police headquarters. Across the road is a bland fountain – a rarity in Bern. Waisenhausplatz hosts a general market on Tuesdays and Saturdays.

Zeughausgasse, to the left, has some shops and hotels, but it is the two buildings near the end that will attract your attention. The

Französische
Kirche

Zeughausgasse 8,
t 031 311 37 32,
www.city-kirche-
bern.ch; open Mon–Fri
9–11 and 2–5, Sat 10–3

first of these, the **Französische Kirche** (French Church), is the oldest house of worship in the city. Originally constructed in the late 13th century as the church of the Dominican monastery, it has had many uses over the years. It was the seat of the Town Council, and sometimes used by the Inquisition Tribunal in the 14th century. After the Reformation, in 1528, it was converted into a hospital, and the Chancel was even used as a granary. The 17th century saw the beginnings of a French-speaking reformed community, which was enlarged after the Nantes Edict in 1685, when Huguenot refugees flooded into the city. In the 19th century the Roman Catholic parish used sections of the church, and in 1875 it became the property of the General Reformed parish of Bern.

Kornhaus

Kornhausplatz 18,
t 031 312 91 10;
www.kornhaus.org

Next is the impressive **Kornhaus** (Cornhouse), one of the city's finest examples of High Baroque architecture. Originally the three upper floors were used to store grain, while barrels of wine were stored in the cellars. It is a multi-purpose venue that stages cultural events and is also a social centre. Pass underneath its arches and the impressive **Stadttheater** (Municipal Theatre) will be to the left, just before the bridge that carries traffic high over the Aare.

09

Bern and the Bernese Oberland | Bern

Eastern Old Town

An interesting street named **Rathausgasse** runs directly to the end of the promontory; it is parallel to, but much quieter than, Kramgasse just to the south. Arcades line either side, populated with quaint shops, hotels and restaurants. But remember to look up. Near the tops of the houses the windows of the small rooms are often adorned with colourful, pretty flower boxes.

Rathaus
t 31 633 13 54; open Mon–Thurs 8.30–12 and 1.15–5

At the end of the street is the building after which the street is named. The **rathaus** (town hall), built between 1406 and 1416, has a most distinct façade, but it was completely restored between 1939 and 1942. It is the seat of the cantonal government. Directly across the road stands the **Vennerbrunnen** (Venner Fountain), dating from 1542, over which a venner, holding the flag of Bern in one hand and brandishing a sword in the other, stands vigil. In medieval times 'venner' was a military/political title. The holder of the position was a very powerful person as he was connected to, and chosen by, a guild and was not only responsible for peace and protection in his part of the city but also for leading local troops into battle.

The street changes name here – as all the streets running towards the end of the promontory do at cross roads – and becomes Postgasse. The architecture continues much as before, if a little bit older, but do pay some attention to the **Antonierhaus** (Antonite House), at number 62. Noticeably different in style to its neighbours, particularly with its curved arches, it was built at the end of the 15th century as the church of the Order of Antonites. Rebuilt in 1939 it has, over its history, been used as a granary, coach-house and even an antiques hall.

At the end of Postgasse you will be able to see clearly how the River Aare doubles around on itself, in the process forming the promontory upon which sits the city of Bern. The church in front of you is the **Nydeggkirche** (Nydegg Church), which was originally built in the mid-14th century over the foundations of the old Nydegg fortress destroyed nearly a century before. It was completely renovated, though, in the 1950s and very little of the original remains.

BärenPark
www.baerenpark-bern.ch; circuit around the Bear Park is accessible 24hrs daily (keepers in attendance 8–5); shop open 8.30–4.30; t 031 357 15 25 to book specialized tour by keepers; book a 'bear-themed' tour through Bern Tourismus (see p.137); adm

Across the Aare by way of Nydeggbrücke is the highlight for most visitors to Bern, the **BärenPark** (Bear Park). As described on p.128, bears have been associated with Bern since its foundation. But it was not until 1513, when Bernese troops returned victoriously home accompanied by a bear, that they were formally kept in the city. And they have been there ever since, except for a brief period when French troops confiscated them. In late October 2009, the two resident bears, Björk and Finn, moved into their luxurious new 1½-acre (6,000-sq m) home. Adjacent to the old pits (which had been there since 1857), this new home slopes down to the river, where there is a pool that they can play and fish in, and various caves and other hideouts if they want a break from people for a while. For visitors there are infrared cameras and webcams in the caves so that the bears can be viewed at all times and an audio or mobile phone tour of the various paths throughout the park is available.

Paul Klee (1879–1940) spent half of his life in Bern and besides being a world-famous artist he was also a musician, teacher and poet. During his life he created over 10,000 works and until 2005 many of his works were on display at the **Kunstmuseum** (see p.131). However, plans were made to create a new, futuristic museum and on 20 June 2005 the Zentrum Paul Klee was opened in the form of three undulating waves of building design on fresh, green land to the east of the city. Catch the no. 12 bus from outside the Bear Park. The bus terminates at the Schöngrün restaurant, just a few minutes' walk away. Besides holding over 4,000 of Klee's works, the largest collection of a single artist of world renown, this is also a leading centre of worldwide research into his life and work.

Take the no. 12 bus back to the Bear Park. Look back at the city from the old **Nydeggbrücke**. The views are fantastic: the city directly ahead with the Münster (Cathedral) spire dominating to the left, the river below and the rolling green hills behind. Notice, also, the row of old buildings on the city side, and to the right of the bridge. The strange one, with no ground floor and steps leading to the river, is the Ländtetor. Dating from the late 13th century, it served as the entrance to the landing stage for boats crossing the Aare.

The main street through the centre of the narrow promontory is **Gerechtigkeitsgasse**, though it changes its name four times before finally reaching the railway station. Colonnaded and arched along the entirety of its length, it is particularly pretty where commercialization isn't so predominant. Antique shops, specialist stores, bars, restaurants and even a hotel or two co-exist in complete harmony and peace. And, this being Bern, you will not be surprised to find another of those colorful water fountains-cum-statues – this time, the **Gerechtigkeitsbrunnen** (Justice Fountain) that originates from 1543.

Bern's Münster (Cathedral) occupies a prime position in a wonderful square near the southern edge of the promontory, where you can stop for a drink at the café, maybe, and then stroll to the edge and enjoy the vistas. Immediately below is a patchwork of picturesque rooftops and then the Aare flowing forcefully through its locks. The way the surrounding countryside wraps itself around the promontory shows clearly what an unusual city Bern is. And, of course, you cannot fail to be enchanted by the immense snow-capped peaks of the Bernese Oberland in the distance. Although it

Zentrum Paul Klee
Monument im Fruchtland 3, t 31 359 01 01, www.zpk.org; open Tues–Sun 10–5; adm

Münster
www.bernermuenster.ch; open winter Mon–Fri 10 –12 and 2–4, Sat 10–12 and 2–5, Sun 11.30–2; summer Mon–Sat 10–5, Sun 11.30–5; last entrance to second tower platform is 30mins before closing

09 Bern and the Bernese Oberland | Bern

is believed that, from Bern's very founding, a chapel has stood on this site, construction of the present cathedral was not initiated until 1421. The 328ft (100m) spire was not added to this, the largest church in Switzerland, until 1893. The bell, which was cast in 1611, is still rung daily. The interior, as the effects of the Reformation dictated more often than not in Switzerland, is rather bland. Look, though, for the sculptured main portal featuring the *Last Judgement*, stained-glass windows from the period 1421–50 and carved choir stalls from 1523. The adventurous and fit may attempt the 344 steps to the second tower platform, where the rewards are unsurpassed views of the city.

Outside the main entrance, the **Mosesbrunnen** (Moses Fountain) was erected in 1790 on the site of an earlier one from 1544. A narrow alleyway, Münstergasse, leads to Kramgasse, an extension of Gerechtigkeitsgasse. Immediately, you will notice an increase in activity, as we are now very near to the centre of Bern.

Einsteinhaus
*Kramgasse 49,
t 31 312 00 91,
www.einstein-bern.ch;
open Jan–Mar,
Oct–mid-Dec Tues–Fri
10–5, Sat 10–4;
April–Sept Mon–Sun
10–5; adm*

Einsteinhaus (Einstein House) is in the second-floor flat where Albert Einstein lived, with his wife and son, between 1903 and 1905. During these years he was working at the Patent Office developing his five key scientific theories. The Albert Einstein society has overseen the restoration of the original furnishings and these, together with other documents and writings, are on display. The visit includes a 20-minute video detailing Einstein's life. Those wanting to learn more about this genius will undoubtedly want to head for the **Historisches Museum Bern** (Bern Historical Museum), within which is the **Einstein Museum**, the world's first museum dedicated to Einstein (*see* p.135).

The Einsteinhaus is sandwiched outside between two fountains. To the east is the **Samsonbrunnen** (Samson Fountain) that dates from 1527, but most visitors' sights will, by now, be riveted to the left. To the west, the **Zähringerbrunnen** (Zähringer Fountain), commemorating the city's founder Berchtold V since 1535, is very elaborate, with a Bern bear in full armour with a bear cub at its foot and Zähringer coat-of-arms.

It is, though, overshadowed, in every sense, by the **Zeitglockenturm** (Clock Tower) directly behind it. This ranks alongside the bears as the city's emblem. The original 12th-century tower, some parts of which still stand, formed the boundary to the first extension of the city. Following the devastation of a fire in 1405 the structure was rebuilt in stone and a tower bell installed. At that time, when the clock chimes had to be struck by hand each hour, it showed the official time and all other clocks were set by it. This practice continued until the advent of modern communications. It was not until 1530 that the Astronomical Clock and humorous figure play were added. And it is the latter, which commences playing four minutes before the hour, which attracts

Albert Einstein

Born in 1879 at Ulm, in what was then a part of the German Empire, Einstein moved to Bern in 1902 where he attained a position as Technical Expert Third Class in the Patent Office. He and his friends formed The Olympia Academy, a club that met weekly to talk about science and philosophy. In 1904 his first son, Hans Albert was born. The following year proved to be his most creative; he began work on the General Theory and developed his Special Theory of Relativity. In 1908 he lectured at Bern University and in 1909 he left his post at the Patent Office to move to Zürich to become an associate professor of theoretical physics at the university there. Einstein considered the years he spent in Bern to be the happiest and most prolific of his life. He was awarded the 1921 Nobel Prize for physics. In 1933 he emigrated to the USA, becoming a citizen in 1940. He died on 17 April 1955.

so many people these days. Less known is the fact that all road distances in Switzerland are measured from this point.

Helvetiaplatz Museums

From the Clock Tower and Casinoplatz, Kirchenfeldbrücke heads south, high over the Aare, to Helvetiaplatz. On a clear day you will have an unobstructed view to the mesmerizing peaks of the Eiger, Mönch and Jungfrau, shimmering on the horizon. The opposite bank of the Aare differs dramatically from the city side. Less densely populated and with large houses, some of which are embassies, there are several museums and the **Schweizerische Nationalbibliotek** (Swiss National Library) in the space of just a few blocks.

Historisches Museum Bern and Einstein Museum
Helvetiaplatz 5, t 31 350 77 11, www.bhm.ch; open Tues–Sun 10–5; adm

Of these, the grand **Historisches Museum Bern** (Bern Historical Museum) is impressive – inside and out. It was originally built to house the Landesmuseum (Swiss National Museum) in 1894, but that was eventually housed in Zürich and this subsequently became the second largest historical museum in the country. It has over 250,000 objects covering prehistory to the present; the Burgundian tapestries from the 15th and 16th centuries and the 6th-century BC Graechwil Hydria Greek bronze vessel are some of the most important.

The first museum in the world dedicated to **Einstein** (*see* box above) is housed within the main museum. It features exhibitions detailing his extraordinary feats of discovery in the 20th century.

Also in the platz is a museum of topographical interest, the **Schweizerisches Alpines Museum** (Swiss Alpine Museum). This gives you a real insight into those magical mountains that attract people from all over the world to Switzerland. Of particular interest are the huge mountain relief maps, as well as exhibitions detailing how the Alps were discovered and how the Swiss who lived in the Alps managed to earn a living. Importantly, too, it explains how ecological factors and tourism are constantly changing the mountain environment.

Schweizerisches Alpines Museum
Helvetiaplatz 4, t 31 350 04 40, www.alpinesmuseum. ch; open Mon 2–5.30, Tues–Sun 10–5.30; adm

Other smaller, specialist interest museums around Helvetiaplatz include the **Schweizer Schützenmuseum** (Swiss Rifle Museum), the

Museum für Kommunikation
Helvetiastrasse 16,
t 31 338 77 77,
www.mfk.ch; open
Tues–Sun 10–5; adm

Schweizerische Parlament
t 031 322 85 22,
www.parlament.ch;
when parliament in
session building is open;
outside of session visit
by guided tour only
Mon–Sat 9, 10, 11, 2, 3, 4,
Thurs 5, 6, 7, book the
day before; take official
identity document
with you

Bundesplatz fountains
operate on the hour
and half-hour
spring–Oct daily 11–11,
Tues and Sat from 2
after markets

Naturhistorisches **Museum** (Natural History Museum) and the Museum für Kommunikation (Museum for Communication). Philatelists will be fascinated by this, the world's largest public collection of postage stamps.

Bundesplatz and Bärenplatz

Back on the promontory, dominating the bank left of the Kirchenfeldbrücke, are four buildings that form an elongated façade accentuated by a central dome. The building to the far right and nearest to the bridge is the very grand **Bellevue Palace Hotel** (a good refreshment stop with fine service and views to match). The others, and there are three, form the **Schweizerische Parlament** (Swiss House of Parliament). Erected between 1851 and 1902, there is very little difference in style between the east and west wings, but the central parliament building, home to the Federal Council and Federal Assembly, truly is architecturally impressive. To get a closer view, turn left at the end of the bridge and then walk along the terrace which runs in front of it.

Just past the domed section of the parliament building, climb the steps that bring you out into Bundesplatz. On 31 July and 1 August 2004 (Swiss National Day) a new-look square was inaugurated with 26 **fountains** – each representing a canton, which are built into the ground and accentuated by lighting patterns. This square, in conjunction with Bärenplatz – which leads out of it – and Waisenhausplatz, mentioned earlier, serve as the sites for Bern's famous markets. Every morning after mid-May there is a colourful geranium market in Bundesplatz. On Tuesday and Saturday mornings the vegetable, fruit and flower markets occupy Bundesplatz, Bärenplatz and their surrounding streets. Between May and October they are in Bärenplatz daily.

In the middle of Bärenplatz, between Marktgasse and Spitalgasse, is the **Käfigturm** (Prison Tower), which was actually used as such until 1897. This was constructed on the site of the second west gate, *c.* 1256, in 1690.

Just down Spitalgasse in the direction of the train station are two more marvellous water fountains-cum statues. You will also see, if the weather's fine, people just sitting and enjoying each other's company on the steps leading to the arcades.

ⓘ **Bern** >
Bern Tourismus:
t 31 328 12 12,
www.berninfo.com;
Bahnhofplatz: open
June–Sept daily 9–8.30,
Oct–May Mon–Sat 9–6.30,
Sun 10–5; BärenPark:
Oct–May Mon–Sun 10–4,
June–Sept Mon–Sun 9–5

Tourist Information and Services in Bern

The BärenPark office offers a fascinating and very clever multivisual 3D show, **BernShow**. Shown every 20mins, it gives a unique view of the history of Bern. CHF 3 adm.

The **BERNCARD**, available at all tourist offices, many museums and most hotels, offers free travel on the transportation system, free admission to most museums and a 25% discount on some official city tours. It costs CHF20 for 24 hours, CHF 31 for 48 hours and CHF 38 for 72 hours.

Bern Three for Two is an accommodation package that offers three nights accommodation for the price of two if arriving in the city on a Thurs or Fri. This can only be booked through *www.berninfo.com*, which lists the available hotels and the prices for single and double rooms in both CHF and euros.

Guided Trips and Tours

Stroll through the Old Town: Leaves from the railway station tourist office; it takes 1½ hours and costs CHF 18. Check *www.berninfo.com* for dates and times.

Tours of the Clock Tower: This 50-min tour starts on the east side of the clock tower and costs CHF 12. Check *www.berninfo.com* for dates and times.

Berne and its Bears: A bear-themed tour that takes in fountains and clocks, among other sights, ending at the BärenPark. Starts from the railway station and costs CHF 20. Check *www.berninfo.com* for dates and times.

Lost Property

Städtisches Fundbüro (City Lost and Found Office), Predigergasse 5, **t** 031 321 50 50; open Mon–Fri 10–4, Thurs till 6.

Fundbüro SBB (SBB Railways Lost Property Office), Bahnhof, **t** 051 220 22 62; open Mon–Fri 8–12 and 2–6.

Medical Emergencies

Medphone, **t** 0900 57 67 47, 24 hours a day.

Market Days

General market: Tues/Sat, Waisenhausplatz.

Vegetables, fruit and flower market: Tues and Sat mornings all year on Bündesplatz, Bärenplatz and adjacent streets, and daily on Bärenplatz May–Oct.

Exhibitions and Festivals in Bern

Early Mar: *Berner Fasnacht* (Bern Carnival).

May: **International Jazz Festival**, *www.jazzfestivalbern.ch*, and **Bern Geranium Market**.

Aug: **Circus Knie** – Swiss National Circus, *www.knie.ch*.

Sept: **Bern International Dance Festival**.

Nov: **Onion Market** (fourth Mon).

Dec: **Christmas Market**.

Shopping in Bern

Under the arcades along Spitalgasse and Marktgasse you will find the latest in high fashion; Münstergasse and Junkerngasse offer more avant-garde fashion; on Kramgasse, Postgasse and Gerechtigkeitsgasse you are more likely to find a wider variety of shops, including some selling antiques.

RailCity, *www.railcity.ch*, a complex above the railway station. Supermarkets and food shops open daily, including Sun, 6am–9pm.

Drinks of the World, RailCity, **t** 031 311 51 10, *www.beerworld.ch*, open daily 9am–10pm. Not only has the widest array of beers, and other drinks, that you can find anywhere, but it is the only place in Bern where you can buy beer, and other alcohol, to take away on Sun.

Swiss Knife Shop, Neuengasse 5, **t** 031 312 13 15, *www.swiss-knifeshop.ch*. Offers wide range of Victorinox and Wenger knives and other products; also has an array of Zwilling J. A. Henckels' kitchen knives etc. Other souvenirs also stocked.

Where to Stay in Bern

Bern is constrained by its topography, and the central area is quite small. Consequently, many of the more economical hotels, guest houses, etc. are located outside the city centre. It is not uncommon to find that the rooms in many hotels are a little on the small side.

Luxury

*****Hotel Bellevue Palace**, Kochergasse 3–5, **t** 031 320 45 45, *www.bellevue-palace.ch*. A member of the Leading Hotels of the World group. This, the largest and most impressive hotel in Bern, is adjacent to the Swiss Parliament building and is used as the official residence of

⊛ Belle Epoque >

visiting dignitaries and parliamentarians. The rooms are tastefully decorated in a variety of styles, and are furnished with every modern facility. The famous La Terrasse restaurant, along with some of the rooms, have marvellous views over the River Aare and to the Alps.

Expensive

****Belle Epoque, Gerechtigkeitsgasse 18, t 031 311 43 36, www.belle-epoque.ch. Situated on one of the most distinguished streets in the quieter part of the Old Town (near the Bear Park), the style of this small, well-designed hotel fully lives up to its name. Each of the 17 rooms, and the public areas, are furnished with original furniture and art from the Belle Epoque era at the turn of the 20th century. The Bar Henri de Toulouse-Lautrec offers light refreshments, while meals are available each lunchtime and evening at the Restaurant le Chariot.

****Bern, Zeughausgasse 9, t 031 329 22 22, www.hotelbern.ch. In the heart of the city, this hotel has a most unusual exterior reflecting its prior use as a fire station. Its 100 rooms are tasteful and thoroughly modern, with high-speed Internet facilities. It has a choice of restaurants, including the gourmet Kurierstube, and bars.

Expensive–moderate

****Bären, Schauplatzgasse 4, t 031 311 33 67, www.baerenbern.ch. A 57-room modern Best Western hotel that is located just around the corner from the parliament building. Investigate the famous display of bear paintings in the Bären Bar or relax in the sauna and solarium.

****Savoy-Garni, Neuengasse 26, t 031 311 44 05, www.hotel-savoy-bern.ch. Close to the railway station, this is a very pleasant hotel – wheelchair accessible too – that has nice rooms with sound-proofed windows and adjustable heating. Air-conditioned rooms available on request.

Moderate

***Hotel Continental-Garni, Zeughausgasse 27, t 031 329 21 21, www.hotel-continental.ch. Very conveniently located in the centre of the city, but still just a few minutes' walk from the railway station. The rooms are clean, comfortable and well appointed.

***Kreuz, Zeughausgasse 41, t 031 329 95 95, www.hotelkreuz-bern.ch. This is a beautiful old town house, with 103 contemporary rooms. Besides the Au Premier restaurant and Kreuz Bar, the Bärenhöfli's 'Öpfuchüechli' (baked apple rings) have become famous!

***Metropole, Zeughausgasse 26, t 031 311 50 21, www.hotelmetropole.ch. Situated on a corner close to the train station, this hotel has 59 medium-sized and nicely furnished rooms. No restaurant, but a nice breakfast buffet.

***Zum Goldenen Adler, Gerechtigkeitsgasse 7, t 031 311 17 25, www.goldener-adler-bern.ch. In the less busy part of the Old Town, this hotel has a long history and the public areas are pleasantly old-fashioned. It has reasonably sized and comfortable rooms.

***City Am Bahnhof, Bahnhofplatz, t 031 311 53 77, www.fhotels.ch. Part of the small Fassbind chain, this is not just very pleasant but also good value. Situated opposite the railway station, expect 58 modern rooms with such perks as parquet floors, translucent partitions between the living and bathroom areas and free Wi-Fi.

***Jardin, Militärstrasse 38, t 031 333 01 17, www.hotel-jardin.ch. Just 10mins from the railway station, on the no. 9 tram, this small hotel offers an alternative for those wanting to be outside the centre. It has a charming restaurant, lounge and patio.

**Goldener Schlüssel, Rathausgasse 72, t 031 311 56 88, www.goldener-schluessel.ch. A small hotel with much character and a central but quiet location. The 34 rooms are comfy but on the small side. Has an Internet corner in the lobby.

**National Am Hirschengraben, Hirschengraben 24, t 031 381 19 88, www.nationalbern.ch. A couple of blocks from the railway station, and slightly away from the Old Town. The distinguished building – that also includes a theatre – dates from 1908, and the wooden lift introduces you to its comfortable, old-fashioned style. Rooms, in various styles and sizes, are basic but comfortable.

Inexpensive

Pension Marthahaus, Wytennbachstrasse 22a, **t** 031 332 41 35, *www.marthahaus.ch*. Outside the town centre. Rooms with one–five beds, garden terrace, free Internet and bikes, and cooking and washing facilities. Take the no. 20 to the second stop (Gewerbe Schule), and the pension is at the end of the first street to the right.

Bern Backpackers – Hotel Glocke, Rathausgasse 75, **t** 031 311 37 71, *www.bernbackpackers.com*. In the heart of old Bern, close to the clock tower, this offers basic accommodation and dorms, and has kitchen facilities, a common room with TV, video and Internet.

Swiss Youth Hostels, Weihergasse 4, **t** 031 326 11 11, *www.youthhostel.ch*. Simple, basic and clean accommodation with two-, four-, five- and six-bedded rooms, as well as two dormitories.

Eating Out in Bern

La Terrasse, Kochergasse 3–5, **t** 031 320 45 45, *www.bellevue-palace.ch* (*very expensive–expensive*). In the summer this is *the* place in Bern to eat. The Terrace of the Bellevue Palace hotel sparkles with crystal glasses full of fine wines, exquisite culinary creations and unparalleled views over the River Aare to the snow-covered peaks of the Alps.

Le Chariot, Gerechtigkeitsgasse 18, **t** 031 311 43 36, *www.belle-epoque.ch* (*expensive*). Like the hotel it is part of (Belle Epoque) this restaurant has some style. And so does the cuisine. At lunch look for *paninis* and fresh salads; in the evening the chef offers a limited, but very tasteful selection of dishes including a speciality or two.

Brasserie Bärengraben, Muristalden 1, **t** 031 331 42 18, *www.brasserie baerengraben.ch* (*expensive/moderate*) Housed in one of the 200-year-old customs houses on the Nydeggbrücke, close to the Bear Park. Eat inside, or out on the small terrace, and enjoy a delightful mix of French-orientated dishes.

Harmonie, Hotelgasse 3, **t** 031 313 11 41, *www.harmonie.ch* (*expensive–moderate*). Step through the doors and step back in time into this charmingly old-fashioned restaurant that has been family-owned since 1915. Although there are other choices, those in the know will order the famous cheese fondue or other traditional Swiss specialities. *Closed Sat and Sun*.

Le Mazot, Bärenplatz 5, **t** 031 311 70 88, *www.mazot-bern.ch* (*moderate*). Sit inside, or at tables outside, and enjoy the best of Valais (Walliser) specialities: a tempting range of fondue, raclette and *rösti* dishes as well as traditional sausage and cheese plates. Those with large appetites can try the Walliser Menu 'Le Mazot' combining raclette, air-dried meat and fondue.

Gourmanderie Moléson, Aarbergergasse 24, **t** 031 311 44 63, *www.moleson-bern.ch* (*moderate*). Founded in 1865, this typical bistro has a logo of two piglets' heads poking out of a lidded pot. The speciality here is Alsatian pies and extravagant desserts, prepared with ecologically grown products.

Klötzlikeller, Gerechtigkeitsgasse 62, **t** 031 311 74 56, *www.kloetzlikeller.ch* (*moderate*). A typical restaurant in the oldest cellar in Bern, dating from 1635. Under the stone arched ceiling pasta, meat and a few fish selections are served, all at reasonable prices.

Brasserie Anker, Schmiedenplatz 1/ Kornhausplatz 16, **t** 031 311 11 13, *www.roeschti.ch* (*moderate*). If you like *rösti*, or want to try more variations of it, this is the place to come.

Altes Tramdepot Brauerei & Restaurant, Gr. Muristalden 6, **t** 031 331 42 18, *www.altestramdepot.ch* (*moderate–inexpensive*). A delightful combination of microbrewery and restaurant in a converted old tram shed next to the Bear Park. Watch the beer being brewed, taste it here or back at your hotel. The cuisine is varied, and includes meat, fish, vegetarian and wok dishes.

⭐ Le Mazot ➤➤

Entertainment and Nightlife in Bern

Stadttheater Bern (Municipal Theatre), Kornhausplatz, **t** 031 329 51 51, *www.stadttheaterbern.ch*. Housed in a magnificent building in the heart of the city, and hosts opera and ballet productions as well as plays.

DAS-Theater an der Effingerstrasse, Effingerstrasse 14, **t** 031 382 72 72, *www.dastheater-effingerstr.ch*. A smaller, more intimate theatre.

Berner Puppen-Theater, Gerechtigkeitsgasse 31, **t** 031 311 95 85, *www.berner-puppentheater.ch*. Perhaps the most interesting of the other theatres in Bern, with puppet productions.

Allegro Grand Casino Bern, Kursaal, **t** 031 339 55 55, *www.grandcasino-bern.ch*. Has 19th-century style décor, and you can try your luck at different games tables and 250 machines, as well as a variety of 'jackpot' systems, including the Swiss Jackpot, which offers millions in prizes. *Open Sun–Wed until 2am and Thurs–Sat until 4am, adm CHF 10, including one complimentary drink.*

The Bar Club Messy, Neuengasse 17, **t** 031 311 30 58, and **Chikito Club of Clubs**, Neuengasse 47, **t** 031 311 62 63, *www.chikito.ch*. The latter was established in 1928 and is considered the most popular in Bern; both offer cabaret shows. *Open till early in the morning.*

Mocambo, Genfergasse 10, **t** 031 311 50 41. Has a striptease show and has similar hours to those above.

Marian's Jazzroom, Engestrasse 54, **t** 031 309 61 11, *www.mariansjazzroom.ch*. In the Hotel Inner Enge and, having hosted numerous international stars, is considered one of the most famous jazz clubs in Europe.

Mahogany Hall, Klösterlistutz 18, **t** 031 331 60 30, *www.mahogany.ch*. Has a special club atmosphere and is popular with a wide range of artists.

Those who fancy a dance have plenty of opportunities in Bern, amongst them:

Gaskessel, Sandrainstrasse 25, **t** 031 372 49 00, *www.gaskessel.ch*. A mix of a cultural centre in an old industrial building. *Open Fri–Sat till 3.30am.*

Club Bonsoir, Aarbergergasse 33–35, *www.bonsoir.ch*. Hosts international DJs, musicians and artists and has a secluded lounge bar.

Wankdorf Club, Papiermühlestrasse 79, **t** 031 333 00 84, *www.wankdorf-club.ch*. An immense 1,500 sq m of space, this is modern and dynamic and considers itself the cutting-edge club of the city.

There is no shortage of late-night bars, either.

Mr Pickwick Pub, Wallgasse, **t** 031 311 28 62, *www.pickwick.ch/bern*. A 'typical' English pub. *Open Mon–Wed 11.30–12, Thurs–Sat 11.30–1.30 and Sun 2–12.*

Pery Bar, Schmiedenplatz 3, **t** 031 311 59 08. Has a cocktail bar on the ground floor and a DJ presents 60s to 90s music. *Open till 1.30am, 2.30am or 3.30am, getting later as the week gets older.*

The Art Café, Gurtengasse 3, **t** 031 311 42 64, *www.artcafe.ch*. Has an elegant bar with DJs playing music. *Open until 3.30am on Thurs, Fri and Sat.*

Eclipse-Bar, Gurtengasse 6, **t** 031 882 08 88, *www.eclipsebar.ch*. Ultra-modern in style and has a large aquarium in the lounge. DJs play music from the 60s onwards and the house cocktails are good. *Open until 3.30am Thurs to Sat.*

Bernese Oberland

Among the many places in Switzerland that have drawn the attention of the world, there is none more acclaimed than the Bernese Oberland. Although there are records of the Romans passing through the area and it was known in medieval times, it has only been since the middle of the 19th century that these often

Getting to the Bernese Oberland

By Car

From Bern the A6 motorway runs south to Thun and around the south side of Lake Thun to Spiez – from where you take the road down to the Lötschberg Tunnel car/rail link. It then continues on to Interlaken – the gateway to the Bernese Oberland villages of Grindelwald, Mürren and Wengen, and on again along the southern shore to the end of Lake Brienz.

By Train

As with the roads, the trains run south to Thun and on to Spiez, where the line splits either going south to the Valais to Visp, or on to Interlaken. Trains arrive at Interlaken West from Basel, the Valais and Bern, with most continuing on to Interlaken Ost (East). Trains from Zürich, via Luzern, arrive at Interlaken Ost (East), with many carrying on to Interlaken West.

At Interlaken you change at the Ost station for Grindelwald or Lauterbrunnen, or for Brienz, along the north side of the lake of the same name, after which the train continues to Luzern.

Getting around the Bernese Oberland

By Car

A car is of limited use in this region as it can only be used to get between Interlaken and Brienz and Thun, and from Interlaken to Grindelwald and Interlaken to Lauterbrunnen and on to Stechelberg.

By Cable Car

Lauterbrunnen to Grütschalp: **Bergbahn Lauterbrunnen-Mürren (BLM)**.
Wengen to Männlichen: **Luftseilbahn Wengen-Männlichen (LWM)**.
Grindelwald to Pfingstegg: **Pfingsteggbahn**.
Stechelberg, Gimmelwald, Mürren, Birg to Schilthorn: **Schilthornbahn**.

By Cog Railway

To reach **Jungfraujoch** take the **Berner Oberland Bahnen (BOB)** from Interlaken Ost (East) to Grindelwald or Lauterbrunnen; from Grindelwald or Lauterbrunnen take the **Wengernalpbahn (WAB)** (via Wengen) to Kleine Scheidegg; from Kleine Scheidegg take the **Jungfraubahn (JF)** to Jungfraujoch.
Wilderswil to Schynige Platte: **Schynige Platte Railway SPB**.

By Funicular

Mürren to Allmendhubel: **Mürren-Allmendhubel (SMA)**.
Interlaken to Harder Kulm: **Harderbahn**.

By Gondola Cableway,

Bort, Grindel to First: **Firstbahnen**.
Grindelwald (Grund), Mittelstation Holenstein, to Männlichen: **Gondelbahn Grindelwald-Männlichen (GGM)**.

By Lake Steamer

Interlaken Ost (East), Ringenberg, Bönigen, Iseltwald, Giessbach See to Brienz: **Thuner und Brienzersee Schiffsbetreib der Lötschbergbahn (BLS)**.
Interlaken West, Sundlauenen, Beatenbucht, Spiez, Oberhofen, Hünibach to Thun: **Thuner und Brienzersee Schiffsbetreib der Lötschbergbahn (BLS)** .

By Narrow Gauge Non-cog Railway

Grütschalp to Mürren: **Bergbahn Lauterbrunnen-Mürren (BLM)**.

By Postbus

Meiringen to Brienz.
Lauterbrunnen, Trümmelbach to Stechelberg.

By Steam Locomotive Rack Railway
Brienz to Brienz Rothorn: **Brienz Rothorn Bahn.**

By Train
Interlaken Ost (East), Niederried, Oberied to Brienz.
Interlaken West, Spiez to Thun.

---

remote valleys and mountains have been opened up to tourism. And since the enterprising locals realized the wealth that lay at their doorstep they have not stopped developing, in the most careful and controlled way, the tourist market.

Not content to rely upon the natural splendour of mounts Eiger, Mönch and Jungfrau, and the lovely serenity of the lakes of Brienz and Thun, they have developed what must be the most eclectic array of transportation possible to link together the towns, villages and mountains. Regular trains and buses lead to rack railways that take you to the highest station in Europe; cable cars, one of which deposits you at a world-famous revolving restaurant 10,000ft (3,048m) up; a steep funicular; the longest gondola cableway in Europe; the quaint steam railway between Brienz and Rothorn; old-fashioned steamer voyages on lakes Brienz and Thun; and, of course, any number of ski and chair lifts. Going one step further, and being not just clever but wise, they decided that the villages of Wengen and Mürren would best retain their character if they were car-free. Following that same line of thinking, some of the roads that traverse the valleys have been reserved for postbuses only.

Interlaken

As the name implies, Interlaken lies between two lakes, Brienz and Thun, at an altitude of 1,870ft (570m) above sea level. As the natural gateway to the famous trio of mountains – the Eiger, Mönch and Jungfrau – and the pretty villages of Grindelwald, Wengen and Mürren, the town grew rapidly during the last century to meet tourists' demands. The luxury accommodation of large and gracious hotels and the diversion of the casino and other attractions have transformed Interlaken into a celebrated resort. Today, this small town with a population of less than 20,000 it is still far and away the largest in the area.

The area closest to Interlaken West station is busy and full of souvenir shops, restaurants and bars. On the way to Interlaken Ost (East), by the Victoria-Jungfrau Grand Hotel and Spa, there is much more parkland and open space, and the buildings and hotels become larger and grander. Besides shopping there is not too much else to do in Interlaken itself, as for most people it will be just

Getting to Interlaken

By Train

Trains arrive at Interlaken West, with most continuing on to Interlaken Ost (East), or vice versa, from Basel and Bern, and Zürich via Luzern, respectively.

By Car

Interlaken is surrounded by mountain ranges to the north and south, so can be accessed by car only from the east or west. To avoid a long, and not always easy, roundabout trip from the Valais region it is highly advisable to take the car/rail link through the Lötschberg tunnel.

Getting around Interlaken

Most people will be happy enough to get around Interlaken on **foot**. However, the two railway stations are quite a distance apart (about 30mins along Höheweg), so you can take a no. 21 **bus** that runs between them; the bus continues on to Beatus and Thun.

09

Bern and the Bernese Oberland | Interlaken

---

a stopping-off point for other destinations or used as a base to explore the Bernese Oberland.

Interlaken has become known for its wide-ranging opportunities for adventure sports. There are many companies based in and around the town that offer bungy jumping, skydiving, ice climbing and river rafting, amongst many others. The activities take place in the surrounding area.

Attractions a Short Distance from Interlaken

St Beatus-Höhlen
t 33 841 16 43,
www.beatushoehlen.ch;
open between Palm Sun
and third Sun in Oct;
guided tours leave on
the half-hour 10.30–5
and last 1 hour; adm

To visit the **St Beatus-Höhlen** (St Beatus Caves) take the BLS steamer from Interlaken West along the north side of Lake Thun to either Sundlauenen or Beatenbucht; the caves are in between these two stops at Beatushöhlen. Thousands of years ago cave dwellers inhabited this area, and you can gain an insight into their lifestyle by visiting this well-presented reconstruction of a prehistoric settlement. What those first settlers called this place no one knows, but the present name was derived more recently – in the 6th century – when, legend has it, an Irish missionary, Beatus, made his home at the entrance to these underground chambers. He reportedly exorcised a dragon from the caves, and preached Christianity to the local heathen population. Visitors venture to a depth of 3,609ft (1,000m) through just a portion of the 5 miles (8.1km) of known paths and trails that wind through numerous caverns and grottos, passing lakes, waterfalls and weirdly wonderful stalactites and stalagmites.

Tell-Freilichtspiele
Höheweg 37,
t 033 822 37 22,
www.tellspiele.ch

Friedrich Schiller's *William Tell* has been performed in the Rugen Woods, very close to Interlaken, every summer since 1912. It is performed at the **Tell-Freilichtspiele** (William Tell Open Air Theatre). Set 700 years ago, in an era during which Switzerland was under the tyrannical rule of Austria, it tells of the Swiss people's hardship and suffering and their heroic struggle for freedom. Over 250 actors, dressed in national costume, re-enact the story against a background of authentic 13th-century wooden houses and towering trees. It is performed primarily on Fridays and Saturdays, between the end of June and beginning of September. Weather conditions need not be a concern as all 2,300 seats are covered.

Bergrestaurant Harder Kulm
t 033 828 73 11,
www.harderkulm.ch

The **Bergrestaurant Harder Kulm** sits at an altitude of 4,337ft (1,322m) in an isolated position on the forested mountain behind Interlaken. You can get there in 10 minutes on the rather unusual small red carriages of the Harderbahn, from the valley station opposite Interlaken Ost train station. Opened in 1908, it is actually a funicular that was constructed along a mile-long winding route – which includes a quarter-mile loop to the summit – to preserve the integrity of the landscape. There is a human-interest story here as well. Two local women, unbeknownst to their husbands, responded when the landlord, Jungfrau Railways, solicited applicants for the restaurant tenancy. What Rosemarie Feuz and Hilde Zurbrügg started as a bit of a joke has now, with much encouragement and support from the railway, become a resounding success. It has become somewhat of a tradition for the locals to meet here for Sunday-morning breakfast, but visitors will enjoy it any time – especially for its breathtaking views across the lakes and over the entire Jungfrau region. An added attraction is the **Alpine Wildlife Park** with its resident Ibex and marmots.

Schynige Platte
www.schynigeplatte.ch

Between late May and late October **Schynige Platte** can be reached on the Schynige Platte Bahn SPB trains that depart from Wilderswil, one stop from Interlaken Ost on the Berner Oberland Bahnen BOB. This is a curious trip into the high alpine pastures, at an elevation of 6,453ft (1,967m), where you will find some diverse attractions. The **Alpengarten** (Alpine Garden) displays over 600 species of alpine flora from above the treeline in their natural habitat. The mountainside area here is ideal for hiking and the hiking-boot manufacturer **Lowa** was quick to recognize these possibilities. At the **Lowa Hiking Boot Test Centre** you can choose from over 200 pairs of boots and test them free of charge for the day.

Alpengarten
t 033 822 28 35,
www.alpengarten.ch;
opening hours match
train schedule; adm
included in train ticket
price

Action and Adventure Around Interlaken

If you have the desire for adventure and adrenalin-fuelled activities, you will be spoilt for choice in Interlaken and the surrounding area. There is a whole host of activities on offer throughout the year. In addition to walking, hiking, cycling and skiing, you can take flight in various forms, take to the water and experience the mountains in a number of different ways.

Note that many activities only take place at certain times of the year, so if you have your heart set on something, make sure you

Jungfraubahnen Pass

The Jungfrau Railways Pass is available from 1 May until 31 October and entitles you to six consecutive days of unlimited travel in the valid area. See *www.jungfraubahn.ch* for a map and details of other offers in conjunction with this pass.

The pass is available to buy from all stations of Jungfrau Railways, Wengen-Männlichen (LWM) and Firstbahn (BGF) Aerial Cableway and the Grindelwald-Männlichen (GGM) Aerial Gondola.

The pass costs CHF 200; or CHF 150 for children, or for adults in conjunction with a Swiss Pass, Swiss Card or Half-fare Card.

check that is on offer when you intend to be in the area. Also do your research and make sure that you understand exactly what the activity entails and that when you choose a certain company to book with that you are satisfied with their credentials and safety procedures.

A helicopter trip in and around the mountains is a breathtaking experience. **Berner Oberländer Helikopter AG** offers a variety of helicopter trips. Their helicopters will whisk you up to and around either the north or south faces of the Eiger, Mönch and Jungfrau mountains. And, if this leaves you begging for more, consider taking the longer trip to Zermatt and the Matterhorn. In summer, flights depart from the airport at Gsteigwiler; in winter, they leave from Männlichen. As you might expect, such flights are not inexpensive, but it will be the adventure of a lifetime.

If you've always wanted to have a go at paragliding, **Paragliding Interlaken** offers flights from nearby hills down to the centre of Interlaken or, for the even more adventurous, from the top of Schilthorn down to Stechelberg.

Hiking across the glaciers to see their splendour close-up is an activity offered by **Swiss Alpine Guides**. They also offer a range of other activities, including rock climbing, snowshoe trekking and mountaineering.

One of the newest activities is zorbing – this involves rolling and careering down hills inside a giant, transparent, plastic ball. **Alpin Center** offer this activity, along with sea kayaking, canyoning, canyon jumping and skydiving, amongst many others.

Berner Oberländer Helikopter AG
between Interlaken and Wilderswil,
t 033 828 90 00,
www.bohag.ch

Paragliding Interlaken
Höheweg 155,
t 033 823 82 33,
www.paragliding-interlaken.ch

Swiss Alpine Guides
Matten-Interlaken,
t 033 822 60 00,
www.swissalpine guides.ch

Alpin Center
Wilderswil,
t 033 823 55 23,
www.alpincenter.ch

ⓘ **Interlaken >**
Interlaken Tourismus: Höheweg 37 (Metropole Hotel building), t 033 826 53 00, www. interlaken.ch; open July–mid-Sept Mon–Fri 8–7, Sat 8–5, Sun 10–12 and 5 –7; mid–Sept–Oct Mon–Fri 8–6, Sat 9–1; Nov–April Mon–Fri 8–12 and 1.30–6, Sat 9–12; May–June Mon–Fri 8–6, Sat 8–4

Tourist Information and Services in Interlaken

A **Visitor's Card** offers various reductions on sights and activities and also entitles you to free travel on public transport (within an area called zone 80). The card is valid in Interlaken and other places in the Jungfrau region (*see www.inter laken.ch* for a full list). Each guest paying visitor's tax in one of the included places is entitled to obtain this card. Ask at your hotel and they should provide one.

Shopping in Interlaken

Kirchhofer's Casino Gallery, Höheweg 73, t 033 828 88 90, *www.kirch hofer.com*. This is the flagship store and headquarters of the renowned Kirchhofer group. Founded in 1944 by Fritz Kirchhofer, who was a watchmaker himself, it is now run by his son Jürg. It offers – confirmed by the Guinness World Records – the largest collection of Swiss watch brands in the world, as well as a collection of famous-name designer leather goods, local souvenirs and home-made chocolate. The staff at Kirchhofer's shops are fluent in 18 languages.

Kirchhofer Haute Horlogerie, Höheweg 46, **t** 033 828 88 93, *www.kirchhofer.com*. Located in the oldest building in Interlaken, dating from 1599, Kirchhofer combines the most sophisticated watch-making technology with the most advanced designs and allows exceptionally skilled craftspeople to exhibit both their skills and watches.

Where to Stay in Interlaken

Luxury

★★★★★Victoria-Jungfrau Grand Hotel and Spa, Höheweg 41, **t** 033 828 28 28, *www.victoria-jungfrau.ch*. A very grand, traditional hotel. The 212 rooms and suites have every modern facility and a classically elegant décor. In the spa you will find a fully equipped health, fitness and beauty centre with whirlpools, steam bath, saunas, massage, gym and a wonderful Art Deco pool area. La Terrasse is a gourmet restaurant of some class and the Jungfrau-Stube is a more informal restaurant. There is also a selection of bars and a nightclub.

(★) **Beatus Merlingen >**

★★★★★Beatus Merlingen, 3658 Merligen-Thunersee, **t** 033 252 81 81, *www.beatus.ch*. Located on the northern shore of Lake Thun (12km from Interlaken), the lake steamers stop right outside the door. The hotel is set in a large park. The south-facing rooms, junior suites, suites and wellness suite all have a breathtaking panorama of lake and mountains and, like the public areas, are traditional in ambience and taste. The restaurants offer light and market-fresh Swiss cuisine with a Mediterranean flavour. The indoor pool, outdoor saltwater pool and spa are a revelation.

Expensive

★★★★★Lindner Grand Hotel Beau Rivage, Höheweg 211, **t** 033 826 70 07, *www.lindnerhotels.ch*. Built around 1874, this was one of the first buildings in the Art Nouveau style. Its latest renovation was in 2003 when the new owners, Lindner, decided on a style that matched the ambience of the traditional building. The 101 rooms and suites have modern facilities. There are two restaurants (one à la carte and the other for half-board guests), the charming Piano Bar and a sun terrace overlooking the Aare river, as well as a spa.

★★★★Metropole, Höheweg 37, **t** 033 828 66 66, *www.metropole-interlaken.ch*. A large, 100-room, tower-block hotel in the centre of town. The rooms are modern, and some have a south-facing balcony with views of the Jungfrau. Guests enjoy the use of an indoor swimming pool, sauna, solarium, indoor shopping arcade, banking facilities and tourist information office. On the 18th floor is the Top o' Met restaurant with panoramic views.

Moderate

Landgasthof Hirschen, Hauptstrasse 11, **t** 033 822 15 45, *www.hirschen-interlaken.ch*. This is a magnificent 16th-century chalet that has been delicately restored to combine traditional style with modern facilities. Surrounded by lawns and gardens with views of the Jungfrau, you will find 20 rooms all with private bathrooms. It also has a restaurant that serves local dishes.

Post Hardermannli, Hauptstrasse 18, **t** 033 822 89 19, *www.post-harder mannli.ch*. Run by the same family for 30 years, this beautiful, 125-year-old chalet has 24 rooms with old-fashioned charm and many have views of the Alps. Decorated with antiques, farming instruments and prize-winning cow bells.

Inexpensive

Heidi's Hostel-Beyer, Bernastrasse 37, **t** 033 822 90 30, *www.heidishostel.ch*. Situated just a short walk from Interlaken West railway station in a quiet location near the woods. It offers nine rooms all with bath/shower, and a nice living room.

Backpackers Villa Sonnenhof, Alpenstrasse 16, **t** 033 826 71 71, *www.villa.ch*. Rooms are divided into three categories, ranging from one–seven beds. Has a kitchen, Internet station and laundry.

Eating Out in Interlaken

⭐ Grand Restaurant Schuh ›

Grand Restaurant Schuh, Hüheweg 56, **t** 033 822 94 41, *www.schuh-interlaken.ch* (*very expensive–expensive*). This hotel has a prime location in Interlaken. Although Johan Ritschard first started the business in 1818, it was taken over by Christian Schuh in 1885. But it was Jacob Schuh who started using the family name and the famous 'Schuh Lady' logo when he took over in 1899. It is now owned by Jürg and Cecelia Kirchhofer, who also own the Kirchhofer's Casino Gallery just across the road. The restaurant offers three types of cuisine – European, Chinese and Thai. If you are just feeling a little peckish

and have a sweet tooth, then pop into the adjoining chocolate and pastry shop. There is an exquisite array of sweet treats on offer and there are 'chocolate shows', too, where you can see how these delicacies are created. Their Schuh Truffles are famous.

Bebbis, Bahnhofstrasse 16, **t** 033 821 14 44, *www.bebbis.ch* (*expensive–moderate*). A fun restaurant decorated in Swiss chalet style and with cuisine to match. Live entertainers, too.

Restaurant Chalet, Höhweg 7, **t** 033 827 87 87 (*expensive–moderate*). Found inside the impressive-looking City Hotel Oberland. A wide array of traditional Swiss specialities, including an assortment of tempting fondues, are on offer at reasonable prices.

Brasserie 17, Rosenstrasse 17, **t** 033 822 32 25, *www.brasserie17.ch* (*moderate–inexpensive*). An integral part of the Happy Inn hostel, this is a fun place to eat. It is famous for its ribs and wings, as well as baked potatoes, salads, soups and veggie dishes. All can be washed down with 20 types of beer, with five on tap.

Grindelwald

The first written mention of Grindelwald is on a document dating from 1146. At that time, King Konrad promised his protection to the Augustinerkloster (Augustine monastery) in Interlaken, which also owned property in Grindelwald. The monks' greed for more and more land occasioned periodic revolts by the citizens of Grindelwald, a conflict that continued until the Reformation in 1528, when the Interlaken monastery was abolished. Thinking that it would augment their independence, the people of Grindelwald allied themselves with the Bernese government – but only on condition that they would not be taxed. The Bernese, however, knew that the monastery was wealthy and didn't want to relinquish this source of revenue. The population of Grindelwald rebelled against this breach of faith, dismissed their Protestant pastor and, in 1528, re-instituted the old faith. Enraged, in their turn, the Bernese dispatched an expedition to Grindelwald that devastated the village. Relations with the Bernese improved during the 18th and 19th centuries when both sides became aware that a cooperative effort could be mutually beneficial.

Getting to Grindelwald

By Cog Railway

Take the **Berner Oberland Bahnen (BOB)** train from Interlaken Ost (East) to Grindelwald.

By Car

From Interlaken travel on the A8; Grindelwald is signposted off this road.

Getting around Grindelwald

In most instances everything in the village can be easily reached on **foot**. However, those taking the gondola cableway to Männlichen may want to avoid a very steep walk, especially on the way back, by taking a return trip on the **Wengernalpbahn (WAB)** train from Grindelwald to Grund.

The late 19th century brought the steam train to Grindelwald, opening the area to convenient travel and bringing in its wake an ever-increasing number of tourists from all over the world.

When you arrive, you will find a beautiful, wide, deep valley squeezed between the north face of the Eiger (and other towering peaks) to the south and lesser peaks to the north. Needless to say, this area is a winter paradise. There is an impressive choice of ski runs, from beginner to expert level, covering 125 miles (200km) and descending from altitudes as high as 9,747ft (2,971m). These are accessed via a combination of no less than 43 mountain railways, ski-lifts, etc. Grindelwald also has approximately 12½ miles (20km) of cross-country skiing, and offers a wide variety of other winter sports.

There has been much development across the valley, although this certainly has not spoiled the ambience. Unlike some of its neighbouring villages, Grindelwald is too large to ban the use of cars, but that does not mean vehicles have the freedom of the valley. They do not. Many of the roads outside the village are reserved for residents and farm vehicles, and only postbuses are allowed on the valley road to Meiringen.

Grindelwald is a starting point for the famous excursion to **Jungfraujoch**. Wengernalpbahn (WAB) trains take you to Kleine Scheidegg to begin the trip (*see* p.156). It is also one of two starting points (the other is Wengen) for a trip to **Männlichen** (*see* p.155). The Gondelbahn Grindelwald-Männlichen gondola cars depart from the Grindelwald Grund station.

Grindelwald First, Bachalpsee and Faulhorn

The original Grindelwald-First chair lift, at its inception in 1950, was the longest in Europe. Just over 40 years later, a combination of age, poor routing, inability to handle the transport capacity and, last but not least, passenger comfort – especially in the colder months – led to its closing on 18 August 1991. Fortuitously, the planning of a replacement had begun in 1986, when it was decided that a modern six-passenger gondola cable car should be introduced. Construction on that system, **Bergbahnen Grindelwald First**, began on 7 June 7 1990 and was completed just two months after the closure of the chair lift. The new system, 3¼ miles (5,226m) in length, takes just 20 minutes to ascend 3,625ft (1,105m) through three stages; Grindelwald to Bort, Bort to Grindel and Grindel to First.

Bergbahnen Grindelwald First
t 033 854 50 50,
www.gofirst.ch

First, at an altitude of 7,113ft (2,168m), sits directly across the valley from four peaks that rise over 13,000ft (3,962m) – the Schreckhorn, Eiger, Mönch and Jungfrau. As a bonus, it is also immediately in front of the famous Grindelwald Glacier, the size of which, even from this distance, is staggering. This stage is a marvellous spot from which to begin a variety of mountain hikes. While you ponder which route you might like to take, sit on the terrace of the **Berggasthaus First** to savour a drink and a snack and the fabulous views around you.

Berggasthaus First
t 033 853 12 84,
www.berghausfirst.ch

The most popular hike, and one that is not too difficult either, is the trek to **Bachalpsee**. Just about an hour away, this mountain lake is particularly popular with photographers as the topography of the land here creates an optical illusion that there is no valley between the lake and the distant mountains. Add to this the verdant foreground, which paints a stark contrast with the distant snow and ice, and a little luck with the weather, and you have a stunning photograph.

The more adventurous could consider pushing on to **Faulhorn**, another hour or so away and at an altitude of 8,796ft (2,681 m), where there is a vantage point almost without equal. The views range from Grindelwald and its majestic mountains to the lakes of Brienz and Thun and even, in the distance, the Black Forest of Germany. Sunsets and sunrises are glorious here and you can enjoy both if you stay overnight at the **Berghotel Faulhorn**, one of the oldest and highest hotels in Switzerland. From the time it opened in 1830 until just recently, the owners relied on mules to deliver supplies and mail. Today, they are airlifted in by helicopter. You, however, will still have to go in on foot!

Berghotel Faulhorn
t 033 853 27 13,
www.berghotel-faulhorn.ch;
open from end June–20 Oct

To return, you have two options. Either return the way you came, or take the path down to Bussalp, where there is yet another mountain restaurant, the **Bergrestaurant Bussalp**, then continue on to Bort – with maybe a stop at the **Berghaus Bort** for refreshments – from where you can make the final descent back on the Firstbahnen.

Bergrestaurant Bussalp
t 033 853 37 51,
www.bussalp.ch

Berghaus Bort
t 033 853 36 51,
www.berghaus-bort.ch

Weather conditions, obviously, will be a major factor when choosing your hike. Obviously, very low cloud cover spoils the view; however, the cloud cover is often quite high and you will need to determine whether it's going to obscure your views from First. If so,

09 | Bern and the Bernese Oberland | Grindelwald

a hike from that point will really not be very enjoyable. But all is not lost if you are determined to get out and about.

If high cloud cover is a problem, stay below it and take the Firstbahnen only as far as **Grindel**, where you can take a break at the modern **Bergrestaurant Schreckfeld**, before doing a gentle hike to **Grosse Scheidegg**. This is an easy undulating walk of 1½ hours, along which the altitude changes only by 23ft (7m), from 6,414 to 6,437ft (1,955 to 1,962m). Even if the peaks across the valley are ensconced in cloud, the ever-changing perspectives, especially of the glacier, will not cease to fascinate. Not far out from Grindel you will come upon a collection of old cow sheds built in the middle of nowhere. While these are of no particular architectural or historical note, you may want to be aware that they serve as public toilets, which you will find, even in such an isolated place, to be spotlessly clean.

When you finally arrive at Grosse Scheidegg don't expect too much of interest; but the **Berghotel Grosse Scheidegg** makes a welcome resting place until the next **Grindelwald bus** arrives to transport you back to Grindelwald. Sit on the left-hand side if you want to see the Grindelwaldgletscher (glacier) just outside Grindelwald.

Bergrestaurant Schreckfeld
t 033 853 54 30,
www.schreckfeld.ch

Berghotel Grosse Scheidegg
t 033 853 67 16,
www.grosse scheidegg.ch

Grindelwald bus
t 033 854 16 16,
www.grindelwaldbus.ch

Pfingstegg and the Glacier

This trip gives you the opportunity to take a close-up look at the glacier. Take the cable car from the Talstation in Grindelwald for the short five-minute ride up to **Pfingstegg**, where you will find the **Bergrestaurant Pfingstegg**, whose terraces offer magnificent views of the glacier. Continue on foot following the path towards the **Oberer Gletscher** (Upper Glacier); this will take about one hour, and on the way to your destination, the **Restaurant at Milchbach** – you will pass through an area known as **Breitlouwina**. The sediments deposited here many millions of years ago have created an amazing variety of strange rock formations. It is the huge mass of the Upper Glacier, though, that will captivate your attention. Relaxing on the terrace of the Restaurant Milchbach, your gaze will be drawn to the grotesquely beautiful shapes the ice has birthed within itself. It is mind-boggling to contemplate that this enormous, solid mass is perpetually, if imperceptibly, in a state of evolution.

Pfingstegg
www.pfingstegg.ch;
website has information about both restaurants

Bergrestaurant Pfingstegg
t 033 853 11 91

Restaurant at Milchbach
t 033 853 14 67

Activities in Grindelwald

Swiss Ski and Snowboarding School, Sportzentrum, **t** 033 854 12 80, *www.grindelwaldsports.ch*. Offers private lessons and ski-guiding. It is necessary to enrol in advance.

Shopping in Grindelwald

Bernet Sport, Hauptstrasse, **t** 033 853 13 09, *www.bernet-sport.ch*. Run by the same family for over 100 years, the current owner is a skiing instructor and mountain guide who has climbed every mountain in Switzerland over 13,000ft (4,000m). The shop offers everything you need, to rent or buy,

ⓘ Grindelwald >
*Grindelwald
Tourismus:
Sportzentrum,
Dorfstrasse,
t 033 854 12 12,
www.grindelwald.ch;
open early Dec–mid-
April Mon–Sat 8–12 and
1.30 –6, Sun 9–12 and
1.30–6; mid-April–early
May Mon–Fri 8–12 and
1.30–6; early May–mid-
June 8–12 and 1.30–6,
Sat 9–12 and 1.30–5;
mid-June–late Oct
Mon–Fri 8–12 and
1.30–6, Sat–Sun 9–12
and 1.30–5; late
Oct–early Dec Mon–Fri
8–12 and 1.30–6*

for skiing, snowboarding, mountaineering and hiking.

Grand Bazar, opposite tourist office, t 033 853 12 88, *www.grandbazar.ch*. In the centre of the village, this store has a wide range of souvenirs. These include the Rosina Wachtmeiser Cat Collection (*www.rosina-wachtmeister.de*, worth a look in its own right), Schleich animals, children's clothes, sports clothes, backpacks, T-shirts and, of course, Swiss Army knives.

Kirchhofer's Collection Grindelwald, Im Tuftli, t 033 854 40 20, *www.kirchhofer.com*. Offers the widest array of name-brand watches in town, along with designer leather goods and other souvenirs.

Where to Stay and Eat in Grindelwald

****Superior Belvedere, t 033 888 99 99, *www.belvedere-grindelwald.ch* (*luxury*). This boasts an enviable location just across the valley from, and almost in the shadow of, the north face of the Eiger. The personality of the Hauser family, owners and operators for over 100 years, is lovingly imprinted on every aspect of this hotel. The rooms are very tastefully appointed and have a

modern feel. You can have the pillow of your choice from the Pillow Bar. The well-equipped spa has both a pool and a jacuzzi with picture windows allowing superb views of the Eiger.

****Spinne, t 033 854 88 88, *www.spinne.ch* (*expensive*). Right in the middle of the village, this has 43 very nice rooms, many with balconies with views over the Eiger. It has four different restaurants featuring Italian/French and Chinese cuisine, two bars, a disco and a wellness centre.

***Fischerblick, Dorfstrasse, t 033 854 53 53, *www.fiescherblick.ch* (*moderate*). This is a charming small hotel that has comfortable, well-equipped standard and superior rooms, Internet access in the lobby and free entry to the Sportzentrum (Sports Centre) of Grindelwald.

Mountain Hostel, Grundstrasse, t 033 854 38 38, *www.mountainhostel.ch* (*inexpensive*). Located down by the Männlichenbahn gondola station and Grund Station, this is the ideal place for those looking for basic, inexpensive accommodation. It has two-, four- and six-bed rooms with running water, but the showers and toilets are centrally located. It also has TV, billiards, table tennis, laundry and an Internet corner.

Wengen

This dramatically beautiful car-free village at 4,180ft (1,274m), with its stupendous views of the Eiger, Jungfrau and the glorious waterfalls that cascade into the valley, is an ideal base for exploring this area of the Bernese Oberland.

In 1834 and 1835 the first licences were issued for the operation of inns over the pass at Kleine Scheidegg to Wengernalp and Kleine Scheidegg respectively. A few years later the first inn was opened in Wengen, and tourism grew. The opening of the railways, Berner Oberland in 1890 and Wengernalp in 1893, brough even more

Getting to and around Wengen

By **train, Berner Oberland Bahnen (BOB)** from Interlaken Ost (East) to Lauterbrunnen, then take the **Wengernalpbahn (WAB)** cog railway train to Wengen.

By **car**, from Interlaken, travel via Zweilütscinen to Lauterbrunnen. As Wengen is car-free, park your car here at the multi-storey car park next to the railway station. Look at *www.jungfraubahn.ch* for details of fees, reservations (recommended), etc. Then take the **Wengernalpbahn (WAB)** cog railway train to Wengen. Once you are in the village everything is very accessible on **foot**.

ⓘ Wengen >
Wengen Tourismus: Dorfstrasse, t 033 855 14 14, www.wengen-muerren.ch; open Easter–late Dec Mon–Fri 9–6; late Dec–Easter Mon–Sat 9–6, Sun 9–12.30 and 1.30–6

Shopping in Wengen

Swiss Made Shop, Dorfstrasse, **t** 033 855 26 27. This offers exactly what you'd expect – a range of souvenirs, all made from natural materials, produced in Switzerland and the surrounding countries. Expect to find Swiss Army knives, cow bells, beer steins, wooden children's toys and fondue pots. There are also home-made tablecloths, which can be made to order in three days, and a Christmas Corner of entirely Swiss-made decorations. On the first floor is an art gallery in which only the art of the mountains is displayed. It's the only one of its kind in Switzerland .

Where to Stay in Wengen

★ Regina

****Regina, **t** 033 855 58 58, *www.hotelregina.ch (expensive)*.

Dating from 1894, this is a luxurious, traditional mountain hotel with uninterrupted views of Jungfrau. The characterful rooms include modern facilities. Relax by the fire on comfortable furniture in antique-laden, wood-panelled public rooms. There is a restaurant, brasserie and bar, plus a beauty centre.

****Silberhorn, **t** 033 856 51 31, *www.silberhorn.ch (moderate)*. In a central position in the village, right across from the train station, this has well-furnished rooms and apartments, a restaurant, a wellness facility, sun terrace and bars.

***Hotel Belvedere, **t** 033 856 68 68, *www.belvedere-wengen.ch (inexpensive)*. Situated at the opposite end of the village to the train station and built in 1912, this magnificent Art Nouveau hotel has all modern comforts. Most of its rooms have balconies with views.

visitors. In 1910 the rail link to Kleine Scheidegg opened up the higher peaks to winter sports.

During the summer Wengen is surrounded by numerous **hiking** possibilities and these are detailed in the map *Lauterbrunnen Jungfrau Region Wanderkarte*, available at the tourist office. The winter season, though, is when Wengen springs to life, with a seemingly never-ending selection of **skiing** and **snowboarding** opportunities. Brush up your skills at the **Schweizer Skischule und Snowboardschule** (Swiss Ski and Snowboard School). There are **winter walking trails**, too, and the tourist office has a brochure detailing these.

Schweizer Skischule und Snowboardschule
Silberhorn Center, t 033 855 20 22, www.skiwengen.ch

Wengen also hosts the world-famous **Lauberhorn Downhill Ski Races** – for the 80th time in January 2010. Covering 2.65 miles (4.26km), this is the oldest and longest downhill ski race in the World Cup calendar.

Wengen is a starting point for the famous excursion to **Jungfraujoch**. Wengernalpbahn (WAB) trains originating at Lauterbrunnen take you to Kleine Scheidegg to begin the trip (*see* p.156). It is also one of two starting points (the other is Grindelwald) for a trip to **Männlichen** (*see* p.155), which begins on the Luftseilbahn Wengen–Männlichen (LWM) cable car.

② Jungfraujoch

Jungfraujoch

Even today, it would take a knowledgeable eye to see a way, other than climbing, to reach the top of the magnificent Jungfrau at

Getting to Jungfraujoch

Begin from either Grindelwald or Lauterbrunnen/Wengen, taking a **Wengernalpbahn (WAB)** train to Kleine Scheidegg. At Kleine Scheidegg listen for the familiar refrain, 'Change for the Jungfraujoch', signalling that a **Jungfraubahn (JB)** train waits to carry you upwards.

13,642ft (4,158m). And that is exactly how it seemed back in 1893 when Adolf Guyer-Zeller, a prominent Swiss industrialist captivated by the towering peaks of the Eiger, Mönch and Jungfrau, had the idea of constructing a railway to the top. Work on this project, based on his notes and sketches, began from Kleine Scheidegg in July 1896. It took two years just to complete the first section of the track, which ran over open ground, to the Eigergletscher station at 7,612ft (2,320m). This became then, and remains today, the operative headquarters of the **Jungfraubahn** (Jungfrau Railway).

From the station onward, the track had to be tunnelled through the mountain. In 1899, a blasting accident claimed six lives. In a subsequent accident, over 29.5 tons (30,000 kilos) of dynamite exploded; no lives were lost, but it is said that the blast was heard in Germany. Work continued, and two other intermediate stations, Eigerwand (9,400ft/2,865m) and Eismeer (10,368ft/3,160m), were completed before the final breakthrough out of the rock at Jungfraujoch in February 1912. Europe's highest railway station, at 11,333ft (3,454m), was finally opened on 1 August 1912.

During the first stage of the journey from Kleine Scheidegg, across open ground to the entrance to the Grosser Tunnel just past the Eigergletscher station, you will be bombarded by a proliferation of alpine vistas so wondrous that you will not know which way to look first. The peaks loom above you, and it will be your first opportunity to see those awesome glaciers close up. There are also tremendous views back across the Lauterbrunnen valley to Mürren and the Schilthorn.

The tunnel, all the way to the top, is 4.4 miles (7.12km) long, but there are two five-minute stops along the way at the intermediate stations of **Eigerwand** and **Eismeer**, each of which offers contrasting panoramas viewed from glassed-in platforms. The first, built into the fearsome north wall of the Eiger, allows you a

09 | Bern and the Bernese Oberland | Jungfraujoch

Good Morning Ticket

Those who want to save on the fare to Jungfraujoch will want to consider the Good Morning Ticket. However, you will have to get up early as it is only valid on the first train, departing Interlaken Ost at 6am between May and October, and also on the second train, departing Interlaken Ost at 7.05am, between November and April. A downside is that between May and October you must start the return journey by no later than 12.30pm.

bird's-eye view of Grindelwald in the valley far below, out over smaller mountains to northern Switzerland and, on occasion, even to the Black Forest in Germany.

The second, at Eismeer, is quite different. Looking out eastwards, behind the Eiger and the Mönch, the surreal and chilling spectre of eternal ice unfolds before you in the forms of the Grindelwald and Fiescher glaciers. And on closer look, as amazing as it might seem, you may see climbers out there as well. A word of warning here – avoid rushing; this rarefied atmosphere, with 16 per cent oxygen, affects almost everyone, especially those with respiratory problems. Those suffering from any form of heart condition should certainly seek their doctor's approval before contemplating this trip.

At Jungfraujoch

Once at Jungfraujoch itself the attractions are numerous. In 1996 the **Sphinx observation hall and terrace** were opened, Europe's highest at an altitude of 11,716ft (3,571m); visitors are transported up 354ft (108m) in an astounding 25 seconds by way of Switzerland's highest-speed lift. From here, the vast Aletsch glacier, Europe's largest at 13.7 miles (22km), fills the wide valley between the towering peaks.

Once you enter the **Top of Europe** complex, you will find a number of attractions. Within the **Ice Palace**, inside the glacier, ice has been sculpted into beautiful patterns and models. This should not be missed.

Before departing, take the opportunity to send a postcard home, franked by Europe's highest **post office**. Not only does it have a special postmark, it has its own postal code as well – CH-3801.

Shopping on Jungfraujoch

Kirchhofer, High Time Jungfraujoch, Sphinx Terrace, *www.kirchhofer.com*. Here at an altitude of 11,716ft (3,571m) you will find the highest watch shop in the world, featuring a wide array of famous-name designer Swiss watches.

Activities on Jungfraujoch

There are numerous activities available on Jungfraujoch. When on Jungfraujoch you should go to the **Adventure Information Desk** in the Top of Europe complex for further details, payment, etc. Information can also be found at *www.jungfrau bahn.ch*. The following activities are open June–mid-September:

Ski & Snowboard Park: for the price of CHF 33 you can rent equipment and use the park.

Snow Disk Run: glide down a specially prepared powder-snow piste on a snow disk. The activity is free, you just have to pay a CHF 5 deposit for the snow disk.

Tyrolienne Jungfraujoch: glide over the glacier attached to a steel cable for CHF 20.

Husky-Drawn Sledge Ride: an exciting ride over the glacier for CHF 8.

For the more adventurous visitor, **Grindelwald Sports**, **t** 033 854 12 90, *www.grindelwaldsports.ch*, offer guided Aletsch glacier hikes and mountain tours on Jungfrau. These are recommended only for fit, suitably equipped and experienced hikers.

Eating Out on Jungfraujoch

There are a number of eateries in the Top of the World complex.

Bollywood, Top of the World Complex, t 033 828 78 88, www.gletscherrestaurant.ch (*expensive/moderate*). This is an Indian restaurant decorated with numerous Bollywood movie posters. This may seem an unlikely setting for an Indian restaurant but there is a logical reason for it. In the past, Bollywood movies were often filmed in Kashmir. However, because of the now volatile situation in this area filming is not possible, so many Bollywood movies are shot in the Bernese Oberland.

Männlichen and Kleine Scheidegg

Männlichen

Männlichen, at an altitude of 7,290ft (2,222m), is the mountain that forms a natural barrier between the valleys of the White Lütschine River of Lauterbrunnen and the Black Lütschine of Grindelwald. Refresh yourself at the **Berggasthaus Männlichen** restaurant (*see* below), between the cable car and gondola stations, and take a few moments to contemplate your surroundings. You will note that the valleys form a contrast in themselves. The White Lütschine, the narrower of the two, can boast little of its unprepossessing peaks. The other valley is longer, much broader and is surrounded by an array of highly impressive mountains, including the north face of the Eiger, 13,025ft (3,970m), which forms its south wall. And it is that scene, directly to the south, that holds the greatest fascination. There, alongside the Eiger, tower the summits of the Mönch, 13,448ft (4,099m), and the Jungfrau, 13,642ft (4,158m), with their respective glaciers, Eigergletscher, Guggigletscher and Giessengletscher.

In the winter this is the starting point for long, wonderful skiing and snowboarding runs down to either Grindelwald or Wengen. In the summer you can get up closer to these mountains by taking a fairly easy, relatively flat 1¼-hour hike to Kleine Scheidegg.

Where to Stay and Eat in Mannlichen and Kleine Scheidegg

Berggasthaus Männlichen, t 033 853 10 68, www.maennlichen.ch/berghaus (*moderate*). A typical mountain hotel with rather basic single or doule rooms, with or without bath. Enjoy lunch in the pleasant dining room, with typical dishes such as fondue, raclette, *Käseschnitte* or a fine plate of dried meats.

Röstizzeria, Restaurante Bahnhof, Kleine Scheidegg, www.roestizza.ch (*inexpensive*). The mountain air certainly gives you an appetite, and this is an ideal place to sample a regional speciality. This '*röstizzeria*' serves variations on Switzerland's famous dish, rösti. Food can be eaten inside or on the terrace.

Getting to Männlichen

From Grindelwald: take the **Gondelbahn Grindelwald-Männlichen (GGM)**, **t** 033 854 80 80, *www.maenn lichen.ch*, from its departure point at **Grindelwald Grund station**. It takes 30mins to travel the 3.4 miles (6.2 km) – making it the longest gondola cableway in Europe – lifting you the 4,199ft (1,280m) up to Männlichen. The ride is taken in comfortable four-seater cabins. Two gondolas, equipped to accommodate the special needs of the disabled, each hold a single wheelchair and have seats for two companions.

From Wengen: the **Luftseilbahn Wengen-Männlichen (LWM)** cable car, **t** 033 855 29 33, *www.maenn lichen.ch*. A cabin with a capacity of 80 whisks you up 3,051 ft (930m) to Männlichen in just 5mins.

Getting to Kleine Scheidegg

You can travel from either Grindelwald or Wengen/Lauterbrunnen by different methods of transportation (*see* below).

Kleine Scheidegg

If you don't want to take the hike there is a very charming alternative. Firstly, walk a few yards from the Berggasthaus to the **Luftseilbahn Wengen-Männlichen (LWM)** cable car. Take the cable car and it will drop you down into the heart of Wengen. Just a couple of minute's walk away is the station from which a **Wengernalpbahn (WAB)** train will wind its way up the mountain, offering spectacular views along the way, to Kleine Scheidegg.

Besides being an important railway junction, Kleine Scheidegg is an interesting small complex of hotels, souvenir shops and restaurants. Rock music blares from open-air bars and, incongruously, there is even an India tepee.

The descent back to your choice of Grindelwald or Wengen can be taken either by Wengernalpbahn (WAB) train, or if the *rosti* has restored your energy, by walking. Both treks are downhill, of course, and each takes around 3½ hours.

Trümmelbach, Schilthorn and Mürren
Trummelbach

If you travel from Lauterbrunnen be sure to get a seat on the right-hand side of the bus because this valley is famous for its waterfalls and soon after passing through the village of Lauterbrunnen there are views on the right side of the **Staubbach Falls** (Staubbachfall). The most magnificent in the valley, they cascade and plunge 945ft (288m) from the rock face above, with much of the water dissipating into fine spray before reaching the valley floor. The water that eventually reaches ground level combines with that of the 70-plus other falls in the valley, and the mountain streams, to feed the eternally fast-flowing White Lütschine river.

Waterfalls are, again, the focus of attention at **Trümmelbach**, just 3km (1.9 miles) from Lauterbrunnen. Cross the road from the bus

Getting to Trümmelbach

By **train**, **Berner Oberland Bahnen (BOB)** from Interlaken Ost (East) to Lauterbrunnen. Then take **postbus** to Trümmelbach, *see* below.

By **car**, from Interlaken via Zweilütschinen to Lauterbrunnen. Park your car here at the multi-storey car park next to the railway station. Look at *www.jungfraubahn.ch* for details of fees, reservations (recommended), etc. Then take **postbus** to Trümmelbach, *see* below.

By **postbus**, **t** 0848 888 888, *www.postbus.ch*, from outside the railway station in Lauterbrunnen or the Schilthornbahn station at Stechelberg.

⭐ **Trümmelbach Falls**
t 033 855 32 32, www.truemmelbach faelle.ch; open July–Aug 8.30–6; April–June, Sept–early Nov 9–5; adm

stop, go around the restaurant/bar and follow the path and a truly impressive sight will come into view. The **Trümmelbach Falls** (Trümmelbachfälle) may be one of the lesser acclaimed spectacles in this area of spectacular sights, but they are certainly one of the most fascinating. Trümmelbach, alone, drains the mighty glaciers of the Eiger, Mönch and Jungfrau. Its drainage area of 9.25sq miles (24sq km), half of which is covered by glaciers and snow, carries off up to 5,283 gallons (20,000 litres) of water per second that transports as much as 20,200 tons (20,524,148 kilos) of rock and other debris per year through the only glacial waterfalls in Europe that are inside a mountain and still accessible. A lift carries you up inside the mountain, and footpaths, sometimes a little precarious, lead you back past 10 different waterfalls, weaving both inside and out of the mountain. The endless current of water can be both visibly and audibly mesmerizing, and the falls' corkscrew paths down the mountain, and the patterns they carve into the rock, are awesome.

Back outside, you have a choice to make. If it will be a while before the next bus departs for Lauterbrunnen or Stechelberg (they usually run once an hour), either pop into the restaurant or, if you prefer, take a pleasant riverside stroll back to Stechelberg. The walk is about 1¼ miles (2km).

⭐ **Schilthorn**

Schilthorn

The cableway that takes you to the summit of the Schilthorn rises from an altitude of 2,844ft (867m) to 9,744ft (2,970m) over 4.3 miles (7km). This is the longest cableway in the Bernese Oberland. The first three sections, including one stretch between Mürren and Birg where the 1.6-inch (40-mm) track cables hang free for nearly 1.2 miles (2km), were completed in 1965. The last leg, ascending to the summit, took two more years to complete. The total journey

Movie Connections

In 1967 the cableway had reached the Schilthorn summit and work had begun on a revolving restaurant, but the company ran out of money. Luckily, the film company planning the next 007 spectacular, **On Her Majesty's Secret Service**, were looking for just such a location. Consequently, the filmmakers finished the building and the revolving restaurant, **Piz Gloria**, and had use of the cableway for three months before turning everything back over to the Schilthorn Aerial Cableway Company in a deal that suited everyone. In turn, the film brought well-deserved international acclaim to the Schilthorn, making it one of Europe's most popular destinations.

Getting to Schilthorn

Take the **Schilthornbahn** cableway, *www.schilthorn.ch*, which starts at Stechelberg. It comprises of four sections: Stechelberg to Gimmelwald, Gimmelwald to Mürren, Mürren to Birg and, finally, Birg to the summit of the Schilthorn.

Piz Gloria
www.schilthorn.ch

time is just 32 minutes. The 80- or 100-person cars depart every half an hour, although this can be increased to every 15 minutes if demand dictates. As you soar skywards, passing an ever-changing array of green pastures, alpine farms, chalets, forests, bare rock face, snow and ice, you will be mindful of the feat of engineering that has enabled such a journey.

The isolation of the Schilthorn affords visitors an unobstructed 360-degree panoramic vista of the surrounding Alps – in excess of 200 peaks, including the Eiger, Mönch and Jungfrau (you can actually see Jungfraujoch just across the valley), plus more than forty glaciers, deep valleys and mountain lakes.

Of course, the weather will have a say in what you see and, to ensure that your trip is not a wasted journey, cameras are installed at each stage to show the conditions at the top. In reality, though, while conditions may appear to be poor, swirling winds can change matters very quickly. Once at the top you can relax and enjoy a meal in the revolving **Piz Gloria** restaurant while enjoying the views, as solar power drives the restaurant slowly to complete one rotation every hour (*see* p.157).

On the way down, you have options if you want to travel to Mürren. The easiest, of course, is to take the Schilthornbahn directly there. Alternatively, weather permitting, you can hike, which will take approximately 5 hours or, much easier, take the cable car to Birg and then trek down, via Blumental (the Valley of the Flowers) to Mürren, which is about a 2½-hour walk.

Mürren

You are sure to be enchanted by Mürren. Traffic-free, like Wengen, but much smaller and more rural, this village sits on a ledge with simply stunning – and more unfamiliar – views across this steep valley to the Eiger, Mönch and Jungfrau. Mürren is famous for its **winter sports**: Switzerland's first ski school opened here in 1930, 1937 marked the opening of the first ski lift service in the Bernese Oberland, and today there are around 31 miles (50km) of pistes and more than 16 downhill ski runs. The most famous of these is the 'Inferno Run', first raced in 1928, which covers a distance of 9¾ miles (15.8km) from the summit of Schilthorn and descends 7,054ft (2,150m) down the valley to Lauterbrunnen.

Hot air ballooning is also popular in Mürren. Eduard Spelterini made the first alpine balloon crossing from here on 12 August 1910, eventually landing in Turin, Italy. And one of the most important summer events is the annual International High Alpine Ballooning Competition, which was inaugurated in 1957.

Getting to Mürren

Take the **Schilthornbahn cableway** from Stechelberg to Mürren; or the **Bergbahn Lauterbrunnen-Mürren** (BLM) cableway from Lauterbrunnen to Grütschalp, and then the BLM railway from Grütschalp to Mürren.

Allmendhubel

Mürren–Allmendhubel funicular
t 033 855 20 42,
www.schilthorn.ch;
usually open mid-June–mid-Sept; mid-Dec–mid-April

A particularly interesting trip from Mürren, when it is open, is on the **Mürren–Allmendhubel funicular**. Opened in December 1912, its original purpose was to service the Allmendhubel toboggan run. Now, however, it raises passengers 846ft (258m) in four minutes, through a tunnel and over arched bridges, to a delightful spot that serves as an origination point for a series of mountain hikes. Alternatively, at this altitude of 6,273ft (1,912m), take life a little easier and enjoy a fondue, perhaps at the mountain restaurant, while admiring the scenery.

There are choices if you're travelling back to Lauterbrunnen. Those with any energy in reserve – and remember ascending and descending mountain peaks is tiring – may elect to **walk** back. It takes a couple of hours and, even though the journey is downhill all the way, it is more difficult than it might, at first, appear. Without doubt, your calves will be screaming for a rest long before, and long after, you reach Lauterbrunnen. Or you can take the narrow-gauge non-cog railway to Grütschalp and then the cable car back to Lauterbrunnen. Both services are run by the **Bergbahn Lauterbrunnen-Mürren (BLM)**. The cable car holds a hundred people and the journey takes just four minutes.

(i) **Mürren >**
Mürren Tourismus:
t 033 856 86 66,
www.wengen-muerren.ch; open Easter–late Dec Mon–Fri 8.30–12 and 1–5; late Dec–Easter Mon–Wed, Fri–Sat 8.30–7, Thurs 8.30–8, Sun 8.30–6

Activities in Mürren

Hiking

The tourist information office has maps and information on hiking in the Schilthorn/Mürren area.

Skiing

There is a small branch of the **Schweizer Ski und Snowboardschule** (Swiss Ski and Snowboard School), t 033 855 12 47, *www.muerren.ch/skischule*.

You can rent equipment from **Abegglen Sport**, Hauptstrasse, t 033 855 12 45, *www.skirental-muerren.ch*.

The tourist information office have information on runs, etc.

Other Activities

The **Alpines Sportzentrum** (Alpine Sportscentre), t 033 856 86 86, offers ice skating, curling, ice hockey and minigolf, amongst others.

Where to Stay and Eat in Mürren

****Hotel Eiger, t 033 856 54 54, *www.hoteleiger.ch* (expensive). Established in 1886, and run by the same family ever since, this offers magnificent views of the Eiger, Mönch and Jungfrau from many of the rooms. The hotel is run with a relaxed personal touch and has an indoor pool, sauna, solarium, a terrace and the Eiger Stübli, an exquisite gourmet restaurant.

***Hotel Jungfrau, t 33 856 64 84, *www.hoteljungfrau.ch* (moderate). Located in the middle of the village, the 29 rooms and one apartment have bath/shower, radio, TV, telephone, and some have a balcony with views over the Eiger, Mönch and Jungfrau. Located next to the ski runs, and offers free admission to the ice rink. The Restaurant Gruebi is open for breakfast and dinner.

Getting to Brienz

By Train

From Interlaken Ost (East) directly to Brienz.

By Lake Steamer

Board a **BLS Company** steamship, t 058 327 48 11, *www.bls.ch*, at Interlaken Ost (East). The journey takes about 1¼ hous. By late afternoon it is more practical to return to Interlaken by train.

Brienz, Rothorn and Ballenberg

Sitting on the eastern edge of Lake Brienz (Brienzersee), Brienz would just be a typically pretty Swiss village if it were not for three attractions: a long-standing cultural tradition that has made the village famous throughout Switzerland and beyond, a very unusual mountain railway and a fascinating open-air museum.

The cultural tradition that Brienz is famous for is woodcarving. This art is explored in detail on pp.29–30.

Across from the dock at Brienz, puffs of steam are the clue that the most well-known attraction of Brienz is just a few footsteps away. These puffs emanate from the small, squat engines of the **Brienz Rothorn Bahn** at the tiny station tucked in next to the mountain. These little engines pull or push passenger carriages for approximately 1 hour as the track twists and turns over a distance of 4¾ miles (7.6km), at an average gradient of 22 per cent, a total of 5,505ft (1,678m). As many as eight steam engines, and a couple of their diesel companions, operate daily. Along the way, the train dodges in and out of the forests, passing through six tunnels and allowing tantalizing glimpses of the lake below and the peaks of the Bernese Oberland beyond it.

Once you disembark at the 7,710-ft (2,350-m) summit the numerous unhampered views of the surrounding countryside are spectacular. Also at the top you will find the **Hotel Rothorn Kulm**, where you can indulge in a fondue at the restaurant. Heavy snowfalls can at times prevent the trains from getting farther than the midway station at Planalp. If this happens you needn't worry, as there are some delightful hiking paths nearby waiting to be explored.

A short bus ride from Brienz station will take you to the **Freilichtmuseum Ballenberg** (Swiss Open-Air Museum Ballenberg).

⭐ **Brienz Rothorn Bahn**
t 33 952 22.22,
www.brienz-rothorn-
bahn.ch; open end
May–end Oct

Hotel Rothorn Kulm
t 033 951 12 21

Freilichtmuseum Ballenberg
t 033 952 10 30;
www.ballenberg.ch;
open early April–Oct
daily 10–5; adm

Brienz by Lake Steamer

The steamers that operate on the lake all have lounges and a restaurant or snack bar. On a warm, sunny day there are few things as relaxing as sitting on the top deck, sipping your favourite drink and marvelling at the scenery. The steamer serenely traverses the lake, which nearly fills this elongated, narrow valley, criss-crossing from one pretty village to another. Pay special attention to the penultimate stop at Giessbach, home to the legendary Giessbach Falls and – you may be able to glimpse it through the forest – the Grandhotel Giessbach.

Shopping in Brienz

ⓘ Brienz >

Brienz Tourismus:
Hauptstrasse 143,
t 033 952 80 80,
www.haslital.ch; open
Mon–Fri 8–12 and 2–6

Kirchhofer Brienz, Hauptstrasse 41,
t 033 951 06 06, *www.kirchhofer.com*.
Besides a very large selection of
famous-name Swiss watches, this
shop also has many music boxes,
cuckoo clocks and woodcarving items
reflecting the culture of Brienz.

Where to Stay and Eat in Brienz

★★★Hotel Brienz, Hauptstrasse 254,
t 033 951 35 51, *www.hotel-brienz.ch*,
(*moderate*). Located just a few
minutes from the lake, this is a
charming family-run hotel that offers
good-sized, modern rooms in different
categories, as well as a rated fish
restaurant.

This offers you a look at Swiss rural life as it was experienced
through the centuries. You will find over a hundred restored old
buildings, cattle, farming exhibitions and country crafts.

Thun

Thun is situated directly south of Bern, at the confluence of Lake
Thun and the River Aare. It has a population of around 40,000 and
is, perhaps surprisingly for such a low figure, Switzerland's tenth
largest city. With its castle dominating the skyline and the
snowcapped Bernese Oberland peaks as a backdrop, it is a quaint
medieval town.

Besides the castle and the art museum, there isn't that much to
visit. Nevertheless, a trip here is worthwhile just to soak up the
atmosphere, and wandering around Thun is a delight. If you want
to stay overnight the choice of hotels is limited, and you won't find
too many fine restaurants to choose from.

As the fastest train trip from Bern takes just 19 minutes, all the
sights of Thun can be seen very easily on a daytrip from that city.

History

In the early 12th century the Barons of Thun are first mentioned
in historical annals. Very late in the same century Duke Berchtold
of Zähringen conquered and expanded the town and also, around
1190, built the castle that still stands today. By 1218 the County of
Kyburg, in eastern Switzerland, had succeeded the House of
Zähringen, though they ruled less than 50 years. In 1264, Countess
Elisabeth of Kyburg granted Thun a City Charter with special
privileges, and these documents are now in safe keeping in the
Rathaus (Town Hall). With the 14th century came a barrage of civic
problems so severe that Thun became a Bernese country town.
Consequently, in 1384 the castle was taken over by the Bernese
authorities as the residence for their governors and mayors.
Among the highlights of the 15th century was the expansion of the
guild that brought with it the construction of the Town Hall and
other new Guildhalls. In the 16th century, Thun joined in the

Getting to and around Thun

Thun is just south of Bern on the mainline to Spiez/Interlaken, and there are fast **trains** from either direction. Thun train station is south of the Old Town, a 5-min walk from the first branch of the Aare. By **car**, Thun is between Bern and Spiez on the A6 motorway.

Reformation movement. It wasn't until 1835 that the first steamboat came to Thun, with the railway following 24 years later.

Outside the Old Town

The one place of interest in Thun that is not directly in the Old Town is situated just to the south of town on the north side of the Aare basin, the area of water between the river and the lake. The **Kunstmuseum** (Museum of Fine Arts) is housed in an impressive building, built in 1875. The focus here is on Swiss and international art, with regular exhibitions on art history themes or focused on the museum's collections of contemporary 20th-century works.

Kunstmuseum
Hofstettenstrasse 14,
t 033 225 84 20,
www.kunstmuseum-
thun.ch; open
Tues–Sun 10–5, Wed till
9; adm

Old Town

For all the other sights, start at Freienhofgasse, the main street on the island between the two branches of the Aare; an anti-clockwise route will take you up to the castle and church on the hill, and then back via the Rathausplatz.

To the north of Freienhofgasse is a two-storey building with three arches at ground-floor level, one of which is differently shaped from the other two. The **Drei Eidgenossen** (Three Confederates) was the former residence of the lords of Amsoldingen. It was rebuilt in 1409 and became an inn from 1798 until 1920, before being renovated in 1989. There is another arched building next to it; however, it is the odd six-sided tower abutting one corner, and its second-floor balcony, that catches the eye. This is the **Rosengarten** (Rose Garden), a late Gothic burgher's mansion that was built around 1480 for Bartholomäus May. It was renovated in the 16th and 17th centuries, and again in 1991.

On the south corner, where the street meets the Aare, stands the Freienhof hotel (*see* p.164). This started life in 1308 as a municipal shelter for travellers, but was rebuilt in 1783 and again in 1957. On the northeast side of the bridge there is a square, neat house, **Oberherren**, which has a metal terrace overlooking the river. This was once the Overlords' Guildhall, but was rebuilt on its foundations in 1749.

Further north, on Obere Hauptgasse, **Schmieden** was first mentioned in 1437 and was the Smiths' Guildhall; the façade, though, dates from 1779. Much more unusual, however, are the **Kirchtreppe** (Church Steps) that were at one time just a steep path. These wooden steps, built with a very low rise and covered with a wooden roof, were originally built by master carpenter Johann Boxdörfer, himself from Thun, in 1818.

Once at the top the dominant building, boasting an impressive clock tower, is the **Stadtkirche** (Town Church) that dates from around 1330 and has frescoes from a century later. In 1738 the master builder, Paulus Nader, rebuilt it for use as a Protestant church. Three nearby buildings are worth a look, too. The nearest is the **Sigristenhaus** (Sexton's House), a chapel until the Reformation in 1528, rebuilt as a private house in 1537 and then as the Sexton's house in 1822. The **Burgtor** (Castle Gate) is the only city gate to have survived from the 13th century, although the roof was added in 1786. The **Helferei** (Curate's House) is rather imposing, and its medieval core might well once have formed part of the nearby castle. What you see dates from the 16th century and the early 19th century, and it was the official residence of the curate intern between 1725 and 1896.

Higher northwest is **Schloss Thun** (Thun Castle), whose history is documented on p.161. The main attraction here, besides the building itself, is the multi-faceted **Schlossmuseum** (Castle Museum), which is housed in the formidable tower. Displayed on several floors, the exhibits are impressively varied and, in addition to giving an insight into the region's cultural development, offer some enlightenment as to how the castle itself evolved throughout the history of Thun. From the tower there are views of the Bernese Oberland in the distance beyond Lake Thun.

Schlossmuseum
*t 033 223 20 01;
www.schlossthun.ch;
open Feb–Mar daily 1–4;
April–Oct daily 10 –5;
Nov–Jan daily except
Sun 1–4; adm*

Follow the steps down and around to the west of the castle, passing an attractive chalet along the way. Pause here for a moment to admire the views, not only of the Alps, but also of a delightfully haphazard collection of red-tiled roofs below. You will soon come across another of those unique covered wooden staircases, but, as you will note on the descent, this is in less than pristine shape and is covered with graffiti. These steps deposit you back into the Old Town and out onto the pretty **Rathausplatz**. The most important building here is the *rathaus* (town hall) on the west side that dates from around 1500, with the Archive Tower added in 1585. The present façade dates from a century later, although it was refurbished both in 1762 and 1964. Going around the square clockwise, you will find the **Velschenhaus** (Velschen House), with a white façade and an overhanging wooden roof. This was first mentioned as early as 1406 as home to a man of the same name; later that century the Thorberg Carthusians moved in from 1464 until 1528. Latterly, it has been used as a restaurant. Across the street is a square-looking building, arcaded at ground level and with pretty window boxes hanging from all of the windows. In 1775 Johannes Deci built the **Burgerhaus** (Burghers' House) as a combination of house and business premises. From 1918 it became the headquarters of the Burghers. Across Untere Hauptgasse the building with a terrace outside, **Metzgern**, was mentioned as early as 1361 and was the original Butchers' Guildhall. Much work was done in the late 16th century, and its

ⓘ **Thun >**

Thun Tourismus:
Bahnhof,
t 33 225 90 90,
www.thun.ch; open
Mon–Fri 9–6.30, Sat
9–4

Activities in Thun

Lake Trips

BLS Thuner-und Brienzersee, t 033 841 16 43, *ww.bls.ch*. While most of the places of interest are nearer Interlaken, or on Lake Brienz, there are possibilities of taking special trips, like fondue cruises, on the lake from Thun.

Where to Stay in Thun

***Krone**, Rathausplatz 2, **t** 033 227 88 88, *www.krone-thun.ch* (*moderate*). Located in the Town Hall square, this has a delightful medieval exterior. Inside, the 27 spacious rooms are contemporary. It has a sun terrace overlooking the Aare, and French and Chinese restaurants.

****Freienhof**, Freienhofgasse 3, **t** 033 227 50 50, *www.freienhof.ch* (*moderate*). This has a marvellous façade, a long history and a privileged position on the peninsula in the Aare river, in a central location in the old part of town. Its 68 rooms have up-to-date facilities.

Eating Out in Thun

Ristorante Al Ponte, Freienhofgasse 16, **t** 033 222 36 42 (*moderate–inexpensive*). As the name implies, this is situated next to the bridge on the island between the two branches of the Aare. Pizza is the order of day, and the menu also includes *antipasti*, soup, pasta, salads, risotto, meat and fish. There is a little terrace next to the river in summer.

Siegfried Röthlisberger ger Marlis, Hauptgasse 72, **t** 033 222 15 27 (*moderate–inexpensive*). This place is easy to miss as the entrance is down a corridor off the street. Even when you find it, it seems out-of-place – a throwback to the way small Swiss country restaurants used to be. Breadsticks and hard-boiled eggs are on each table, and the menu is pure Swiss.

Kaffeebar Mühleplatz, Mühleplatz 1, **t** 033 222 01 50 (*inexpensive*). This is located right next to the Mühlebrücke and has a rather limited menu of snacks and salads. However, it has a much more impressive list of cocktails and other drinks, and it is a great place to soak up the atmosphere.

present look came about in 1770. Directly across from the town hall the long façade belongs to the **Platzschulhaus** (School on the Square) that was built in 1793–7 as a hospital, but was used as a school from 1806 until 1909. The last building, with another of those six-sided towers that was rebuilt in 1972, was the former Bakers' Guildhall. Since 1822 it has been the **Krone** (Crown) hotel.

Between the town hall and the Krone a path leads to the inner Aare, and that leads on to the **Mühleplatz**, a small plaza. Stop and enjoy the tranquillity of the surroundings. Swans and ducks move gracefully over the clear water while the typical Swiss centuries-old houses stand vigil over their comings and goings. Cross the water via the old wooden-covered sluice bridge immediately to the east and this will bring you to the road back to the railway station.

Central Switzerland

This region is dominated by the Vierwaldstättersee, the lake of Luzern, the largest of several lakes in the region. The scenery all around the lake is never less than gloriously pretty and always, though usually in the distance, snow-capped mountain peaks are in view. A cruise around the lake on a steamer is a must. This, combined with its history and culture, makes Luzern one of the most attractive and most visited cities in Switzerland.

There are mountain adventures to be had in this region. Mount Pilatus, just to the south of Luzern, is full of mysteries, but for a high-peak experience it is necessary to travel much farther south. At the end of a very long valley is Engelberg, a pretty alpine village. From here, a revolving cable car takes you up to a world of ice and snow.

10

Don't miss

① Music to your ears
KKL, Luzern **p.170**

② Mural to amaze and inform
Bourbaki Panorama, Luzern **p.173**

③ Iconic sight
Kapellbrücke, Luzern **p.175**

④ Mythical mountain
Mount Pilatus **p.181**

⑤ 360° mountain spectacular
Titlis Rotair, Engelberg **p.183**

See map overleaf

Central Switzerland

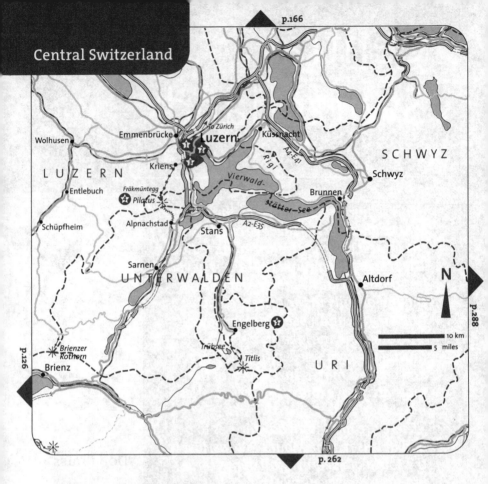

p.166

p.288

p.126

p. 262

Wolhusen

Emmenbrücke

To Zürich

Luzern

Küssnacht

SCHWYZ

Kriens

Rigi

Schwyz

L U Z E R N

Vierwald-

Entlebuch

Fräkmüntegg

Pilatus

Brunnen

Schüpfheim

Alpnachstad

Vätter-See

A2-E35

Stans

Sarnen

U N T E R W A L D E N

Altdorf

N

Engelberg

Brienzer
Rothorn

Trübsee

Titlis

U R I

Brienz

10 km

5 miles

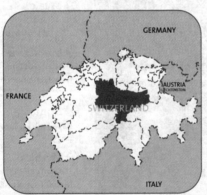

GERMANY

FRANCE

AUSTRIA
LIECHTENSTEIN

SWITZERLAND

ITALY

Don't miss

⭐ KKL, Luzern **p.170**

⭐ Bourbaki Panorama, Luzern **p.173**

⭐ Kapellbrücke, Luzern **p.175**

⭐ Mount Pilatus **p.181**

⭐ Titlis Rotair, Engelberg **p.183**

Getting to Central Switzerland

The city of Luzern is situated at the centre of this region, and details of how to get there are on p.168.

Getting around Central Switzerland

By Car

The motorway system leads to central Switzerland and also circles the lakes. A regular road runs along the north and east shores of Lake Luzern from the city to Altdorf via Küssnat, and Brunnen, from where the road leads north to Einsiedeln.

By Lake Steamer

The **Lake Lucerne Navigation Company (SGV)**, Vier-waldstättersee, **t** 041 367 67 67, *www.lakelucerne.ch*, offers any number of opportunities to cruise around this splendid and beautiful lake at the heart of central Switzerland.

By Train

With the exception of the direct line between Luzern and Engelberg and the rather roundabout line to Einsiedeln (*see* p.88), trains are of limited use in this region.

Luzern

Besides being one of Switzerland's most attractive cities, Luzern (Lucerne in French) is also famous for the arts. It boasts many fascinating museums and an international Festival of Music that began in 1938 and today attracts music lovers from all over the world. The arcades and cafés of the Reuss River promenades are a lively meeting place, and visitors can browse or shop to their hearts' content in the Old Town. Both the city government and private donors spent large sums renovating Luzern on the occasion of its 800th birthday in 1978. And, if all this was not enough of an attraction, the town benefits from a beautiful location in the heart of Switzerland, at the northern end of the beautiful lake of Luzern (Vierwaldstättersee), with panoramic views of the surrounding Alps.

Tell-Pass Regional Pass for Central Switzerland

Available between 1 April and 31 October from any tourist office or train or boat station, this pass is a necessity for those planning to spend more than two days travelling from Luzern to attractions in central Switzerland such as Pilatus, Titlis Rotair and Rigi, for example (**t** 041 367 67 67, *www.tell-pass.ch*).

It gives you two options: either 2 days' unlimited travel on days of your choice within a 7-day time period or 5 days within a 15-day time period. In either case, you receive a 50% discount for travel on the remaining days.

The cost for the 2-day pass is either CHF 158 or CHF 180 for 1st class. The cost for the 5-day pass is either CHF 210 or CHF 244 for 1st class. You can use your Swiss Pass/Swiss Card to obtain a discount.

Getting to Luzern

By Air
Luzern doesn't have its own **airport**. The nearest ones are at Zürich, Basel and Geneva; these are, respectively, 50mins, 1hr 13mins and 3hrs 17mins away.

By Car
Luzern is situated in the centre of the country and, likewise, is at the centre of a network of motorways connecting the city to all other major Swiss cities, as well as international destinations.

By Train
From Geneva there are direct services and others that incur a change at either/both Bern and Olten; from Bern there are either direct services and others with a change at Olten; from Basel and Zürich there are direct services; from Lugano there are direct services and others with a change at Arth-Goldau; from St Moritz the best services mean changes at Chur and Thalwil; from St Gallen there is a direct service, but a faster one with a change at Zürich.

Getting around Luzern
Everywhere, except the **Verkehrshaus der Schweiz** and the **Richard Wagner Museum** – both accessible by **bus** and **lake steamer**, and the former also by train – is within walking distance.

By Bicycle
Bicycles can be hired at the Bahnhof SBB from **Rent a Bike**, **t** 051 227 32 61, *www.rentabike.ch*.

By Car
While you do not need a **car** to explore Luzern itself, you may want to hire one to explore the region further. There are many car hire companies in the city including **Avis**, Schachenstrasse 38, Kriens Luzern, **t** 041 310 16 16, *www.avis.ch*; **Europcar**, Inseliquai 12, **t** 041 210 57 22, *www.europcar.ch*; **Hertz**, Luzernerstrasse 33, **t** 041 420 02 77, *www.hertz.ch*.

History
The first mention of Luzern, *Luciaria* as it was know at the time, was made in AD 840. Early on it was christened the 'city of lights', a reference to a miracle in which, legend has it, an angel guided its early citizens with a heavenly light to the place where they were to erect a chapel in honour of St Nicklaus, patron saint of sailors and fishermen. Around 1220, this small fishing and monastery village was catapulted to international importance when the opening of the nearby Gotthard Pass facilitated a lucrative trade between the north and south. From that time on, rich merchants, pilgrims, diplomats and messengers either prepared for their journeys or started one from the city of Luzern so that, by 1450, it was home to over 400 inns and restaurants. It was the resulting exposure to a wealth of international influences that endowed this city with its adventurous and outward-looking character and led, in turn, in the 18th century to a great emphasis not only on trade, but on a keen educational awareness of foreign cultures. The 19th-century completion of the European rail network was the key that finally opened the door for travellers from all over the world to discover the charms of Luzern – and many they are.

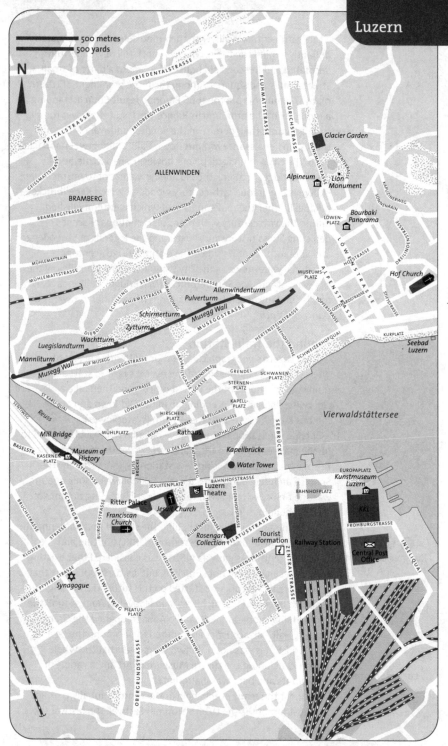

Late 14th-century walls, with their nine defensive towers, stand defiantly behind the town, which is chock-full of wonderfully decorated and frescoed old houses that adorn a maze of small streets, lanes and squares. Among the more prominent of Luzern's many monuments are the 1666 Baroque **Jesuit Church**, standing as a reminder of the profound influence the Jesuits had over the city from 1574 until their demise in the Sonderbund War of 1847, and the Italian Renaissance *rathaus* (town hall), built between 1602 and 1606. The city's main focal points, however, are two medieval covered bridges that link the old and new areas of town: most well known is the unique 14th-century wooden covered **Kapellbrücke** (Chapel Bridge), the roof supports of which were embellished during the 17th century with triangular paintings of scenes depicting Swiss history and illustrating the legends of St Leodegar and St Mauritius. At its side is the distinctive 13th-century octagonal water tower – the city's signature landmark. Below the city walls stands the **Spreuerbrücke** (Mill Bridge), built in 1408; its roof is similarly decorated with a series of paintings known as the *Dance of Death*.

Around the Train Station

Given Luzern's geographical situation, with most places of interest being on either side of the river, it's best to start at the train station – home of the tourist office – and then take a clockwise circular route, ending up in the Old Town and at the famous Kapellbrücke and Wasserturm (Water Tower).

Outside the station is a decorative old arch which, in fact, used to be the main entrance to the station. However, there was a major fire in 1971, and the resulting new station, an innovation by the Spanish architect Santiago Calatrava built between 1984 and 1991, was the first of what proved to be an ever-increasing number of modern buildings in Luzern.

⓯ **Kultur und Kongresszentrum (KKL)**
Europlatz 1, t 041 226 70 70, www.kkl-luzern.ch; guided tours at weekends, except Aug–Sept; adm

The dominant building just behind the station, and bordering the lake, is the **Kultur und Kongresszentrum (KKL)** (Culture and Congress Centre). As early as 1980 it was considered that existing cultural facilities were not sufficient, but it wasn't until 1995 that ground-breaking work was started on this futuristic building designed by the French architect Jean Nouvel. In August 1998 the Berlin Philharmonic, under Claudio Abbado, opened the Grand Concert Hall – its acoustics are reputed to be among the best in the world. But it was not until two years later that the whole complex, including the **Luzern Museum of Art** and a variety of restaurants and bars, was inaugurated.

Luzern Summer Festival
t 041 226 44 00, www.lucernefestival.ch

Amongst the many events held at the centre annually, perhaps the most famous is the **Luzern Summer Festival**. The festival takes place in August and September and is one of the world's leading classical and contemporary music festivals. World-famous orchestras and conductors hold around 30 symphony concerts as well as 60 other events, attended by audiences of over 100,000.

Kunstmuseum Luzern
Europaplatz 1,
t 041 226 78 00,
www.kunstmuseum luzern.ch; open Tues and Thurs–Sun 10–5, Wed 10–9; adm

The **Kunstmuseum Luzern** (Luzern Museum of Art) is an integral part of the centre. This museum's focus is primarily Swiss art from the Renaissance to the present day. It includes works from the early and high Baroque periods, a comprehensive display of 18th-century work and landscape paintings from the 19th century. The early 20th century is represented by the likes of Hodler, Emmenegger and Valloton and, thanks to a donation by Dr Walter and Alice Minnich, the museum received an important collection of Vlaminck, Soutine and Pechstein in 1937. There are also important works from the Swiss 'Art Informed' from the 1950s and 'Zürich Concrete Artists' from the 1980s and 1990s. Also important, is Central Swiss artists' work, such as André Thomkins, Urs Lüthi, Walker and Markowitsch. These, and the museum's international paintings, are not on permanent display, but shown in changing exhibitions.

Old Town

Nearby, just a few minutes' walk to the west, is Luzern's newest museum. You can't miss it as it is a distinguished Empire-style neo-classical structure dating from 1924 that was once home to the Swiss National Bank. Since March 2002, however, it has housed the

Sammlung Rosengart
Pilatusstrasse 10,
t 041 220 16 60,
www.rosengart.ch;
open April–Oct daily 10–6; Nov–Mar daily 11–5; adm

Sammlung Rosengart (Rosengart Collection). This museum displays Angela Rosengart's own collection of over 200 important works by more than 20 world-famous 19th- and 20th-century masters, including Cézanne, Monet, Picasso, Matisse, Klee, Miró and many more. Angela Rosengart, who was born in Luzern in 1932 and still lives here, started working with her father, an art dealer, at age 16 and eventually became a co-owner of the business in 1957. In 1978 she and her father donated seven paintings and a sculpture by Picasso to the city in honour of its 800th anniversary, and these became the foundation of the **Picasso Museum**, which has been substantially added to since. The Picasso Museum was housed in the Am-Rhyn house, one of the city's most beautiful buildings, but it moved to this museum in 2008. Its exhibits include important works created by the artist in the last 20 years of his life and also includes an exhibition of over 200 photos of Picasso by David Douglas Duncan.

Luzerner Theater
Theaterstrasse 2,
t 041 210 33 63,
www.luzerner-theater.ch

Just a block or two north is an area with four more places of interest. The first of these is the **Luzerner Theater** (Luzern Theatre), close to the Chapel Bridge. Luzern has a long theatrical history, with Easter plays being regularly presented in the Weinmarkt as

10

Central Switzerland | Luzern

long ago as the 15th century. In later centuries these took place in the Jesuit Theatre, and in 1838–9 one of the first municipal theatres in Switzerland was built on this spot. In 1924 a fire caused much damage, and only the middle section of the façade facing the Reuss is original.

However, it is the tall, elegant onion-domed façade of the Jesuitenkirche (Jesuit Church) that will attract your attention most. Constructed between 1666 and 1673 and considered to be the first sacred Baroque structure in Switzerland, it is said to be on the site of the first two collegiate churches in Luzern. The main spires are a creation of H. V. von Segesser and date from 1893. It has a rather complex interior design with a beautiful central ceiling painting of St Francis Xavier, a red marble stucco High Altar dating from 1681 and it has the vestments of the famous Swiss, Brother Klaus.

Jesuitenkirche
Bahnhofstrasse 11a,
t 041 210 07 56; open
daily 6am–6.30pm

Directly to the west lies another church with a simpler façade, but a long history. The Franziskanerkirche (Franciscan Church) dates from around 1270 and is considered to be the oldest building in Luzern. Of interest inside is the cycle of flags on the north nave wall and the fresco above the choir arch.

Franziskanerkirche
t 041 210 14 67

Between that and the river is a rather beautiful building that was modelled after the Renaissance palaces of Italian nobility. The **Ritterscher Palast** (Ritter Palace) dates from 1556–7 and is named after the person who began the construction, Mayor Lux Ritter. Originally, this belonged to the Jesuits, but since 1804 it has been utilized as a government building and is now the seat of the Luzern cantonal government. Its main hall was added in 1841–3, and the three-storied Tuscan patio is also of note.

A little farther along the river it is impossible not to notice the strange **Water Spikes** in the middle. Up until the middle of the 19th century the Reuss Steps channelled the water over the city mills. They were then replaced by these mechanical 'spikes', which are lowered by hand to regulate the water flow. These are connected to another wooden river crossing, the **Spreuerbrücke** (Mill Bridge), altogether less pristine than the Chapel Bridge. Completed in 1408 as part of the city's fortifications, it came by its name from the ruling that only chaffs of wheat were to be thrown into the river from this bridge. It is embellished by 67 paintings depicting the *Dance of Death*, which are the work, between 1626 and 1635, of Kaspar Meglinger, and a shrine stands in the middle of the bridge. Interestingly, neither this nor the Chapel Bridge were built to service pedestrian traffic but, rather, to close the gap over the water in the city's walled fortifications.

Before crossing the bridge, though, there is a museum to be explored nearby. The Historiches Museum (Museum of History) is

Historiches Museum
Pfistergasse 24,
t 041 228 54 24,
www.hmluzern.ch;
open Tues–Sun 10–5;
adm

located in the old arsenal and has a wide and interesting range of exhibits detailing the history of Luzern and Switzerland, including a mail shirt of Duke Leopold III from 1386. Visitors receive a scanner – when you scan the barcode by each piece in the collection, information about the piece appears on the screen.

Across the river, the impressive, and remarkably well-preserved, city walls of 860 yards (786m) now beckon – and their formidability is awesome. To get a closer perspective, walk away from the city and then ascend the steep steps by the closest, and quite small, tower. These take you behind the **Museggmauer** (Musegg Wall) where you will note, perhaps with some surprise, that the steep adjacent fields leading up to them are occupied by grazing cows. These walls were built between 1350 and 1408 as part of Luzern's medieval fortifications, and of the nine remaining *türme* (towers), six are quite different from each other. One of these towers, the **Zytturm**, is the proud host of the oldest clock in Luzern, visible from a great distance. The respect endowed upon it by the city is such that it is this clock's privilege to chime one minute before all others. This, the Männli and Schirmer towers and some battlements are open to the public, but only in the summer from 8am to 7pm.

Towards the western end of the walls a memorial chapel and a fountain with a strange, water-emitting head greet you before a pathway, Schirmertoweg, leads under an archway, decorated with two lions and a shield, to the city side of the walls. A little farther to the east Löwenplatz, a strange traffic junction with a combination of old and new structures, is home to the **Bourbaki Panorama**. This is the largest (1,315.6sq yd/1,100sq m) round mural in the world and, painted by Edouard Castres, it depicts the retreat and internment of General Bourbaki's French Eastern Army at Les Verrières in Switzerland during the Franco/German War of 1870–1.

The predominance of tourist shops in what is a less than inspiring area of Luzern signal the presence of three most unusual attractions. The **Löwendenkmal** (Lion Monument) was designed by the classicist Danish sculptor, Thorvaldsen, and was carved in 1820–1 from natural sandstone indigenous to this area by a stonemason from Constance, Ahorn (1789–1856). In addition to agriculture and town crafts, mercenary and military service was an important and gainful trade during the era of the old Confederation, and at the beginning of the French Revolution in 1789, about 40,000 Swiss were serving under foreign banners. The Lion Monument is dedicated to the Swiss mercenaries who were either killed during the invasion of the Tuileries in Paris, seat of Louis XIV, on 10 August 1792 or executed by guillotine on 2 and 3 September 1792 for their part in that heroic but unsuccessful

10

Central Switzerland | Luzern

🎯 **Bourbaki Panorama**
Löwenstrasse 11, t 041 412 30 30, www.panorama-luzern.ch; open April–Oct Mon 1–6, Tues–Sun 9–6; Nov–Mar Mon 1–5, Tues–Sun 10–5; adm

revolt. The inscription *helvitorium fidei ac virtuiti means*, 'to the loyalty and bravery of the Swiss'. Measuring 6.6yd (6m) high by 10.9yd (10m) long, it was dedicated on 10 August 1821 and purchased by the town of Luzern in 1882.

Gletschgarten

Denkmalstrasse 4,
t 041 410 43 40,
www.gletscher
garten.ch; open
April–Oct daily 9–6;
Nov–Mar daily 10–5;
adm

Almost next door, the **Gletschgarten** (Glacier Garden), discovered in 1872, is one of the oldest of natural wonders. Gigantic potholes and rocks carved in the strangest of shapes by the Ice Age, 10,000 years ago, co-exist with fossilized remains from over 20,000,000 years ago when Luzern was a subtropical palm beach. Also to be seen on display are the oldest relief map of Switzerland, a historical model of Luzern, a variety of other geological exhibits and, incongruously, a Hall of Mirrors based on a juxtaposition of aspects of the Alhambra in Granada, Spain. This was created in 1896 for the Swiss National Exhibition in Geneva and has been here since 1899.

Alpineum–3D-
Alpen-Panorama

Denkmalstrasse 11,
t 041 410 62 66,
www.alpineum.ch; open
April–Oct daily 9–12.30
and 1.30–6; adm

The last of the three attractions is the **Alpineum-3D-Alpen-Panorama** (Alpineum–3D-Panorama of the Alps). Although most visitors will have seen or will be seeing the Alps for real themselves, this large and panoramic painting from around 1900 gives a surreal 3D glimpse of Switzerland's most famous peaks.

Back down towards the lake front, you can't miss the imposing façade of the **Hofkirche** (Hof Church). A Benedictine monastery was founded here, with the earliest reference being the year 735, and subsequently a collegiate Romanesque church dedicated to Sts Leodegar and Mauritius was constructed around 1345. However, a fire destroyed most of that in 1633 and only the two distinguished spires – dating from 1504 and 1625 – survived and were incorporated into the new late Renaissance church that was built between 1634 and 1639. In fact, it is the only religious building of late Renaissance times in Switzerland. There is a *Mount of Olives* painting, with late Gothic figures, in a niche on the north tower, and the interior is ornately decorated.

Contrary to popular belief, Switzerland can get quite hot in the summer and the attraction of the cool, crystal-clear waters of the lake has led to a tradition of open-air swimming here. If you look at the lake, in the direction of the Palace hotel, you will see a curious wooden building reached by a creaky footpath. Closer inspection will reveal a genuine Luzern institution, the **Seebad Luzern**. This is the cheapest, and coolest, attraction Luzern has to offer.

Seebad Luzern

Nationalquai, t 041
410 18 12, www.seebad-
luzern.ch; if the weather
is fine it is open daily
May–Sept daily 10–7,
July–Aug from 9; adm

Three squares are of particular note: the **Weinmarkt** is where the citizens of Luzern swore a federal oath with the cantons of Uri, Schwyz and Unterwalden; the **Hirschenplatz** is named after a medieval inn; and the main features of the **Kornmarkt** are the prettily painted Pfistern guildhall and the **Town Hall** (Rathaus). The latter was built in 1602–6 in the Italian Renaissance style, and has a Bern farmhouse roof; the open façade facing the Reuss still serves today as a weekly marketplace.

Lake Cruises

No trip to Luzern is complete without taking a cruise on the beautiful lake. The **Lake Lucerne Navigation Company (SGV)**, Vierwaldstättersee, **t** 041 367 67 67, *www.lakelucerne.ch*, manages Switzerland's largest shipyard right here in the centre of Luzern. There are 35 boat stations spread around the lake, and SGV operate any number of regular routes as well as excursions that leave from the quayside outside the train station.

Kapellbrücke

⊛ Kapellbrücke (Chapel Bridge)

Of course, the main attraction in Luzern is the wooden, covered Kapellbrücke (Chapel Bridge). Named after the nearby St Peter's Chapel, it was built in the early 14th century as part of the city's fortifications. Take time to admire the unusual paintings that adorn its gabled roof. Dating from the 17th century, they are the creations of Heinrich Wägmann and depict representations of Swiss and local history, including the martyrdom of Luzern's two patron saints, Mauritius and Leodegar. Hans Rudolf von Sonnenberg and Renward Cysat wrote the accompanying verses. The **Wasserturm** (Water Tower), dating from the beginning of the 14th century and situated about two-thirds of the way across the bridge, is a formidable 111.5ft- (34m-) tall octagonal stone tower that was originally part of the city wall. Subsequently utilized as an archive, treasury, prison and torture chamber, these days the base – as might be expected – houses a tourist shop. It is also used as the Guildhall of the Artillery Association. The water tower and the bridge have long been the most photographed monuments in Switzerland. However, being made of wood, the bridge has always been susceptible to the danger of fire. And, tragically, that danger materialized in the early hours of 18 August 1993 when a fire destroyed two-thirds of the bridge and 65 of the 111 gable paintings. Sadly, only 30 of the paintings could be restored, though facsimiles supplied by Ilford, the camera/film maker, and made on fadeless Ilfachrome Classic Deluxe materials, have temporarily replaced the originals. The substructure of the bridge was undamaged, however, enabling it to be rebuilt and reopened to the public on 14 April 1994.

Outside Town

There are two more attractions to be found just outside the centre of Luzern, one on the north side of the lake and the other on the south.

Verkehrshaus der Schweiz
Lidostrasse 5, t 041 370 44 44, www.verkehrshaus.ch; open April–Oct 10–6; Nov–Mar 10–5; adm

As the one on the north is closer, and being far more multi-faceted is likely to be of more interest, start with the **Verkehrshaus der Schweiz** (Swiss Museum of Transport and Communication). Take the no. 6, 8 or 24 bus from the centre of Luzern; alternatively you can travel by train or lake steamer.

Opened in 1959, this has evolved into the most diverse museum of its kind in Europe, its exhibitions and collections all related to the development and significance of transport and communication – as well as other attractions. It's a fascinating place, with a varied collection of planes, boats and trains as well as cars, model ships, engines, a space station and even a horse-drawn coach that used to operate as the Grimsel Pass mail coach. The **Planetarium** was opened in 1969 by the astronaut John H. Glenn via the Early Bird news satellite, and over 6.7 million visitors have attended shows since then. The **IMAX Filmtheater** has a 82 x 62ft (25 x 19m) screen – the largest in Switzerland – and uses a 2.75in (70mm) film format; the sound blasts out with 22,000 watt power. The last part of this fascinating museum is perhaps the most unexpected, the **Hans Erni Museum**. Erni, born in 1909, is Switzerland's most popular artist, and made his name in 1939 when he painted *Switzerland, Holiday Land of Nations*, which was exhibited at that year's national exhibition. A dedicated humanist, he has more than 300 of his varied works – paintings, graphic art and sculptures – displayed here, with the most prominent being the *Panta Rhei*, a 86osq ft (8osq m) mural in The Auditorium.

Richard Wagner had been to Luzern several times before, but it was in 1866 that he and his then partner Cosima von Bülow (she was at that time still married to the conductor and pianist Hans von Bülow) discovered a charming, although rundown, villa at Tribschen, a headland on the lake southeast of town. After renovating it, they moved in and stayed until 1872, a period he considered the happiest of his life. During these years not only did he complete *Meistersinger* and *Siegfried* and begin composing *Götterdämmerung*, but *Siegfried Idyll* was first performed as a present to Cosima – by then his wife – on the birth of their son, Siegfried. These days it is home to the **Richard Wagner Museum**. Take the no. 6 or 8 bus to the Wartegg stop or travel by boat – during the summer months – from the quay by the railway station.

Here you will find original manuscripts, scores and paintings as well as other exhibits, and on the upper floor there is a historic collection of rare wind and stringed instruments gathered by Henry Schumacher in the 19th century.

Richard Wagner Museum
Richard Wagner Weg 27, t 041 360 23 70, www.richard-wagner-museum.ch; open mid-Mar–Oct Tues–Sun 10–12 and 2–5; adm

Tourist Information and Services in Luzern

The **Luzern Card** offers unlimited travel on the city's public and local regional transportation facilities, a 50% discount on some museum admission fees, and a variety of other discounts. It can be purchased at the Tourist Information Office, all partner museums and the train station. It costs CHF 10 for 24 hours, CHF 27 for 48 hours and CHF 33 for 72 hours.

(i) Luzern >

*Luzern Tourismus:
Zentralstrasse 5,
t 041 227 17 17,
www.luzern.com; open
April–Oct Mon–Fri
8.30–7.30, Sat–Sun 9–7,
but mid-June–mid-
Sept Mon–Fri
8.30–7.30, Sat–Sun
9–7.30; winter hours
Mon–Fri 8.30–5.30, Sat
9–6, Sun 9–1*

Guided Tour

City Train Luzern: t 041 220 11 00, *www.citytrain.ch*, is one of those ever-popular little 'trains' offering multi-language commentaries on a 40-minute tour of Luzern in April 2, 3; May 11, 12, 1, 2, 3 4; June–Aug 10, 11, 12, 1, 2, 3, 4, 5, 6, 7; Sept 11, 12, 1, 2, 3, 4, 5; Oct 2, 3, 4. Catch it in front of the Hotel Schweizerhof.

Lost Property

Fundbüro, Hirschengraben 17b, **t** 041 208 78 08

Market Days

Fish market: every Tues, Fri and Sat 7–1, Unter der Egg.

Flowers, fruit and vegetables: Tues and Sat mornings alongside the Reuss river.

Flea market: May–Oct on Sat at Burgerstrasse, Reussteg and Ruessplatz.

Handicraft market: April–Nov 7–4, first Sat at Weinmarkt; in Dec there is a Christmas market.

Medical Emergencies

Pharmacy: t 041 211 33 33

Emergency service Luzern: t 041 211 14 14

Festivals in Luzern

Jan: Mozart Days Luzern.

Mid-Feb: Carnival.

Late Mar: Honky Tonk Bar and Restaurant Festival, *www.honky-tonk.ch*.

Late Mar–early April: Luzern Festival Ostern, classical music festival, *www.lucernefestival.ch*.

Early May: FUMETTO, Luzern's Comix-Festival, *www.fumetto.ch*.

June: Corpus Christi Day.

Mid-July–late Aug: Open-Air Cinema Luzern.

Late July: Blue Balls Festival 03, *www.blueballs.ch*.

Mid-Aug: Lucerne Summer Festival, *www.lucernefestival.ch*.

Late Sept: World Band Festival, *www.worldbandfestival.ch*.

Early Nov: Lucerne Blues Festival, *www.bluesfestival.ch*.

Mid-Nov: Comedy Festival.

Late-Nov: Lucerne Festival Piano.

Dec: Barstreet-Festival, every weekend.

Shopping in Luzern

Swiss Lion, Löwenplatz 11, **t** 041 410 61 81, *www.swisslion.ch*. Suitably close to the Swiss Lion monument and in the same building as the Bourbaki Panorama, it has a wide variety of Victorinox knives etc., plus other souvenirs and an extensive selection of fine watches, including AP and Omega.

Where to Stay in Luzern

Luxury

*****Palace Luzern, Haldenstrasse 10, **t** 041 416 16 16, *www.palace-luzern.com*. Located on the shores of the lake, and just 5 minutes' walk from the Old Town. Its eight-storey façade, distinguished by elegant turrets, French windows and balconies, has graced the Luzern skyline since 1906. All of its 168 rooms and suites, whilst still having state-of-the-art technology, radiate an Art Nouveau style with Ionic columns, arched ceilings, intricate tapestries, rich brocades and glittering chandeliers – as do the charming public areas and bars. Its Jasper restaurant is considered the best in town.

*****Schweizerhof-Luzern, Schweizerhofquai, **t** 041 410 29 71, *www.schweizerhof-luzern.ch*. This hotel, built in 1845 and owned by the same family since 1861, has a prime lakeside location. Guests over the years include emperors and empresses, kings and queens and writers and musicians; Tolstoy wrote a book and Wagner completed *Tristan and Isolde* here. The interior reflects 19th-century splendour but rooms have all modern facilities. It has two restaurants and its famous outdoor terrace overlooks the city and lake.

****The Hotel, Sempacherstrasse 14, t 041 226 86 86, www.the-hotel.ch. Situated in a pleasant square, close to the train station, this is a most unusual deluxe boutique hotel. Designed by the French star architect, Jean Nouvel, the 25 studios and suites combine elegance and design with a fascinating interplay of nature (wood) and technology (steel). An extra quirk is that film scenes, of 25 movies from Jean Nouvel's personal background, are projected on to the ceilings.

Expensive

****Art Deco Hotel Montana, Adligenswilerstrasse 22, t 041 419 00 00, www.hotel-montana.ch. This was one of the last classical hotels built in Luzern (in 1909–10), on a hill just behind the Palace Hotel. With the help of the acclaimed Zürich architect Pia Schmid, it has been converted into an Art Deco-style building. Its 62 rooms, ranging from standard to the two acclaimed Tower suites, have a décor that plays on stripes, squares and rectangles combined with warm colours and sharp black and white effects.

****Hôtel Des Balances, Weinmarkt, t 041 418 28 28, www.balances.ch. This is located in the former Guildhall, in a distinguished position in the Old Town, and has an attractively painted façade. The 57 rooms are decorated and equipped to the highest standards; the best are those that overlook the Reuss River, Chapel Bridge and the Jesuit Church.

Moderate

***Krone, Weinmarkt 12, t 041 419 44 00, www.krone-luzern.ch. This is a charming hotel with 25 rooms and four apartments, boasting a great riverside location in the Old Town, a lovely restaurant with a fantastic sun terrace. Offers a high degree of comfort at reasonable rates.

***Gefängishotel Löwengraben, Löwengraben 18, t 041 417 12 12, www.jailhotel.ch. Dating from 1862, this was actually used as a jail until 1998. Some 50 cells have been

transformed into rooms with up to four beds and four suites – much larger and good value – that were once the visitors' room, the jail warden's office, the prison library and the games room.

Inexpensive

***Baslertor, Pfistergasse 17, t 041 249 22 22, www.baslertor.ch. Close to the Jesuit Church, this hotel has 30 rooms mixed as singles, twins and doubles; all have Internet connections and some have air-conditioning. Unusually and refreshingly, it has a nice small pool.

***Weinhof, Weystrasse 10, t 041 410 12 51, www.hotel-weinhof.ch. In the Old Town, close to the Lion Monument, this has modern, if rather small, rooms. It also offers a typical Swiss restaurant and two bowling alleys.

Tourist Hotel Luzern, St Karliquai 12, t 041 410 24 74, www.touristhotel.ch. This fairly basic hotel is located alongside the Reuss River, a short distance behind the town centre. It has 30 rooms in a combination of single, double, 3 and 4 bedrooms as well as a suite for 6. Choose between private or shared bathrooms.

**Goldener Stern, Burgerstrasse 35, t 041 227 50 60, www.goldener-stern.ch. Located in a traditional old building, just across from the Franciscan Church, this is a small, family-run hotel in a fine location with 16 rooms of different sizes.

Pickwick, Rathausquai 6, t 041 410 59 27, www.hotelpickwick.ch. Directly next to the Reuss River, and with its own sun terrace, this is the best located budget hotel in Luzern. Associated with the Pickwick pubs that serve typical pub-style food, this has double-, twin- and three-bed rooms and family room, with some having a balcony; most are en suite.

Rösli, Pfistergasse 12, t 041 249 22 77, www.roesli.ch. Just across the road from – and part of – the Baslertor (it's where you have to check in). Just 6 rooms, and a good economical choice.

Backpackers Lucerne, Alpenquai 42, t 041 360 04 20, www.backpackers lucerne.ch. About 10mins from the station, this has rooms with two beds, two bunks and dormitories for four with bunks female/male mixed. Free kitchen facilities, laundry and a bar with games and books.

Eating Out in Luzern

A local speciality to look for is *Kügelipastete*. This creamed, meat-filled shell is made from a recipe imported by mercenary soldiers who fought in Spain.

Very expensive

Jasper, Haldenstrasse 10, t 041 416 16 16, *www.palace-luzern.com*. Has established itself as one of the best restaurants in Luzern. With its low-intensity Mediterranean minimalist style, it is quite a contrast to the Palace Hotel, of which it is part. The cuisine is sublime. Expect starters like *Gröstel* of octopus with spring onions and dried tomatoes, followed by a main course of duck breast with confit of San Marzanno tomatoes and *chantrelles*. The Jasper Menu consists of three to six courses and there is also a speciality vegetarian menu.

Expensive

Rotes Gatter, Weinmarkt, t 041 418 28 28, *www.balances.ch*. In the Hotel Des Balances, this restaurant has the very best location in Luzern as it is set on a covered private terrace right next to the Reuss River. Chef Andy Fluri creates interestingly mixed menus to match the ambience. The Rotes Gatter Fondue, with veal, maize poulard, lamb entrecôte, king prawns and fillet strips of red mullet, salmon, pike and perch, is an interesting selection for two people. Leave room for *tartes flambées*.

Bam Bou & More, Sempacherstrasse 14, t 041 226 86 86, *www.the-hotel.ch*. As eclectic in style and cuisine as the hotel (The Hotel) it is in. With a definite Asian influence, the menu has a selective range of choices. Try the three home-made snacks – Peking duck roll, Indonesian crêpes and Thai spring rolls for a starter. Followed, maybe, by finely sliced duck, marinated Indonesian-style, and served on wok-fried spaghetti with artichokes and roasted red peppers and Joseph's famous Makhanwalla sauce.

Li Tai Pe, Furrengasse 14, t 041 410 10 23. A particularly fine Chinese restaurant, which has established for itself a great reputation in Luzern that is well deserved indeed. The dishes, well prepared and plentiful, can be ordered à-la-carte or through a selection of menus. Some specialities, including Peking Duck and Braised Whole Carp, must be ordered in advance and reservations are definitely recommended.

Old Swiss House, Löwenplatz 4, t 041 410 61 71, *www.oldswisshouse.ch*. Next to the Lion Monument, in a beautiful house with a wood-partitioned façade that dates from 1859, this restaurant, full of antiques – many of which date from the 17th century – is a Luzern landmark. The house speciality, served by staff in traditional Luzern dress, is a deluxe Wienerschnitzel with veal escalopes dipped in a highly secret mixture of beaten egg, Swiss cheese and herbs. *Open Tues–Sun 9am–12.30am.*

Expensive–moderate

Helvetia, Waldstätterstrasse 9, t 041 210 44 50, *www.helvetialuzern.ch*. Another of the group of restaurants in this part of Luzern, slightly away from the tourist area. Its speciality is home-made pasta cooked daily, along with a fine selection of salads, vegetarian dishes and veal. For dessert they offer some unusual *tartes flambées*. Eat inside or on the square.

Taube, Burgerstrasse 3, t 041 210 07 47, *www.taube-luzern.ch*. In a building over 500 years old that, in 1772, became a restaurant named the Pigeon (Taube). Up until 1998, when it reverted to the Pigeon name, it was known as the Pot of Valais (Walliser Kanne). These days it specializes in popular regional and seasonal dishes.

Moderate

Chill's Food Engineering, Waldstätterstrasse 3, t 041 210 55 00, *www.chills.ch*. A delightful little restaurant that specializes in Thai and Asian cuisine. Look for starters like satay and wonton soup, with curries featuring as main dishes, and such things as fried bananas and coconut ice cream for dessert.

Moderate–inexpensive

Rathaus Brauerei, Unter der Egg 2, **t** 041 410 52 27. A very popular brewery right on the banks of the Reuss near the town hall. The usual food is available – salads, sausages, Bratwurst and French fries, along with filled pretzels, cold and vegetarian dishes. The beer is served in various sizes, including 2-litre bottles to take away.

Bourbaki, Löwenplatz 11, **t** 041 412 16 35. A combination of modern restaurant, bar, bistro and takeaway that is located underneath the Bourbaki Panorama. It has a variety of daily specials, including a vegetarian menu.

Inexpensive

Fischerstube, Mühlenplatz 11, **t** 041 410 99 98. This is a local, apparently working-class, pub, and the favourite of some rather unusual characters.

More of a social experience than a gastronomic one.

Café Bar Salu, Am Helvetiagarten, **t** 041 210 67 77. Another small place on this popular little square that specializes in home-made fresh soups, salads and sandwiches. Make your choices at the bar, and then take them to the outside tables.

Mahlzeit/Barock, Winkelriedstrasse 62, **t** 041 210 08 83. Very small and a little out-of-the-way, but it offers very good deals on couscous, kebabs and falafel.

Entertainment and Nightlife in Luzern

Grand Casino Luzern, Haldenstrasse 6 (next to the Palace Hotel), **t** 041 418 56 56, *www.casinoluzern.ch*. Minimum age 20, CHF 10 adm from 4pm; has American roulette, blackjack, mini punto banco, stud poker, craps and slot machines, as well as a variety of bars and a restaurant. *Open 12pm–4am.*

Pilatus – A Daytrip from Luzern

This trip, the **Goldene Rundfahrt** (Golden Round Trip), encompasses a famous mythical mountain and an impressive array of transportation. Although the distances covered are not particularly great you should plan to dedicate a full day to it in order to enjoy it to the full; all information from the local tourist office (*see* p.182) and from the Luzern tourist office (*see* p.177). As it is a roundtrip it can be taken in either direction, but only if you visit between May and mid-December, as during the winter months the cogwheel railway (*see* p.182) is closed.

Depart from Luzern on the no.1 bus for the 15-minute, 2-mile (3.1-km) trip to Kriens. Follow the signposts to the gondola station, from where a gondola cabin will silently whisk you from Kriens, 1,692ft (516m), through the middle station of Krienseregg at 3,366ft (1,026m), and on to the upper station of Fräkmüntegg, at an altitude of 4,642ft (1,415m). Fräkmüntegg is itself the starting point for numerous hikes, as well as for the longest **toboggan run** in Switzerland that winds back down to the valley. This run is normally open between April and October/November and tickets can be purchased at the gondola car ticket office.

The ultimate stage of the ascent is made by cable car. The distance of 4,557ft (1,389m) is travelled at 21ft (6.5m) a second and is covered in just five minutes. You have now reached your destination, the Pilatus Kulm station at an altitude of 6,791ft (2,070m).

⭐ Mount Pilatus

The first mountain in Switzerland to be given a name, **Mount Pilatus**, the dominant natural landmark of Luzern, stands isolated from the main ranges of the Alps. It is not the prettiest of peaks – in fact it is rather forbidding, both physically and mythically. Despite this, and despite the fact that it is far from being the highest in Switzerland, more has been written about this mountain than any other in the country.

Legend has it that in the lake on this 'mountain of dragons' are interred the remains of the Roman Governor Pontius Pilate – hence, its name. The legend goes on to tell that his anguished spirit surfaced annually, on Good Friday, in an unsuccessful attempt to cleanse his bloodied hands. Long before Pilate lived, however, this mountain, then known as the Broken Mountain (Fraactus Mons), was believed to be inhabited by dragons, which could be either benevolent or terrifying. Numerous stories have been told of these flame-spitting, flying creatures, and of a dragon-stone, said to be endowed with miraculous healing powers. There is also a legend of the *Modmilchloch* (Moon Milk), which was considered a universal cure for the infirmities of mankind.

The sum total of these myths led the government of Luzern to declare Pilatus a 'forbidden' mountain, with even the local shepherds placed under oath that they would not approach the waters of the lake. In 1585, however, a determined parish priest from Luzern and some brave citizens ascended Pilatus. Their goal was the exorcism of the spirits there. In continuation of the purgation begun by their mission, the lake, believed to be a home of spirit beings, was completely drained in 1594. It remained a dry bed for 400 years, until it was dammed again in 1980.

The views from Pilatus are absolutely magnificent: a horizon of glorious mountain peaks and glaciers, Lake Luzern (known locally as Vierwaldstättersee) and its tributary rivers glistening below. This scene is enchanting, but is especially remarkable at sunset and sunrise, so you may want to think about spending a night at one of the hotels on the mountain (*see* p.182).

On the terrace at the Hotel Pilatus Kulm, you will no doubt be enchanted by the black birds with bright yellow beaks and red feet, which can be so tame that they will take food directly from your hand. The *Täche* (mountain crows) are found all over Switzerland

10

Central Switzerland | Luzern: Pilatus – A Daytrip from Luzern

Tourist Information in Pilatus

ⓘ Pilatus >
Pilatus-Bahnen:
Schlossweg 1,
t 041 329 11 11,
www.pilatus.ch

The tourist office supplies information about this trip, as well as accommodation, restaurants and hikes.

Where to Stay on Pilatus

Hotel Bellevue, t 041 329 12 12 (*moderate*). Built in the shape of a circle and perched precariously on the ridge of the mountain. Each of the comfortably furnished double rooms has private bath or shower, toilet and TV.

Hotel Pilatus Kulm, t 041 329 12 12 (*moderate*). The smaller of the two, with a less dramatic location. It is also more basic; the double rooms have hot and cold running water, but showers and toilets are located within separate rooms on each floor.

Eating Out on Pilatus

Trendrestaurant Express, Hotel Bellevue, **t** *as above* (*moderate*). The setting is an original cogwheel railway carriage, and fresh pasta is the speciality here.

Panorama-Restaurant, Hotel Pilatus-Kulm, **t** *as above* (*inexpensive*). Offers traditional Swiss cuisine along with unique views of the mountains.

Spiesshüsli, Hotel Pilatus-Kulm **t** *as above* (*inexpensive*). Situated on an open-air terrace, this is the ideal choice for a quick snack such as a tasty Bratwurst sausage and a refreshing beer.

and tend to live at high altitudes. When they go down to the lower villages it is a warning that snow is on the way.

Pilatus is the starting point for numerous hikes, and you may, if you are very fortunate, catch a glimpse of an elusive chamois perched precariously on a cliff face or come face-to-face with a shy marmot.

The journey back to Luzern is attractive, too. As long ago as 1889, a remarkable **cogwheel railway**, which operates on a rack and pinion system, opened between Pilatus Kulm at 6,791ft (2,070m) and Alpnachstad at 1,430ft (436m) on the shores of Lake Luzern. This dramatic trip along the mountainside, which takes 30 minutes when ascending and 40 minutes when descending, still retains the distinction of being the steepest rack railway in the world – with an average gradient of 42 per cent and a maximum of 48 per cent. Down at Alpnachstad you can choose between a quick 20-minute return to Luzern on the Brünig railway or a 70-minute cruise across the lake.

Engelberg

The Engelberg valley was civilized in 1120 when Baron Konrad von Sellenbüren of Zürich founded a Benedictine monastery that was soon renowned for its scientific and artistic activity. The history of the valley and the monastery remained inexorably entwined, with

Getting to Engelberg

By Car
Engelberg is at the end of a valley that can only be accessed by exiting the A2 motorway south of Luzern, near Pilatus, at the Stans-Süd exit then following signs to Engelberg for approx. 20km (12.5 miles).

By Train
Engelberg is at the end of a branch line from Luzern and this is the only way to reach the resort by train. An hourly service from Luzern is operated by **Zentralbahn t** 051 228 85 85, 0900 300 300 (recorded timetable information), *www.zentralbahn.ch*.

Getting around Engelberg

The centre of Engelberg is small enough to walk around comfortably, but from late June to mid-Oct a **shuttle bus** runs every half-hour from the railway station to the village. The service is free with a Guest Card or if you have a train ticket; small charge payable without.

Engelberg retaining its status as a 'state in miniature', under spiritual auspices, up to the time of the French Revolution. Suitably, two brothers from the monastery were the first to climb Mount Titlis in 1744 (forty years before Mont Blanc was conquered).

However, it wasn't until the middle of the 19th century that Engelberg was commercially developed as a summer tourist resort, with winter sports facilities added at the beginning of the 20th century. Initially, in 1913, a funicular was opened between Engelberg and Gerschnialp, and fourteen years later the first aerial cable car in Switzerland, connecting Gerschnialp and Trübsee, began operation. In the mid-1960s this was extended from Trübsee to the top of Titlis itself. Engelberg's main claim to international fame, though, originates from 1992, when the Rotair, the world's first revolving cable car, was installed between Stand and Titlis.

Titlis Rotair

 Titlis Rotair
t 041 639 50 50,
www.titlis.ch; open
8.30–5 daily, last ascent
3.40pm, last descent
4.50pm; closes for 2 wks
in Nov for maintenance

Engelberg's **Titlis Rotair** not only provides the highest viewpoint in central Switzerland but also, much more innovatively, is the first revolving cable car in the world. Beginning on the valley floor at an altitude of 3,280ft (1,000m), a gondola car glides across the lower pastures and rises up to the first stage, Gerschnialp, at 4,265ft (1,300m), and then continues up to Trübsee at 5,905ft (1,800m). Here you must make a change onto a cable car that whisks you up to Stand – 8,038ft (2,450m) – in just five minutes, and then there's the final leg from Stand to Titlis, at 9,908ft (3,020m).

Deciding that a spectacular ride over glacier falls and ice crevices among craggy mountain peaks was not sufficiently exciting, the authorities decided to add another thrilling aspect to the last five minutes of the trip. In 1993 the installation of two revolving Rotair cable cars was completed, and these were – and still are – a worldwide innovation. The mechanism used is similar to that of revolving restaurants: shortly after the trip begins the cabin floor begins to revolve, leaving only a central podium and the walls fixed. Thus, the spectacular alpine scenery all around you may be viewed from an unparalleled variety of angles. Certainly, this is quite an experience, but a vertiginous one for those not blessed with a head for heights.

At the summit there is a wealth of things to do. In addition to the ever-captivating views that reach out over the Alps and, on a clear day, to the Black Forest in Germany, there are numerous restaurants plus the Ofenbar, considered the highest in Europe. Relax on the sun terrace of the wind-protected Toporama, or take a walk into the **Glacier Grotto** that traverses into the highest point of the Titlis Glacier. You will find that the temperature inside the grotto varies only between -1 and -1.5°C (30.2 and 29.3°F), regardless of the outside conditions. The more adventurous may opt for a walk out onto the glacier, or even take the **Ice-Flyer** chairlift down to the unique **Glacier Ice Park** (closed till May 2010) and slide down the slopes on snow tubes or other unusual sledges.

On the descent to the valley some may be tempted to stop at **Trübsee**, where, in the summer months and weather permitting, there are enchanting horse-drawn carriage rides around idyllic Lake Trübsee. Most visitors will finish their trip to Titlis the easy way, by taking the gentle gondola ride back down to Engelberg. But a more unusual way to descend is to rent a Trotti bike, actually more like an old-fashioned scooter, which can be used on the descent from Gerschnialp to Engelberg. But remember, cows have the right of way!

Other Attractions

The journey up to Titlis is an exciting trip, and certainly will be the highlight of a visit to Engelberg; those coming for a daytrip, or even staying overnight, will be satisfied with going up Titlis and then spending some time in the pleasant village. However, Engelberg – the largest summer and winter resort in central Switzerland – has much more to offer in either season, including other cable and gondola cars. In summer, you can explore over 224 miles (360km) of marked **walking and hiking paths**, many more miles of mountain bike trails and a wide variety of outdoor activities. In winter, downhill and cross-country **skiers** have the run of over 28 miles (45km) of marked ski pistes and 25 miles (40km) of cross-country tracks. Other facilities include a sledge and toboggan run, and indoor pool.

Tal Engelberg Museum
t 041 637 04 14; open Mon–Sun 2–6; adm

Benediktinerkloster
Wed–Sat 10–4; film show Wed at 10; adm

Schaukäserei Kloster Engelberg
t 041 638 08 88, www.schaukaeserei-engelberg.ch; open daily 9–6.30, Sun and hols till 5; cheese production 11–5

Alpkaserie Gerschnialp
Gerschnialp, t 079 431 52 45; reservations essential; adm plus towel hire

In either season learn more about the history and life of the high alpine valleys at the **Tal Engelberg Museum**. Arrange, by appointment, a guided tour in English of the **Benediktinerkloster** (Benedictine Monastery), and its famed library. Or visit Switzerland's only demonstration dairy operated in a monastery, **Schaukäserei Kloster Engelberg**.

The **Alpkaserie Gerschnialp** (Alpine Dairy) offers something a little different: a whey bath, big enough for two, set up in a pasture at the foot of the Titlis. This dairy is about a 45-minute uphill hike from the centre of the village or take the gondola car and get off at the first stop, Gerschnialp. Whey contains vitamins and minerals and is thought to aid healthy skin, hair and nails. A by-product of cheese-making, the whey is pumped directly from the factory and is pleasantly warm. After taking a shower in the changing room, next to the bath, just lay back and relax among the alpine scenery. Most probably the most unusual and most memorable bath you will ever experience.

Tourist Information and Services in Engelberg

(i) **Engelberg >**
Engelberg Titlis Tourismus AG: Klosterstrasse 3, t 041 639 77 77, www.engelberg.ch

The tourist information centre can provide all of the necessary information on the many activities available in the area including **skiing, snowboarding, hiking, cycling, Nordic walking, golf, pony riding** and many more.

Shopping in Engelberg

R. Blatter, t 041 639 50 39, is a delightful souvenir shop that has been run by the same family for four generations and nearly 100 years. Besides stocking everything you would expect and more, the son is an expert woodcarver (having trained at Huggler in Brienz) and his father is a wood-turner, and their handiwork is on sale.

Cristallina Sport, Titlis-Zentrum, t 041 637 11 78, and Dorfstrasse 39, t 041 637 01 41, www.cristallina-sport.ch. Has all the equipment you need to rent for either skiing or snowboarding, a snowboard test-centre as well as a wide range of clothes and hiking boots.

Bike'n Roll, Dorfstrasse 31, t 041 638 02 25, www.bikenroll.ch. Offers crossroad, hardrail, full suspension and freeride bikes, as well as children's bikes, for rent by the hour or day, and also organizes bike tours.

Where to Stay in Engelberg

****Ramada Hotel Regina Titlis**, Dorfstrasse 33, t 041 639 58 58, www.ramada.com (*moderate*). A modern hotel with 128 rooms, located right in the centre of the village; has a Swiss/Italian restaurant and the lively Regina Bar.

***Edelweiss**, Terracestrasse 10, t 041 637 07 37, www.edelweissengelberg.ch (*moderate*). A few minutes from the centre, this charming, family-run hotel offers 43 well-equipped rooms and spacious public areas.

Eating Out in Engelberg

No visit to Engelberg is complete without taking lunch or refreshment at the top of Titlis. Outlets include the à la carte **Titlis Stübli**, the **Mamma Mia** pizzeria, the **Panorama Self-**

service Restaurant, **Sandwich Bar** and the **Ice Cream Boutique**.

Schaukäserei Bistro, Klosterhof, **t** 041 638 08 88, *www.schaukaeserei-engelberg.ch* (*moderate*). This bistro is located within the famous cheese-making factory. The speciality, of course, is cheese dishes, along with salads, cakes and tarts.

Duke's Restaurant, Bahnhofstrasse 7, **t** 041 637 02 73, *www.dukes-restaurant.ch* (*expensive–moderate*). One of the smallest restaurants in Engelberg. It serves a wide variety of international cuisine using quality, fresh ingredients. *Open all day Tues–Sun.*

Lake Geneva Region

Lake Geneva (Lac Léman) is located in the far southwest of Switzerland and is the country's largest lake. Geneva – on clear days dominated by Mont Blanc in France – wraps around the lake in the far southwestern corner and is the most important place along its shores. Between Geneva and Lausanne, to the northeast, the scenery on the Swiss side doesn't have too many points of interest but looking through the haze of the lake towards France there are beautiful snow-covered peaks on the horizon.

After Lausanne the uneven patterns of the Lavaux vineyards dominate almost to Vevey/Montreux. Just inland from Montreux is the quaint village of Gruyères, famous of course for its cheese. As the lake narrows towards the Valais region more and more Swiss peaks appear leading to Les Diablerets, where there is a whole array of activities on offer no matter what the season.

11

Don't miss

1 European HQ
United Nations, Geneva **p.202**

2 Relive the records and runs
Musée Olympique, Lausanne **p.213**

3 Island castle
Château de Chillon **p.218**

4 Medieval cheese-making village
Gruyères **p.223**

5 Panorama of peaks
Les Diablerets, Glacier 3000 **p.226**

See map overleaf

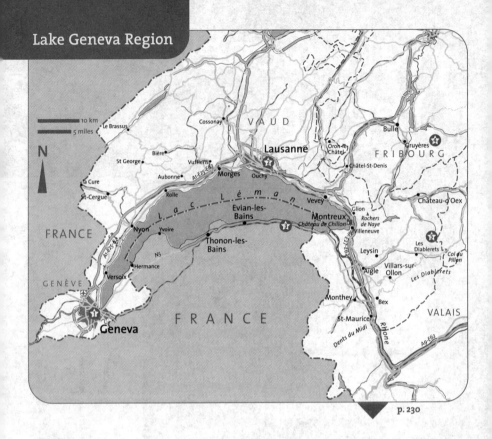

p. 230

Don't miss

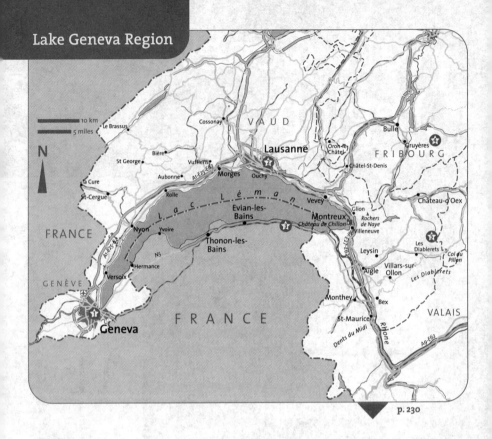 United Nations, Geneva **p.202**

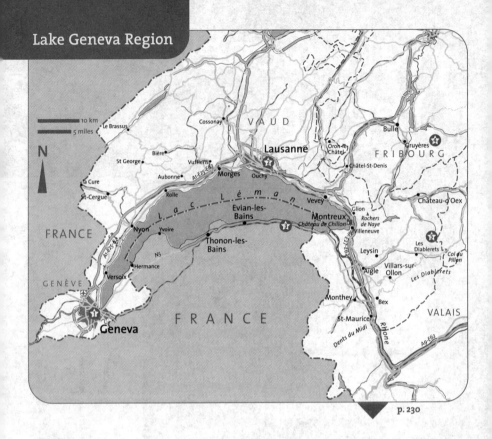 Musée Olympique, Lausanne **p.213**

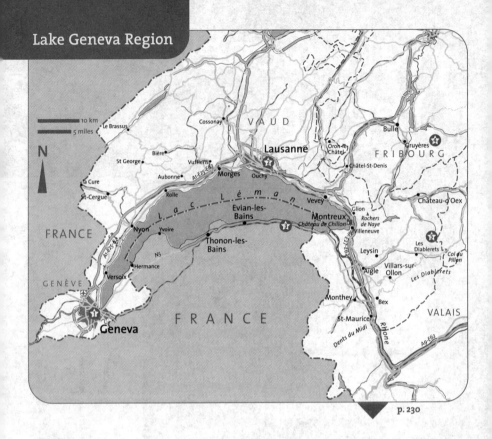 Château de Chillon **p.218**

 Gruyères **p.223**

 Les Diablerets, Glacier 3000 **p.226**

Geneva

Geneva – Genève in French and Genf in German – has a marvellous location at the southwestern end of Lake Geneva (known locally as Lac Léman) surrounded by mountains, particularly the grand but elusive Mont Blanc, and is blessed by a genial climate. It also has a history of welcoming foreigners. It is no wonder, then, that politicians, ambassadors and royalty, not to mention affluent businessmen – a group never prone to self-denial – found themselves attracted by the city's charms. As far back as 1864 Geneva initiated its role in international diplomacy by becoming the home of the International Red Cross, founded by the Swiss Henri Durant. This role was extended greatly after the First World War, when the city was chosen as the site for the headquarters of the League of Nations, and later, after the Second World War, as the European headquarters of the new United Nations organization. These days it is home to over 200 international organizations, one-third of the population – of 180,000 – emanates from 157 different nations. Consequently, Geneva is far and away the most cosmopolitan city in Switzerland, and an interesting side product is the abundance of restaurants offering a tasteful array of international cuisine. The downside for tourists is that with such a community of super-rich international diplomats, civil servants and tax exiles, there is a demand for expensive hotels, restaurants and shops. As a consequence, the city has a reputation for being somewhat expensive. However, in return, it has gained affluence and a cosmopolitan ambience – a fascinating combination considerably enhanced by a decidedly Gallic flair. Art and culture flourish here, too; Geneva hosts more than 40 museums, plus numerous art galleries, exhibiting a variety of prestigious collections, and is justly proud of its musical conservatories and opera.

As it is the place where the lake – the largest freshwater one in western Europe – flows speedily into the Rhône, the city is effectively cut into two parts. The left bank of Geneva is dominated by the Old Town and its cathedral topping the hill, and is also home to many museums, an upmarket shopping area and the Jardins Anglais and the Jet d'Eau, both set alongside the lake. The right bank is home to the Cornavin train station, and between that and the lake it has its own shopping areas as well as the majority of the city's hotels and ethnic restaurants. Alongside the lake, there are numerous five-star hotels, piers for lake steamers and, slightly farther away, wonderful parks that lead to the botanic gardens and the United Nations complex, and a couple of museums.

Owing to its geographical location, squeezed into a tight corner of Switzerland and rather surrounded by France, there aren't many

Getting to Geneva

By Air

International flights from Europe, North America and worldwide arrive at **Geneva's International Airport**, **t** 022 717 71 11, *www.gva.ch*, which is 5km from the city centre. You can take a **train** from the station within the airport to Geneva Cornavin station, journey time 6mins, or travel on the no. 5 or 10 bus.

By Car

The A1 motorway runs from St Gallen, Winterthur and Zürich, picking up the motorway from Basel on the way to Bern, Lausanne and Geneva. From the Valais the A9 motorway runs around Lake Geneva to Lausanne where it joins with the A1 motorway on to Geneva.

By Train

There are mainline connections from St Gallen, Winterthur, Zürich, Basel, Bern and Lausanne to Geneva Cornavin station and on to the airport. From the Valais and beyond mainline trains run via Aigle, Montreux, Vevey and Lausanne to Geneva Cornavin station and on to the airport.

Getting around Geneva

Public transport in and around Geneva is convenient and efficient. However, most places, with the exception of the area around the United Nations, are within walking distance.

By Bicycle

Genèveroule, Place de Montbrillant, **t** 022 740 13 43, *www.geneveroule.ch*, offers bike rentals or free bike loan for 4 hours at five centres in the city. Open May–Oct daily 8–9, Nov–April Mon–Sat 8–6.

By Mini-Train

STT Trains Tours, **t** 022 781 04 04, *www.sttr.ch*, operate several tours of which the most popular are: Old Town, International and Panoramic, both departing from the place du Rhône; and the Parks and Residences tour departing from the quai du Mont Blanc.

By Boat

Mouettes Genevoises Navigation, quai du Mont Blanc 8, **t** 022 732 29 44, *www.mouettesgenevoises.ch*, operate the ever-popular little yellow ferryboats that run on four routes in the inner harbour area. Tickets cost CHF 2 for one journey and CHF 3 valid for 1 hour.

Compagnie Générale de Navigation sur le Lac Léman (CGN), **t** 0848 811 848, *www.cgn.ch*, operates services to cities and towns in both Switzerland and France up and down the whole length of the lake, and they set sail from the quai du Mont-Blanc (however the train is a better option for many of the more distant places).

---

opportunities for easy, short trips – other than to Yvoire – outside Geneva. That doesn't present a problem, however, as there is more than enough to see and do in this delightful and interesting city to keep anyone occupied for at least three days, or even more.

History

The geographical location of Geneva, set in the far southwestern corner of Lac Léman where the fast-flowing River Rhône leaves the lake and continues its meandering way to the Mediterranean, has made it a strategically important site for thousands of years. There is evidence of human occupancy around the shores of Lake Geneva, as the locals prefer to call it, dating back to around 3,000 BC. It is likely, though, that it wasn't until nearly 500 BC that the Celtic

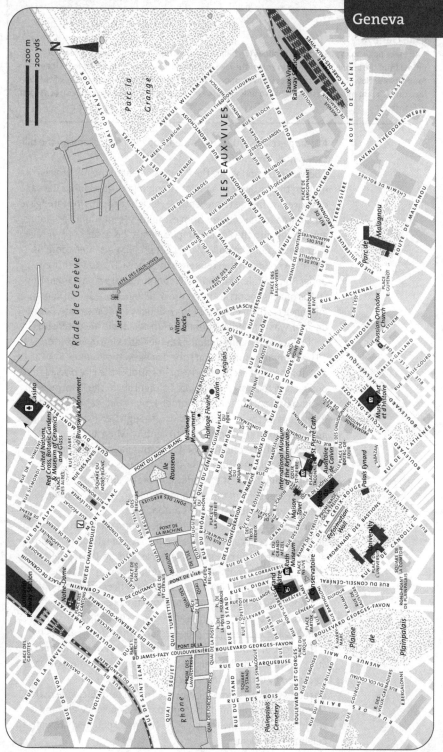

Lake Geneva

The lake holds 19,577,263,102,000 gallons (89 billion m³) of water, which represents 11 years of inflow from the Rhône at the eastern end of the lake. Therefore, it also takes that long to fill it and for the water flowing in to travel the relatively short distance down to Geneva. The surface of the lake covers 223sq miles (582sq km) – 134sq miles (348sq km) in Switzerland and 90sq miles (134.3sq km) in France.

Allobroges clan settled in the area, and built a stockade on the hill that is now the Old Town.

Between 122 and 120 BC the Romans defeated the Allobroges, making the settlement a major stronghold. In 58 BC Julius Caesar destroyed its bridge to prevent the Helvetic people, who later gave their name to the country, from escaping the invading Barbarians and fleeing into the Roman Empire. In fact, his account of the event in *Comments on the Gallic Wars*, penned six years later, contains the first known written reference to Geneva. The town thrived under Roman rule, and shortly before AD 400 it was awarded the status of a bishopric, at the centre of a huge diocese. The Roman influence is still in evidence today: Geneva's oldest square, Bourg-de-Four, was formerly a Roman Forum, and there are extensive, well-restored remains underneath the Cathedral of St Pierre.

The Germanic Burgundian tribe displaced the Romans in AD 443 and, for the next six hundred years, control of the city passed from one faction to another. From the 11th century to the Reformation, Geneva was part of the Holy Roman Empire, yet was governed by its bishops as their own seigneury. Although Geneva didn't gain any real importance until the 15th century, when its trade fairs placed it on the world's map, it was continually under threat from the neighbouring House of Savoy. The attacks were particularly strong during the first three decades of the 16th century, when reinforcements from the cantons of Fribourg and Bern were necessary to preserve the city's autonomy.

The year 1536 saw the triumph of the Reformation, and Geneva attained the political status of a republic. A year later Jean Calvin arrived to live in the city and, under his leadership, the republic was elevated to 'Mother of the Protestant Church'. From that time forward large numbers of Protestants, many fleeing persecution in neighbouring countries, found their way to Geneva, establishing it as a city of faith and learning. These influences led, in 1559, to Calvin founding the Academy, the predecessor of the current university.

The night of 11 December is the anniversary of an event that is still commemorated in Geneva to this day. On this date in 1602, forces led by Charles-Emmanuel, Duke of Savoy, tried unsuccessfully to storm the city. The French term *Escalade* makes reference to this ill-fated attempt to scale Geneva's walls, and is the name given to the three-day festival weekend held annually to celebrate the event.

The 18th and 19th centuries were periods of prosperity for Geneva, as it blossomed into an important centre for industry – particularly watchmaking, commerce, banking, arts, medicine and science. Among its more prominent citizens of that era were Jean-Jacques Rousseau, Voltaire and the biologist Charles Bonnet. In 1798 French troops entered and annexed Geneva (where Napoleon stopped for one night on 9 May 1800) and it remained a part of France until the defeat of the French forces resulted in its freedom on 31 December 1813. Determining the time to be right, Geneva joined the Swiss Confederation and became a canton on 19 May 1815. Yet another, and the last to date, revolution took place in 1846, when James Fazy overturned the government of the Restoration; the new constitution forged from that conflict is still in use today.

Old Town

The Old Town in Geneva is full of character, and there are numerous attractions among the many boutiques, antique shops, restaurants and bars. The most important is the **Cathédrale St Pierre** (Cathedral of St Peter). The cathedral was built between 1160 and 1232 and is somewhat of an architectural hybrid, with elements of Romanesque, Gothic and Graeco-Roman styles. Although of grand proportions, it reflects the effects of the Reformation, like most churches in Switzerland, and is rather austere inside. Enlightened by beautiful stained-glass windows, the main attractions are the amazingly intricate tomb of the Duke of Rohan, leader of the French Protestants who died in 1638, the cleverly sculptured stone choir and Calvin's chair. The tower, with its 157 steps, affords marvellous views of Geneva. Visitors wanting to investigate the art from the cathedral more fully should visit the **Musée d'Art et d'Histoire** (Museum of Art and History) (see p.196).

Do not leave, however, before exploring underneath the cathedral, where you will find one of the largest European subterranean archaeological sites open to the public, the **Site Archéologique de la Cathédrale St Pierre** (Archaeological Site of St Peter's Cathedral). The size and array of exhibits is most impressive, and includes the portal of the old Romanesque cathedral dating from 1000 and other items dating back as far as AD 350.

Just outside the cathedral is the **Musée International de la Réforme** (International Museum of the Reformation). Here you will find manuscripts and portraits of both Genevese personalities and people linked with Geneva covering four centuries of history, and documents of all kinds relating to the international Reformation movement. An underground passageway connects it with the archaeological site underneath the cathedral and the cathedral tower.

The rather austere, but not unattractive, building on the corner of the place de la Taconnerie, just across from the cathedral, is worth

Cathédrale St Pierre
cours Saint-Pierre; open June–Sept Mon–Sat 9.30–6.30, Sun 12–6.30; Oct–May 10–5.30; adm for tower

Site Archéologique de la Cathédrale St Pierre
cours Saint-Pierre, t 022 310 02 05, www.site-archeologique.ch; open Tues–Sun 10–5; adm

Musée International de la Réforme
rue de Cloître 4, t 022 310 24 31, www.musee-reforme.ch; open Tues–Sun 10–5; adm

11

Lake Geneva Region | Geneva

**Auditoire
de Calvin**
*place de la
Taconnerie,*
t 022 909 70 00;
open Mon–Sat 10.30–12
and 2–5

some attention. This is the historic **Auditoire de Calvin**. There used to be a 5th-century church here that was built over the Roman walls, but that burnt down in the 11th century. It was replaced in the 13th century by a parish church – of which some traces can be seen in the present nave – which, in turn, was replaced by this small, Gothic-style chapel that dates from the 15th century. At the beginning of the Reformation the building was deprived of its name, and even its use as a church. However, reformers and reformed exiles from many other European countries didn't just gather here to pray in their own language – as some, like the Church of Scotland and the Dutch and Italian Reformed Churches do today – but also listened to prominent Reformers such as Calvin, Knox and de Bèze. Between 1556 and 1559 British refugees led by John Knox printed a new English translation of the Bible here – the first with explanatory notes – known as the Geneva or Breeches Bible, which was largely used in the preparation of the King James Authorized Bible. The Auditory was also the heart of the university; John Calvin and his successors lectured here for 200 years, hence its name meaning Calvin's lecture theatre.

Just around the corner is the **Hôtel de Ville** (town hall), originally constructed in the 15th century – the Tour Badet is the only remnant from that era – but with substantial additions over the next two centuries. It is the administrative seat of Geneva's government, and boasts international connections, too. In 1864 the First Geneva Convention on the Red Cross met here. Eight years later the international arbitration between the USA and Great Britain to resolve their 'Alabama' dispute was held in what is now known as the 'Alabama Room', and on 15 November 1920 the initial assembly of the League of Nations met here. Note the unusual square ramp of the staircase that enabled horsemen to ride the three floors without dismounting, and provided access for sedan chairs and their like.

Back outside, and actually more striking, is the building directly across from the town hall. On the open ground-floor area stand five original cannon, three with wheels and two without, that date from the 17th and 18th centuries. Once part of Geneva's artillery, they give a strong clue as to one of the building's former uses. Though built as a granary in the 15th century, it was converted for use as an armoury in 1720 and was used for that purpose until 1877, hence the name **Arsenal**. The three mosaics adorning the walls behind the cannons, by Alexandre Cingria in 1949, depict the arrival of Julius Caesar in Geneva, Middle Ages fairs at the Bourg-de-Four and the arrival of the Huguenot refugees in the city. The rooms above the wooden-beamed ceiling serve as the state archives. If you happen to be in Geneva during the *Escalade* festivities in

December, make a point of coming here to buy some vegetable soup, which is sold in commemorative bowls.

Maison Tavel
rue du Puits-Saint-Pierre 6,
t 022 418 37 00;
open Tues–Sun 10–5;
adm temporary
exhibitions

Just a short walk from the cathedral is the Maison Tavel (Tavel House). This was originally constructed by the Tavel family as their private residence during the 12th century, and is the oldest private house in Geneva. With the exception of the cellars, however, it was destroyed by a fire in 1334 and rebuilt by the Tavels, who proceeded to make it a combination of fortified mansion and urban palace. Subsequently owned by eminent local families over the centuries, it was acquired by the City of Geneva in 1963. Tastefully restored, from the cellars to the attic, it is now devoted – by way of objects, drawings, photographs, furniture and other such exhibits – to demonstrating the daily life of urban Geneva from the Middle Ages to the early 20th century. One of the highlights is the Magnin Model, a huge scale model that reconstructs how Geneva looked, including the fortifications, before the 1850s.

Don't leave the Old Town before taking a break in the **place du Bourg-de-Four**. This square has traditionally been one of the city's main meeting places, starting in the Roman era, carrying on through Middle Ages fairs and into the present day. A strange bronze statue of a nymph welcomes you on arrival. Take a seat at one of the many cafés to soak up the atmosphere, and admire, too, marvellous examples of 16th-, 17th- and 18th-century architecture, the façade of the Palais de Justice and the 18th-century fountain. As a bonus, you may get a sighting of the towering waters of the Jet d'Eau fountain, if you happen to look down rue Verdaine.

Place Neuve, Promenade des Bastions and Surrounding Museums

The place Neuve is best reached from the Old Town by way of the rampe de Treille, dating from the 16th century. Yes, *rampe* does mean 'ramp', and it is quite steep too; but the chestnut trees offer considerable shade and the architectural characteristics of the houses to the right provide an interesting diversion. The long, rectangular promenade at the top, embellished with a statue of the diplomat Pictet de Rochemont (1755–1824), instrumental in the Treaty of Paris in 1814 and the Congress of Vienna in 1815, offers an ideal vantage point from which to gain a better perspective of the place Neuve and Promenade des Bastions below, and the surrounding hills in the distance. This should give a clue to its earlier use as an observation and artillery post for the defence of Geneva. Interestingly, one of the trees is Geneva's 'official' chestnut tree, and tradition dictates that its first blossoming marks the arrival of spring.

The **place Neuve** is a square new in name but older in character. Located just outside the city walls, it is surrounded by some

Musée Rath
place Neuve 2,
t 022 418 33 40; open
Tues, Thurs, Fri, Sat, Sun
10–5, Wed 12–9; adm

memorable buildings and has become something of a focal point of Genevese culture. The Musée Rath (Rath Museum) is considered to be the first building in Switzerland dedicated to exhibiting the fine arts. It was donated as a gift to the people of Geneva by two sisters, Jeanne-Françoise and Henrietta Rath, and is housed in an impressive building combining French taste and Italian style. There are no permanent exhibitions, as this museum specializes in temporary exhibitions of international and Swiss art.

Grand Théâtre
boulevard du Théâtre
11, t 022 418 30 00,
www.geneveopera.ch

Conservatoire de
Musique de
Genève
boulevard Saint-
Georges 36

To its right are two other delightful buildings. First is the Grand Théâtre, Geneva's opera house that was inspired by the Paris Garnier Opéra and inaugurated in 1879. In 1951 it was destroyed by fire, but after a 10-year restoration it re-opened grander than ever. Then comes the Conservatoire de Musique de Genève, a delightful Byzantine-style building decorated with muses and antique divinities, that was constructed between 1856 and 1858. In the centre of the square stands an equestrian statue of Genevese **Général Henri Dufour**, a national hero and cartographer of the first geographical map of Switzerland.

Take a few moments, now, to explore the **Promenade des Bastions**, chosen in 1816 as the site of Geneva's first botanical gardens. Although that garden is now officially housed elsewhere, lovely plants and trees remain as testimony to its former role. However, the most important thing here is built into the ramparts of the Old Town. Construction of the 492ft (150m) **Mur des Réformateurs** (Reformation Wall) began in 1909 to mark the 400th anniversary of the birth of Jean Calvin and the 350th anniversary of the foundation of the Academy of Geneva. At its centre, at a height of 16½ft (5m) each, are statues of the four great figures of the Reformation: **Guillame Farel** (1489–1565), one of the first to preach the Reformation in Geneva; **Jean Calvin** (1509–64), the leader of the Reformers; **Théodore de Bèze** (1513–1605), the first rector of the Academy of Geneva, and **John Knox** (1513–72), the founder of Presbyterianism in Scotland. Behind them you will read the motto of both the Reformation and Geneva, *Post Tenebras Lux* – After the Darkness, the Light: 'darkness' referring to the times before the Reformation and 'Light' to those after, when they believed the Bible was finally understood. To each side, there are further statues and reliefs of important Protestant figures of the many Calvinist countries, and crucial moments in the development of the Reformation.

Musée d'Art et
d'Histoire
rue Charles-Galland 2,
t 022 418 26 00,
www.ville-ge.ch/mah;
open Tues–Sun 10–5

Back around the Promenade des Bastions, on the other side of the Old Town, is another museum and an interesting church. The Musée d'Art et d'Histoire (Museum of Art and History) is everything you would expect in a museum: a grand, very classical façade, elegant staircases and a marvellous inner patio – and that's just the building itself. Built between 1903 and 1910, this structure was donated by Charles Galland (1806–1901), a benefactor of the city. It also happens to be Switzerland's only museum whose exhibits, numbering in excess of 1,000,000 – and organized in three sections comprising archaeology, fine arts and applied arts – relate to the entire span of Western culture from its origins to date. Not-to-be-missed exhibits are the 15th-century altarpiece by Konrad Wilz and stained-glass windows that were originally in the cathedral.

A right turn out of the museum will take you across another bridge and into an area of elegant houses. Your curiosity will soon be aroused by the sight, down one of the turnings to the left, of a genuine **Église Orthodoxe Russe** (Russian Orthodox Church). In 1859 the many Orthodox Russians living in Geneva were given permission to build a church, and were lucky in that another resident, the Grand Duchess Anna Feodorovna, sister-in-law of Tsar Alexander I and aunt of Queen Victoria, became their patron. The site granted them was once the home of an ancient Benedictine priory, which had been destroyed in the 16th century. The Byzantine Muscovite-style edifice that replaced it in 1866 is easily identifiable by the golden, glittering cupolas. Don't miss the experience of going inside. It's very small, domed, dark and ornate with brown walls adorned by inlaid crosses, modern stained-glass windows, the aroma of incense and, of course, numerous candles. If you want a souvenir they will gladly sell you a CD or tape of Russian Orthodox music.

Église Orthodoxe Russe
rue Toepffer 9,
t 022 346 47 09;
open daily

Bay of Geneva and the Jet d'Eau

Essentially, this section covers the attractions on both sides of the lake closest to the city itself, in the area where the lake siphons into the River Rhône .

Among the first things you will notice along the attractive quai du Mont-Blanc are the steamers moored on the lake, indicative of the many trips originating from here. But your attention, most certainly, will soon be drawn to the unusual monument in a little park, the place des Alpes. The elaborate **Brunswick Monument** is actually the tomb of Charles d'Este-Guelph, Duke of Brunswick. Born in 1804, he was a fine linguist, horseman and musician, but in 1830 this also paranoid and eccentric man was chased into Parisian exile. Establishing himself as a talented investor he accumulated a large fortune and spent the last three years of his life in Geneva, where he died in 1873. He bequeathed a large part of his fortune to the City of Geneva, but specified that it should establish an eminent and worthy location and commission the finest artists of the era to create an exact replica of the Scaligeri Mausoleum in Verona, where his remains would be interred. This elaborate and well-placed monument should see him rest in peace.

In this immediate area you will notice several five-star hotels, only a few of Geneva's impressive tally of such establishments. However, the dominant feature of the Bay of Geneva, the towering **Jet d'Eau**, lies on the other bank with – on fine days – a backdrop of the Alps. And in summer you do not have to walk all the way around the bay to get there. Between March and October, simply head for the nearby Pâquis Pier and take one of the popular little *Mouette* ferry boats that cross every 10 minutes to the Gustave-Ador Pier, right next to the Jetée des Eaux-Vives that leads to the fountain (but beware of the spray).

You will by now be in no doubt, even if you were previously unaware of the fact, that the massive fountain of water emitting from the Jet d'Eau is the symbol of this city. Surprisingly, what is now a picturesque scene familiar to people throughout the world was conceived as a matter of practicality. Towards the end of the last century the turbine house on the Rhône had excess water on days when industrial demand was light. A quick-thinking engineer, Butticaz by name, designed a way to divert this excess water to a fountain, reaching a height of 98ft (30m), outside the plant. In 1891 the first solely decorative fountain, reaching a height of 295ft (90m), was created in its present position on the lake. This was raised in several stages, and today it gushes 132 gallons (500 litres) a second at a speed of 124 miles (200km) per hour at the nozzle, through an independent pump to an elevation of 459ft (140m). But don't expect to see it year-round. It is turned on to celebrate the coming of spring, usually to coincide with the Motor Show at the beginning of March, and operates, high winds permitting, until the second Sunday in October. Beginning on the week of Ascension Thursday in May, until closing, it is illuminated each night with eight 13,500-watt projection lights.

Follow the lakeside back towards the city centre. In the summer months the surrounding quays are delightful places to sunbathe, or just pass the time of day, while swans, ducks, small boats and lake steamers glide over the glistening waters. In those waters, though, are two blocks of stone that could easily be overlooked. Named **Neiton** and **Neptune**, these 'Niton' rocks emerged at the end of the Ice Age, and were even used during the Bronze Age for celebrations of rites and even sacrifices. More recently, the largest was represented by General Henri Dufour (whose equestrian statue is in the place Neuve) as the basis, at 1,225ft (373.6m) above sea level, for his land survey and his famous 1:100,000 map of Switzerland in 1864.

Soon after, the **Jardin Anglais** (English Garden), dating from 1854, offers a variety of attractions. The most spectacular, without doubt, is the **Horloge Fleurie** (Flower Clock), installed in 1955 to commemorate Geneva's long and illustrious watchmaking

Day Trip to Yvoire

A day trip to the absolutely charming medieval French village of **Yvoire** is well worth considering. Take a CGN boat (see p.190) from the quai du Mont-Blanc.

The voyage itself is pleasant enough, especially at the weekend when the lake seems to come alive as the sails of hundreds of yachts flutter in the breeze and the shores are dotted with sunbathers in the pretty villages on the French side of the lake. Yvoire is something special. A fortified medieval town, with an interesting castle as well, its narrow lanes are crowded with wooden and stone buildings that are literally covered with bright, colourful flowers. Browse or shop in delightful craft boutiques and dine in one of the many restaurants, most of which specialize in lake perch fillets. Yvoire's charms have not gone unnoticed, however, and this small village often gets just a little too crowded. Even so, it is a charming place that merits a visit, and you will come away with lovely memories.

tradition. With a diameter of 16.4ft (5m), a circumference of 51.5ft (15.7m) and a second hand measuring 8.2ft (2.5m), it took no small technical expertise to get the second hand to travel 10.6 inches (27cm) each second to compensate for the speed of rotation varying between the rising and descending phases of this inclined clock. The floral decoration changes as well, with as many as 6,500 plants of varying varieties that change with the season, comprising each setting of eight concentric circles. The Jardin Anglais also features a statue of Gustav Ador (1845–1928), with an inscription telling you he was president of just about every organization going, and the nearby Four Seasons Fountain, featuring Neptune with ladies below and children at the top.

Between the gardens and the Mont-Blanc bridge is where the **National Monument** has stood since its inauguration in 1869. It features two young ladies, carrying double-edged swords and with their arms encircling each other's waist. The one with the crenellated headwear represents the Republic of Geneva and the other is Helvetia (Switzerland). The symbolism is the date, 12 September 1814, when Geneva joined the Swiss Confederation.

Just away from the left bank of the lake is one of the most important shopping areas in Geneva, especially along the rue du Rhône. But hidden in there is the **place Molard**, the modern city's answer to the place du Bourg-de-Four, which is just a few hundred feet away up the hill. Lined with outdoor cafés, the square is graced by an octagonal fountain with a marble obelisk dating from 1771 and the Tour du Molard that originates from the 14th century when it was part of the surrounding wall. The Tour was rebuilt in 1591, restored several times later, and has a painted frieze showing the coats-of-arms of the main medieval figures and the Reformation, and a tablet indicating 'Geneva, City of Refuge'.

In the middle of the Pont des Bergues there is a most unusual little island. The **Ile Rousseau** was created in 1583 as a defensive fortification, and in 1628 it became a shipyard. An island until as late as 1832, when the footbridge the Pont des Bergues was built, it was then that it was named after one of Geneva's most illustrious citizens, the philosopher/writer Jean-Jacques Rousseau, whose statue you will find in the grounds. These days the little park is a haven for ducks and swans, and from here it is interesting to note just how fast the waters flow away from the lake into the river.

North of the River Rhône

Paquis-Express Mini-Train
STT Train Tours, boulevard St-Georges 36, t 022 781 04 04, www.sttr.ch; operates Mar–Oct daily; Nov and Dec weekends only

It is fun to take the Paquis-Express Mini-Train that steams off from the Rotunde du Mont-Blanc on the quai du Mont-Blanc. The journey is called the Parks and Residences Tour, and takes 35 minutes. As it rolls on its way, the quai du Mont-Blanc transforms itself into the quai Wilson by the **Pâquis Baths**, a feature of life here since 1932 – now featuring a sauna, massage and Turkish baths. All along the quai are huge luxury hotels, the casino and the imposing Palais Wilson. Soon there begins a whole series of delightful parks, whose imminent arrival is announced by a graceful bronze of *L'Adolescent et le Cheval* (The Youth and the Horse). These days the parks are continuous and, in fact, have no discernible boundaries. Still, each has its own separate identity and intriguing history, and most include a structure, or structures, of not inconsiderable architectural interest. The history of each park is lengthy and complicated, and very well documented by a multilingual commentary (and sign-boards along the way). One interesting note, though, is that two of the properties, the Moynier and Perle du Lac, were purchased by the League of Nations in 1926. But, unable to acquire enough land for their needs, they subsequently deeded these to the city in exchange for a portion of the Barembé estate. History aside, these parks are a delight. Competing for your attention are a wealth of beautiful buildings, statues, fountains and arrays of trees, plants and shrubs, along with all the activity on the lake.

Conservatoire et Jardin Botanique
chemin de L'Impératrice 1, t 022 418 51 00, www.ville-ge.ch/cjb; open daily April–Oct 8–7.30; Nov–Mar 9.30–5; greenhouses daily 9.30–4

Cheat a little, though, and get off at the stop for the Conservatoire et Jardin Botanique (Conservatory and Botanic Gardens). The botanic gardens have clearly thrived since being moved from the Promenade des Bastions in 1904 and, as delightful as the nearby parks are, the gardens are more so. As well as the abundant plantlife (more than 16,000 species), you will find deer, flamingoes, aviaries, ponds, fountains, statues, a 19th-century mansion (Le Chêne), a special conservatory for the herbarium (La Console) and a variety of greenhouses, including a beautiful domed one. There is even a 'scent and touch garden' for visually impaired visitors. It is home, too, to a botanical library and a world-famous scientific institute. This is a quiet place to relax in before moving on to the United Nations complex, and more museums.

Take the exit from the gardens on the city side farthest away from the lake, turn right on to avenue de la Paix and follow it to the oversize 39ft- (12m-) high chair with a broken left leg. The symbolism here, as conceived by the humanitarian organization, Handicap International, is to encourage all nations to sign up to the Ottawa landmine ban treaty. This, the place des Nations, is also the main entrance to the United Nations complex. However, this is not the entrance for ordinary visitors; that is farther up and around the hill, and along the way a special treat awaits in the **Ariana Park** to the right.

This, once, consisted of a surface area of 62 acres (25.1 hectares) forming part of the Barembé estate, which was the property of Gustave Revilliod, a prominent Genevese. Extensively travelled, he represented the Swiss Federation at such events as the inauguration of the Suez Canal in 1869. Revilliod also had an inveterate passion for collecting, and he amassed a phenomenal number of objects on his journeys. In 1877 he decided to build the Italian Renaissance-style **Ariana Museum** in the grounds to house his treasures, naming it Ariana after his mother, Arine de la Rive, a member of one of Geneva's oldest families. Upon his death, in 1890, the property and CHF 1,000,000 for its upkeep were bequeathed to the city. Fourteen years later, in 1904, the Botanical Gardens were established in the lower part of the grounds, below the railway lines. The remainder of the estate, with the exception of the museum and the immediate land around it, were given to the League of Nations in 1928 in exchange for the two lakeside properties, as described on p.200.

This acquisition enabled the organization to build its headquarters, but at the cost of the Revilliod family home, which was demolished along with various outbuildings and a small zoo. Fortunately, someone had the good sense to preserve the museum, and in 1954 the city opened an International Ceramic Academy in the building. And the **Musée Suisse de la Céramique et du Verre** (Swiss Museum of Ceramics and Glass), really is a gem! The classical lines of the domed exterior, attractive in their own right, enclose an interior that is as beautiful as it is unusual. Its design is deceptive as well; from the outside there is no indication that the main two-storey hall is oval in shape. Enter now, stepping on to the brown marble floor of the ground level, the perimeter of which is encircled by attractive marble pillars of similar colouring, which support the lone upper floor. But, as your attention is drawn upwards, your surroundings pale somewhat into insignificance in comparison with the intricate beauty above you. Around the second floor, elegant wrought-iron railings connect eighteen marble pillars, each sculpted in a unique, but complementary, helicoidal design. Crowning this majestic display is a ring of stained-glass windows, with one set into the light blue dome above each archway between the columns. The only museum of its

Musée Suisse de le Céramique et du Verre
avenue de la Paix 10,
t 022 418 54 5;
open Wed–Mon 10–5

kind in Switzerland, and one of the most important in Europe, it has over 20,000 objects covering a span of seven centuries of ceramics. Capitalizing on this delightful scene, the authorities have had the insight to create a small café/bar on the higher level where you can sit on the terrace overlooking the UN complex.

Just outside the building you will find a majestic Japanese bell, which has an interesting story in its own right. The original bell, dating from 1657 and the property of a temple in Shinagawa, was lost during the troubled period of Japanese history preceding the fall of the feudal regime around 1867. In 1873, unaware of its origin, Revilliod rescued the bell from a meltdown and placed it in the museum. In 1930 it was returned home to Japan, and a grateful Shinagawa offered Geneva a consecrated replica that was installed in 1991.

Security, as you might expect, is stringent at the Portail Pregny Gate entrance to the **United Nations**. Expect a request for identification, which will be held by security until you exit. Once approved, you may pass through and walk down to the visitors' service area located in the main building. Among the highlights of what you will learn during the hour-long guided tour, conducted in any one of 18 languages, are the following. The League of Nations was founded by President Woodrow Wilson in 1920, and this complex, completed in 1936, has a larger surface area than the Palace of Versailles, just outside Paris. After the Second World War the League of Nations was succeeded by the United Nations, whose responsibilities are divided between New York (where the political decisions are made) and Geneva (where all humanitarian facets are considered). Note, also, that materials for the construction and furnishings of the old Palais des Nations were donated by different countries around the world. You will see an introductory film, the Grand Assembly Hall with its bronze doors, the Salle des Pas Perdus (The Hall of Lost Steps, the main foyer of the Assembly Hall), conference rooms in the new building, and some gifts donated by various countries to the UN. A tapestry from China will most certainly catch your eye, with its optical illusion that a door appears always to be facing you, whatever angle you look at it from. All in all this is a very informative tour; before leaving you may want to sign the Golden Book for Peace, demonstrating your support for the United Nations' never-ending crusade for peace.

Philatelists will enjoy the UN also. In 1962 the **United Nations Philatelic Museum** was opened to house the Charles Mistelli collection. This Genevese doctor began collecting postage stamps, envelopes, etc. relating to the League of Nations in 1919, and those relating to the United Nations and its specialized agencies in 1951. His collection was purchased using funds raised by the sale of a

⓫ United Nations
avenue de la Paix 14,
t 022 917 48 96,
www.unog.ch; open
April–June, Sept–Oct
daily 10–12 and 2–4;
Nov–Mar 10–12 and
2–4; it is best to confirm
before visiting, however,
as these times, and the
itineraries, are subject
to change according to
the demands of the
conference programme;
adm

special stamp issued by the Swiss Post Office and sold on premises provided by the United Nations Organization. The exhibition is now enhanced by audiovisual presentations, a 'readers' corner' with philatelic publications from around the world, and various temporary displays.

Musée de la Croix-Rouge et du Croissant-Rouge
avenue de la Paix 17,
t 022 748 95 25,
www.micr.ch; open
Wed–Mon 10–5; adm

Almost directly across from the United Nations is the **Musée de la Croix-Rouge et du Croissant-Rouge** (International Red Cross and Red Crescent Museum). This modern museum uses state-of-the-art audiovisual demonstrations to showcase the organizations' activities over their 130-year history.

To get back to the town centre just walk back down avenue de la Paix, passing the impressive white walls and metal gates of the Federation of Russia, to place des Nations, and catch a bus back to the Gare de Cornavin.

Carouge – A Taste of the Mediterranean by the Lake

If you want a trip out of the centre of Geneva take tram 12 or 13 to **Carouge**. Back in 1754 this small suburb of the city was granted to the king of Sardinia who later developed a city plan, with the help of Italian architects, around a tree-planted axis – the place du Marché. It has a Mediterranean ambience, with beautiful houses and gardens. There are also trendy shops, boutiques, restaurants and dynamic nightlife, leading to it being referred to as Geneva's Greenwich Village.

Musée de Carouge
place de Sardaigne 2,
t 022 342 33,
www.carouge.ch;
open Tues–Sun 2–6

The area also has an interesting musuem. The **Musée de Carouge** is housed in a magnificent Louis XVI mansion dating from around 1789. It has permanent collections of earthenware made by Carouge Pottery from 1810 to 1930, Noverraz Art Deco from around 1930–1960 and some more contemporary works. The museum is open only during the annual four temporary exhibitions, but the charming Sardinian garden has handicraft shops.

Tourist Information and Services in Geneva

(i) **Geneva >**
Genève Tourisme et Bureau des congrès:
rue du Mont-Blanc 18,
t 022 909 70 70,
www.geneva-tourism.ch; open Mon 10–6, Tues–Sat 9–6, Sun 10–4

Genève Tourisme offers special weekend **hotel package rates** (*Forfait Week-end)* that include accommodation in a double or single room with bath or shower (but only in hotels that participate in the plan), with breakfast, a 2-hour guided city tour and voucher booklets offering certain privileges and reductions. These range in price, for one night, from CHF 74pp at a 2-star hotel to CHF 164pp at a 5-star hotel.

Walking Tour

Genève Tourisme offers a self-audioguided walking tour, which includes 25 points of interest. You are given a pamphlet and a map and then you can either pay CHF 15 and download the guide to your MP3 player or rent a CD and CD player. The rental cost is CHF 10 and you have to pay a CHF 50 deposit and present either a passport or identity card. The tour takes about 2½ hours.

Market Days

Books: April–Nov, Fri at place de la Fusterie
Crafts: Thurs at place de la Fusterie

Flower market: daily at place du Molard

Flea market: Wed and Sat at Plaine de Plainpalais

Fruit and vegetables: Tues, Fri and Sun morning at Plaine de Plainpalais

Medical Emergencies

Chemist/pharmacy emergency service, t 022 420 64 80.

Doctor's emergency service, t 022 748 49 50.

Festivals in Geneva

Early Mar: Motor Show, www.salon-auto.ch.

Early April: International Exhibition of Inventions.

Late April: International fair for books.

Late April: Europ'Art, www.europart.ch, international art fair.

Mid-June: Bol d'Or Regatta on the lake, www.boldor.ch.

4 July: one of the largest **celebrations of American Independence** outside the USA.

End July/mid-Aug: Fêtes de Genève, www.fetes-de-geneve.ch, the Geneva Festival, fairs, fun and one of the largest fireworks displays in Europe.

1 August: Swiss National Day.

Last week Aug/first week Sept: La Bâtie Festival, www.baties.ch, a music and theatre festival that opens the dance season in Geneva.

Early Oct: International Fair of Minerals, Fossils and Gems.

11/12 Dec: the *Escalade*, commemorating the attempt by the Duke of Savoy to invade Geneva in 1602.

Shopping in Geneva

On the right bank the area of rue du Rhône and rues de la Confédération, du Marché and de la Croix-d'Or (these last three known as the rues Basses) is the fashionable shopping district. Also on the right bank, many antique shops, art galleries and boutiques etc. can be found in the Old Town. On the left bank, most of the shops are between the train station, Cornavin, and the quai du Mont-Blanc –

particularly along the rue du Mont-Blanc.

Main train station: the shops here open daily 8–8.

Airport, Les Galeries d'Aéroport, Centre Commercial: 60 shops open daily 8–8, bars and restaurants open daily 6–11.

Swiss Corner, rue des Alpes 7, t 022 731 06 84, open daily. The widest array of souvenirs in Geneva, with a great selection of cuckoo clocks, T-shirts, watches, knives, etc.

Coutellerie du Jet d'Eau, Pastore Frères, rue du Mont-Blanc 7, t 022 731 45 19, www.coutellerie.ch. Has the finest selection of Swiss Army knives, scissors and other such things. It is also home to the first Victorinox Corner in Geneva, which features a full range of their products.

Where to Stay in Geneva

Luxury

*******Beau-Rivage**, quai du Mont-Blanc 13, t 022 716 66 66, www.beau-rivage.ch. Founded in 1865, this is the last privately owned 5-star hotel in Geneva, and is still run by the Mayer family. The location is superb, overlooking both the Brunswick Memorial and the lake, and the style is purely classical. This is reflected in the five-storey atrium in the lobby, where a restoration revealed fragments of the Pompeian frescoes dating from the opening. Rooms and suites are spacious, and the private balconies offer spectacular views.

Expensive

******Ambassador**, quai des Bergues 21, t 022 908 05 30, www.hotel-ambassador.ch. This is the only 4-star hotel directly on the right bank of the Rhône. Privately owned, it overlooks a little square. All of its 64 rooms are modern in style and have the latest technological facilities.

******The New Midi**, place Chevelu 4, t 022 544 15 00, www.hotel-du-midi.ch. This eight-storey building is situated in a quiet location near the Rhône. It has 78 well-equipped and fairly spacious rooms with modern facilities.

Moderate

Résidence Mont-Blanc, rue Thalberg 4, **t** 022 716 40 00, *www.residence-mont-blanc.ch*. A fine location just a minute or so away from the lake. Modern studios and apartments offer an alternative to hotel accommodation.

***Astoria, place Cornavin 6, **t** 022 544 52 52, *www.astoria-geneve.ch*. Very central, opposite the train station. All of the rooms offer modern facilities as well as a modem plug, safe and soundproofing.

***Excelsior, rue Rousseau 34, **t** 022 732 09 45, *www.excelsior-geneva.ch*. In a central, but less busy area, the 54 rooms and 2 suites in this hotel have a charming old-fashioned ambience along with modern facilities like free Wi-Fi and a café with reasonably priced dishes as well as a coffee shop.

⭐ Le Chat-Botté >>

Inexpensive

***At Home, rue de Fribourg 16, **t** 022 906 19 00, *www.hotel-at-home.ch*. A block away from the station on a street full of good restaurants and Internet cafés. With singles, doubles, triples as well as studios, suites and apartments, all have a shower or bath, and are nicely furnished and equipped.

Bel'Esperance, rue de la Vallée 1, **t 022 818 37 37, *www.hotel-bel-esperance.ch*. Situated on the slopes of the Old Town, this has 40 comfortable and very nice rooms. Single, double, triple and family rooms and studios, owned and managed by the Salvation Army, so don't expect any alcohol.

Hotel des Tourelles, Boulevard James-Fazy 2, **t 022732 44 23, *www.destourelles.ch*. In a charming 19th-century building, this is the only hotel of its class that overlooks the Rhône. Its 23 comfortable, but sometimes small, rooms combine a flavour of the past with modern comforts.

*Hôtel de la Cloche, rue de la Cloche 6, **t** 022 732 94 81. This has a surprisingly good location, in an old house in one of the side streets just off the quai du Mont-Blanc. A B&B hotel with just eight rooms.

Home St Pierre Petershöfli, cours St Pierre 4, **t** 022 310 37 07, *www.home stpierre.ch*. In the heart of the Old Town, this building is immersed in history and owned and supported by the German Lutheran Church and the Swiss-German Reformed Church of Geneva. It was founded in 1874 to provide a refuge for German and Swiss-German women who came to the city to improve their French. Still catering only to women, it has single and double rooms and two dormitories.

Eating Out in Geneva

Very expensive–expensive

Le Chat-Botté, quai du Mont-Blanc 13, **t** 022 716 66 66. An unusual name – Puss in Boots – for a gourmet restaurant located within the Hotel Beau-Rivage that has décor resembling a country house library. The chef, Dominique Gauthier, combines tradition and creativity by using the freshest produce. The wine list here is exceptional, as is the *sommelier*, who will diplomatically advise you to try wines that otherwise you may never have heard of.

Expensive–moderate

Café du Centre, place du Molard 5, **t** 022 311 85 86, *www.cafeducentre.ch*. With its window full of tempting fish and shellfish, this restaurant would not look at all out of place on a Paris boulevard. This is a fish lover's paradise, and irresistible to those who simply can't say no to such temptations.

Au Pied de Cochon, place du Bourg-de-Four 4, **t** 022 310 47 97, *www.pied-de-cochon.ch*. As the name implies, this is the place to make a pig of yourself, especially if you like pig's trotters. But don't let that put you off; there are plenty of other tasty selections available, to be eaten in the old and characterful dining room or on the terrace.

Hung Wan, quai du Mont-Blanc 7, **t** 022 731 73 30, *www.hung-wan.ch*. With a prominent position alongside the lake, this is a classical and authentic Chinese restaurant with the highest standards of cuisine and service.

Le Lacustre, quai Général-Guisan, **t** 022 317 40 00, *www.molino.ch*. Designed like the interior of an old ship, and with a great location overlooking the water by the Molard Pier. The speciality here is perch (although they don't come from the lake), and Swiss and international dishes. There is a wonderful lakeside terrace, too.

Edelweiss, place de la Navigation 2, **t** 022 544 51 51. In the hotel of the same name, this really does look, and feel, like a typical Swiss chalet. There are fondues of different varieties – including chocolate – and plenty of other tasty choices like country pâté, air-dried meats, perch, a range of meats, chicken and duck. All accompanied by Swiss yodelling too!

Swiss Cottage, rue Barton 6, **t** 022 732 40 00. The main dining room on the upper level is a real attraction. The walls are embellished with very imaginative murals of typical Swiss scenes, and prove a perfect backdrop to an equally imaginative array of fondues, raclette, fish and meat dishes.

Moderate–inexpensive

El Ruedo, rue de Fribourg 5, **t** 022 732 65 08. Named The Ring, this has the traditional bullfight and Real Madrid décor common in Spanish restaurants. Fish and seafood, along with grandmother's cooking (*Cocina Abuela*) featuring Galician-style cod and octopus (*pulpo*) are the specialities – as are *paella valenciana* and an enticing array of tapas and good wines. *Open daily*.

Manora, rue Cornavin 6, **t** 022 909 44 10. This has an unlikely location in the Placette department store, but shouldn't be missed. The food is self-served from innovatively arranged separate areas that each specialize in a different type of food.

La Grappe d'Or, rue des Pâquis 19, **t** 022 732 75 16. This unpretentious place, with a café in the front, restaurant at the back and six tables outside, is open all day long and has a surprisingly inventive menu: perch

fillets, steak, chicken and lamb, salads, pasta dishes, small and large plates of cold and mixed meats, as well as fondues. *Open daily*.

Lord Nelson Pub, place du Molard 9, **t** 022 311 11 00, *www.lordnelsonpub.ch*. Not really a good imitation of an English pub, but they do brew some tasty beer and it does have a good location in this popular square. Expect a good mix of dishes, along with the usual pub sandwiches and daily specials. *Open daily*.

Shahi Restaurant, place de Cornavin 2, **t** 022 738 44 44, *www.shahifood.ch*. Located on the first floor of a building diagonally opposite the railway station, this serves spicy Indian and Pakistani dishes, and offers an impressive hot buffet at lunchtimes. You can order takeaways too.

Entertainment in Geneva

SEG Geneva ARENA, routes des Batailleux 3, **t** 022 710 90 90, *www.geneva-arena.com*. Located close to the airport, it has a capacity of 9,000 people and hosts international stars, musicals and other top shows.

Orchestre de la Suisse Romande (OSR), Place du Cirque 2, **t** 022 807 00 00, *www.osr.ch*. Created in 1918; its classical music has a great tradition in Geneva, where it is also the regular orchestra of the Grand Théâtre.

The Grand Théâtre de Genève, boulevard du Théâtre 11, **t** 022 418 30 00, *www.geneveopera.ch*. This is the home of international opera and ballet productions. In recent years the ballet company has started a new, and successful, initiative of working with contemporary creators.

Association pour la Danse Contemporaine (ADC), rue des Eaux-Vives 82–84, **t** 022 320 06 66, *www.adc-geneve.ch*. A contemporary dance company.

Orchestre de Chambre de Genève (L'OCG), *www.locg.ch*. Relatively young, having been founded in 1992, but it is making a name for itself and its concerts take place at the following places, amongst others: **Victoria Hall**,

Rue du Général-Dufour 14, t 022 418 35 13, Geneva's main home for symphonic music; **Bâtiment des Forces Motrices**, place des Volontaires 2, t 022 322 12 20, *www.bfm.ch*, a former hydro-electric power plant now cleverly converted to a concert hall.

Contrechamps Ensemble, rue de la Coulouvrenière 8, t 022 329 24 00, *www.contrechamps.ch*. This is the place to go for contemporary music, and they also organize the annual Archipel Festival, *www.archipel.ch*.

AMR Association, rue des Alpes 10, t 022 716 56 30, *www.amr-geneve.ch*. Offers jazz amateurs the opportunity of improvised concerts and jam sessions.

Le Contretemps, rue des Savoises 1, *www.jazz-agmj.ch*. Managed by local artists, it hosts traditional jazz every Friday.

Le Chat Noir, rue Vautier 13, t 22 343 49 48, *www.chatnoir.ch*. Located in Carouge, this famous bar and concert hall offers jazz, rock, pop and other music concerts and festivals.

Ateliers d'Ethnomusicologie, rue de Montbrilliant 10, t 022 919 04 94, *www.adem.ch*. Specializes in world music. During the summer it organizes free concerts with both established and up-and-coming artists in various open-air locations, such as the Ella Fitzgerald Stage in the Parc la Grange.

Nightlife in Geneva

White'n Silver, Glacis-de-Rive 15, t 022 735 15 15, *www.whitensilver.ch*. Offers its rather chic guests an ultra-modern environment to dance the night away.

Platinum, quai du Seujet 18, *www.platinum-club.ch*. The 'in-spot' with high-class service for prestigious trendsetters.

Le Scandale, rue de Lausanne 24, t 022 731 83 73, *www.lescandale.ch*. Has a resident DJ, guest performers and themed nights.

The Java Club, Grand Hotel Kempinski, quai du Mont-Blanc 19, t 022 908 90 88, *www.javaclub.ch*. The largest club in town.

LA SIP, rue des Vieux-Granadiers 10, *www.lasip.ch*. Located in an old factory, this is a gay-friendly venue.

Lausanne

Lausanne, with a population of around 125,000 or 250,000 in the metropolitan area, is the provincial capital of the canton of Vaud in the French-speaking part of Switzerland. It has a dramatic location, being built on three hills – the **Cité**, **Bourg** and **Saint Laurent** – overlooking Lac Léman (Lake Geneva's offical name) and the French Alps beyond it.

Literary personalities such as Victor Hugo, Jean-Jacques Rousseau and Lord Byron all lived for many years here, as did the musicians Igor Stravinsky, Ernest Ansermet and Clara Haskill. Consequently, Lausanne has deep cultural traditions, and is home to more than 20 museums, its own opera company and chamber orchestra, and the Béjart ballet company founded by choreographer Maurice Béjart. There are numerous theatres, too, led by the Vidy-Lausanne Theatre.

Sports-wise, too, it is internationally famous. In 1915, Baron Pierre de Coubertin, founder of the modern Olympics, established the first headquarters of the International Olympic Committee (IOC) in Lausanne. The very impressive Olympic museum was opened in

Getting to Lausanne

By Car

The A9 motorway runs around Lake Geneva and through the Valais, and at Lausanne it joins with the A1 motorway that goes north to Bern, Solothurn, Zürich, Winterthur and St Gallen, with a connecting motorway to Basel.

By Train

It is on the mainline running from Geneva around the lake to Lausanne, Vevey and Montreux and then from Aigle to Brig through the Valais. There are connections from Lausanne on to Basel, Bern, Geneva and St Gallen.

Getting around Lausanne

Lausanne is set upon three levels: **Ouchy** is the area down by the lakeside; the **Old Town**, **cathedral**, many **museums** and the **town hall** and **shopping** area centred around the place de la Palud are on the upper level; and the **Gare CFF** (Central Railway Station) is nestled between the two. Of course, it is possible to walk or take the bus from one level to another, although the roads are steep and the routes meandering. The fastest and most direct mode of transport is the **Métro** – actually a rather steep funicular that runs from the lake-level station of Ouchy to the train station stop and then on and up to the Flons top by the rue de Grand-Chêne, the closest stop to the Old Town.

1993 and in 1994 the city was given the official sobriquet 'Capitale Olympique'. Numerous other international sports federations have also made Lausanne their home.

Service organizations of banking, insurance and tourism and other multinational companies, such as Alcoa and Reynolds, have made Lausanne their headquarters. The Beaulieu exhibition complex plays host each September to the Swiss National Fair.

As a consequence of all this, Lausanne is not short on hotels – some of which are pretty luxurious – and there are many top-class restaurants, both in the town and the smaller communities either side of it along the lake.

Lausanne also has the reputation of being Switzerland's youngest city, mainly due to the fact that there are so many schools here, including the university (the largest in Switzerland), Federal Institute of Technology and many other professional and private institutions. Such youth has brought with it a lively, cosmopolitan vitality, and there are numerous clubs and discos, many of which are in the old warehouses of the Le Flon area south of the station.

History

The area in and around Lausanne has an ancient history. A necropolis dating from between 6500 to 4500 BC has been discovered beneath the Roman ruins of *Lousonna* at Vidy, and there is evidence that lake dwellers, *lacustrians*, lived in villages built on piles along the lakeshore for nearly 3,000 years.

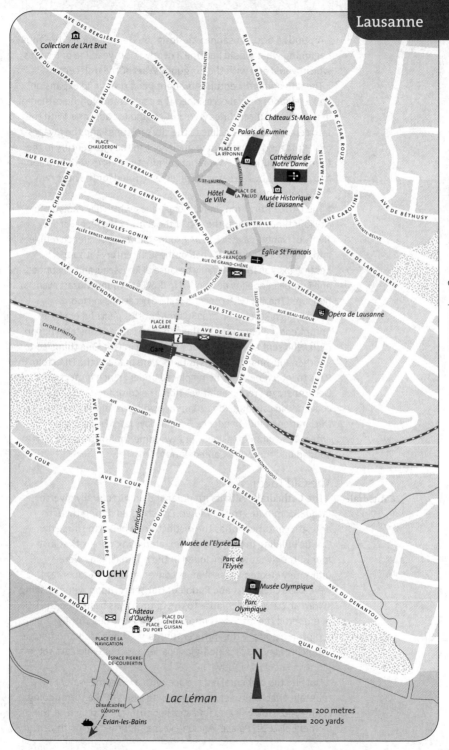

AVE DES BERGIÈRES

Collection de L'Art Brut

RUE DU MAUPAS

AVE DE BEAULIEU

RUE ST-ROCH

AVE VINET

RUE DU VALENTIN

RUE DE LA BORDE

PLACE CHAUDERON

RUE DES TERRAUX

RUE DU TUNNEL

Château St-Maire

RUE DR CÉSAR ROUX

Palais de Rumine

RUE DE GENÈVE

PLACE DE LA RIPONNE

MADELEINE

Cathédrale de Notre Dame

PONT CHAUDERON

RUE DE GENÈVE

RUE DE GRAND-PONT

R. ST-LAURENT

PLACE DE LA PALUD

Hôtel de Ville

Musée Historique de Lausanne

RUE ST-MARTIN

AVE DE BÉTHUSY

RUE CAROLINE

RUE SAINTE-BEUVE

AVE JULES-GONIN

RUE CENTRALE

ALLÉE ERNEST-ANSERMET

AVE LOUIS RUCHONNET

CH DE MORNEX

PLACE ST-FRANÇOIS

RUE DE GRAND-CHÊNE

Église St Francois

RUE DE LANGALLERIE

RUE DE PETIT-CHÊNE

AVE DU THÉÂTRE

CH DES EPINETTES

AVE STE-LUCE

RUE DE LA GROTTE

RUE BEAU-SÉJOUR

Opéra de Lausanne

PLACE DE LA GARE

AVE DE LA GARE

Gare

AVE W. FRAISSE

AVE D'OUCHY

AVE JUSTE OLIVIER

AVE EDOUARD -

DAPPLES

AVE DE LA HARPE

AVE DES ACACIAS

AVE DE MONTCHOISI

AVE DE COUR

AVE DE COUR

AVE DE SERVAN

AVE DE LA HARPE

AVE DE L'ELYSÉE

Funicular

AVE D'OUCHY

Musée de l'Elysée

OUCHY

Parc de l'Elysée

Musée Olympique

AVE DU DENANTOU

AVE DE RHODANIE

Parc Olympique

Château d'Ouchy

PLACE DU PORT

PLACE DU GÉNÉRAL GUISAN

QUAI D'OUCHY

PLACE DE LA NAVIGATION

ESPACE PIERRE-DE-COUBERTIN

N

DÉBARCADÈRE D'OUCHY

Evian-les-Bains

Lac Léman

200 metres
200 yards

Around AD 600, Lausanne was designated a Cathedral City – thus beginning what would become a nearly 1,000-year line of bishops which would end with the Burgundy Wars of the 16th century.

The 12th and 13th centuries brought good times and expansion, and a religious revival occasioned the consecration of the cathedral in 1275. The next centuries were not so kind to Lausanne. With the 14th century came a decline in the city's fortunes and the ravages of the plague. Devastation reigned early in the 15th century in the form of the Burgundy Wars that culminated in 1536 with invasion and conquest by the Bernese forces, who ruled for the next two and a half centuries.

The 17th century brought further plagues, which devastated the city four times. Towards the end of the century, the repeal of the Treaty of Nantes gave rise to an exodus of over 1,000 French refugees into Lausanne. In the latter half of the 18th century Lausanne became fashionable, primarily because of Rousseau, and celebrities and European nobility descended in droves. A young Mozart even honoured the city with concerts on two occasions in 1766.

The French Revolution of 1789 brought this peaceful era to an abrupt end. Celebrations by the populace caused consternation in Bern, who sent troops to occupy the town in 1791. One thing led to another and, finally, representations were made to the Directoire in Paris to intervene. After being placed under French protection on 18 December 1797, representatives from the communities in Vaud convened in Lausanne on 24 January 1798, proclaiming a Declaration of Independence. Several days later French troops entered Lausanne to a liberators' welcome. In 1803 the canton of Vaud joined the Swiss Confederation.

The Old Town

Cathédrale
t 021 316 71 61; open Mon–Fri 7–7, Sat–Sun 8–7; Oct–Mar closes 5.30

The **Cathédrale**, with its irregular and architecturally diverse façade, dominates the Old Town. Constructed during the 12th and 13th centuries, it has the distinction of being the largest Gothic building in Switzerland; an interesting note is that just four of the five towers included in the original plans were ultimately erected. Present at its consecration in October 1275 were Pope Gregory X and Rudolf of Habsburg, upon whom, having sworn an oath of allegiance to the Church, was bestowed the title of emperor. The interior is impressive; note the beautifully sculptured portals, the 16th-century carved choir stalls, numerous sepulchres and 105 stained-glass panes, most of which are set in a glorious circular window.

Outside the cathedral is a terrace, with a welcome water fountain, that offers yet more imposing views of the surrounding countryside. You will also find a rather aristocratic structure, the former Episcopal Palace (Ancien-Evêche), adorned by a 13th-century

Musée Historique de Lausanne
place de la Cathédrale 4, t 021 315 41 00; open July–Aug daily 11–6; all other months closed Mon; adm

fortified tower, which was home to the bishops of Lausanne until the early 15th century. Today it houses the **Musée Historique de Lausanne** (Lausanne Historical Museum). One of the main exhibits is a 28.7sq yd (24sq m) scale model, complete with sound and lighting effects, of the Old Town as it looked in the 17th century. It also features regular temporary exhibitions that can be as diverse as headdresses and bonnets from the late 18th to early 20th centuries to the art of erotic bookplates.

The other end of the Old Town is dominated by the 15th-century **Saint-Maire castle**, now the seat of the government of the canton of Vaud. In between, there are any number of quiet cobbled streets full of attractive medieval buildings that have been converted into tempting boutiques, galleries, restaurants and bars. And if you happen to be around here between 10pm and 2am you can hear, from the bell tower, Europe's last nightwatchman shouting out his traditional 'All's Well' cry.

Place de la Riponne and Place de la Palud

Palais de Rumine
place de la Riponne 6

Musée Cantonal des Beaux-Arts
t 021 316 34 45, www.beaux-arts.vd.ch; open Tues–Wed 11–6, Thurs 11–8, Fri–Sun 11–5; adm, first Sat of month free

Musée Monétaire Cantonal
t 021 316 39 90, www.musees-vd.ch; open Tues–Thurs 11–6, Fri–Sun 11–5; adm, first Sat of month free

Musée Cantonal d'Archéologie et d'Histoire
t 021 316 34 30, www.musees-vd.ch; open and adm as Musée Monétaire

Musée Cantonal de Géologie
t 021 692 44 70, www.unil.ch/mcg; open and adm as Musée Monétaire

Just outside the main doors of the cathedral, the 160 steps of the Escaliers du Marché – a wooden roofed stairway similar to two seen in Thun – take you down to another open set of steps that lead into the place de la Riponne. This large plaza, adorned by a marvellous fountain from which spout dozens upon dozens of jets of water, is totally dominated by the huge, classical façade of the **Palais de Rumine** (Rumine Palace). Named after its donor, this Florentine Renaissance-style structure was built in 1906 as the principal building of Lausanne University. Presently, however, besides being a market place it is also a centre of culture as it is home to an eclectic collection of the following museums. The **Musée Cantonal des Beaux-Arts** (Cantonal Fine Arts Museum), the second oldest such museum in Switzerland, displays works by French-Swiss artists like Ducros, Bocion, Gleyre, Vallotton and Soutter from the 18th, 19th and 20th centuries. These are complemented by the donations of D. Widner of works by Matisse, Cézanne, Renoir, Bonnard and Vuillard, among others. The **Musée Monétaire Cantonal** (Cantonal Money Musuem) has over 60,000 items from the cantonal collection from antiquity to the modern day. Other exhibits relate to the history of European, Swiss and regional monetary history. **Musée Cantonal d'Archéologie et d'Histoire** (Cantonal Museum of Archaeology and History), has local exhibits from the end of the last Ice Age, through the Bronze Age and the Celts to more modern times, and has an interesting mix of traditional objects, models and thematic explanations in either slide or video shows. The **Musée Cantonal de Géologie** (Cantonal Geological Museum) traces the geological evolution of

Musée Cantonal de Zoologie
*t 021 316 34 60,
www.zoologie.vd.ch;
open and adm as
Musée Monétaire*

this region. It features a virtual trip through the Alps, fossils and exhibitions on minerals and crystals. Finally there is the **Musée Cantonal de Zoologie** (Cantonal Zoology Museum).

Place de la Palud, one of the city's traditional meeting places, is due south of the place de la Riponne, following rue Madeleine out of the plaza and down, past some shops. This really is quite an interesting square. Upon the 17th-century *hôtel de ville* (town hall), the pre-eminent structure, is an ornamental clock that has become a Lausanne landmark. It strikes on the hour between 9am and 7pm with a parade of mechanical figures depicting the region's history. This overlooks the elegant and colourful Fountain of Justice, that dates from 1726. Try to time your visit to coincide with one of the two lively market days (Wednesday and Saturday). This is also the centre of the modern shopping district, which crosses the busy rue Centrale and extends up to the **Place St-François**, dominated by the 13th-century church, with a 15th-century bell tower, of the same name. This once served as the sanctuary of a monastery, but has been Protestant since the Reformation. Place St-Francois is encircled by pavement cafés, restaurants, shops and there is a post office.

West of the Old Town

Collection de L'Art Brut
*avenue des Bergières 11,
t 021 315 25 70,
www.artbrut.ch; open
Tues–Sun 11–6; adm, first
Sat of month free*

The **Collection de L'Art Brut** (Art Brut Museum) is dedicated to Art Brut, meaning 'raw art'. It is a term created by French artist Jean Debuffet to describe artwork produced by artists outside the mainstream, particularly that of artists in asylums and prison. When this museum opened in 1976 it was the first of its kind in the world. The collection is housed inside an 18th-century mansion whose interior is shrouded in black, in keeping with the atmosphere in which the artworks were created. There are some 5,000 pieces from Debuffet's collection on display.

Ouchy

Just outside the Ouchy Métro, the imposing neo-Gothic castle-like structure to the left, a former defensive building dating from 1893, today houses the 3-star Château d'Ouchy hotel, surrounded by gardens running down to the lake. Immediately behind, and south, of the hotel are more gardens that lead to the embarkation point for the lake steamers, **Débarcadère d'Ouchy**.

To the west is the **place de la Navigation**, and the **Éspace Pierre-de-Coubertin** with a combination of shallow water ponds and fountains abutting the small inner harbour. The ponds are most popular with the children of Lausanne and their parents bring them here at the weekends to play in the cool water. There is also a children's adventure tower, public chess games and a giant,

C-shaped weather vane. It is also a popular meeting place and, if you are lucky, you may find that you have chanced upon the European Beer Festival.

The main attractions of Ouchy, however, are to the east of the Métro station. Lausanne does not come by one of its nicknames, the Garden City, without reason. And nowhere is this more apparent than along the lakeside promenade of quai d'Ouchy where, in 1901, nearly 1,100 yards (more than 1km) of trees and flowerbeds were planted. In fact, Lausanne has a total of 790 acres (319.7 hectares) of public gardens, of which 250 acres (101.2 hectares) are at the lakeside. The city employs no fewer than 270 gardeners, who, during the cooler months, raise 650,000 plants under glass for planting in the spring. There are over 5 miles (8km) of promenades, and strolling along the quai d'Ouchy you will see far more than just plants and trees. Interspersed between these are a host of fountains and statues of every kind, including one of General Henri Guisan, leader of the Swiss defensive army in the Second World War. To the north, away from the lake, is an eclectic array of expansive buildings some of which, like the Beau-Rivage Palace and the Royal-Savoy, now serve as luxury hotels. To the south, the Alps glisten in the distance.

⭐ **Musée Olympique**
quai d'Ouchy 1,
t 021 621 65 11,
www.olympic.org; open
daily 9–6, closed on
Mon Oct–April; adm

As the headquarters of the International Olympic Committee, Lausanne's **Musée Olympique**, opened in 1993, is the world's greatest centre of information on the Olympic movement. You can reach the museum by taking a pathway that winds its way past an ever-increasing number of Olympian sculptures. Alternatively, if you need a rest, take the escalators up and wander down once you have explored the museum. The architectural futurism of this ultra-modern structure, faced with Thassos marble, is complemented by its use of technology: admission and exit, both to the museum and to the individual exhibitions within, is by a computer-coded key. Permanent exhibitions spotlight a multitude of familiar athletes, their respective events, and, in some cases, the equipment that played a role in their victories. These, as well as whatever temporary exhibits are on offer, are enhanced by a variety of innovative audio-visual effects. This impressive museum is guaranteed to be a winner for children of all ages. In addition to the Olympic Archives, the Olympic Documentation Centre has 150,000 books, 250,000 photos, and film and video totalling 7,000 hours of viewing. There is also a museum shop, but beware, the prices can hit Olympian heights.

Musée de l'Elysée
avenue de l'Elysée 18,
t 021 316 99 11,
www.elysee.ch; open
Tues–Sun 11–6; adm,
free on first Sat of
the month

Just north of the Olympic Museum is Switzerland's main photography museum, the **Musée de l'Elysée**, located in a picture-perfect 17th-century mansion set in gardens adjacent to the Olympic Museum.

Evian-les-Bains, France

Compagnie Générale de Navigation sur le Lac Léman,
avenue de Rhodaine,
t 021 614 62 00,
www.cgn.ch

Lake steamers operated by the **Compagnie Générale de Navigation sur le Lac Léman** set sail from the port d'Ouchy-Débarcadère. The sailing across the lake takes around 40 minutes and is a delight in itself as the French Alps draw ever closer.

Located directly across Lake Geneva from Lausanne, Evian is one of those curious places that is world-famous even though most people haven't been there and indeed would be hard-pressed to say where it actually is. The claim to fame, of course, is derived from its most important export, **mineral water**. It was not until the latter 18th century that the news of Evian's refreshing natural spring water began to circulate throughout Europe. For over a century, the wealthy and the aristocratic flocked to this peaceful mountain town to take the waters by day and indulge themselves in what became a glittering and elegant social whirl by night.

The first mineral water development company and the first spa water establishment were both opened in 1826. In 1869, the Public Limited Company of Les Eaux Minérales d'Evian-les-Bains was founded. That same year, Cachat water was approved by the Academy of Medicine and won honours at the Universal Exhibition.

Evian has made an ongoing effort to build upon its natural attributes – the beautiful mountains and lovely lake, refreshing water, pure alpine air, a moderate mountain climate and low atmospheric pressure – by constructing extensive spa and sports facilities. Visitors will also enjoy wonderful restaurants, an array of interesting shops and a variety of cultural activities – not to mention Evian's delightful ambience. It is an ideal retreat from the hustle and bustle of daily life.

Wander around this very pretty flower-filled town at your leisure, strolling along the lakefront promenade and admiring the beautiful houses. Because of the timings of the sailings many of the shops may be closed for lunch, but you could enjoy a long, leisurely French meal instead, as many Swiss do. The cuisine in Evian is very much lake-influenced, with char, perch fillets, trout and fera making tasty dishes. And the surrounding high country of the Savoie means that fondue and raclette also feature on menus. The cheeses of Reblochon, Abondance, Vacherin and Tomme are particularly popular, as are the white wines of Marin, Marignan Crepy and Ripaille. The local cherry orchards produce an excellent variety of kirsch, and Muratore liqueur, made from alpine plants, is a local speciality. **Le Franco-Suisse** is a pleasant restaurant right in the middle of the main pedestrian-only street, specializing in the traditional cuisine of the Savoie.

Le Franco-Suisse
place Jean Bernex,
t 04 50 75 14 74,
www.kamira.net

Tourist Information and Services in Lausanne

ⓘ Lausanne >
*Lausanne Tourisme:
avenue de Rhodanie 2,
t 021 613 73 73,
www.lausanne-
tourisme.ch; open
Mon–Fri 8–5*

*main hall of SBB
railway station, place
de la Gare 9; open
daily 9–7*

The **Lausanne Transport Card** gives any guest staying in Lausanne free and unrestricted access to all public transport services in the city (bus, train, metro). This personalized card is given to each visitor at their hotel or guest house on arrival. It is valid for the duration of your stay, including arrival and departure days.

Guided Trips and Tours

Guided **walking tours** are offered by Lausanne Tourisme and concentrate on the area around the Cathedral, place de la Palud and the Old Town. They take place May–Sept Mon–Sat (except hols) at 10 and 3. The walks last between 1 and 2 hours, depart from outside the Hôtel de Ville on the place de la Palud and cost CHF 10.

Trips on **lake steamers** are operated by the **Compagnie Générale de Navigation sur le Lac Léman**, avenue de Rhodaine, t 021 614 62 00, *www.cgn.ch*. The most popular trip is to Evian-les-Bains, the pretty French town (*see* p.214). Another option is to travel to Montreux and the Château de Chillon (*see* p.218). The lake steamers, in effect, act as buses around the lake, west towards Geneva or east to Montreux.

Lost Property

Bureau des Objets Trouvés (Lost Property Office), place de la Riponne 10, t 021 315 33 85/86, open Mon–Fri 8–5.30, Sat 8–12.

Market Days

★ Beau-Rivage
Palace >>

Christmas Market, dates vary each year, place St-François.

Craftsmen Market, first Fri of the month and first three Fri of December at place de la Palud.

Flea Market, Thu from 9.30–7 at the place Chauderon.

Fruit and Vegetables, Wed and Sat mornings at the place de la Palud.

St Louis Market for Flowers and Honey, for two days at the end of Aug 6am–7pm at Derrière-Bourg.

Festivals in Lausanne

Late Jan–early Feb: Prix de Lausanne, *www.prixdelausanne.ch*, an international young dancers competition.

Late April: Carnival of Lausanne.

Late June: Fête de la Musique, free concerts in the streets.

Late June: Fête à Lausanne, a popular event in the city centre.

Early to mid-July: Festival de la Cité, *www.festivalcite.ch*, 250 free outdoor events in the Old Town.

Shopping in Lausanne

The principal shopping areas in Lausanne are centred between the place de la Palud and the place St-François. You can find everything from large department stores to fashionable boutiques, and much more.

Coutelleries du Petit-Chêne, Petit-Chêne 22, t 021 312 01 86, *www.swiss-knife.com*. Has the most extensive collection of Swiss Army knives, as well as numerous pen knives, scissors, kitchen knives, sewing sets with thimbles, corkscrews and an array of collectors' swords.

Heidi's Shop, Petit-Chêne 22, t 021 311 16 89, 22, *www.heidi-shop.ch*. Provides quite a contrast, and here there is an excellent array of Lötscher cuckoo clocks, backpacks, mugs, soft toys, dolls, sweatshirts and much else.

Where to Stay in Lausanne

Luxury

*****Beau-Rivage Palace**, place du Port 17–19, t 021 613 33 33, *www.brp.ch*. Has been Switzerland's finest hotel for 150 years since its opening in 1861. One of the country's most important historical landmarks, it is a grand building in its own picturesque park adjacent to the lake. It has 169 rooms, of which 33 are suites – some, such as the Art Deco suite, are famous in their own right. In addition there are two exquisite restaurants, two bars and the fabulous Cinq Mondes Spa, as well as an outdoor and indoor pool and tennis courts.

*****Lausanne Palace and Spa**, Grand-Chêne 7–9, **t** 021 331 31 31, *www.lausanne-palace.com*. This is a palace by name and by nature. Opened in 1915, it is in the heart of the business and shopping district and yet offers fantastic views over Lake Geneva and the Alps. On the exterior is a beautiful, classical façade; the interior features 150 large and spacious rooms and suites, each distinctively decorated with fine fabrics in a traditional style. There are even two toilets in each room, and heated mirrors in the bathrooms that won't steam up! It has the largest wellness centre in the Lake Geneva region, with an indoor pool and specialized beauty treatments.

Expensive

****Royal-Savoy**, avenue d'Ouchy 40, **t** 021 614 88 88, *www.royal-savoy.ch*. This stylish building is set in its own grounds close to the lakeside. An established hotel with a fine reputation, all of its 99 rooms and 9 suites are spacious and have modern facilities within the antique décor. Many also have balconies with lake views.

Moderate

***Hôtel du Port**, place du Port 5, **t** 021 612 04 44, *www.hotel-du-port.ch*. This hotel, close to the Ouchy Métro stop, has a colourful and irregularly shaped façade. Run by the same family for over 40 years, it has 22 modern rooms and junior suites.

***City**, rue Caroline 5, **t** 021 320 21 41, *www.fassbindhotels.ch*. This is in the heart of the Old Town area between the cathedral and the rue de Bourg. They advertise, and justifiably so, that they offer 4-star service at 3-star prices. The Art Deco lobby sets the style for the rest of the hotel. Fifty-one guest rooms, some with kitchenettes, each have a bath/shower, a TV with free video, computer connections and a mini-bar.

Inexpensive

Jeunotel, chemin du Bois-de-Vaux 36, **t** 021 626 02 22. Situated to the south of the city, by way of a no.2 bus from Ouchy to the Bois-de-Vaux stop. It has a total of 110 rooms offering modern combinations of accommodation, with or without en suite facilities.

Lausanne Guesthouse and Backpacker, chemin des Epinettes 4, **t** 021 601 80 00, *www.lausanne-guesthouse.ch*. Just a few minutes' walk south of the train station, this is in a gracious old house. It has a range of room combinations, all clean and comfortable: quadruples (with or without sheets), doubles (with or without sheets and with a private or semi-private bathroom) and singles (with a private or semi-private bathroom).

Eating Out in Lausanne

La Rotonde, place du Port 17–19, **t** 021 613 33 33, *www.brp.ch* (*very expensive*). This is the celebrated restaurant of the Beau-Rivage Palace hotel that holds one Michelin star. Here, in marvellous surroundings, you will find an array of exquisitely prepared and presented dishes created by the imaginative chef David Sauvignet, accompanied by a wine list of 75,000 bottles including 600 *crus* of which 150 are available in half-bottles and more than a dozen by the glass.

Le Table d'Edgard, Grand-Chêne 7–9, **t** 021 331 31 31, *www.lausanne-palace.ch* (*very expensive*). As expected of a restaurant affiliated with the Lausanne Palace and Spa hotel, this one Michelin-starred restaurant is one of the finest places to dine in the city. An intriguingly contemporary classical décor is enhanced by expansive vistas over the lake and Haute-Savoie Alps, especially from the terrace. The chef is an advocate of light cuisine that is typical of the region, and presents a tantalizing array of exotically flavoured and beautifully prepared and presented dishes.

Brasserie Bavaria, rue du Petit-Chêne 10, **t** 021 323 39 13, *www.labavaria.ch* (*expensive–moderate*). This is a typical German-style drinking house, with painted murals and dark wooden ceilings. Look for a wide selection of foreign beers, sandwiches and breadsticks on the bars, and regional specialities such as *choucroute* and *rösti*.

Le Lacustre, port d'Ouchy-Débarcadère, quai Dapples 1, t 021 617 42 00, *www.lelacustre.ch* (*moderate*). This French restaurant and brasserie has a fantastic location right next to the lake, with stunning views of the French Alps – especially from the large terrace. It has an interesting menu, too, that includes a selection of fish from the lake.

El Chiringuito Café-Restaurant, Saint Laurent 38, t 021 312 73 47 (*moderate– inexpensive*). A Spanish snack bar in the middle of a pedestrian shopping area not far from the Old Town. You'll find authentic tapas and other Spanish dishes on the menu.

Entertainment in Lausanne

Casino de Montbenon, allée Ernest-Ansermet 3, t 021315 21 50, just 5mins' walk from the city centre, was built in 1908 and renovated in 1981.

Opera, Music and Dance

Opéra de Lausanne, avenue du Théâtre 12, t 021 310 16 16, *www.opera-lausanne.ch*.

Orchestre de Chambre de Lausanne, rue St-Laurent 19, t 021 345 00 20, *www.regart.ch*. Led by Christian Zacharias.

Lausanne Sinfonietta, avenue du Grammont 11 bis, t 021 616 71 35, *www.sinfonietta.ch*.

Association des Concerts de Montbenon, Casino de Montbenon, t 021 318 71 71.

Béjart Ballet Lausanne, chemin du Presbytére, t 021 641 64 80, *www.bejart.ch*. World-famous ballet.

Nightlife in Lausanne

For cabaret shows try:

La Belle Epoque, rue de Bourg 17, t 021 312 11 49, *www.belleepoque.ch*. Live shows and music and two spectacular scenes. *Open daily 6pm–5am.*

Le Tiffany, rue de l'Ale 15, t 021 312 52 01, *www.belleepoque.ch*. *Open daily 6pm–5am.*

On the club and bar scene there is:

Chorus Jazz, avenue Mon-Repos 3, t 021 323 22 33, *www.chorus.ch*.

Cult Club, place Chaudron 18, t 021 311 95 30, *www.cultclub.ch*.

Atelier Volant, côtes de Montbenon 12, Le Flon, t 021 624 84 28, *www.atelier volant.ch*.

Montreux and Vevey

While nowadays Montreux is the better known of the two towns, it is Vevey that has the older history. The Romans established a trading post called *Vibiscum* at the junction of the road that led from their Helvetian capital of *Aventicum* (today, Avenches) and the road that connected Lausanne to Martigny, on the way to Italy. Thus, the founding and growth of Vevey was based, primarily, around trade.

Montreux, unlike many other towns in Switzerland, was not formed around a church, but rather was established as a miniature confederation of the small villages that were physically separated from one another by the area's many vineyards.

The area that encompasses Montreux and Vevey was, from early on, primarily under the control of the Counts of Savoy, whose presence was symbolized by the nearby Château de Chillon. The year 1536, however, brought dramatic change. On 29 January over 6,000 Bernese troops blitzed the château, subsequently taking control of the whole of the Vaud and

Getting to and around Montreux and Vevey

The A9 motorway runs around Lake Geneva and through the Valais, and at Lausanne, some 20 miles (32km) west of Vevey, it joins with the A1 motorway that goes north to Bern, Solothurn, Zürich, Winterthur and St Gallen, with a connecting motorway to Basel.

Both Montreux and Vevey are on the main **rail** line running from Geneva around the lake to Lausanne, Vevey and Montreux and then from Aigle to Brig through the Valais. There are connections from Lausanne on to Basel, Bern, Geneva and St Gallen.

Both places are small enough to **walk** around, although to get between them and to **Château de Chillon** it might be easier to take the train or the lake steamer.

bringing with them the Protestant religion. This had far-reaching consequences – in 1685 the French revoked freedom of religion, and many thousands of French Protestants, known as Huguenots, fled to Switzerland, many of them settling in Vevey. In 1798, after more than 250 years of domination by the Bernese, the Vaudois Revolution – which came in the wake of the French Revolution – restored the region's freedom.

In the early decades of the 19th century, artists, writers, musicians and others of like mind began to discover the unique natural charms of this far eastern section of the Lac Léman. Beautifully situated, with the peaceful lake and the soaring peaks of the Haute Savoie as a background, it also enjoys a mild climate. The Rochers de Naye at 6,700ft (2,042m) immediately behind (reached by train and famous for its Alpine Garden and Marmot Park) protect the slopes and lake shore from the northerly winds, giving rise to a microclimate that ranks as one of the sunniest in Switzerland. Visitors will be amazed at the numerous vineyards and the abundance of palm trees and tropical flowers that grow along the 9 miles (15km) distance from Villeneuve to Vevey – truly meriting its name, the 'Flowered Path'. The springtime is especially delightful when the fields blossom with thousands of fragrant narcissi. Is it any wonder, then, that the likes of Byron, Jean-Jacques Rousseau, Stravinsky and Charlie Chaplin fell in love with this place?

Over the years, Montreux and Vevey have established for themselves a worldwide reputation as a centre for arts and culture. Today, a variety of events and festivals (see p.221) follow one after the other throughout the year. Not to be overlooked, either, are the handful of museums in both towns.

🏰 Château de Chillon

t 021 966 89 10, www.chillon.ch; open daily April–Sept 9–6; Mar and Oct 9.30–5; Jan, Feb, Nov and Dec 10–4; adm

Around Montreux and Vevey: the Château de Chillon

Firstly, the majority of visitors to Montreux and Vevey will want to see the **Château de Chillon**. Situated on a little island jutting into the lake this château is a signature landmark, not only of this portion of the Vaud, but of the country of Switzerland as well. You can get there by various means: lake steamer is best, but a no. 1 bus is a good alternative from Montreux. The site has long been considered of strategic importance by virtue of its position guarding the narrow stretch of land between the lake and the mountains, along which ran the road that traversed the Great St Bernard Pass and continued on to Italy. It is generally believed that the Romans established an outpost here, although the first documentation of a castle on this site dates much more recently, from 1150.

First owned by the bishops of Sion, the castle was built as a base from which to collect taxes on the goods that passed along the road. It was enlarged in the 13th century when it came under the control of the Counts of Savoy. It was Peter II of Savoy, the master of Chillon from 1255 to 1268, who was responsible for the size and appearance of the structure as it is seen today.

In 1536, it was captured by the Bernese who used it, amongst other things, as a depot, armoury and residence for their bailiffs. During this period it suffered damage from a violent earthquake that occurred in 1584. The castle remained under Bernese control until the Vaudois Revolution of 1798, following which it became the property of the Canton of Vaud.

A century later, in 1897, the renowned restorer and archaeologist, Albert Naef, was appointed as the architect in charge of renovating the château. Seeking to carry out his task as authentically as possible, he consulted numerous archive documents that described much of the work that had been done since the end of the 12th century. What has evolved today is an irregularly shaped oval fortress, guarded by numerous towers and graced by three inner courtyards that are surrounded by a variety of grand rooms that overlook the lake and defensive positions. This is an intriguing place and as you investigate the carefully reconstructed chambers and listen to the sound of the water lapping at the walls it is almost possible to imagine that you have been transported back through the centuries to the castle's days of glory.

The château has inspired countless writers to put pen to paper – Jean-Jacques Rousseau, Shelley, Victor Hugo and Alexandre Dumas, to name a few. The most famous words written about it in a hotel in Lausanne were composed by Lord Byron in *The Prisoner of Chillon*, his poetic recounting of the imprisonment of Bonivard during the 16th century. This Prior of St Victor's in Geneva was chained for five years to the fifth pillar from the entrance because of his outspokenness in favour of the independence of Geneva. Byron's name is still visible where he inscribed it, upon the third pillar.

Montreux

Montreux is more commercialized and developed than its neighbour Vevey, with grand hotels lining the lakefront and interspersed with numerous upmarket boutiques and shops. It is sandwiched between the mountains and the lake, with the railway line separating **Les Planches** (the Old Town) from the new. The former is contained within quite a small area and is worth exploring. The **Musée du Vieux Montreux** (Historical Museum of the Swiss Riviera) is located within a collection of 17th-century houses. Its exhibits chronicle the development of the region from the Palaeolithic period to the modern days of tourism.

Of the many celebrities who have settled in Montreux, the rock star Freddie Mercury, of the rock group Queen, is perhaps the most unlikely. Nevertheless, the group recorded their last albums here before Freddie died of AIDS in November 1991, and a bronze statue on the quayside was erected as a permanent memorial to him. If you want to know more, then check out *www.montreux music.com*.

Musée du Vieux Montreux
*rue de la Gare 40;
t 021 963 13 53,
www.musee montreux.ch; daily Apr–early Nov 10–midday, 2–5; adm*

Vevey

Vevey has an entirely different character, and the town is somewhat older. The lakefront is less commercialized and there are a number of museums that may be of interest, notably the dual **Musée Historique du Vieux Vevey** (Museum of Old Vevey) and **Musée de la Confrérie des Vignerons** (Museum of the Brotherhood of Wine Growers). The château dates from 1599 and served as a home for bailiffs during the period of Bernese rule. Exhibits, dating from Celtic times, are varied and include memorabilia from the various Vevey Wine festivals, famous local celebrations that were instituted in the 17th century and continue today.

Also worth a visit is the **Musée Jenisch** (Jenisch Museum), housed in a neoclassical-inspired building. It has art by Swiss and foreign painters, including 700 works by the Expressionist master Oskar Kokoschka, and the cantonal print room with master prints from many periods.

Musée Historique du Vieux Vevey
*rue du Château 2,
t 021 921 07 22,
www.museehistorique vevey.ch; open April–Oct Tues–Sun 11–5; Nov–Mar 2–5.30*

Musée de la Confrérie des Vignerons
*rue du Château 2,
t 021 923 87 05,
www.fetedesvignerons. ch; open April–Oct Tues–Sun 10.30–12, and 2–5.30; Nov–Mar closed in the morning*

Musée Jenisch
*avenue de la Gare 2,
t 021 921 29 50,
www.museejenisch.ch; open Tues–Sun 11–5.30; adm*

Lavaux Vineyard Terraces

Starting just west of Vevey, and continuing for about 20 miles (32km) to Lausanne, the slopes of the north bank of Lake Geneva are covered with vine-planted terraces. Although there is some evidence that vines were cultivated here in Roman times, these terraces date to when the Benedictine and Cistercian monasteries dominated the area during the 11th century.

This is one of Switzerland's most famous wine areas and there is a good reason why very little is known about it outside the country – the Swiss drink most of the wine themselves. These vineyards have been in the possession of the same families for many generations and the ways of working have evolved over the centuries; any changes have to be in keeping with local traditions.

Cully is the capital of the Vignoble de Lavaux and amongst the most important wines, red and white, are Dézaley, St Saphorin and Espesses. In June 2007 the Lavaux vineyards were designated a UNESCO World Heritage site.

Services in Montreux and Vevey

ⓘ **Montreux >**
Montreux-Vevey Tourisme: Pavillon d'information, place de l'Eurovision, t 0848 86 84 84, www.montreux-vevey.com; open mid-May–mid-Sept Mon–Fri 9–6, Sat–Sun 9.30–5; mid-Sept–mid-May Mon–Fri 9–12, 1–5.30, Sat–Sun 10–2

ⓘ **Vevey >**
Montreux-Vevey Tourisme: Grand-Place 29, t 0848 86 84 84, www.montreux-vevey.com; open mid-May–mid-Sept Mon–Fri 9–6, Sat 8.30–12.30; mid-Sept–mid-May Mon–Fri 9–12, 1–5.30, Sat 9–12

Guided Tours

Walking tours of Montreux (April–Sept on Wed, Thurs, Fri and Sat) and Vevey (May–Sept on Wed, Thurs and Fri) take place at 10am, cost CHF 10 and are organized by Montreux-Vevey Tourisme.

There are many different **guided tours** to the Lavaux vineyard terraces. Mini-trains, the **Lavaux Express**, www.lavaux-express.com, depart from Cully and Lutry (both towns can be easily reached on the train from Montreux/Vevey or Lausanne).

There are lots of **self-guided trails** that wind through these vineyards allowing stops for wine-tasting along the way. These routes are shown in detail on the Lavaux website, www.lavaux.com.

Festivals in Montreux and Vevey

April: Montreux, **Montreux Choral Festival**, www.choralfestival.ch.
July: Montreux, **Montreux Jazz Festival**, www.montreuxjazz.com.

Founded by Claude Nobs in 1967, this two-week festival has become one of the premier events in Switzerland. It incorporates other styles of music besides jazz and attracts top artists from around the world.

Aug: Vevey, **Festival of Street Artists**.
Sept: Montreux, **Classical Musical Festival**.
Nov: Montreux, **Art Gallery**.
Nov: Vevey, **St Martin's Fair**, dating from the 1500s and one of Switzerland's oldest.
Nov: Montreux, **Brass Band Competition**.
Dec: Montreux, **Comedy Festival**, www.montreuxfestivaldurire.
Dec: Montreux, **Christmas Market**, www.montreuxnoel.ch. Rapidly becoming one of the area's most popular events with more than 100 chalet-style stalls along the quayside.

Shopping in Montreux and Vevey

Bazar Suisse, Grand Rue 24, Montreux, t 021 963 32 74, www.bazarsuisse.ch. The best place to buy Swiss Army knives; also on sale are music boxes, cuckoo clocks with lovely wood carvings and a host of other items. It also has a 'Freddie Mercury Corner' that features souvenirs including world-exclusive items.

Where to Stay in Montreux and Vevey

Montreux

****Eden au Lac**, rue du Théâtre 1, t 021 966 08 00, *www.eden montreux.ch* (*expensive*). This has a wonderful location on Lake Geneva, conveniently close to the centre of Montreux. Behind a delightful Victorian façade, the interior has a Louis XVI décor while preserving the original style. Each of the 105 rooms has ultra-modern facilities. A fine restaurant, too, plus a large garden and pool.

***Tra La La**, rue du Temple 2, t 021 963 49 73, *www.tralalahotel.ch* (*moderate*). Located in the Old Town, this hotel started life as the home of an affluent villager nearly 400 years ago, became a hostel in 1900 and in 2008 it was renovated using the musical heritage of Montreux as its theme. Each of the 33 rooms and 3 suites is dedicated to an artist who has contributed to the city's reputation, and they offer a harmonious combination of comfort and elegance. Has a small restaurant, lounge and wine bar.

***Splendid**, Grand-Rue 52, t 021 966 79 79, *www.hotel-splendid.ch* (*moderate*). This is a charming Victorian hotel in a privileged position across from the lake. The 24 rooms, many with private balcony or loggia, have an old-fashioned ambience. There is a pleasant lounge and a dining room that offers fine cuisine.

Vevey

*****Hotel des Trois Couronnes**, rue d'Italie 49, t 021 923 32 00,

⭐ Hotel des Trois Couronnes >

www.hoteldestroiscouronnes.com (*luxury*). With a 150-year tradition, this is a charming hotel by the shores of the lake, close to the centre. Its rooms, suites and junior suites are spacious with traditional décor and balconies overlooking the lake; the public areas are stately and marble-colonnaded. In the summer months, dine on culinary French masterpieces in the terrace restaurant. Also a Puressens spa and health centre with underwater music in the pool.

Auberge Du Raisin, place de l'Hôtel de Ville 1, Cully, t 021 799 21 31, *www. aubergeduraisin.ch* (*expensive*). The less than totally convenient location (in Cully) and the small effort involved in getting here will quickly be forgotten once you arrive. The setting on the Lavaux shore of Lac Léman and at the foot of the vineyard of the same name is lovely and the hotel itself is delightful. The owners have filled a wonderful old house with period furniture and paintings by Old Masters. The 7 rooms, suite and apartment are beautifully and classically decorated and there is also a pleasant, shady terrace.

Hostellerie de Genève, place du Marché 11, t 021 921 45 77, *www. hotelgeneve.ch* (*inexpensive*). A charming small hotel located in the centre, just a moment's walk from the lake. It offers 10 pleasant rooms, a shady terrace and a restaurant that specializes in Italian and classic cuisine.

Eating Out in Montreux and Vevey

Montreux

Café-Restaurant et Caveau les Vignerons, rue Industrielle 30 bis, t 021 963 25 70 (*very expensive*). A quaint bodega-style restaurant on the edge of the Old Town. Look for traditional regional specialities such as fondues, raclette and *entrecôte du vigneron. Closed on Sun.*

White Horse Pub, Grand Rue 28, **t** 021 963 15 92 (*very expensive*). Quite a realistic interpretation of an English pub with a fantastic location on the main street and just across from the lake. From Mon–Fri, between 12–2, the *menu du jour* is good value.

Le Palais Oriental, quai E.-Ansermet 6, **t** 021 963 12 71, *www.palais oriental.ch (moderate)*. An unusual Oriental restaurant whose specialities include Moroccan, Lebanese and Iranian cuisine. They also offer imported Iranian caviar from the Caspian Sea.

Vevey

Restaurant Denis Martin, Rue du Château 2, **t** 021 921 12 10, *www. denismartin.ch (very expensive)*. Denis Martin has crafted for himself and his restaurant an international reputation for avant-garde cuisine

with Asian flavours. Constantly experimenting to achieve unusual, memorable dishes, the results are always exceptional. For an unforgettable gastronomic experience partake of the 26-course Evolution Menu at an eye-watering CHF 310. *Open for dinner only at 7pm. Closed Sun and Mon, mid-Jul–mid-Aug, two weeks over Christmas and New Year.*

The Auberge Du Raisin, place de l'Hôtel de Ville 1, Cully, **t** 021 799 21 31, *www.aubergeduraisin.ch (moderate–inexpensive)*. Within the small hotel of the same name are two beautiful dining rooms where you can expect creative cuisine, particularly with game and fish. The desserts are exquisite. The cellar features wines from Switzerland (including the local St Saphorin), France and America. This is a truly special restaurant where you can expect a culinary experience, not just a meal.

✪ Gruyères

Gruyères

Gruyères is synonymous with Switzerland's world-famous product, cheese. However, there is more to Gruyères than just cheese. Set on an isolated hill that dramatically controls the broad valley, and with towering mountains looking down upon it, it is a charming, fortified medieval village with an intriguing history and a famous castle.

Nineteen counts of the dynasty of Gruyères resided here beginning in the 11th century and ending when the last, Michael I, left the castle in 1554 and died in exile. The cantons of Fribourg and Bern subsequently divided the county between them, and the castle was used as a residence of the bailiff of Fribourg from that time until 1798. In 1848 it passed into private hands and the families of Bovy and Balland, and the many important artists who also lived there from time to time, left an unusual heritage of their own. Since 1938 the structure has been maintained by the canton of Fribourg.

Getting to and around Gruyères

A look at a map will verify that Gruyères is due north of Montreux/Vevey, but the topography of this area makes the journey by **road** somewhat indirect. Take the N12 autoroute north to the Bulle exit and then loop around south to Gruyères. The village itself, however, is car-free, so you are obliged to leave your car in the large car park just below the village on the hill. Alternatively, from the north, take the motorway from Bern that bypasses Fribourg and then exit to Bulle from where Gruyères is just a few kms away.

A combination of **trains** and a **bus** may be taken from Vevey to Gruyères, though it is a little complicated. The first leg is by bus, which departs from Vevey train station for the 25min trip to Châtel-St-Denis train station. From there a train journey of approximately the same duration will take you on to Bulle, where another train takes you on to Gruyères. However, you are not there yet! Gruyères' train station is not centrally located and it's either a long uphill walk or a short bus ride up to the village itself.

No option really, you have to **walk** to get around the village itself.

You will need a **car** for the trip to Moléson-sur-Gruyères.

A visit to Gruyères, with its population of just 1,500, is like taking a trip back in time, and a walk through the uncluttered village could best be likened to strolling through a living museum. Obviously tourism plays a major part in the village's existence, but while visitors' needs are certainly catered to – there is even a boutique or two – it is not obtrusive. The restriction of automobiles, too, marvellously enhances the ambience.

Perched at an altitude of 2,625ft (800m) Gruyères basically consists of just one street with a castle at the end. Three gates give access to the village, but most will enter from the north through the Chavonne gate. From this vantage point, where the cobblestone street widens somewhat, the castle, framed by the Dent-de-Broc mountain, dominates the background. Without doubt, the castle should be your first destination.

Château de Gruyères
t 026 921 21 02, www.chateau-gruyeres.ch; open April–Oct 9–6; Nov–Mar 10–4.30; adm, combined with the Museum H. R. Giger; request a brochure in English

The **Château de Gruyères** offers an array of ancient courtyards and rooms exhibiting eight centuries of architecture, history and culture. The Medieval Garden is a must-see. There is also a multimedia show, *Gruyères*, which through a combination of high-definition images, music, light and sound tells the story of the castle. The show is 18 minutes long and is shown at regular intervals throughout the day in the projection room.

Museum H. R. Giger
t 026 921 22 00; www.hrgigermuseum.ch; open April–Oct 10–6; Nov–Mar Tues–Fri 1–5, Sat–Sun 10–6; adm, combined with the castle

This castle is also home to the **Museum H. R. Giger**, where you can immerse yourself in the world of fantastic art. In 1980, H. R. Giger, a Swiss artist, won the Oscar for Best Visual Effects for his work on the film *Alien*. The museum contains the biggest existing collection of the artist's works, in the form of paintings, sculptures, furnishings and film sets. Between reality and fiction, past and future, H. R. Giger takes you on a journey into the fascinating world

ⓘ Gruyères >
La Gruyères Tourisme:
place des Alpes 26,
t 0848 424 424,
www.la-gruyere.ch;
open April, May, June
and Sept daily
9.30–12.15 and 1–5.30;
July–Aug 9.15–5.45

Where to Stay and Eat in Gruyères

***Hostellerie St Georges, t 026 921 83 00 (*moderate*).** This is a delightful inn, located in the centre of the village. The rooms are spacious and comfortable, and there are a couple of restaurants, a bar and a large covered terrace. Staying here on a half-board basis is the best option in Gruyères.

Le Chalet, t 026 921 34 34, *www. chalet-gruyeres.ch* (*moderate*). This traditional restaurant is a great alternative for fondue or raclette, however.

of your imagination. The H. R. Giger Bar, opposite the museum, is also well worth visiting.

La Maison
du Gruyère
t 026 921 84 00,
www.lamaisondu
gruyere.ch; open
June–Sept 9–7;
Oct–May 9–6;
cheesemaking at 9, 11,
12.30, 2. 30; adm

As for the rest of the village, just wander around, discover its charms and stop for a cheese fondue or raclette for lunch. The local cheese is for sale in many shops, but you may want to get it directly from the dairy. Just down the hill from the village, at Pringy-Gruyères, **La Maison du Gruyère** has a visitors' gallery from where you can observe the making of the cheese. While this is a commercial dairy, it still adheres to traditions that date back to the 12th century. There is a shop and the Restaurant de la Fromagerie, which serves regional dishes.

Moléson-sur-Gruyères

Moléson-sur-
Gruyères
www.moleson.ch

To get a different perspective of the area, move on down the valley a few kilometres to **Moléson-sur-Gruyères**, from where a combination of funicular and cable car will whisk you up to the summit of Moléson at 6,568ft (2,002m). There are panoramic views, which can be seen through the world's most powerful binoculars at the Observatory on the summit.

Les Diablerets

Although the Auberge de la Poste became a modest guest house in 1789 (and is still run by the same family to this day), it wasn't until 1856 that the first hotel saw the beginning of real tourism in Les Diablerets. Over a century later, in 1964, the first cable car was constructed. Cleverly, Les Diablerets has managed the growth of tourism very well indeed, building upon its original infrastructure, adding new facilities and developing a whole array of outdoor activities for every season – all without impinging upon the ambience of this charming country village.

Getting to and around Les Diablerets

There are only two ways to access Les Diablerets by **car**. The easiest is to take the Aigle exit off the A9 motorway that runs around Lake Geneva and through the Valais, turn northeast towards Ormont Dessous and then take the road east to Les Diablerets. Alternatively, the only other way in is to take the road south from Gstaad via Gsteig.

The only **train** access to Les Diablerets is via a branch line running from Aigle. Aigle is on the mainline running from Geneva around the lake to Lausanne and Montreux, and then from Aigle to Brig, in the eastern part of the Valais.

This is a very small village and most of the attractions begin some distance outside the village itself, particularly access to the Glacier 3000 and Lac Retaud, so it's advisable to have a **car**.

Both Col du Pillon (the starting point of a trip to Glacier 3000) and Lac Retaud can be accessed by the Les Diablerets to Gstaad **bus**, but at best services run hourly and often less frequently.

Glacier 3000
*t 024 492 09 23,
www.glacier3000.ch*

Whatever the season the highlight of a visit to Les Diablerets is the **Glacier 3000**. The first cable car here, the Glacier des Diablerets, was built in 1964. It was replaced by new cable cars in November 1999. The trip begins outside the village at **Col du Pillon**, 5,072ft (1,546m), where the first of two cable cars will be waiting to whisk you up to the summit. This, one of the highest vantage points in Switzerland – nearly 10,000ft (3,000m) – offers a vast panorama of mountain peaks, including the Matterhorn 14,692ft (4,478m) and Mont Blanc at 15,771ft (4,807m). It is also a winter and summer skiing area with a network of chair lifts, ski lifts and cross-country trails.

Once you reach the Glacier 3000 there are any number of exciting activities – some more energetic than others. Everyone will enjoy a ride on the Snow Bus across the glacier itself and it is also possible to take a husky dog sled ride. There is also the world's highest bobsleigh track, the Alpine Coaster, 1,000m long with ten turns, six waves, three jumps and two bridges. It is possible to hike and cross-country ski across the glacier, but this should only be undertaken by experienced, fit people, who have the correct equipment. Both start by taking the chairlift down to the ice from Glacier 3000. Most people though, will be content to enjoy a snack and a drink while enjoying the views.

In the summer there are over 124 miles (200km) of **hiking paths**. A favourite excursion is to take the cable car up to Isenau, from where a gentle walk of around a half-hour or so will bring you down to **Lac Retaud**. Really, it is not much of a lake, but the restaurant of the same name not only has some delicious dishes (it specializes in local mushrooms) but it also serves a home-made fruit-flavoured *liqueur de maison* (liquor of the house) that is guaranteed to refresh you. Another easy walk down deposits you on the main road that, if you decide not to wait for the postbus, leads back to the village.

Another interesting possibility is to take the chair lift to **Les Mazots**, where you will not only find a traditional restaurant but, also, the Fromagerie. Here, you can see – and later taste – how the famous mountain cheese L'Etivaz is made.

Winter-sports lovers will have difficulty deciding what to do first in the Les Diablerets area. There are more than 75 miles (20km) of ski runs serviced by an array of transportation, including more than 50 ski lifts. The Swiss Ski and Snowboard School, located in the tourist office, is there to help you out. Cross-country skiing, ice-skating, curling, tobogganing and bobsleighing are also on offer.

Festivals in Les Diablerets

(i) **Les Diablerets >**
Diablerets Tourisme: Maison du Tourisme, rue de la Gare, t 024 492 33 58, www.diablerets.ch; open high season Dec–April, July–Aug Mon–Sun 8.30–6.30; low season May–June, Sept–Nov Mon–Fri 8.30–6, Sat 8.30–12.30, 2.30–6, Sun 9.30–1

26 July: Devil's Night – a traditional village festival.
July/Aug: Rösti Festival at Isenau.
Late Sept: International Alpine Film Festival.
Mid-Oct: Folk Music Festival.

Shopping in Les Diablerets

Holiday Sport, t 024 492 37 17. Almost directly across from the tourist office, has a full range of skis, snowboards, snowshoes and sledges available for hire, as well as mountain bikes, hiking boots, etc.

Where to Stay in Les Diablerets

****Eurotel Victoria, t** 024 492 37 21, *www.eurotel-victoria.ch (moderate).* A large, modern hotel, just outside the village centre. Its rooms are contemporary in style and have all the facilities expected in a 4-star hotel. Pleasant public rooms and fine restaurants, plus an indoor pool and sauna.

***Les Sources, t** 024 492 01 00, *www.hotel-les-sources.ch (moderate).* Just outside the centre of the village within spacious private grounds, this offers rooms equipped with shower, toilet, telephone, radio and TV. Other amenities are the La Marmotte restaurant, an on-site bar, a lounge with an open fireplace and a leisure room with TV/games.

Auberge de la Poste, rue de la Gare, t 024 492 31 24, *www.auberge delaposte.ch (inexpensive).* A typical flower-bedecked Swiss chalet in the heart of the village, which has been run by the same family since 1789. Doubling as a small restaurant (whose speciality is raclette and cheese fondue), its rooms are for either one, two, three, four or five people.

Eating Out in Les Diablerets

Alpine Restaurant Oldegg, Glacier 3000, t 024 492 09 23, *www. glacier3000.ch (moderate).* This is found at an elevation of just under 10,000ft (3,000m) and has a large sun terrace with fantastic views over the glacier. Expect a daily menu and snacks.

Les Mazots, Restaurant Fromagerie, Col de la Croix, **t** 024 492 10 23, *www.diablerets.ch* (*moderate*). Located at an altitude of 5,633ft (1,717m), this is a traditional mountain restaurant (*see* p.227).

Lac Retaud Restaurant, **t** 024 492 31 29 (*moderate*). Overlooking the small lake of the same name, at an altitude of 5,577ft (1,700m) (*see* p.226). In addition to the usual regional dishes and mushroom specialities, they serve strawberries and cream and meringues. Try also the home-made jam and the *liqueur de maison* (*see* p.226). *Closed Nov–early May.*

Valais

The Valais is one of Switzerland's most emblematic regions. The Alps protecting this valley divide the country and form an almost impenetrable border with the rest of Switzerland to the north and Italy to the south. The Valais begins in the east, close to where the Rhône Glacier gives birth to what becomes the mighty river of the same name. Then it takes a southwesterly course, descending past attractive villages towards Brig, which strategically controls access to the Simplon Pass and Italy.

From Brig the Valais follows the Rhône almost due west to Martigny, another historically important town. Although this stretch of the Valais is not particularly attractive in itself, it is the gateway to numerous valleys, running north and south, that most certainly are. These lead to such world-famous villages as Zermatt and Verbier and the lesser-known Lötschental and Val d'Anniviers. Only one resort in the Valais isn't in a valley: Crans-Montana sits on a south-facing, sun-drenched shelf parallel to the Valais itself. From Martigny the Rhône and Valais take a sharp northernly course until it officially ends a little before Lake Geneva.

12

Don't miss

⚀ **Museums and sculpture park**
Fondation Pierre Gianadda, Martigny
p.236

⚁ **Beautiful valley**
Lötschental p.248

⚂ **Unique spot for lunch**
Drehrestaurant, Saas-Fee p.252

⚃ **Mount magnificent**
Klein Matterhorn, Zermatt p.257

⚄ **Incredible vista**
Gornergrat, Zermatt p.257

See map overleaf

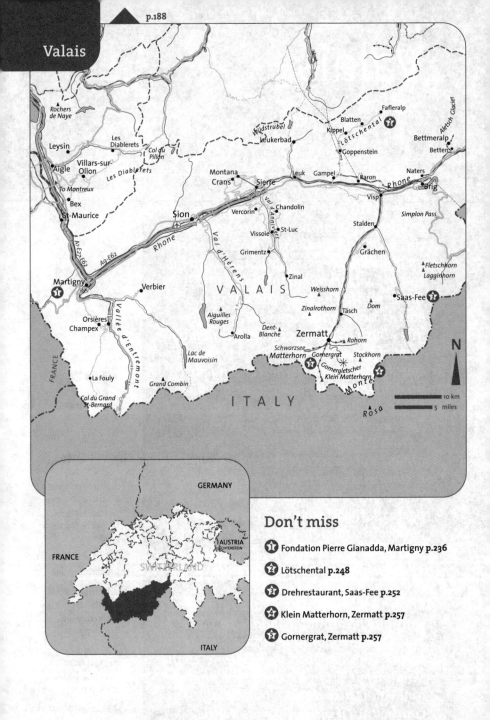

p.188

Rochers de Naye
Leysin
Les Diablerets
Aigle
Villars-sur-Ollon
Les Diablerets
Col du Pillon
To Montreux
Bex
St-Maurice
Martigny
A1-E27/E62
A9-E62
Rhone
Verbier
Orsières
Champex
Vallée d'Entremont
La Fouly
Col du Grand St-Bernard

Montana
Crans
Sion
Vercorin
Val d'Anniviers
Chandolin
Vissoie
St-Luc
Grimentz
Zinal
Weisshorn
Zinalrothorn
VALAIS
Aiguilles Rouges
Arolla
Dent-Blanche
Lac de Mauvoisin
Grand Combin
Val d'Hérens
Sierre
Leuk
Gampel
Raron
Rhone
Visp
Stalden
Grächen
Fletschhorn
Lagginhorn
Saas-Fee
Dom
Täsch
Rohorn
Zermatt
Schwarzsee
Matterhorn
Gornergrat
Gornergletscher
Klein Matterhorn
Stockhorn
Monte Rosa

Wildstrubel
Leukerbad
Blatten
Kippel
Lötschental
Goppenstein
Fafleralp
Bettmeralp
Betten
Aletsch Glacier
Naters
Brig
Simplon Pass

FRANCE
ITALY
N
10 km
5 miles

GERMANY
FRANCE
SWITZERLAND
AUSTRIA
LIECHTENSTEIN
ITALY

Don't miss

1. Fondation Pierre Gianadda, Martigny **p.236**

2. Lötschental **p.248**

3. Drehrestaurant, Saas-Fee **p.252**

4. Klein Matterhorn, Zermatt **p.257**

5. Gornergrat, Zermatt **p.257**

Getting to the Valais

Access to the Valais is limited by its geographical constraints.

By Air

Sion has a small airport, *www.sionairport.ch*, and a limited winter schedule offered by **Snowjet**, *www.snowjet.co.uk*, operating from London Stansted.

By Train

Trains on the following routes run to Visp and Brig: from the east there is direct access from the Lake Geneva region throughout the length of the valley; from the west, trains run from Andermatt; and from the north, you can travel from the Bernese Oberland through the Lötschberg Tunnel – the world's longest under land. If you are travelling from Italy, trains from Domodossola and Milan also run into Visp and Brig.

By Car

From the east the A9 motorway cuts through the Valais to Sierre/Siders, and on to Brig by regular roads. From the west a rather more difficult road runs from Rhône Glacier to Oberwald, and then down the Valais to Brig. From Brig the road runs south via the Simplon Tunnel or Pass to Domodossola, Italy. Also from the south, there is access from Aosta, Italy via the Grand Saint Bernard Pass or Tunnel north to Martigny, and from Chamonix, France via the Forclaz Pass to Martigny. There is no direct road access from the north; cars need to be loaded on trains and transported through the Lötschberg rail tunnel.

Getting around the Valais

The train system directly along the length of the valley stops at almost all places along the way. Other than that, trains only run south from Visp to Stalden-Saas – where it's necessary to change for a bus to Saas-Fee, and on to Zermatt, and from Martigny to Le Châble, where a bus continues to Verbier. It is necessary to use **postbuses**, *www.postbus.ch*, for all other destinations, except you can take a **funicular** between Sierre/Siders and Crans-Montana.

Considered to be the oldest of the alpine passes, the Grand Saint Bernard pass runs northeast–southwest through the Valais. It has been used since the Bronze Age and, reputedly, Hannibal and his famous elephants crossed it in 217 BC. In 57 BC the Romans, under the command of Julius Caesar, arrived in Martigny to conquer the local Celts, naming the area *Vallis Poenina*.

By 580 the bishop of Valais chose Sion as his headquarters, and by the late 9th century this area came under the control of the kingdom of Jurane Burgundy. In 999 the bishop of Sion was given all the land by the Burgundian king, Rudolph III. In later years the Lower Valais passed to Savoy and from then on, known as the counts of the Valais, the bishops faced a continuing struggle with the dukes of Savoy, culminating with a victory in 1475. The Lower Valais was in their control until 1798.

The Valais region has always been overwhelmingly Catholic and, as such, the Protestant Reformation didn't take hold here. The Valais became an associated member of the Swiss Confederation in March 1529, and led by the count-bishops became a republic in 1628. The count-bishops managed to retain power until Napoleon's army invaded in 1798 and pronounced a revolutionary Republic of Valais. Very soon after in the same year it was incorporated into the

Helvetic Republic, which evolved into the Rhodanic Republic in 1802. Eight years later it was annexed and made a department by Napoleonic France, but independence was quickly regained in 1813 and in 1815 the Valais became a canton in the Swiss Confederation. More problems seemed likely when, in 1845, the Valais joined up with the Catholic separatist league Sonderbund, but two years later, and without any fighting, the Valais submitted to confederate forces.

Sion

Sion (Sitten in German) is the capital of the Valais and makes for an impressive sight. In the centre of the wide Rhône valley, it sits at the foot of two isolated, castle-topped hills surrounded on both sides – and for long distances – by majestic snow-capped mountains whose lower slopes are covered with vineyards, producing the fine wines that are one of the area's claim to fame.

These wines, and an interesting history, make Sion an attractive proposition in its own right. However, in winter time the town is also important as a gateway to the majestic winter sports resorts of the Valais, such as Verbier (see p.238), Crans-Montana (see p.239), Saas-Fee (see p.251) and Zermatt (see p.254).

History

After Julius Caesar's campaign, the citizens of *Sedunum* – both locals and Romans – lived at the foot of the twin towers, Valère and Tourbillon. The fledgling city underwent several changes of status, and in 377 was home to the first Christian inscription in Switzerland – praising the magistrate Asclepiodotes for replacing an imperial building by an even more sumptuous one. On the main route to Italy, the city remained prosperous until the Barbarian invasions, which caused the bishop of canton Valais to move from Martigny (*Octodurum*) to Sion in 580. King Rudolph III provided the bishops with a regular subsidy from 999, and early the following century, in 1032, Sion became the Imperial City, with the bishop ruling over the whole of the canton of Valais from Martigny to the Furka. This was reinforced early in the 12th century with the construction of the church of Valère.

However, the proximity and overlapping of territory of the Counts of Savoy – the rulers of the Lower Valais – led to more than one war. Finally, in 1475, after having been overrun by the Savoyards, federal troops retook Sion after the Battle of La Planta, thus reuniting the Valais with Sion as its political and geographical capital. From then until the late 1700s the powers of the bishops

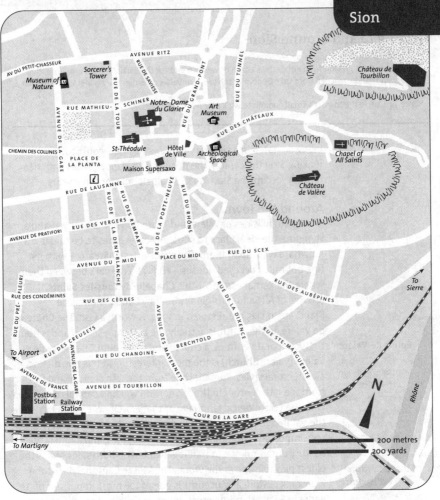

were relentlessly watered down in favour of civil power, with the brief exception of 1516–22 when Bishop Mathew Schiner was promoted to cardinal. However, in 1780 and to great joy, the Valais renewed its alliance with the seven Catholic cantons and the citizens of the Lower Valais claimed Sion and demanded equal rights. Napoleon, seizing upon this and wanting to keep the access to Italy under his control, annexed Valais to France as the 'Simplon Department', and Sion became a prefecture with a mayor.

The emperor was defeated in 1815 when the valley of the Rhone joined the Swiss Confederation, but the Lower Valais claimed its own political rights, with Sion becoming the capital of the French-speaking district and Sierre the capital of the German-speaking people. Nevertheless, problems continued with the Upper Valais

Getting to and around Sion

For information on arriving by air *see* p.231.

Trains pass through Sion from either the eastern or western ends of the Valais, and via Brig from Italy.

By **car**, Sion can be reached from Lake Geneva or the western Valais on either the A9 and/or the regular road.

Once you are in the town it's small enough to **walk** around.

being defeated in a civil war in 1840 and a new constitution making Sion the capital. The people of the Upper Valais had their revenge, occupying Sion in 1844 – albeit only for three years.

Around the Town

The twin hillsides of Valère and Tourbillon dominate Sion and are therefore the ideal place to start, although it has to be said it is a long hard walk up to them. The avenue des Châteaux – with its fine but much decayed houses – ends at a car park between them, where the Romanesque/Gothic **Chapelle de Tous-les-Saints** (Chapel of All Saints), originally built by Canon Thomas de Blandrate in 1325 but restored in 1964, is worth a visit. The **Château de Valère**, to the south, is actually the better preserved and is home to two separate entities, a church and a museum. The **Église de Valère** (Valère Church) is the most interesting. It has two distinct architectural styles: Romanesque from the 12th century and Gothic from the 13th century. In the former you will find capitals decorated with the teratological language of that era. Of note in the latter are the painted tomb of Guillaume de Rarogne, bishop from 1437 to 1451; important 15th- and 16th-century frescoes; and a rare 14th-century organ, unique in that it is painted on both sides and is the oldest playable one in the world. The **Musée Cantonal d'Histoire** (Cantonal Historical Museum), is one of the most important of its genre in Switzerland. Its most important exhibits are the objects from the excavations of Roman *Octodurum* in Martigny, including the head of a Mithraic bull, and medieval collections featuring a liturgical chest and sculptures.

Église de Valère
t 027 606 47 15; open June–Sept Mon–Sun 10–6; Oct–May Tues–Sun 11–5; adm; guided tours mid-Mar–mid-Nov 10.15, 11.15, 12.15, 2.15, 3.15, 4.15

Musée Cantonal d'Histoire
t 027 606 47 15, www.vs.ch/musees; open Tues–Sun 11–5; adm

Another steep climb up the opposite, northern hill brings you to the ruins of the **Château de Tourbillon**. Originally built by Bishop Boniface de Challant between 1290 and 1308, it was almost completely destroyed by the Patriots of Valais in 1461. The Bishop of Raron, Guillaume VI, rebuilt it in 1477, but a major fire destroyed it once more in 1788.

Château de Tourbillon
t 027 606 47 45; open Tues–Sun 10–5

Back westwards down the hill there are two more museums. The **Musée d'Art** (Art Museum) is located in two wonderful old houses. The exhibits here are devoted to local and national art from the 17th century to date, with representations of Baroque, romantic and primitivist work and also abstract, kinetic and minimalist

Musée d'Art
place de la Majorie 15, t 027 606 46 90, www.vs.ch/musees; open Tues–Sun 11–5; adm

works by the likes of Dubuis, Duarte and Zuber. Just to its south is the **Espace d'Archéologie** (Archeological Space). Here you will find extensive collections documenting the occupation of the Valais from 30,000 BC to the end of the Roman era in the 5th century, and important objects from the Bronze Age.

Espace d'Archéologie
rue des Châteaux 12,
t 027 606 47 00,
www.vs.ch/musees;
open Tues–Sun 1–6;
adm

All of the remaining attractions in Sion are found within a small area bounded by the rue du Grand-Pont (to the east), avenue Ritz (to the north), avenue de la Gare (to the west) and rue de Lausanne (to the south).

Hôtel de ville
Grand-Pont 12

The **hôtel de ville** (town hall) has a façade dating from 1660 that is adorned by an astronomical clock. Inside, in the entrance hall, is the earliest Christian inscription in Switzerland that dates from 377 and praises the munificence of the magistrate Asclepidotes. Upstairs, behind magnificent wooden carved doors, the Salle de la Bourgeoisie has equally wonderfully carved panels and portraits of two great rivals: George Supersaxo, champion of the French party, and Mathew Schiner, the bishop and cardinal who championed the Empire.

Maison Supersaxo
passage Supersaxo

Across the road is another Supersaxo connection, in the form of the **Maison Supersaxo** (House of Supersaxo), dating from 1505, which features a Gothic staircase, carved doors and a beautiful carved and painted ceiling by Jacobinus de Malacridis. In this immediate area there are also several other Baroque or classical homes of old aristocratic families. One of the most important, on rue de Lausanne, is the **Kalbermatten House** – known as 'The Prefecture' – that was the house of the French ambassador, Chateaubriand.

Notre-Dame du Glarier
Cathédrale 13,
t 027 322 80 66

Église St-Théodule
rue St-Théodule 14

There are also two churches found next to each other, with the most important being the **Notre-Dame du Glarier**, whose Romanesque tower indicates that it was started in the first half of the 12th century. However, wars in succeeding centuries meant that it was completed in the late Gothic style by the bishops Supersaxo, Jost de Silenen and Nicholas Schiner between the years 1457 and 1522. The other church, **Église St-Théodule**, dedicated to the patron saint of the Valais, dates from 1514–16 and was constructed by the master sculptor Ulrich Ruffiner under the patronage of Mathew Schiner.

Musée de la Nature
avenue de la Gare 42,
t 027 606 47 30,
www.vs.ch/musees;
open Tues–Sun 1–5; adm

Tour des Sorciers
rue de la Tour

The last two attractions are situated in the northwest of this quadrant. The **Musée de la Nature** (Museum of Nature) exhibits, amongst other things, the last specimens of important species like the bear, wolf and bearded vulture that once inhabited the area. The **Tour des Sorciers** (Sorcerer's Tower) is now all that is left of the walls that once encircled the city.

Tourist Information in Sion

(i) Sion >
Sion Tourisme:
place de la Planta,
t 027 327 77 27,
www.siontourism.ch;
open Mon–Fri 9–6, Sat
9.30–4, Sun 9–12.30

Tours

The tourist office organizes various guided walks, including around the Old Town and the Château Valère.

Le P'Tit Sédunois, is one of those little 'trains' offering round trips in the city, Mon–Sat, from the train station via the tourist office to Valère and back.

Where to Stay in Sion

★★★Europa, rue de l'Envol 19, **t** 027 322 24 23, *www.hoteleuoropa-sion.ch* (*moderate*). This, the largest hotel in Sion with 65 contemporary rooms, is located on the west side of town towards the airport. An interesting selection of dishes is available at the Grissini Pizzeria and Ristorante.

★★★Atlantic, route de Sion 38, **t** 027 455 25 35, *www.hotelatlantic.ch* (*moderate*). As there isn't much of a selection of hotels in Sion itself, this hotel, just a few miles to the east in Sierre, is a very good alternative. Besides 38 rooms with modern facilities, it offers a very fine restaurant (with a fantastic shrimp dish) and a large garden with an oversize swimming pool that is overlooked by vineyards.

Eating Out in Sion

Le Jardin Gourmand, avenue de la Gare 22, **t** 027 323 23 10 (*expensive– moderate*) *www.lejardin gourmand.ch*. An elegant restaurant with a terrace in the city centre. It offers imaginative cuisine based around market-fresh produce and it has an enticing array of special menus.

Grotto de La Fontaine, Grand-Pont 21, **t** 027 323 83 77 (*expensive–moderate*). A charming, informal – expect long marble tables – restaurant whose specialities are dishes from Ticino and northern Italy: from traditional pizzas to dishes featuring white truffles, quail, rabbit and pigeon ravioli.

West of Sion

Martigny

Martigny, the first important town heading east into the Valais, sits under the Château de la Bâtiaz alongside the Rhône River. The town itself is quite small and not particularly impressive, but it has important historical and wine connections.

Martigny, situated at a crossroads between Switzerland, France and Italy, is famous for its Roman history. Julius Caesar's army was defeated here in 57 BC, and *Octodurum*, as Martigny was then known, was an important trading post. The Emperor Claudius, had an imperial forum here in 47 BC, and the settlement, then called *Claudii Vallensium*, became the capital of the Pennine Alps.

★ Fondation
Pierre Gianadda
rue du Forum 59,
t 027 722 39 78,
www.gianadda.ch; open
June–Nov daily 9–7;
Nov–June daily 10–6;
adm

The best way to gain a greater understanding of the history of the town is to visit the acclaimed Fondation Pierre Gianadda. This place has a curious history: in 1976 whilst planning to build a house on a plot of land that he owned, Léonard Gianadda

Getting around West of Sion

Martigny is on the main **train** line that runs the length of the Valais. By **car**, from the north it is reached on the A9 motorway from Lac Léman; from the southeast you can travel via the Forclaz Pass from Chamonix, France; from the south there is access from Aosta, Italy via the Grand Saint Bernard Pass; from the east it is reached from Brig along the main road, and the A9 via Sion. Everything here is accessible on **foot**, although the Château de la Bâtiaz and the Fondation Pierre Gianadda can also be reached on the little tourist train, **Le Baladeur**, which departs from the place Centrale. The latter can also be reached by bus, which departs from the train station.

For **Verbier, trains** operate from Martigny to Le Châble, from where a **bus** or **cable car** will take you on to the town. By **car**, take the road from Martigny towards the Grand Saint Bernard Pass, then turn off for Le Châble and on up to Verbier. A free **shuttle bus** operates within the resort.

---

discovered the remains of an ancient Celtic temple, the oldest of its kind in the country. Very soon afterwards his brother died in the aftermath of a plane crash and Léonard decided that it would make a fine memorial to his brother, Pierre, if he set up a foundation in his name based around the temple. The foundation has four areas of interest. The most important is **Le Musée Gallo-romain** (Gallo-Roman Museum), built around the temple, which exhibits Roman relics including the Great Bronzes of Octodurus in the form of a three-horned bull. The foundation itself is a part of a fascinating archeological walk that includes the 5,000-seat Domus Minerva amphitheatre, a shrine to Mithras and thermal baths. In the beautiful gardens there is **Le Parc de Sculptures** (Sculpture Park), which features a permanent collection of pieces by world-renowned artists such as Rodin, Brancusi and Moore. Also within the grounds is the fascinating **Cour Chagall** (Chagall Court), the highlight of which is one of Chagall's few mosaics, inaugurated on the 25th anniversary of the foundation. **Le Musée de l'Automobile** (Automobile Museum), the finest in Switzerland, displays 50 veteran vehicles dating from 1897–1939, all of which are in working order; many are the only surviving examples of their kind.

Musée et Chiens du Saint Bernard
rue du Levant 34,
t 027 720 49 20,
www.museesaintbernard.
ch; open daily 10–6; adm

Just a short walk away you will find the **Musée et Chiens du Saint Bernard** (St Bernard Dog Museum). Housed in an old military warehouse this museum explains the story behind the Great St Bernard Hospice and these world-famous dogs. On the ground floor are kennels where you can see the dogs, and on the first floor, by way of innovative exhibitions and a film called *François the Pilgrim*, you can learn about their fascinating history.

Château de la Bâtiaz
rue des Moulins 13,
t 027 721 22 70,
www.batiaz.ch; open
May–June, Sept–Oct
Fri–Sat 11, Sun 11–6;
July–Aug Mon–Thurs 2,
Fri–Sat 11, Sun 11–6

Dominating Martigny is the unusual round tower of the **Château de la Bâtiaz**. It was constructed in 1260 and was fought over continuously by the House of Savoy and the Count-Bishops of Sion. This is the town's only remaining medieval monument.

ⓘ **Martigny >**
Martigny Tourisme:
avenue de la Gare 6,
t 027 720 49 49,
www.martigny.com;
open Nov–April
Mon–Fri 9–12, 2–6, Sat
9–12; May–June,
Sept–Oct Mon–Fri 9–12,
1.30–6.30, Sat 9–12,
1.30–4.30; July–Aug
Mon–Fri 9–6.30, Sat
9–5, Sun and hols
10–12.30, 3–5

Shopping in Martigny

Distillerie Morand, rue de Plaisance 2, t 027 722 20 36, *www.morand.ch*. Fruit brandy is a local speciality, and to gain the AOC symbol of authenticity the fruit must be grown, picked and distilled at this distillery.

Where to Stay in Martigny

Motel des Sports, rue du Forum 15, t 027 722 20 78, *www.moteldes sports.ch* (*moderate*). This modern motel, just a short walk away from the Fondation Pierre Gianadda, offers 38 very pleasant rooms with full amenities and park views. It also has a restaurant featuring a seasonal menu,

and is close to such facilities as the ice arena and swimming pool.

Hotel-Restaurant Forclaz-Touring, rue du Léman 15, t 027 722 27 01, *www.hotelforclaztouring.ch* (*moderate*). Located close to the train station, this hotel has 100 recently renovated modern rooms, two restaurants and bars.

Eating Out in Martigny

Restaurant Les Tres Couronnes, place du Borg 8, t 027 723 21 14 (*expensive/moderate*). Situated in a charming square in a pleasing auberge dating from 1792. Seasonal regional cuisine is served in the characterful inside dining area or on the terrace.

Verbier

Situated in the southwestern Valais and on a south-facing terrace at an altitude of nearly 5,000ft (1,500m), Verbier, in the municipality of Bagnes, is one of the largest ski resort areas in the Alps. It is famous for its off- and semi-off-piste runs and has seven different ski and snowboard schools. The resort attracts a broad clientele including celebrities and royalty who frequent the trendy bars and restaurants, and adrenalin junkies who are in search of perfect powder.

In the summer months there are more than 250 miles (400km) of hiking trails and a further 125 miles (200km) of mountain-bike trails to be explored.

If you want to take a break from physical activities and learn a little about local culture, combined with fine arts exhibitions, visit the **Musée de Bagnes**.

Musée de Bagnes
Le Châble,
t 027 776 15 25; open
July–late Aug Wed–Mon
2–6; late Aug–late Sept
Wed–Sun 2–6

Activities in Verbier

Verbier Sport Plus, t 027 775 33 63. Offers a full range of instruction for winter and summer sports in and around Verbier.

European Snowsport, located in Mountain Air, halfway up hill between place Centrale and the Médran, **t** 027 771 62 22. A small, specialist school offering ski and snowboard instruction and courses.

Events and Festivals in Verbier

Late Mar: Nissan Extreme, *www.xtremeverbier.com*, the most prestigious event in the freeride world with only the top-ranked riders participating.

Mid-April: FIS World Cup Final, *www.xspeedski.net*, the Swiss championship of speed skating.

Late July–early Aug: Verbier Festival, *www.verbierfestival.com*. Started in 1994, this event attracts over 40,000

(i) **Verbier** >

Verbier/Bagnes Tourisme: place Centrale, t 027 775 38 88, www.verbier.ch; open July–Aug Mon–Sat 8–12 and 2–6.30, Sun 9–12 and 3–6.30; mid–Dec–April Mon–Fri 8–12.30 and 2–6.30, Sat 8.30–7, Sun 9–12 and 3–6.30; May–early July, Sept–mid-Dec Mon–Fri 8–12 and 2–6.30, Sat 9–12 and 4–6.30, Sun 9–12

(i) **Le Châble** >

Verbier/Bagnes Tourisme: ch. de la Gare 2, t 027 775 38 88, www.verbier.ch; open July–Aug Mon–Sat 8–12 and 2–6.30, Sun 9–12 and 3–6.30; mid-Dec–April Mon–Fri 8–12.30, 2–6.30, Sat 8.30–7, Sun 9–12, and 3–6.30; May–early July, Sept–mid-Dec Mon–Fri 8–12 and 2–6.30, Sat 9–12 and 4–6.30, Sun 9–12

spectators to listen to young artists perform in this innovative music festival.

Where to Stay in Verbier

*****King's Park Hôtel, rue de la Poste, t 027 775 20 10, *www.kings verbier.ch* (*luxury*). One of the finest hotels in Verbier, it has just 18 large and luxurious suites, some of which have fireplaces; all have magnificent views. The King's Restaurant offers gourmet cuisine, the King's Café is more informal and the King's Cocktail Bar will serve you exotic drinks in a room with 1960s décor. *Open July–Aug, Dec–April.*

***Les Chamois, 1936 Verbier, t 027 771 64 02, *www.hotel-chamois.ch* (*moderate*). This chalet-style hotel has been run by the Oreiller family for 30 years. It offers spacious and comfortable rooms, some suitable for families, with alpine views and has an inviting restaurant with large fireplace. It's just a 2-min walk to the ski lifts and the centre of the resort. *Open June–July, Nov–April.*

**Mirabeau, rue de la Tintaz, t 027 771 63 35, *www.mirabeauhotel.ch* (*moderate*). Operated by Chris Stuckelberger, a Norwegian, since 1974, this bed and breakfast establishment is centrally located and

offers 23 rooms, most of which have a balcony with mountain views. There are also two suites that are suitable for families. It has a Turkish bath and sauna (payable).

Eating Out in Verbier

King's Bar and Restaurant, rue de la Poste 8, t 027 775 20 35 (*very expensive–expensive*) Located in the hotel of the same name, this comfortable restaurant serves a wide range of excellently prepared and presented dishes supplemented by wine from the extensive cellar.

Au Vieux Verbier, rue de Médran, t 027 771 16 68 (*expensive–moderate*). Next to the Médran base station, this restaurant (one of the few not in a hotel) is popular with skiers just off the slopes and those wanting a relaxing atmosphere and traditional cuisine later in the evening.

Bar

Pub Mont Fort, chemin de la Tinte 10, t 027 771 48 98, *www.pubmont fort.com*. This lively place is very popular for après-ski. Offers cocktails, a beer of the month and half-price drinks during happy hour between 4 and 5. In the winter the Shots Bar mixes a new, enticing, concoction each month. Serves food between 4 and 10 each evening.

East of Sion

Crans-Montana

Crans-Montana – actually the two adjoining villages of Crans and Montana located just north of Sierre – are unique in the fact that, unlike other illustrious villages in the Valais, they are situated on a ledge overlooking the Rhône valley with a Mediterranean microclimate, and not at the end of an adjacent valley. Unique, too, in the fact that they have no discernible history as, until the end of the 19th century, these sun-blessed southern slopes of the Bernese Alps, at an altitude of 4,921ft (1,500m), were nothing but summer pastures for Swiss cows.

This scenario soon changed, though, when two hunting partners from the region, Louis Antille and Michel Zufferey, realized the area's potential and were behind the opening of the first hotel, the

Getting to and around Crans-Montana

Take any train from the east or west Valais to Sierre and then transfer to the **funicular** that takes 12–20 minutes, depending on the number of stops, before arriving at Montana station.

An **SMC**, www.cie-smc.ch, bus runs from Sierre train station to Montana via Mollen, and Crans via Chermignon.

A free **shuttle bus** operates between all the important places in these villages.

By **car**, although it is closer from Sierre, Crans-Montana can also be reached from Sion, but in both cases the roads aren't easy to drive.

du Parc, in 1893. Within three years the first road suitable for vehicles was opened and, incongruously, within a decade, in 1906, golf was introduced here by the Englishman, Sir Henry Lunn. Two years later Crans-Montana inaugurated the world's highest 18-hole golf course. By 1939 the Plan Bramois golf course, still considered the best in Switzerland, was hosting the first Swiss Open, and has seen such illustrious players as Nicklaus, Ballesteros and Faldo stride its greens. In fact, the specialist magazines *Golf Monthly* and *Golf Magazine* both classified its 7th hole as one of the finest 40 in the world. These days, the sport has progressed to the point that there are three 9-hole courses in the area – one designed by Jack Nicklaus – and a golf simulator, driving swing analyzer and video facilities are also available.

Further progress came quickly. In 1911 the longest funicular in Switzerland, at 2.6 miles (4.2km), was opened to connect to Sierre in the valley in less than an hour. That same year, Lunn's son, Arnold, put Crans-Montana on the world skiing map by organizing the Earl Robert of Kandahar Challenge Cup, the first genuine downhill event in the history of skiing. And the skiing scene hasn't looked back; there are now 100 miles (160km) of synchronous pistes, and in 1987 Crans-Montana hosted the World Alpine Ski Championship.

Notwithstanding these outdoor attractions, Crans-Montana has gone one better and established itself as a major shopping venue, with every big designer brand available, as well as all the important Swiss master watch and clock makers. The town also has an impressive convention centre, Le Régent. It plays host to the leading lights of the world's political and economic scene.

Not the least of Crans-Montana's attractions are the fantastic views down and across the Rhône valley to a literal wall of snow-capped Valaisanne peaks that stretch as far as the eye can see from east to west. This may be the 'longest' mountain view anywhere in the Alps.

Crans-Montana has come a long way in a short while and is quite a delight to visit. Everything here is man-made – including the large lakes in the village.

Sightseeing and Outdoor Activities

The whole resort of Crans-Montana and the villages below offer many opportunities for sightseeing: not only the natural surroundings – pastures, mountain lakes and waterfalls – but also museums, such as the open-air architectural museum in Lens, **Le Grand Lens** and the **Swiss Model Train Foundation.** The **Musée d'Alpage de Colombire** (Colombire Alpine Museum), reached on the free SMC bus, is well worth visiting in order to explore the secrets of Alpine life. Alpine pastures (*alpage*) are stretches of grassy land situated at high altitude and snow-covered in winter. Over 10,000 alpine pastures occupy 20 per cent of Switzerland, and the Valais boasts 700 of them, covering 25 per cent of the canton. In this museum you will learn about the day-to-day life of both the people and their animals.

Musée d'Alpage de Colombire
rue de la Moubra,
t 027 485 04 04,
www.ecomusee-
colombire.ch

Almost everything else to do here, with the exception of shopping of course, is an outdoor adventure. In the winter **skiers** and **snowboarders** will be in their element. There are over 40 slopes – 17 blue, 20 red and 4 black, and a 2½-mile (4-km) floodlit slope from Cry d'Er to Signal – served by an amazing array of 328 ski lifts, a *funitel* from Les Vilettes to the Plaine-Morte Glacier, 4 cable cars, 12 drag lifts and 6 chair lifts, and also 3 drag lifts on the golf course, which transforms in wintertime to a paradise for children and beginners. There is also a 12½-acre (50,000-sq m) snow park at La Tsa, Aminona, 19 miles (30km) of classic cross-country skiing, a 3.7-mile (6-km) tobogganing/sledge run, 5 trails of 6.2 miles (15km) for snow shoe enthusiasts and 41 miles (65km) of walking paths. Five Swiss Ski Schools will teach you the necessary skills.

In the summer **hikers** can choose from 174 miles (280km) of marked paths including four botanical walks. There are eight marked trails totalling 95 miles (152km) for **mountain bikers**, as well as a permanent 5-mile (8-km) downhill route. There is also the impressive and exciting **Bike Park**. Located in the car park of the Crans Cry d'Er, this is a sort of 'obstacle course' for mountain bikers, where you can improve your skills. For a thrilling adventure in the treetops for the whole family, try the **Fun Forest**, which is situated at the southern end of Moubra Lake. This is an adventure park that has a number of trails for children of different ages (minimum height requirements apply), one of which for older children can be completed with adults joining in. Other sports such as archery,

Fun Forest
impasse de la plage 3,
t 027 480 10 10,
www.funforest.ch; open
mid-June–mid-Sept
daily 10–6; mid-
Sept–end Oct weekends
1–6; adm

12

Valais | East of Sion: Crans-Montana

Golf in the Valais

Golfers, as has been noted, have a choice of one 18-hole course and three 9-hole courses, and details of green fees etc. can be obtained from the **Golf-Club Crans-Sur-Sierre** (*www.golfcrans.ch*) or the tourist office. It might come as a surprise to realize that there are also courses at **Leuk** (*www.golfleuk.ch*), **Obergesteln** (*www.golf-source-du-rhone.ch*), **Riederalp** (*www.golfclub-riederalp.ch*), **Sierre** (*www.golfsierre.ch*), **Sion** (*www.golfclubsion.ch*), **Verbier** (*www.verbiergolf.ch*) and **Zermatt** (*www.golfclubmatterhorn.ch*).

beach volleyball, ten-pin bowling, fishing (seven lakes), horse-riding, paragliding, squash, swimming and tennis are well represented. For those who want to relax, the **beach** has recently been brought to the mountain in the centre of Montana. The Ycoor ice-skating rink is transformed into the **Trop'Yc** beach, with deck chairs, palm trees, a shady bar and musical performances.

Trop'Yc
place d'Ycoor; open early July–mid-/end Aug

(i) **Montana >**
Crans-Montana Tourisme: av. de la Gare 22, t 027 485 04 04, www.crans-montana.ch; open mid-July–early Sept, mid-Dec–early Jan, early Feb–mid-Mar Mon–Sat 8.30–6, Sun 10–12.30 and 3–6; early Sept–Oct, late Nov–mid-Dec, early Jan–early Feb, late Mar–mid-April, early June–mid-July Mon–Fri 8.30–12 and 2–6, Sat 8.30–12 and 2–6, Sun 10–12.30 and 3–6; most of Nov, mid-April–early June Mon–Fri 9–12 and 2–5, Sat 10–12.30 and 3–6

(i) **Crans >**
Crans-Montana Tourisme: rue Centrale 7, t 027 485 04 04, www.crans-montana.ch; open mid-July–early Sept, mid-Dec–early Jan, early Feb–mid-Mar Mon–Sat 8.30–6, Sun 10–12.30 and 3–6; early Sept–Oct, late Nov–mid-Dec, early Jan–early Feb, late Mar–mid-April, early June–mid-July Mon–Fri 8.30–12 and 2–6, Sat 8.30–12 and 2–6, Sun 10–12.30 and 3–6, most. of Nov, mid-April–early June Mon–Fri 9–12 and 2–5, Sat 10–12.30 and 3–6

Tourist Information in Crans-Montana

The tourist office offers interesting guided activities such as mornings on the alpine pasture of Colombire/Merdechon, walks on the glacier, nature discovery trails for kids and an aromatic herbs walk.

Event in Crans-Montana

Early Sept: Omega European Masters, *www.omegaeuropeanmasters.com*; an important stop on the PGA European Tour and regarded as the most important European golf tournament after the British Open.

Shopping in Crans-Montana

René Rey, t 027 481 25 44. In the centre of Crans and a part of the Intersport scheme, this store has everything you may need to hire, including 1,000 skis of all categories, snowboards, mountain bikes and golf clubs. It also has a good choice of sports clothing and hiking boots.

Where to Stay in Crans-Montana

*****Hôtel Royal, t 027 485 95 95, *www.hotel-royal.ch* (*luxury*). Has an excellent location just a few minutes' walk from the centre of Crans-Montana. Within this beautiful chalet-style building you will find 54 elegant rooms with modern facilities and private balconies with glorious alpine views. The Promenade du Royal restaurant serves French cuisine with Italian and Mediterranean influences,

and you can relax in the pool and enjoy other spa facilities.

Hostellerie du Pas de l'Ours, t 027 485 93 33, *www.pasdelours.ch* (*luxury*). Located in Crans in an attractive building, this has nine individually furnished suites with Jacuzzi and fireplace. The Restaurant de l'Ours is run by the excellent young chef, Frank Reynaud, and you can get great bar food at the Bistrot des Ours. There are also spa facilities and treatments and a winter/summer pool.

***Hôtel du Lac, t 027 481 34 14, *www.hoteldulac-crans-montana.ch* (*moderate*). Has an excellent location on the lakeside and 30 rooms with balconies and spectacular mountain views. It also offers a fine restaurant, cosy lounge and bar, Turkish bath and sauna, and pedalo hire.

Auberge Crans-Sapins, t 027 483 14 41 (*inexpensive*). Near the centre of Crans, this is a small, unpretentious place where all the twin-bedded rooms have private bathroom facilities, whilst the single ones do not. Offers excellent southward views.

Eating Out in Crans-Montana

Café Restaurant du Centre, t 027 481 36 68 (*expensive–moderate*). A charming little place full of alpine ambience and serving good value Valaisanne specialities like fondue, raclette and *grillades*. In the high season, there is music nightly.

Le Tirbouchon, t 027 480 26 08 (*expensive–moderate*). A cosy little wine bar in the middle of Montana where you can find an excellent selection of local vintages – and there are many – with a weekly 'by the glass' list on a board, as well as some interesting choices of *eaux-de-vie*.

Entertainment and Nightlife in Crans-Montana

Casino de Crans-Montana, allée Katherine Mansfield 1, t 027 485 90 40, www.casinocransmontana.ch. With gaming tables for roulette, black jack and stud poker, and slot machines. Minimum age of 18, entrance with photo ID. *Open daily 10am–4am; Fri and Sat 10am–5am; gaming tables open 7pm; restaurant 12 noon–2pm and 7pm–1am.*

Val d'Anniviers

Situated immediately to the south of Sierre and one of the least known of many such valleys in this region, the Val d'Anniviers is an incredibly beautiful area with numerous attractions.

The road into the valley leads first to Vissoie, a charming little village that is considered the unofficial capital as it controls access to all the other villages. This section concentrates on the villages of St-Luc and Chandolin on the western side of the valley. Other villages, though, have their own attractions: there is Vercorin; Grimentz, with its 15th-century Maison Bourgeoisiale; and Zinal, sitting at the foothills of the imperial crown of five mountains (the Weisshorn, Zinalrothorn, Obergabelhorn, Matterhorn and Dent-Blanche), with its interesting Lée Cooper Mine.

St-Luc

Funiculaire Tignousa
t 027 476 15 50, www.funiluc.ch; open late-May–early July, late Aug–early Nov 8–5, service every hour; early July–late Aug 8–6, service every 30 mins

François-Xavier Bagnoud Observatory
t 027 475 58 08, www.ofxb.ch; open May, June, Sept, Oct 1.15; July–Aug 11.15 and 1.15; adm

Les Moulins du XVIIIᵉ
t 079 610 92 71; open mid-July–mid-Sept, Tues and Thurs; adm

In the centre of the village of St-Luc there is a very interesting work of art featuring *Les Lavandières* (*The Washerwomen*), which reflects an old social custom of this area. In the old days, women were forbidden to enter bars and their only real social meeting place, from which they in turn barred men, was the public washhouse where once or twice a week they could meet and exchange village news and gossip. These washhouses quickly disappeared with the introduction of running water and washing machines, but this dignified sculpture ensures that the custom will forever be remembered.

Also in the village is the station for the **Funiculaire Tignousa**. Just a short distance above the Tignousa station you will find the **François-Xavier Bagnoud Observatory**. In this, the largest observatory open to the public in Switzerland, you can observe the sun and, on occasion, they have astronomy evenings (which must be booked in advance at the tourist office). It is a pleasing, gentle walk back from Tignousa to St-Luc, if you so choose.

Back just outside St-Luc **Les Moulins du XVIIIᵉ** (18th century Watermills) are of real interest. Here you will find a corn mill,

Getting to and around the Val d'Anniviers

By **car** the only route into, and around, the Val d'Anniviers is the entrance to the valley immediately south of Sierre.

Buses run from Sierre train station to Vissoie, where it is necessary to change for buses on to St-Luc, Chandolin, Ayer-Zinal and Grimentz.

walnut press, two rye and wheat mills and a cloth-fulling mill. Mills bring to mind bread, and the baking of rye bread in the communal oven is another tradition of St-Luc. Once a year each family prepares, according to recipes passed down through the generations, their own rye bread. You, too, can enjoy this fun, which takes place once a week, by contacting the St-Luc tourist office.

Chandolin

Chandolin, at an altitude of 6,562ft (2,000m), about 1,050ft (320m) higher than St-Luc, has its own attractions, too. The ecosystem is different here to the extent that it has its own micro-climate, and its rich diversity of flora includes several species that are rare even in other parts of the Anniviers, let alone the Valais itself. To explore this subject in detail, between spring and autumn, it is fun to take one or more of the **Promenades Botaniques** (Botanical Walks) between altitudes of 6,561ft (2,000m) and 8,858ft (2,700m). There are 22 information posts

Cow-fighting

The most unusual event in these villages, and others in the valley, takes place on a Saturday in mid- to late June and late September. Unfortunately, though, the exact date is variable – you have to check with the tourist office beforehand and be reliant upon favourable weather conditions. June is the time when the cows are taken from the villages up to alpine pastures to feast on the fresh grass, and this ceremony – the **Inalpes** – is quite a celebration. The cows leave the villages at 7am on what can be a rather long procession to pastures (*alpage*) that can be quite remote. Once there, at 10am, the Combats de Reines takes place – the local Valais tradition of cowfighting.

These, though, are not the average cows seen grazing all over Switzerland. They are, in fact, the black – often dark brown – Hérens breed that originate in the Valais and the Aosta valley in northern Italy, and have been around for thousands of years. These strong animals have retained their instinct for hierarchy, and all the cows in the herd fight against each other to determine a ranking. The queen, the one that defeats all the others, takes pride of place at the head of processions and retains that position until she, in turn, is defeated. In reality, they don't seriously hurt each other as they stand head-to-head attempting to push the other out of the way. The prizes, suitably enough, are usually cowbells, but the farmer can sell the offspring of a winner for up to ten times the price of an ordinary calf. Winners, too, can go on to competitions, categorized by weight and age, with the ultimate winner being called the Queen of the Valais.

In September the reverse process, the **Desalpes**, takes place when the cows leave the alpine pastures at 9am to return to the village, where more celebrations take place at 11am, as the cows are housed in their indoor barns for the winter.

The Sierre Anniviers tourist office, *www.sierre-anniviers.ch*, can arrange accommodation for these events at St-Luc and Chandolin, as well as at Grimentz, Vercorin and Ayer-Zinal.

Ella Maillart (1903–97)

Ella Maillart was one of the most extraordinary female travellers of the 20th century, having explored, in extremely trying conditions, such places as Asia, China and Tibet. In 1946 she decided that she would spend six months, from the first to last snow, in Chandolin and the ancient chapel has, since 1998, played host to an exhibition that traces the achievements of her life.

positioned along the way that indicate, among other things, that there are no less than 24 species of orchid to be seen, and you may pass the 860-year-old larch tree. Along the way you will find fauna observation posts equipped with binoculars and educational panels. A more detailed guide about the walks can be purchased at the tourist office. In fact, in this area there are over 90 miles (150km) of hiking paths.

Between the end of June and mid-September it is possible to take the Télésiège Le Tsapé (chairlift) from Chandolin up to **Tsapé** at an altitude of 8,038ft (2,450m). From here there are some nice walks, particularly up to Lac Noir. The Restaurant Tsapé – at the top station of the chairlift – is a fine place for a breather, particularly during the Fête du Remuage at the end of July.

Télésiège Le Tsapé
open late June–early July, late Aug–late Sept Mon–Fri 9–9.30, 11–2 and 4–5; early July–late Aug and every weekend from late June–late Sept 9–5 non-stop

Discount Ticket in the Val d'Anniviers

An **all-day pass** for the postbus (PTT) and all lifts for the Upper Vissoie is available at a cost of CHF 20.

ⓘ **St-Luc >**
Office du Tourisme de St-Luc: t 027 475 14 12, www.saint-luc.ch; open Mon–Sat 9–12 and 3–6

Shopping in the Val d'Anniviers

Chabloz Sports, rue Principale, St-Luc, t 027 475 16 18, *www.chabloz-sports.ch*. Has a full range of skiing and snowboarding equipment, snowshoes and sledges available for hire, as well as mountain bikes. Hiking boots, sports clothes and other equipment in stock.

ⓘ **Chandolin >**
Office du Tourisme de Chandolin: t 027 475 18 38, www.chandolin.ch; open Mon–Sat 9–12 and 3–6

Salaisons d'Anniviers, Vissoie, t 027 475 21 21, *www.salaisons-anniviers.ch*. Dry-cured meat has been a speciality in this area for centuries. Marc Genoud offers cured products and 15 different kinds of tasty sausages for tasting and purchase. *Open Mon–Fri 7.30–12, 1.30–6.*

Where to Stay and Eat in the Val d'Anniviers

***Bella-Tola**, rue Principale, St-Luc, t 027 475 14 44, *www.bellatola.ch*

(*expensive*). This, the luxury hotel of the area, was originally opened in 1859. However, by 1883 demand exceeded supply and this grand building was constructed on the foundations of a Roman villa on the outskirts of St-Luc. These days you can choose from 33 rooms and one suite, each one individually decorated and all the furnishings original and dating from the opening of the hotel. It also has a gourmet French restaurant and the Tzambron, a typical mountain restaurant specializing in regional dishes.

**Le Beausite, t 027 475 15 86, St-Luc, *www.lebeausite.ch* (*moderate*). On the road just before, and under, the village, this is a delightful small hotel and fully lives up to its name. All of its 24 rooms and two studio apartments with kitchenettes are more than comfortable, fully equipped and have balconies with lovely views. The restaurant has a décor of light pine and cuisine that features specialities of the valley.

(*See also* Atlantic hotel, p.236. This is a fine place from which to start or finish a trip to the Val d'Anniviers.)

> **Thermal Springs in Leukerbad**
> From an altitude of around 9,842ft (3,000m), rainwater seeps down through the mountains to about 1,640ft (500m) below sea level. After 40 years thermal energy causes the water, by then enriched by calcium and sulphate, to rise up. At a temperature of 123.8°F (51°C) it fills 60 springs at the rate of 857,880 gallons (3.9 million litres) daily.

Leukerbad

Leukerbad, at an altitude of 4,629ft (1,411m), has quite a different ambience from its next-door neighbour, the Lötschental (*see* p.248), due to a quirk of nature – thermal hot springs.

It wasn't until 1478, when the mineral water springs and baths became the property of the bishop of Sion, Jost von Silenen, that the first inns were opened. In 1850 a road was opened to the village, and that is still the only way to access it as the electric train that started services in 1915 made its last trip in 1967. These days, there are two main ways of enjoying these waters: in the citizen-owned Burgerbad, finally completed in 1989, or at the Alpentherme attached to the Lindner Hôtel.

Amongst the many personalities who have visited Leukerbad over the years are Goethe in 1779, Mark Twain in 1878, Pablo Picasso and Paul Valéry in 1933, and James Baldwin, who stayed in the village from 1951–53.

The Baths and Cable Cars

Taking the waters will naturally be high on everyone's agenda. The baths are the largest of their kind in the Alps, and there are two main places to experience them.

Burgerbad
Rathausstrasse 32,
t 027 472 20 20,
www.burgerbad.ch;
adm

The community-owned **Burgerbad** is a multi-level, multi-pool, multi-attraction facility that, especially with its 230-ft (70-m) water slide, is more along the lines of a water park. There are also sport and wellness facilities, a self-service restaurant and American Bar.

Lindner Alpentherme
Dorfplatz,
t 027 472 10 10,
www.alpentherme.ch

The **Lindner Alpentherme**, however, is an altogether more sophisticated place, and offers a wide range of eclectic experiences. Most obvious are the two large pools, both at 96.8°F (36°C), with the open-air one being 360 sq yards (300sq m) and the indoor a third smaller. Both of these have a number of integrated facilities such as neck douches, underwater massage jets, a hot-water pool at 104°F (40°C) and built-in bubble-bath loungers and seats. There is also a competition pool, with four 27-yard (25-m) lanes at a slightly lower temperature. Admission costs CHF 23 for a 3-hour ticket, with a supplemental CHF 3.50 for each extra 30 minutes, while a day ticket costs CHF 30.

Undoubtedly, though, the most interesting and sensual experiences are to be had in the **Roman-Irish bath** – one of just two in Switzerland (the other being in Scuol, *see* p.295). Around a separate, elegant Roman-style atrium you will be pampered for over two hours with an array of cold-water, sauna and steam baths

Getting to and around Leukerbad

Buses run from Leuk railway station directly to Leukerbad. By **car**, the road north from Leuk leads directly to Leukerbad. The only sensible way of getting around this small town is by **walking**.

ranging from 53.6°F (12°C) to 154.5°F (68°C), a 10-minute massage, and finally 30 minutes of rest and relaxation. All this for just CHF 74.

Don't overlook the **Lindner Alpentherme Wellness Centre** either, where you can treat yourself to any number of intriguingly enticing treatments. Some, like massages, etc. are familiar, but others, certainly, are rather unusual. A thalasso treatment of algae and sea salts can be taken in the form of a purifying bath of bubbling seawater, or perhaps as an algae body-pack to enhance the beauty of your skin. Ayurveda – the science of long life – features a range of treatments including synchronized massages, relaxing oil treatments and effective vegetable remedies. These, though, just scratch the surface of the range of treatments available here; others that may entice are the hayflower wraps, natural mud packs and aroma baths.

These bathing experiences can be taken individually, or as combination packages with the Lindner Hôtel, or other hotels.

Torrent-Bahnen
t 027 472 81 10,
www.torrent.ch

There are also cable cars in Leukerbad. The **Torrent-Bahnen** station is just outside the village to the east and takes you up to the **Restaurant Rinderhütte**, at 7,677ft (2,340m). Although with a slightly less dramatic location than the Gemmi (see below), it has spectacular views back across the Valais to the wall of gigantic peaks including the Matterhorn and Monte Rosa. Apart from skiing, its other main attraction is the modern Rinderhütte itself, a great place for lunch. Not only does it have a fine sun terrace, but the menu includes a good selection of local dishes at reasonable prices.

Gemmibahn
t 027 470 18 39,
www.gemmi.ch

The **Gemmibahn** takes you up to the ledge that is just north of, and literally overlooking, the village at an elevation of 7,710ft (2,350m). The Berghotel Wildstrubel offers basic accommodation and a nice terrace restaurant, and there are many good hikes from here – especially around the Daubensee lake.

Incongruously, there is also an 18-hole golf course in Leukerbad, but most visitors will want to try and schedule their time here to coincide with two far more local events. The last Sunday morning

Leuk

The pretty medieval town of Leuk is located at the junction of the road that leads north to Leukerbad. The town is dominated by the **Bischofschloss** (Bishop's Castle), *www.schlossleuk.ch* (*not open to the public*). The building was first mentioned as far back as 1254, when it served as a house for the mayor. The castle and its neighbouring tower, Viztum, were almost completely destroyed during the troubles of 1415. Some 60 years on it was reconstructed as the bishop's summer residence, and even went on to become the meeting place for the Valais parliament. In the early 17th century the rebel Anton Stockalper was tried here, as were many witches. Declared a listed building in 1934, it is currently being restored by the acclaimed Ticino architect, Mario Botta (*see* p.271). One of the first features he added was the distinctive glass dome that acts as an odd, yet attractive, contrast to the brick tower.

ⓘ Leukerbad ›
*Leukerbad Tourismus:
Rathaus, t 027 472 71 71,
www.leukerbad.ch; open
early Nov–early Dec
Mon–Sat 9–12 and
1.15–5.30; early Dec–early
April Mon–Fri 9–12, 1.15–6,
Sat 9–6, Sun 9–12; early
April–early July Mon–Sat
9–12 and 1.15–5.30; early
July–end Oct Mon–Fri
9–12 and 1.15–6, Sat 9–6,
Sun 9–12*

Where to Stay and Eat in Leukerbad

****Lindner Hôtel & Alpentherme**,
Dorfplatz, t 027 472 10 00,
www.lindnerhotels.ch (luxury). A
traditional hotel with a combination
of 136 rooms and suites that are well
furnished and have up-to-date
facilities. Also two restaurants, a piano
bar, garden terrace, indoor and
outdoor thermal pools, grotto bath,
sauna, solarium and steam bath, as
well as a direct underground
connection to, and free use of, the
Lindner Alpentherme and the
shopping arcade.

***Hôtel de la Croix-Fédérale**,
Kirchstrasse 43, t 027 472 79 79,
www.croix-federale.ch (inexpensive).
Located in a typical chalet in the
village centre, this is a small hotel
with just 10 traditionally styled rooms.

in July, at precisely 11.30am, the annual **Shepherds Festival** enlivens the meadows around the Daubensee. Shepherds arrive with their flocks from both the Valais and Bernese Oberland and, until that hour, the sheep, maybe 1,000 of them, are held back whilst the shepherds spread Glack – a mixture of bran and salt – around the lakeside. It being a particular favourite of these creatures, they stampede down the mountainside to get to it. Incidentally, they are given this treat just three times during the grazing season – and then only 3.2 ounces (100g) per sheep. Huge wheels of raclette cheese are melted in special raclette ovens and served with boiled potatoes, pickles and onions, all washed down with the local Fendant white wine. Also on show are local bands, yodelling, alpine horn-blowing, flag-throwing and local wrestling competitions.

At the beginning of summer, cows from different regions and farms are led up the mountain to share the same pastures and, as they are not familiar with each other, this leads to territorial conflicts between the animals (*see also* p.244). Fighting with their horns, a winner finally emerges that then becomes the leader of the herd. Very early in August the cows are brought back down to Leukerbad for the annual **Summer Cow-fight**; check with the tourist office for the exact date.

㉔ Lötschental Lötschental

Surrounded by lofty alpine peaks, the Lötschental is a beautiful, narrow, attenuated valley (*tal* is the German word for valley), whose people, until the railway reached the head of the valley very early in the 20th century, lived an isolated lifestyle, and still choose to retain a host of centuries-old traditions. The people of the valley speak a very unusual German dialect, which is difficult for other German-speaking people, let alone foreigners, to understand. Large families equal small fields here: staunchly Catholic families with nine or ten children are not abnormal, and as a consequence, with so many children and such little land to pass down, you will notice that the fields here are particularly small.

The villages of Ferden, Kippel, Wiler and Blatten – each at a slightly higher altitude than its predecessor – have retained their delightful characters. As dramatic as the valley is, however, its apex

Getting to Lötschental

Trains run from the Bernese Oberland and Visp to Goppenstein, from where it is necessary to change to a **postbus** that operates the length of the valley to Fafleralp – but only as far as Blatten in the winter months.

By **car**, leave the main road through the valley at Steg and drive north to Goppenstein, and then on to Lötschental.

is even more so. The road comes to a dead end at Fafleralp that, at 5,889ft (1,795m), is literally surrounded by peaks that rise to majestic pinnacles of between 12,192 and 14,022ft (3,716 to 4,274m) – a sight to be savoured in any season. Switzerland is so small that few places with outstanding natural scenery remain virtually unknown; Lötschental is one of those places.

Outdoor Activities

Lötschental is a place most suited to those who enjoy outdoor activities, in summer or winter. During the warmer months the valley offers activities to suit all ages and levels of fitness. Serious hikers will find no end of high mountain trails to explore, either within the valley or venturing as far as Leukerbad and Kandersteg over the mountains. For those intent on exploring in this manner the *Lötschental Touring Map*, available at the tourist office, is a necessity. Visitors seeking easier paths will want to take the cable car to Lauchernalp, and walk down from there, with Fafleralp being a popular destination. Fafleralp is also the best place for a more gentle hike, particularly up to the small, ice-cold lake of Grundsee and then on to the foot of the large glacier. Similarly, a *Mountainbike-Karte* is also available for mountain bikers.

Skiing and/or snowboarding enthusiasts will wish to base themselves close to the **Lauchernalp cable car**, which was opened in 1972. From there a combination of chair lifts and ski lifts rise to Gandegg, at an altitude of 8,858ft (2,700m) and then continue on up to Hockenhorngrat to reach 10,206ft (3,111m). There is a wide variety of ski runs, for beginners through to experts.

Lauchernalp cable car
t 027 938 89 99, www.lauchernalp.ch

Local Festivals

With luck your visit will coincide with one of the colourful local traditions. The strangest of these is the **Tschäggätä**. No written records have been found relating to this custom; the tradition has its roots in a story that has been passed down orally through the generations. Legend has it that just across from Wiler, many centuries ago, there was a settlement – **Schurtendiebe aus dem Giätrich** – that was inhabited by very strange people. Under cover of night these people, dressed in often hideously carved wooden facemasks and a fur costume with a large bell tied around the waist, would attack the more prosperous citizens of Wiler. The University of Basel has in fact excavated ruins that confirm that

Ghost Story

Of course, there has to be a ghost story in the Lötschental. It is the story of Ferden, an old farmer who was killed in mysterious circumstances and whose restless spirit was reputed to return to chase the animals through the mountains and valleys of the Faldum, Resti and Kummen Alps. After days and nights of relentless pursuit the totally exhausted animals gave up red milk. The inhabitants of the village of Ferden, to which these particular Alps belonged, tried in vain to exorcise the farmer's spirit. Finally, the villagers agreed to donate two days' milk production to the poor folk of the valley. This act of generosity must have appeased the spirit of the farmer Ferden, and he bothered them no more. The custom has been celebrated for centuries since in the community house of Ferden, where the women and children receive a gift of cottage cheese and bread, and drink red wine out of wooden cups.

such a settlement did exist. Today, a re-enactment of the tradition continues, but one of the strict rules is that only bachelors can participate. After the 2 February Maria Candlelight Mass the young men prepare themselves, and their expensive costumes, for the festivities, the highlight of which is a carnival parade through Wiler on the Saturday before Ash Wednesday.

Another colourful, but far less grotesque, custom is that of the **Herrgottsgrenadiere** – the 'Red Soldiers'. For many centuries men of the Lötschental worked as mercenaries for foreign armies, and it is recorded that as far back as 1644 six men were killed in the Battle of Lérida, in Catalonia, Spain. They also have fought for the kingdoms of Naples and Versailles, and it is from that era that the red and white uniforms originate. Proud of their service with these armies, the soldiers saved their parade uniforms to wear at church services and parades when they returned to the Lötschental. In further remembrance of those times a white silk banner, bearing a red cross and imprinted with the year 1625, is stored in the archives of the church in Kippel. During the celebrations of Corpus Christi, the descendants of these soldiers don scarlet red frocks with golden buttons, white trousers, a white criss-cross holder for swords and bullets and a peaked cap adorned by a tall feather. After the morning church service, with rifles at their shoulders, they parade through the town accompanied by their famous brass band. The Lötschental women, in their own traditional costumes, join in the festivities, too, and it is a resplendent sight.

If you thought these two customs strange and unusual enough to satiate these people's penchant for the bizarre, you'd be wrong. The New Year brings with it the festival of the Three Kings, **Chinigrosslinu**, during which three young men of military age dress themselves and their steeds in a manner imitating the Three Kings. And not content with 'traditional' tradition, they are chaperoned by two other men dressed in bright and amusing costumes – basically whatever comes to their minds. This colourful entourage is in turn joined by a children's choir, and they go from house to house singing joyous songs until late in the night.

Shopping in Lötschental

ⓘ Lötschental >
*Lötschental
Tourismus: located
next to the cable car
station at Wiler,
t 027 938 88 88;
www.loetschental.ch;
open Mon–Fri 8.30–12
and 1.30–5.30, Sat
8.30–11.30*

Maskenkeller, t 027 939 13 55, *www.maskenkeller.ch.* Located in the heart of Wiler and operated by Agnes and Ernst Rieder-Jerjen, this has the most amazing collection of gruesomely erotic masks – some of which are over 100 years old. The young men of the valley can rent their masks here for the Tschäggätä (*see* p.249) – a different one every year to protect their anonymity – and they also have plenty of smaller ones, and models, that make most unusual souvenirs.

Where to Stay in Lötschental

Moderate

★ Fafleralp >

★ Berg-Restaurant Hockenalp >>

★★★Fafleralp, t 027 939 14 51, *www.fafleralp.ch.* This typical mountain hotel is located in a delightfully isolated position off the road, at the very end of the valley. All of the clean, very comfortable guest rooms, as well as the charming public rooms and dining areas, are decorated with wood panelling. Be advised, the road up from Blatten is closed in winter. *Cash only, no credit cards accepted.*

★★Edelweiss, Blatten, **t** 027 939 13 63, *www.hoteledelweiss.ch.* Located in Blatten, one village back from Fafleralp, this is a fairly large traditional hotel with modern amenities. Its restaurant is famed for its Valais cuisine and fine wines. For those travelling with children, family rooms are available where guests pay extra for children according to their age.

★★★Nest-Und Bietschhorn, between Ried and Blatten, **t** 027 939 11 06, *www.nest-bietsch.ch.* One of the largest hotels in the valley. In a traditional house, it offers home-style comforts, a restaurant renowned for its Valais specialities and an in-house sauna. Special excursion packages, including snow safaris, ski-packages and cultural weeks, are also available.

★★★Hotel-Restaurant zur Wildi, Lauchernalp, **t** 027 939 19 89, *www.zur-wildi.ch.* A fairly isolated, small, typical mountain hotel and restaurant reached via the Lauchernalp cable car. An ideal choice for those interested in summer hikes or winter sports.

Eating Out in Lötschental

Berg-Restaurant Hockenalp, t 027 939 12 45 (*moderate–intermediate*). About 45mins' walk from the Lauchernalp cable car upper station, this is run by the owner/cook Thomas Murmann. There are no formal opening hours, but he is there most of the time between May and the first snow in the middle of October. His speciality is a delicious cheese bread topped with a fried egg – *käseschnitte* – washed down with a large glass of white wine, Hocken-Ballon. The brave will finish with *kaffee perlig* – a mind-blowing mix of coffee and a local Schnapps. All the dishes are washed in the outside water fountain.

Saas-Fee

It is strange that two villages, sitting near the ends of adjacent valleys in the far southern Valais, could be so different in character. While its neighbour, Zermatt, is hemmed into a fairly narrow and very steep valley, Saas-Fee sits beautifully in a natural bowl at an altitude of 5,906ft (1,800m). It is surrounded by no less than 13 mountains that rise to over 13,123ft (4,000m), including the Dom which, at 14,911ft (4,545m), is the highest mountain wholly in Switzerland.

Getting to and around Saas-Fee

Trains run from Visp to Zermatt, but it is necessary to change at Stalden-Saas for a **postbus** to Saas-Fee.

A **postbus** service runs from Visp to Saas-Fee, via Stalden-Saas.

By **car** from Visp, travel south down the valley to Stalden-Saas then take the eastern branch of the road to Saas-Grund where there is a turn-off for Saas-Fee. Saas-Fee is a car-free village and all vehicles have to be parked in the large car park at the entrance to the village. Call your hotel and they will send someone to pick you up in an electric golf-cart-type vehicle.

Saas-Fee is a small village and all places are easily accessible on **foot**.

This charming glacier village, which has preserved many of its customs and traditions, has a population of just under 1,500. And as recently as 1850 there were just 236 inhabitants, in part because access to the village was difficult. The first road to Saas-Fee was opened in 1951, but then only on the condition that the village itself remained car-free. Of course, Saas-Fee has accumulated its share of shops, but they are manageable in number. It also has a variety of bars and restaurants but, very wisely not wanting to spoil the peaceful and harmonious setting, no noise or music is allowed on the village streets after 10.30pm.

Outdoor Activities

Saas-Fee has a particularly impressive mountain transport system (some of which is closed, though, between seasons). Two large cable cars and three smaller ones, 18 ski lifts, two chair lifts and a 'Metro Alpin' funicular compete for your attention. One particular trip, in winter or summer, is a must: take the cable car from Saas-Fee to Felskinn, at an altitude of 9,843ft (3,000m), then change on to the 'Metro Alpin' – the highest funicular in the world – for the 1,526ft (465m) ascent to **Mittelallalin**.

On arrival, at an altitude of 11,483ft (3,500m), you will find two 'highest in the world' places. The **Drehrestaurant**, which seats 220 people and revolves 360 degrees every hour, is a unique place to enjoy a meal and watch as a panoramic feast of alpine peaks and glaciers slowly reveal themselves to you in all their glory. It is the highest revolving restaurant in the world. It is then possible to go down deep into the glacier and visit the world's highest and largest **ice pavilion**. Inside, beneath a ceiling of pure ice that averages a thickness of 33ft (10m), you will learn much about glaciers – and you can touch as well. Regular visitors will notice, too, the effects of almost imperceptible but constant change – the annual movement of both the glacier and ice pavilion is 10.6–11.8 inches (27–30cm).

⭐ Drehrestaurant

The overriding appeal of Saas-Fee, regardless of the season, is a magnificent natural setting offering **outdoor sports** of all kinds. Mountain hikers and mountain bikers will be in their element in the summer. There are over 174 miles (280km) of pathways that vary in difficulty, and the tourist office has brochures, panoramic maps and the *Saastal* hiking map available for visitors. From Saas-Fee, cable cars ascend to your choice of Plattjen, 8,432ft (2,570m), Längfluh, 9,416ft (2,870m), or Hannig, 7,710ft (2,350m). Each of these has a restaurant/bar where you can indulge in a bit of refreshment before beginning the downhill treks back to the village. Be sure to take along some raw carrots; along the way you are bound to encounter some of Saas-Fee's trademark tame marmots, and these chubby, furry creatures love nothing better than a carrot snack.

Alternatively, take the postbus up to Mattmark, where you will see Europe's largest dam, perhaps continuing on to the Monte Moro Pass, at 9,409ft (2,868m), before returning to Saas-Fee the same way.

Winter-sports enthusiasts can have the best of both worlds, as the glaciers around Mittelallalin allow for summer skiing as well. During winter there are over 62 miles (100km) of ski slopes – 50 per cent red, 25 per cent blue and 25 per cent black runs as well as three off-piste (yellow) runs. There are also 36 miles (60km) of winter hiking paths, and 22 miles (36km) of cross-country ski runs. During summer the runs are reduced to 12.4 miles (20km) of slopes, for average to very good skiers.

Those interested in learning more about the history and culture of Saas-Fee will wish to visit the **Saaser Museum**. Housed in an early 18th-century home, the main exhibit is the original study of the German writer Carl Zuckmayer, who adopted Saas-Fee as his second home. Look, also, for traditional costumes, a sacred art collection, folklore articles, a collection of minerals and an exhibition on glaciers.

Saaser Museum
t 027 958 18 58; open July–Aug daily 10–11 and 1.30–5.30; June, Sept, Oct Tues–Sun 10–11.30 and 1.30–5.30; mid-Dec–end April Tues–Sun 10–11.30 and 2–5; adm

12 Valais | Saas-Fee

ⓘ **Saas-Fee** >
Saas-Fee/Saastal Tourismus: opposite post office and bus station, t 027 958 18 58, www.saas-fee.ch; open Mon–Sat 8.30–12 and 2–6, Sun 10–12 and 4–6, with slight seasonal variations

Tourist Information in Saas-Fee

Many all-season packages, put together by the tourist office in brochures and on the website, are available in advance of your visit.

Shopping in Saas-Fee

Haus der Geschenke, just across from the Ferienart Resort and Spa, t 027 957 25 06. Has by far the widest range of souvenirs and toys in Saas-Fee.

César Sport, t 027 957 14 16, *www.cesarsport.ch,* and **Alpin Sport,** t 027 957 37 33, *www.alpinsport.ch.* Members of the INTERSPORT scheme; offer everything you need, to either rent or buy, for skiing, snowboarding, mountaineering and summer hiking.

Where to Stay in Saas-Fee

⭐ Ferienart Resort and Spa >

****Ferienart Resort and Spa, t 027 958 19 00, www.ferienart.ch (luxury). Behind its chalet-style façade is a warm, stylish and extremely congenial hotel. The rooms are innovatively designed and usually wood panelled, beautifully decorated and extremely well equipped. Dine in your choice of the three restaurants, including the fine Le Gourmet, and afterwards dance to live bands in the bar. There is also an extensive on-site spa and grotto pool.

**Chalet-Hotel Gletschergarten, t 027 957 21 75, www.hotelgletschergarten.ch (inexpensive). This is a charming old wooden hotel in the village centre, just down from the Ferienart, that has been run by the same family for three generations. The traditional panelled bedrooms all have private bathrooms and balconies and there is a small dining room, restaurant and lounge area and an attractive sun terrace with lovely views.

Eating Out in Saas-Fee

Waldhotel Fleschhorn, t 027 957 21 31, www.fletschhorn.ch (very expensive). Markus Neff is the accomplished chef here, and his creative cuisine has gained him a Michelin star listing. The Markus Neff menus feature six or nine different dishes and Les Plats de Résistance are specialities. Over 45,000 bottles of 1,150 different kinds of fine wine are available here, including the best Valais vintages and others of international acclaim.

Drehrestaurant Metro-Alpin, t 027 957 17 71, www.drehrestaurant-allalin.th (moderate). At an elevation of 11,483ft (3,500m), this is the world's highest revolving restaurant. Making a full 360-degree rotation once every hour, it affords an unparalleled panoramic vista of the surrounding mountain peaks and glaciers.

Nightlife in Saas-Fee

Saas Fee is not the hottest place in Switzerland for nightlife; in fact noise on the streets at night after 10pm is frowned upon. Nevertheless, there is action to be found, including at the following: Popcorn, Hotel Dom, t 027 958 77 06, www.popcorn.ch; Nesti's Ski-bar, t 027 957 42 11, Pic-Pic Bar, t 027 957 25 35.

Zermatt

Zermatt is located in the far south of the Valais, nestling up against the Italian border. Roman coins have been found on the Theodul Pass, indicating that soldiers used this as a means of access to Gaul and Helvetia from 400–200 BC. It is accepted that the area was populated in the early years of Christendom. Not until 1280, however, does the first documentation mentioning Zermatt, then known as Protobornum, originate. A seal of the municipality bears a similar name, Vallis Prato Borni, the translation of which somehow leads to 'zer Matt', which was first found on a map dated 1495. Although the valley was, traditionally, under the jurisdiction of the bishop of Sion, those rights were frequently transferred to

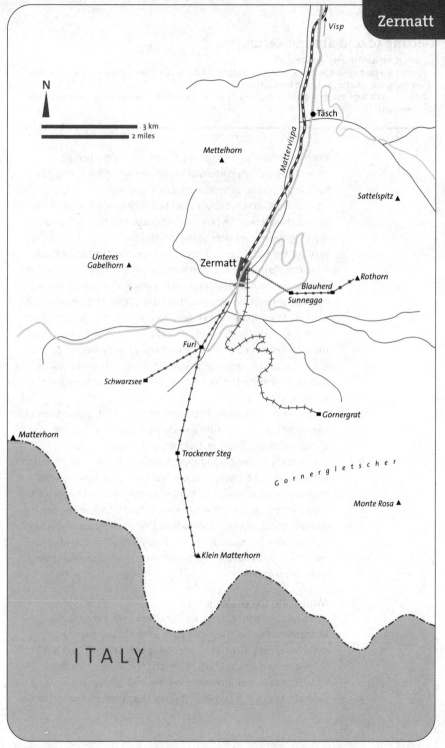

N

3 km
2 miles

Visp

● *Täsch*

Mettelhorn
▲

Sattelspitz ▲

Mattervispa

Unteres
Gabelhorn ▲

Zermatt

▲ *Rothorn*
Blauherd
Sunnegga

Furi ■

Schwarzsee ■

■ *Gornergrat*

▲ *Matterhorn*

■ *Trockener Steg*

G o r n e r g l e t s c h e r

Monte Rosa ▲

▲ *Klein Matterhorn*

ITALY

Getting to and around Zermatt

Trains run from Visp directly to Zermatt.
Zermatt is a **car-free** village and all vehicles have to be left at Täsch, 3 miles (5km) down the valley, from where trains will shuttle you to and from Zermatt.
Zermatt isn't a large village and all places are easily accessible on **foot**, although there are electric golf-cart-type **taxis**.

the most powerful baron of the period. Finally, the people of Zermatt, as was the custom of the day, bought their liberty, paying for it in an ancient Swiss currency, *Mörserpfund*.

Life in Zermatt was fairly uneventful until the early part of the 19th century, when the first tourists discovered the Matterhorn in 1820. Eighteen years later a surgeon, Dr Josef Lauber, opened the first inn, the Hotel Cervin, later to be known as the Monte Rosa, which had just three beds. Zermatt, boasting an enviable southern position, yet protected from the wind and with excellent snow conditions, never looked back. These days, Zermatt is synonymous with the Matterhorn, and visitors from around the world flock to see the most distinctive, and some say most beautiful, mountain in the Alps. Renowned as both a summer and winter resort, Zermatt is famous, also, for having the longest skiing season in the Alps. The authorities have acted to preserve the character of the village by banning all traffic.

As more tourists arrive, so the infrastructure has grown to meet their needs, and this in turn gives rise to other changes. The upmarket shops, hotels, restaurants and discos, originally appendages to scenery and sport, have now become an attraction in their own right. Daylight hours find the few streets crowded with shoppers, and nightfall brings popular bars and discos alive until the early hours of the morning. Zermatt is, therefore, not the quietest of places, but is somewhere that combines, and uniquely so, dramatically beautiful alpine scenery and unparalleled year-round skiing possibilities with very refined hotels, specialist shops and lively nightlife.

Mountain Excursions

Without any doubt, the main attraction here is the magical **Matterhorn**. Even in the presence of a host of commanding mountain peaks, 36 of which ascend to over 13,000ft (4,000m), it is the magnetism of the Matterhorn, and the Matterhorn alone, which draws huge numbers of visitors from all over the world to Zermatt. At 14,692ft (4,478m), it is not the tallest mountain in the area but, unusually shaped, it stands alone and seems to rise from nowhere.

The easiest way to get unobstructed, and closer, views of the Matterhorn is to start by taking one of the eight-seat **Matterhorn-Express** gondola cars from Zermatt at 5,315ft (1,620m) up to **Furi** at 6,115ft (1,864m). From there you have two options. Either take the Matterhorn-Express up to **Schwarzee**, 8,471ft (2,582m), where a small lake and a mountain hotel with the same name sit right on the foothills of the Matterhorn. Or, alternatively, take the cable car up to **Trockener Steg** at 9,642ft (2,939m). The sundeck that winds around the restaurant here is not only a great place for refreshments, but also offers glorious 360-degree views of the surrounding peaks and glaciers. The sheer face of the Matterhorn rises imposingly on one side. To the south stands a veritable wall of mountain peaks, and flowing interminably from them are vast glaciers. Time, now, to take the highest cable car ride in Europe to

✪ Klein Matterhorn

Klein Matterhorn itself, reaching 12,532ft (3,820m). The views from this vantage point are, simply stated, unforgettable, and the panorama that unfolds around you takes in everywhere from Mont Blanc to Austria, and everything in between.

This is a great area for summer skiing, and the Theodul Glacier and its surroundings offer a natural amphitheatre of over 8,960 acres (3,626 hectares) of perpetual snow. There are 15 miles (24.1km) of safe marked runs, including one of 4 miles (6.4km) with a vertical descent of 3,290ft (1,003m).

Another fascinating trip is on a Gornergratbahn (GGB) train – preferably in an open carriage – beginning at the second of Zermatt's train stations located directly across from the main station. From here, the cog-rail trains make a 43-minute ascent to

✪ Gornergrat

Gornergrat at 10,269ft (3,130m), making it Europe's highest totally open-air railway. The initial part of the journey twists and turns through the forested slopes up to the open mountain side, offering ever-changing views of this glorious alpine scenery. In the warmer seasons you might see marmots scampering around. Upon reaching Gornergrat, you will marvel at the unparalleled vista of

12

Valais | Zermatt

Half 'n' Half

On the journey up the valley to Zermatt – and in other places in the Valais too – you will no doubt see some odd-looking goats. Their head and front half are black and the rear half is white. These are **Walliser Schwarzhalsiege** (Valais Blacknecks), and as of 2007 there were estimated to be just 250 breeding males and 2,300 breeding females in Switzerland. Generally, they are kept in mountainous regions and graze in the high Alps during the summer.

A Bird's-eye View of the Matterhorn

The most spectacular views of the Matterhorn are from an Air-Zermatt helicopter, t 027 966 86 86, www.air-zermatt.ch. They offer 20-minute trips, for CHF 210 per person, that takes you as close as you can get to the summit without actually climbing it. If you are lucky, you might even see climbers. On the same trip, you will also be taken closely over a huge and imposing glacier.

the massive Monte Rosa and her sister peaks, each of which is well over 13,123ft (4,000m). Directly behind you, but in the distance, you will see another range of peaks of equal stature, amongst which is the Dom at 14,911ft (4,545m). Yet even these magnetic mountains will be unable to distract you from the magnificence of the Matterhorn, splendidly isolated in the distance. Directly in front is the Gornergletscher, and from this vantage point you will be able to clearly define the path along which this massive glacier slowly meanders its way down, as well as its confluences with other, smaller, glaciers. Incidentally, the Kulm Hotel Gornergrat here is the highest hotel in the Alps, and its terrace is a great place for a snack.

Another mountain trip starts at the Standseilbahn in Zermatt, just across the river from the Gornergratbahn. The first stage is on the **Métro Sunnegga Express**, a funicular that ascends inside the mountain itself to the plateau of Sunnegga, at 7,546ft (2,300m). From there a gondola cable car travels up to **Blauherd**, 8,619ft (2,627m), and the final stage is by cable car that climbs to **Rothorn** (a common name in Switzerland for a mountain), at 10,180ft (3,103m). Besides being the starting point for numerous walks, it also boasts splendid views in its own right.

Hiking is, of course, a favourite pastime here, and there are numerous routes to choose from; these can last from just an hour or so to a full day. **Mountain biking**, also, is becoming immensely popular, and there are miles of specially laid-out, well-marked, bike trails. Further information regarding both hiking and mountain bike trails is available through the tourist office.

In this wind-protected southern location, Zermatt has three skiing areas that offer excellent snow conditions. There are more than 245 miles (394km) of ski slopes, ranging from the simplest to the most complicated runs, that are accessible by an ever-growing myriad of transport alternatives. There are also snow parks, fun parks, sledding runs, snowshoe walking tours and 28 miles (30km) of prepared winter hiking paths.

Tourist Information in Zermatt

(i) Zermatt >
*Zermatt Tourismus:
Bahnhofplatz 5,
t 027 966 81 00,
www.zermatt.ch; open
mid-June–end Sept
Mon–Sat 8.30–6, Sun
8.30–6; end Sept–mid-
Dec Mon–Sat 8.30–12
and 1.30–6, Sun 9.30–12
and 4–6; mid-Dec–early
April Mon–Fri 8.30–12
and 1.30–6, Sat 8.30–6,
Sun 9.30–12 and 4–6;
early April–mid-June
Mon–Sat 8.30–12 and
1.30–6, Sun 9.30–12 and
4–6*

Multi-lingual summer and winter information brochures, detailing all manner of activity packages, are available to visitors in advance. Contact the tourist office and check their website.

Shopping in Zermatt

WEGA gift shops, Bahnhofplatz and other locations in Zermatt, **t** 027 967 21 66. The best places to buy Swiss Army knives – they will engrave the knives free of charge. Also on sale are watches, clocks, music boxes, cowbells, books, T-shirts, etc.

Bayard, Bahnhofplatz 4 (and at four other locations in Zermatt), **t** 027 966 49 50, *www.bayardzermatt.ch*. Members of the Swiss rent-a-sport rent-and-go scheme; offer everything you need either to rent or buy for skiing, snowboarding, snowshoeing, sledging, mountaineering, mountain biking and summer hiking.

Horu Käserei; Oberhäusen 6, Chalet Friedheim, **t** 027 967 39 75, *www.horu-kaserei.ch*. Take a look at this cheesemaker at work and taste these local specialities before deciding which ones to buy for lunch.

Where to Stay in Zermatt

Luxury

(★) Alex >

****Alex**, Bodmenstrasse 12, **t** 027 966 70 70, *www.hotelalex zermatt.com*. No other hotel in Zermatt has more ambience and character than the Alex. It is also steeped in the history of Zermatt and its mountains. The maternal grandfather of the founder, Peter Taugwalder, was the first person to climb the Matterhorn. At the age of 19 his grandson, Alex Perren, became the youngest person from Zermatt to qualify as a ski instructor and mountain guide. Tragedy struck seven years later when, after an accident, Alex had to have his left leg amputated below the knee. Turning his energies to a different career he opened the Hotel Alex in 1960, and soon after he fell in love with the hotel's Austrian girl Friday, Gisela Becwar and they married in 1964. Gisela's charismatic charm and Alex's down-to-earth practicality made for a formidable combination and the hotel went from strength to strength. Setting many new trends, it became, as it still is, the 'in place' to stay in Zermatt. These days Alex and Gisela are semi-retired, but they still take breakfast in their own 'Mr and Mrs Alex corner' by the bar. There's no pompousness or stuffiness here, but there is plenty of luxury. Rooms range from small singles to oversize deluxe Jacuzzi suites decorated with warm colours and indulgent fabrics, making for a cosy atmosphere. The public areas have a similar feel, with hand-turned furniture, brocade curtains, exquisite woodcarvings, valuable paintings of the Matterhorn and numerous antiques. The romantic grotto indoor pool is next to a health club that offers a range of pampering treatments guaranteed to relax body and soul. The very fine Alex Grill restaurant, which has a magnificent woodcarved ceiling, has just been completely renovated. The service, attention and care given to the guests here is exemplary.

Expensive

****Alpenroyal**, Riedstrasse 96, **t** 027 966 60 66, *www.alpenroyal.ch*. This is a typical mountain-style hotel found in an elevated and peaceful location with excellent views of the Matterhorn. A family-run establishment, there are 30 very comfortable rooms, good food and an indoor pool with sauna and whirlpool.

Moderate

Kulm Hotel Gornergrat, **t 027 966 64 00, *www.matterhorngroup.ch*. Sitting in splendid alpine isolation at an altitude of 10,286ft (3,100m) and only accessed via the Gornergrat railway, this is the highest hotel in Europe. A typical mountain hotel, the rooms are rather basic, but the views are unparalleled and the restaurant serves wine from the highest vineyard in Switzerland. (Not an advisable place to stay for those with breathing difficulties.)

Inexpensive

Le Mazot, **t 027 966 06 06, *www.lemazotzermatt.ch*. Located by the river, just a couple of minutes from the centre, this has 2 single and 7 double rooms that have excellent facilities. Also a nice restaurant with fondue specialities.

Bahnhof, **t 027 967 24 06, *www.hotelbahnhof.com*. Right next to the station, this has a mix of rooms ranging from singles to four beds – with or without private shower and dormitory accommodation.

Eating Out in Zermatt

Restaurant Weisshorn, **t** 027 967 57 72 (*moderate–inexpensive*). A nice place right by the bridge next to the church on the main street. A varied menu features such delicacies as home-made soups, cooked in a large pot outside by the tables, as well as *rösti*, fondue and *käseschnitte*, all at reasonable prices.

Elsie's Bar, Kirchplatz 16, **t** 027 967 24 31, *www.elsiebar.ch* (*expensive–moderate*). Centrally located, this bar has a typical Valais feel. Dishes served include oysters, snails and spaghetti with caviar, enhanced by a fine selection of whiskies, cocktails and wines from the bar.

Heimberg Zermatt, Bahnhofstrasse 84, **t** 027 967 24 31, *www.heimberg-zermatt.ch* (*expensive–moderate*). Located on the main street in Zermatt, the interior was created by local artist, Heinz Julen. On the menu you'll find rack of veal with smoked eel and marinated carpaccio of summer deer, as well as a wide selection of risottos.

Nightlife in Zermatt

Most of the action in Zermatt takes place around the Bahnhofstrasse.

Hotel Post, Bahnhofstrasse 41, **t** 027 967 1931, *www.hotelpost.ch*. A mix of five bars and clubs, and the hot place in town.

Other bars and pubs of interest are: **Papperla Pub**, Steinmattenstrasse 34, *www.papperlapub.ch*, for the younger crowd; **Elsie's Bar**, contact *see* above, a little more on the upmarket side; **Vernissage**, Hofmattstrasse 4, **t** 027 967 66 36, *www.vernissage-zermatt.ch*, a combo of art gallery, cinema and bars; and **GramPi's**, Bahnhofstrasse 70, **t** 027 967 77 75, *www.grampis.ch*, a late-night hangout. The **Star Bar**, Hotel Zermatterhof, Bahnhofstrasse 55, **t** 027 966 66 00, *www.zermatter hof.ch*, offers a quieter ambience, with singers and cocktails.

Ticino

Isolated from most of the rest of the country by mountains – except for Graubünden to the east – and surrounded by Italy, Ticino is Switzerland's most distinct region. Situated south of the Alps, with a much milder climate and with historical ties to Italy, Ticino has a Mediterranean culture and ambience.

The greater part of the canton in the north is sparsely populated. The capital, Bellinzona, and the major towns of Lugano and Ascona/Locarno are situated in the south. The towns are located on the lakeside.

Ticino is famous for its beautiful isolated valleys. The Valle Maggia, beginning by Ascona/Locarno, splinters into sub-valleys that end at the foot of the Alps bordering Italy and the rest of Switzerland. Also beginning by Ascona/Locarno, but this time running west to Domodossola, Italy, is the spectacularly beautiful Centovalli, itself fed by numerous valleys from the north and south.

13

Don't miss

⭐ **Historic fortress**
Castelgrande, Bellinzona
p.265

⭐ **Important works of art**
Chiesa di Santa Maria degli Angioli, Lugano
p.269

⭐ **Lake trip to islands**
Brissago Islands **p.278**

⭐ **Captivating valley scenery**
Monte Comino, Centovalli **p.281**

⭐ **Natural rural beauty**
Valle Maggia **p.282**

See map overleaf

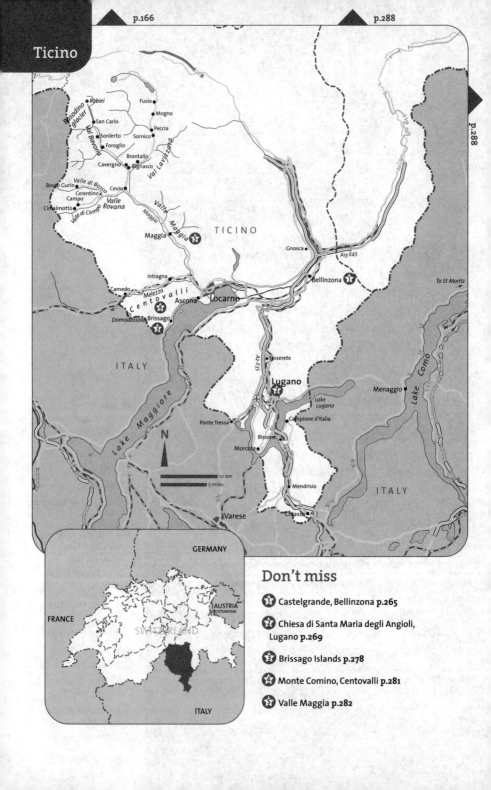

Ticino

p.288

Bosodino glacier
Robiei
Fusio
San Carlo
Mogno
Val Bavona
Sonlerto
Peccia
Foroglio
Sornico
Brontallo
Cavergno
Bignasco
Valle di Bosco
Cevio
Bosco Gurin
Cerentino
Campo
Valle
Cimalmotto
Rovana
Valle di Campo
Maggia

TICINO

Gnosca

A13-E43

Bellinzona

To St Moritz

Intragna
Camedo
Melezza
Centovalli
Ascona
Locarno
Domodossola
Brissago

ITALY

Tesserete
A2-E35
Lugano

Lake
Lugano

Menaggio

Lake Como

Ponte Tressa
Campione d'Italia
Bissone
Morcote

N

10 km
5 miles

Mendrisio

ITALY

Varese
Chiasso

GERMANY

FRANCE

AUSTRIA
LIECHTENSTEIN

SWITZERLAND

ITALY

Don't miss

Getting to Ticino

By Air

Although Lugano has an airport, **Agno Airport**, *www.lugano-airport.ch*, there are no direct scheduled international flights from the UK or USA. Within Switzerland, **Swiss**, *www.swiss.com*, operate a service from Zürich, and **Darwin Airline**, *www.darwinairline.com*, and Flybaboo, *www.flybaboo.com*, have flights from Geneva.

The nearest airports with flights from the UK and USA are Zürich, Basel and Geneva, respectively 2hrs 50mins, 3hrs 50mins and 5hrs 40mins away by train (*see* below).

By Train

Lugano is directly on the Zürich–Luzern–Milan line. Travelling to Locarno station involves a change at Bellinzona. If you are travelling from Geneva, the train connection to Locarno/Lugano takes you via Zürich; this is a roundabout way but is the simplest and quickest route.

By Car

When approaching from the **north**, take the St Gotthard Tunnel to the N2 autoroute, which cuts a north/south axis through Ticino until you reach the capital city of Bellinzona. From there, follow the signs to Locarno/Ascona or, alternatively, continue south to Lugano.

When approaching from the **west** (e.g. Geneva, Lausanne, Montreux and Zermatt) the trip is a bit more complicated. Follow the main Valais road to Brig, traversing the Simplon Pass to Domodossola, Italy. From there the road, rather tricky at times, follows the Centovalli to Ascona/Locarno. If you wish to continue on to Lugano, go via Bellinzona.

From **eastern** Switzerland, particularly the Upper and Lower Engadine, the route is more than a bit complicated but very interesting. Head southwest from St Moritz and, just past the lakes, the road drops precipitously at the Malojapass, crossing into Italy shortly before you reach Chiavenna. Continue on around the western side of Lake Como as far as Menaggio, where you turn inland to Lugano or carry on due north to Locarno/Ascona, via Bellinzona. An alternative route is via the San Bernadino Pass, where you can take the N13 motorway to Bellinzona, and from there travel on to Ascona/Locarno or Lugano.

Ticino (Tessin in French and German), making up 7% of Switzerland's land territory, is located across the 46th parallel equidistant from the North Pole and the equator. It has the distinction of being the only one of the country's twenty-six cantons situated entirely south of the Alps, and its geographical isolation has proved to be a significant factor in its development and history. Fossilized remains from the Triassic period – 200 million years ago – found in the fossil beds of Mount San Giorgio indicate that this area was once a part of the sea bed. And, the first evidence of human life dates from the Stone Age. Ticino's shape can best be described as an upturned triangle, with the base being the Alps and the apex – just fifty kilometres from Milan, Italy – extending into Italian territory. And it is that southernmost point of land that has been the derivation of a multitude of problems throughout the area's history. Of course, the Romans left behind their typical inheritance but, even following their departure and up until the 14th century, the history of Ticino, and its people *Ticinesi*, was inextricably linked with the Italian regions of Lombardy and Piedmont. During this era, Ticino, coveted because of its commercial and strategic prominence, came under the control of either Como or Milan.

Eating Style in Ticino

Special mention must be made here that dining is after the Italian manner. An appetizer, *antipasto*, is followed by a first course, *primo* (most often pasta), and a second, *secondo* (usually a meat dish). The meal culminates with cheese then a dessert, possibly *torta di pane* (a bread cake) or *torta della nonna* (a sugar tart). The choice of wine is wide, but most won't want to leave the area without sampling the famous *Ticino Merlot*, a claret wine, or its rarer white vintage. End, of course, with a *grappa* or *nocino*, a walnut-based liqueur.

In the mid-13th century, during their initial organization and consolidation period, leaders of the Swiss cantons realized that control of the St Gotthard road was of paramount importance. The Swiss Confederation's 'Gotthard policy' was not implemented swiftly or without tragic consequences, however, and it took until the early 16th century before Ticino passed indisputably into their control. The status quo persevered until the close of the Napoleonic Wars when, in 1803, it became a free and independent Swiss canton.

Even as late as 1860 nearly a third of the population dwelt in the mountain villages, a figure that, over the last decades has, gradually, diminished to 10%. The foremost factor in effecting this redistribution was the completion, in 1882, of the St Gotthard railway tunnel which, finally, broke the bonds of isolation, opening routes of travel and lines of communication to other parts of Switzerland and, indeed, the world. Even today, Ticino has only around 300,000 inhabitants, just over 4% of the country's total, with the bulk of the population centered around the communities of Lugano, Locarno, Chiasso, and the capital city of Bellinzona.

Ticino's claim to international fame arises from its magnificently varied scenery and mild climate which, when compared to other areas of Switzerland, could be termed 'warm'. The temperature averages 15.5 degrees Celsius (60 degrees Fahrenheit) and the region is blessed with about 2,300 hours of sunshine each year. In the north are untamed mountains and valleys forged by ice and icy rivers which, in turn, spill into and replenish Lake Maggiore and the other lakes in the region. These natural characteristics, in concert, endow Ticino with what can best be described as a Mediterranean ambience – tiny, palm-treed villages cling precariously to steep mountain sides and pretty, oftentimes pastel-coloured, houses and villas line the balmy lakes. In addition, the area boasts many sites of architectural importance – in large part built by the *Ticinesi*, who are celebrated for their craftsmanship in such areas, and many places of historical interest.

Although politically Swiss, 85% of the people in Ticino are Italian speaking and this may, occasionally, cause some difficulty in communicating; but many *Ticinesi* understand English as well.

Getting to and around Bellinzona

See 'Getting to Ticino', p.263 for information on how to get to Bellinzona.

Bellinzona is a small town and you can **walk** around its centre. However, the **Castello di Montebello** and **Castello di Sasso Corbaro** can be reached by a no. **4 bus** from the train station, which stops at Montebello and then goes on to Artore, which is a 15-min walk away from Sasso Corbaro. Note that the service is irregular, with long gaps between buses.

Bellinzona

Bellinzona is the seat of the cantonal government and parliament and therefore the capital of Ticino. Visitors approaching the town will notice its three dominant castles and will quickly realize that it holds a strategic position between the Alps and Italy. It is thought that it was first settled some 7,000 years ago, although most of what can be seen today dates from the medieval period and later, with examples of elegant 19th-century houses and piazzas. Also known as the Turrita (City of Towers), it has been fought over by the Romans, Longobards, rulers of Como and Milan and even the French and Swiss.

In 2000 Bellinzona was added to the UNESCO World Heritage list and it has a special website, *www.bellinzonaunesco.ch*, to commemorate that prestigious award.

Undoubtedly, the dominant feature of the town is the fortress, **Castelgrande**. It can be reached by steep footpaths from the Piazza Collegiata, or more easily by a lift at the Piazzetta della Valle. Work began on the castle in the 13th century, with the two main towers, the Torre Bianca (White Tower) and Torre Negra (Black Tower) dating from the 13th and 14th centuries. It was enlarged in the late 15th century by the Sforza dukes of Milan, who extended the battlements down into the town. The castle has been restored several times, with the lastest extensive renovations completed in 1984–91. The castle houses two museums – one of historical art, the other, archeological.

Some 295ft (90m) above the Castelgrande, where the defensive walls of the town originate on the Montebello hill, sits the **Castello di Montibello**. The inner castle is thought to have been constructed by the Rusconi family of Como in the 13–14th centuries, with the external courtyards and towers added by the Sforzas in the late 15th century. In the late 18th century it was acquired by the Ghiringhelli family, who donated it to the canton to coincide with the centenary of independence in 1903. The **Museo Civico Archeologico** (Civic Archeological Museum) is within the castle.

The third castle, **Sasso Corbaro**, again named after the hill it dominates, is even higher at an altitude of 755ft (230m). It was built by the Sforzas after the defeat of the Milanese at the Battle of Giornico in 1479. Supposedly it was completed in just six months

⓫ Castelgrande
Monte San Michele,
t 091 825 81 45,
www.castelgrande.ch;
inner court open
Jan–Dec Mon 10–6,
Tues–Sun 9am–10pm;
museums open
Nov–Mar daily 10–5,
April–Oct daily 10–6;
castle walls open
summer 10–7, winter
10–5; adm, combined
for the three castles

Castello di Montebello
Salita ai Castelli,
t 091 825 13 42; castle
open Mar/April–Nov
daily 8–8; museum
open Mar/April–Nov
daily 10–6; adm,
combined for the three
castles

Castello di Sasso Corbaro
t 091 825 59 06; open
Mar/April–Nov Mon
10–6, Tues–Sun 10–10;
adm, combined for the
three castles

13

Ticino | Bellinzona

Where to Stay and Eat in Bellinzona

ⓘ Bellinzona >

Bellinzona Turismo e Eventi: Palazzo Civico, t 091 825 21 31, www.bellinzonaturismo. ch; open Mon–Fri 9–6.30, Sat 9–12

***Hotel Unione,** Via G. Guisan 1, t 091 825 55 77, www.hotel-unione.ch (*moderate*). Has a very good location just a few minutes from the station and the Castelgrande fortress. All of the rooms are pleasantly decorated, but be sure to ask for one of the twelve with views to the castle.

Traditional local food is served in the restaurant.

Ristorante Castelgrande, t 091 826 23 53, www.castelgrande.ch. The castle has two restaurants. One is a gourmet restaurant (*expensive*) featuring a daily business lunch, dinner or a special tasting menu in luxurious surroundings. The other, the Grotto San Michele (*moderate–inexpensive*), is more casual and in the summer food is served on the terrace.

Civica Galleria d'Arte

Villa dei Cedri, Piazza S. Biagio, t 091 821 85 20, www.villacedri.ch; open Jan–Dec Tues–Fri 2–6, Sat–Sun and hols 11–6, first Thurs of month open until 8; adm; grounds open summer daily 8–8, winter daily 8–5

under the instructions of the military engineer Benedetto Ferrino, who died of the plague before it was finished. The castle walls are massive, being 15½ft (4.7m) at their thickest. The castle doesn't particularly have any grounds to walk around, but there are magnificent views stretching to Lake Maggiore to the south.

The **Civica Galleria d'Arte** (Municipal Art Gallery) opened in 1985 and has a collection of mainly 19th- and 20th-century paintings, along with a small selection of contemporary pieces. Still being added to, the collection mainly features artists from the Lombardy region.

Lugano

Perhaps because of its relatively remote location and small size, Lugano is often overlooked by visitors to Switzerland – a mistake if you consider its fabulous location surrounded by mountains and nestled against the lake.

Culturally, like the canton it is part of, this delightful city is far closer to Italy than the rest of the country. And this, along with a pleasantly benign climate that delivers about 2,300 hours of sunshine annually, gives the city a decidedly Mediterranean feel. Spring comes early here, usually by mid-March, and with it a burst of colour that contrasts sharply with the surrounding snowcapped mountains.

Besides the interesting museums and churches, it is a delight to wander through the narrow streets of the Old Town, or simply sit at an outdoor café, watching the animated conversation and Mediterranean style of the Italian-orientated Swiss. At each end of the bay on which Lugano sits are two small mountains – San Salvatore to the south and Monte Bré to the northeast – that, by way of a funicular, offer spectacular views not only of the city, but

Getting to and around Lugano

See p.263. A **shuttle bus**, **t** 079 221 42 43, *www.shuttle-bus.com*, departs from Agno Airport after all passengers have left the departure lounge and will take you either to the railway station or to the Piazza Manzoni.

The **train station** is located in Piazzale della Stazione in an elevated position slightly above the town centre; the quickest – and cheapest – way down is on the **funicular** to the Piazza Cioccaro in the heart of the Old Town.

Lugano is quite small enough to **walk** around. The only bus that you might want to take is the no. 1 that runs around the lakeside and through the city centre, from Paradiso to Castagnola.

Although many places around the lake can be reached by **train** or **bus**, the best option is to take one of the **steamers**.

also of the surrounding mountains for many miles around. And because most of the places of interest are located in between them – with the exception of a few places just a block or so away – Lugano is an easy place to explore. Another major attraction is the places nearby that can be visited by lake steamer, especially between April and October.

As tourism has been important here since the mid-19th century, there is a wide range of hotels to choose from, including one or two really special five-star ones. You won't go hungry, either, with many Italian restaurants to choose from.

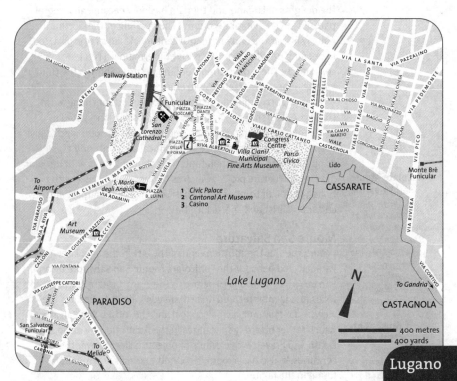

1 Civic Palace
2 Cantonal Art Museum
3 Casino

Lake Lugano

400 metres
400 yards

Lugano

History

There are indications that a rural borough existed here as long ago as the 10th century, and up until the late 13th century it was the property of Como. However, from then and until the very beginning of the 16th century, control alternated between Como and the Duchy of Milan. During the last period of control by the latter, however, from 1434 to 1501 it actually had its own Counts of Lugano. From 1513 to 1798 it became part of the Bellinzona district of Switzerland. In 1798 the Ticino area asked to remain within the Helvetic Republic, rather than becoming a part of Napoleon's Cisalpinian Republic that emerged in 1803. Lugano then became part of the free and independent Swiss canton of Ticino. During the 18th century Lugano played a large part in the struggle for a united Italy. Prominent citizens like the Ciani brothers organized networks of Italian refugees escaping from Austrian repression, and the Villa Ciani became the centre of that activity.

Ticino and its people, the *Ticinesi*, have been inextricably linked with the Italian regions of Lombardy and Piedmont, and this is reflected in the fact that the official language is Italian, spoken by 84 per cent of the population.

In the second half of the 19th century tourists began to discover the delights of Lugano, and tourism has now become an integral part of the city's vibrant economy. The opening of the Gotthard railway line at the end of the 19th century played a large part, too, in opening up what was, up to that time, mainly a rural community. These days, Lugano, perhaps surprisingly, is the third largest financial market in Switzerland.

The year 2003 brought the prospect of important changes to Lugano. A referendum – a Swiss political institution – voted in favour of a new Lugano whereby eight city states combined to give Lugano a new administrative and political authority and a population of 50,000 inhabitants. This change brings with it major new infrastructure projects such as high-speed rail links with the Italian region of Lombardy, reconstruction of Agno Airport and new cultural, tourist and sports facilities.

Monte San Salvatore

Start, then, at the southern end of the city in the area known as Paradiso and head for the **Funicolare Monte San Salvatore** (Monte San Salvatore Funicular). The trip to the 2,992ft (912m) summit takes just 12 minutes, and once there you will find – besides the views – a restaurant, a small chapel and the **Museo San Salvatore**, which rather bizarrely specializes in the Archfraternity of Good Death and Prayer, with exhibits of objects collected over the centuries. It also has a room dedicated to fossils and minerals found in the region.

Funicolare Monte San Salvatore
*t 091 985 28 28,
www.montesan
salvatore.ch; open mid-
Mar–mid-Nov; first
service up departs 8.30
and every 30mins
thereafter; in summer
last return trip is
at 11pm*

Museo San Salvatore
*open Wed–Sun 10–12,
and 1–3; adm free with
funicular ticket*

You will notice that beautiful villas are a particular feature of this city and one of them, the **Villa Malpensata**, is just a few moments away if you walk back in the direction of the town. This typically grand 19th-century villa in lovely grounds passed out of private ownership when, in 1893, it and the collection of paintings, sculptures and other pieces of art it contained were bequeathed to the city by Antonio Caccia, a writer and art collector. There was a proviso, however. The income from the estate was to be used to found a fine arts museum bearing the name of the donor. Such a museum was opened in 1912 but, just 21 years later, it was relocated to the Villa Ciani (see p.271). From that point forward, the Villa Malpensata has been utilized in a variety of ways and now houses the **Museo d'Arte** (Art Museum). You will find works of art from the 20th and 21st centuries only, with the emphasis on Expressionism; the museum particularly favours artists who focus their work on elements of humanitarianism. While there is a permanent collection on display, the museum's fame arises from its reputation as a host for major touring exhibitions that have included the likes of Chagall, Kirchner, Modigliani, Munch and their peers.

Museo d'Arte
Riva A. Caccia 5,
t 058 866 72 14,
www.mda.lugano.ch;
open Tues–Sun 10–6;
adm

Continuing back towards town, it would be entirely possible to overlook the church of **Santa Maria degli Angioli**, but that would be a mistake. Completed in 1500 and consecrated 15 years later, this is one of Lugano's most important buildings. Initially it was aligned with the St Francis Rule Fathers Franciscan monastery, but after 1602 it changed to the Reformed Fathers from Milan. Most notable here is the wall separating the nave from the chancel, which is entirely overlaid with an immense fresco. Created by Bernardino Luini in 1529, this gloriously depicts the *Passion and Crucifixion of Christ*. However, two other works by the same artist, *The Last Supper* and *The Madonna with Child*, are considered more important.

❷ Chiesa di Santa Maria degli Angioli
Piazza Luini 3

The Old Town

Via Nassa diverges from the lakeside here, and runs almost parallel to it. In the old days this was where fishermen used to hang their nets to dry, but not so now. Expect to find, instead, upmarket jewellers, boutiques, supermarkets and a host of bars and restaurants on this pedestrian and part-arcaded street. At its end, and almost surrounded by outdoor restaurants and bars, is the **Piazza della Riforma**, Lugano's main square. The large, impressive building on its lakeside is the **Civic Palace** that dates from 1844; it was built to provide a home to the cantonal government. The 1814 constitution allowed for Lugano, Locarno and Bellinzona to alternate every six years as the capital of the canton, and when it wasn't used for that purpose it became a hotel. Eventually Bellinzona became the permanent capital, and in 1890 this became home for the Municipal Assembly, Town Council and the respective administrative offices. Look at the four statues adorning the pediment: created by the renowned 19th-century Lombardian artist Francesco Somaini (1795–1855), they represent, from left to right, *Religion, Concord, Strength* and *Freedom*. Take a peek inside, too, and admire Vincenzo Vela's (1820–91), powerful statue of Spartacus. The tourist office is in a corner of the building facing the lake, and the embarkation pier for the **Società Navigazione del Lago di Lugano** lake steamers is just across the road.

The side streets and alleys of the Old Town around here are full of charm, and not far away is the **Sant'Antonio Abate** church; although it opened in 1651 it wasn't entirely completed until the early 18th century. The Somaschi boarding school was attached to the church, until it became the cantonal high school in 1852 before being demolished in 1908. And it is that connection, despite a portrait of St Antonio on the vault of the choir, that it is most known for, as it is a place of memorial to the famed Italian writer, Alessandro Manzoni, who studied at the school.

Chiesa di Sant'Antonio Abate
Piazza Dante

Cattedrale San Lorenzo
Via Cattedrale

The **Cattedrale San Lorenzo**, atop a nearby hill, has a history dating back over 1,000 years as it is thought a church existed here as long ago as 875. What you see, on the outside, is a Renaissance façade dating from 1517, with 15th-century vaults replacing the original wooden ceiling. Some parts of the original construction can still be identified inside.

Museo Cantonale d'Arte
Via Canova 10, t 091 910 47 80, www.museo-cantonale-arte.ch; open Tues 2–5, Wed–Sun 10–5; adm

Before heading back to the lakeside, cross Via della Posta into the Canova quarter to find the **Museo Cantonale d'Arte** (Cantonal Art Museum). Housed in a group of buildings that date from the Middle Ages and are noteworthy in their own right, this museum boasts a collection of works by Swiss-Italian and Italian artists of the late 18th, 19th and 20th centuries. The work of those who had a connection with the Ticino region is particularly highlighted. The museum also hosts a rolling programme of temporary exhibitions.

Chiesa di San Rocco
Piazza San Rocco

Nearby is another church to explore – one with a fascinating history. **San Rocco** was originally built in 1349 and was then dedicated to St Biagio. In 1512–27 and then again in 1528 Lugano, little more than a large village at the time, suffered two devastating plagues. Its citizens asked that the church be rebuilt, and the new church was re-named after St Rocco as he was believed to be able to keep plagues away. Given the previous problems, it was also designed for use as a leprosy hospital. Inside, the frescoes on the nave date from the 17th century, but the neo-Baroque façade is much more modern and has only existed since 1909.

On the Lakefront

San Carlino
Rivetta Tell

The **San Carlino**, by the lake just before the Parco Ciani, was erected in 1999 and meant to be a temporary attraction. However, this real curiosity has proved so popular that it has now been made permanent. Francesco Borromini built the original San Carlino in Rome, and this museum-piece replica of half the church, designed in turn by the world-renowned Ticinese architect Mario Botta and made of 32,000 pieces of wood and 108ft (33m) tall, commemorates the 400th anniversary of his birth.

Parco Ciani (Ciana Park) is the largest open area on the lake, and the house and its extensive gardens are named after two brothers, Giacomo and Filippo Ciani. Although their family originated from the Ticino, the brothers were born in Milan. As important figures in liberal politics, and very enterprising entrepreneurs, they played a major role in the political and economic development of Lugano, becoming among its most prominent 19th-century citizens. In fact, they founded, in 1844, the first kindergarten in Lugano for children of the working classes. Between 1840 and 1843, they acquired, expanded and refurbished an existing 17th-century home, fashioning it into the Villa Ciani, as it is known today. The municipality compulsorily purchased the property in 1912 and initially used it to house the local history museum. In 1933, it metamorphosed into the **Museo Civico di Belle Arti** (Municipal Fine Arts Museum), but currently it is only open for temporary exhibitions.

Monte Brè

**Funicolare
Monte Brè**
*t 091 971 31 71,
www.montebre.ch*

Move on east now – on a no. 1 bus if you prefer, to the ACT Cassarate stop – and then walk behind the impressive Grand Hotel Villa Castagnola to the **Funicolare Monte Brè**. The first stage of the journey is an automatic service between Cassarate and Suvigliana that takes four minutes; the second stage uses cars that have been restored to their original 1912 style, and takes you to the top, 3,061ft (933m) above sea level. There, the Ristorante Vetta Monte Brè allows you to sit, rest and admire truly wonderful views that, on a clear day, can include the peaks of the Bernese and Valais Alps. The

13

Ticino | Lugano

Mario Botta

Born in 1943 in Mendrisio, Ticino, Botta was an architectural apprentice in Lugano before studying in Milan and Venice – where he met and worked for Le Corbusier and Louis I. Kahn. In 1970 he started his first projects in Ticino before extending his reach worldwide, attaining international acclaim and numerous important awards. Amongst his many works are the San Francisco Museum of Modern Art (SFMOMA), the Museum Tinguely in Basel (*see* p.104), the Cymbalista Synagogue and Jewish Heritage Centre in Tel Aviv, the Kyobo Tower in Seoul, South Korea, and restoration of the Teatro alla Scala opera house in Milan. In 1996 he created and founded the new academy of architecture in Ticino, and has current projects in such diverse places as North Carolina, Beijing and Naples.

more adventurous can wander the short distance to the local village, that has been restored in typical Ticinese style.

Trips from Lugano

One of the many attractions of Lugano is the fact that there are several places of interest nearby that can be reached by boat (and train or sometimes bus). Between March and the end of October/November many of these trips are run by the Società Navigazione del Lago di Lugano.

Società
Navigazione del
Lago di Lugano
Viale Castagnola 12,
t 091 971 52 23,
www.lakelugano.ch

The closest place is the charming village of **Gandria**, once a fishing village, which is just around the bay about 3 miles (5km) from Lugano (although it is possible to get to and from Gandria by the Porlezza–Lugano bus, stopping by the post office in Castagnola and the Gandria restaurant in Gandria). Sitting at the foot of Monte Brè on the steep mountainside, this community of narrow streets and old-fashioned ambience is a car-free haven. The more active could consider taking the footpath alongside the lake back to Castagnola, a walk of about an hour. This is known as the Olive Tree Path, and new, recently fruiting olive trees have been reintroduced to supplant the ancient ones that used to grow here. Along the way, there are 18 panels explaining everything about olive trees and olive oil that you could possibly want to know. At Castagnola, you can hop on the no. 1 bus back to the town centre.

Another of these trips, further along the lake in an isolated position near the Italian border, is a very curious museum, the Museo delle Dogane Svizzere (Swiss Customs Museum). It is accessible only via a lake steamer that departs from Lugano Giardino at 1pm. The history of this museum revolves around – and this is the curious part – smuggling. Smuggling is an illegal activity that, inevitably, afflicts every border to some degree, and the physical features of this particular coast were certainly conducive to its success. In fact, it was a local way of life that has only recently come to an end. During 1856, in an effort to control this epidemic, the Swiss authorities constructed the first customs house on the steep slopes of Monte Caprino. The present building, which replaced the original in 1904, continued in operation until 1935, when it became a museum that has something for people of every age, including an interactive exhibition.

Museo delle
Dogane Svizzere
Cantine di Gandria,
t 091 923 98 43,
www.ezv.admin.ch/ezv;
open April–Oct
1.30–5.30

Two other lakeside attractions are between Lugano and Capolago – although they can't really be managed on the same day. The first of these is the closest: **Swissminiatur**, which children of all ages will find fascinating. You can get there by lake steamer, train or bus, getting off at Melide. Here, the entire landscape of Switzerland is replicated in miniature to a scale of 1:25 over an area of 2.7 acres

Swissminiatur
Via Cantonale,
Melide, t 091 640 10 60,
www.swissminiatur.ch;
open mid-Mar–Oct
9–6; adm

(11,000sq m). This enables you to formulate a mental vision of the country as a whole and to understand better either where you are going or where you have been. Model train lovers will certainly be on track: a model railway 1.86 miles (3.5km) long has been constructed, and the whole network is centrally controlled.

The second attraction entails taking a lake steamer or train to Capolago and then boarding an old-fashioned cog-wheel steam-powered railway on a 40-minute trip to Vetta, the summit of **Monte Generoso**. This is the highest summit in the region, at 5,591ft (1,704m), and besides having a marvellous perspective of the various branches of the lake it is also possible to see, to the south, the Lombard plain as far as the Apennines and the alpine range including the Eiger, Matterhorn, Jungfrau and Monte Rosa northwards. Relax at one of the cafés or restaurants, or maybe stroll around and try and sight one of the rare species of animal and plant life that have survived here since the last Ice Age.

Finally, there is a small but important museum within the Casa Carmuzzi complex in Montagnola, approximately 10 minutes west of Lugano. You can reach it by postbus to Montagnola, departing from the Via Sorengo just 150 yards from the train station via the underpass. The **Fondazione Hermann Hesse Montagnola** (Herman Hesse Foundation) was inaugurated on 2 July 1997 on the 120th anniversary of this painter, poet, novelist and Nobel Prize winner's birth. One of four museums in the world dedicated to his memory (this is considered the third most important), it contains memorabilia from the last 43 years of his life until his death in 1962, during which time he lived in Ticino. Expect to find some watercolours and a documentary showing the man at work; recitals of his works can be heard on Sundays.

Monte Generoso
*t 091 648 11 05,
www.montegeneroso.ch*

13
Ticino | Lugano

Fondazione Herman Hesse Montagnola
Torre Camuzzi, t 091 993 37 70, www.hessemontagnola.ch; open Mar–Oct daily 10–6.30; Nov–Feb Sat–Sun 10–5.30; adm

ⓘ **Lugano >**
Lugano Turismo: Riva Albertolli – Palazzo Civico, t 091 913 32 32, www.lugano-tourism.ch; open April–early May, late Sept–late Oct Mon–Fri 9–7, Sat 9–5, Sun and hols 10–5; May–Sept Mon–Fri 9–7, Sat 9–6, Sun and hols 10–6; Nov–Mar Mon–Fri 9–12 and 2–5.30, Sat 10–12.30 and 1.30–5

Tourist Information and Services in Lugano

Lugano Regional Pass: available from hotels and respective transport and tourist offices for either 3 days for CHF 92 or 7 days for CHF 108. It offers 100 per cent free local transport on buses, lake steamers, the Monte Brè and San Salvatore funiculars and some other places. Expect, also, 50 per cent reductions on other attractions and transport, including the airport shuttle bus.

Guided Tours

The **Trenino Turistico 'La Freccia Rossa'** ('The Red Arrow' Tourist Train), t 091 940 29 40, departs from the Piazza A. Manzoni, near the Burger King. Operating between mid-March and mid-October, the train leaves every half-hour between 10am and 6pm for a 40-min trip covering 6¼ miles (10km).

A number of free **guided walks** leave from the tourist office, including the Classic Tour, Parks and Gardens, Buildings and Mount Brè. The walks operate at different times of the year, so check the tourist information website for current information.

(★) Principe
Leopoldo Hotel
and Spa >>

Lost Property
Ufficio Oggetti Smarriti (Lost
Property Office, City of Lugano Police),
Via Beltramina 20b, **t** 058 866 82 50.

Market Days
Flowers, fruit and vegetables: Tues
and Fri mornings at Piazza Riforma.
Antiques and flea market: all day Sat
in the Canova quarter.

Medical Emergencies
Emergency doctor/dentist, t 1811.

Exhibitions and Festivals in Lugano

Late Mar: Camellia and magnolia
exhibition.
Easter Week: traditional processions.
April: start of the three-month **Lugano
Classic Music Festival**.
Late June–Aug: *Lungolago Al Pedoni*,
entertainment along the lakeside in
the evenings.
July: **Estival Jazz Festival**,
www.estivaljazz.ch, through the
streets.
1 Aug: **Swiss National Day**,
celebrations and a large firework
display.
Late Aug: **Blues to Bop Festival**,
www.bluestobop.ch.
Early Oct: *Festa d'Autunno*, Autumn
Festival in the city centre.
Mid-Oct: *Mercato delle Cipolle*, Onion
Market at the Piazza Riforma.

Shopping in Lugano

Shops are usually open Mon–Fri
8–12 and 1.30–6.30 – although some
extend their hours until 9pm on Thurs
– and Sat 8–12 and 1.30–5.
Department stores have longer hours,
usually Mon–Fri 8–6.30, and close a
little earlier on Sat.

The main shopping area is along
the Via Nassa up through the Piazza
Dante and in the surrounding side
streets. Fashion, particularly of the
Italian style, is king around here,
especially in the numerous small
boutiques and other clothing stores.

An interesting area to check out is
the Quartiere Maghetti, in the streets
just off the piazza of the same name.
This older part of Lugano has been
completely renovated and has now
become the equivalent of a shopping
mall – although outdoors. There are
all kinds of shops, restaurants and
bars here.

Where to Stay in Lugano

Luxury
*****Principe Leopoldo Hotel and
Spa, Via Montalbano 5, **t** 091 985 88
55, *www.leopoldohotel.com*. This
exquisite hotel combines history with
magnificent views. It is an 18th-
century neoclassical-style mansion
constructed by a prince and cavalry
general of the German Hohenzollern
dynasty, with wonderful views over
Lugano and the lake from its position
on Collina d'Oro (Golden Hill). The
hotel exudes an enchanting
ambience. The 37 rooms and suites are
beautifully furnished, and the
luxurious spa and exquisite
restaurants complete the package.

Expensive
****Villa Sassa Hotel Residence and
Spa, Via Tesserete 10, **t** 091 911 41 11,
www.villasassa.ch. This beautifully
restored 19th-century mansion has a
similar hilltop location to the
Leopoldo. Its 49 rooms, including 28
suites, are spacious and furnished to
the highest standards. The Ai Giardini
di Sasa restaurant offers innovative
cuisine, and in the summer meals are
served on the terrace overlooking the
lake. The Wellness Club has inviting
indoor and outdoor pools as well as
whirlpools, sauna and Turkish bath.
****Lido Seegarten, Viale Castagnola
24, **t** 091 973 63 63, *www.hotellido-
lugano.com*. Architecturally
impressive, this is the only hotel in
Lugano that has a lakeside location. It
has large and modern rooms; the best
are those that overlook the outdoor
restaurant and pool, with the latter
having a ramp down to the lake itself
and a floating deck a few yards
offshore.

Moderate

***Acquarello**, Piazza Cioccaro 9, **t** 091 911 68 68, *www.acquarello.ch*. This has an excellent location in the heart of the Old Town, and right next to the funicular to and from the train station. Quite a nice style, too; its 59 rooms all have ISDN connections.

Eating Out in Lugano

Very expensive

Principe Leopoldo, Via Montalbano 5, **t** 091 985 88 55, *www.leopoldo hotel.com*. This is the gourmet restaurant of the hotel of the same name. Swiss-Italian cuisine with Mediterranean flavours is the order of the day. The risotto is excellent, the seafood very tempting, and other main courses include duck, veal, pigeon, lamb and beef. The wine list is extensive – there are even two and a half pages of champagnes and *spumanti* – but don't overlook the white merlots. If the weather's fine, take a seat at one of the outdoor gazebos looking directly down on the lake.

⭐ Al Portone >

Al Portone, Viale Cassarate 3, **t** 091 923 55 11, *www.ristorantealportone.ch*. Just north of the Parco Civico, this could easily be overlooked from the exterior. It is, however, without any doubt the best non-hotel restaurant in Lugano. Run by Roberto and Doris Galizzi and their son Silvio, it serves up some of the finest and most beautifully presented examples of Swiss-Italian cuisine with all the subtle flavours of the Mediterranean. There are two *degustazione* menus or you can select what you fancy from the menu. The wine list specializes in the finest Ticino vintages.

Arté, Piazza Emilio Bossi 7, **t** 091 973 48 00, *www.villacastagnola.com*. Although technically a part of the Grand Hotel Villa Castagnola, just 100 yards away, this is much more modern in style. As you step down into the dining room it gives the optical illusion that you are about to walk directly into the lake just the other side of the large windows. The *chef de cuisine* here, Frank Oerthle, specializes in innovative gourmet cuisine, including many fish dishes.

Orologio, Via Nizzola 2, **t** 091 923 23 38, *www.ristorante-orologio.ch*. Opened in 1907, this has traditionally been one of the city's finest restaurants. Now, completely renovated and furnished in a minimalist style, it continues to serve classic Mediterranean cuisine. Look for interesting specials, too.

Expensive–moderate

Trani, Via Cattedrale 12, **t** 091 922 05 05, *www.trani.ch*. At the top of a steep pedestrian street is this fascinating complex of restaurant, wine bar and wine shop. The name originates from an Italian town famous for its wine production; producers from there have set up 'Trani' shops in northern Italy that have become a cultural institution. In the curved brick-ceilinged dining room you'll find a small but interesting menu, which may include seasonal specialities like asparagus or artichoke. At the wine bar try the Tavolozza, a method of trying six different quality wines and keeping notes on them – then buy the ones you like at the shop.

Grand Café Al Porto, Via Pessina 3, **t** 091 910 51 30, *www.grand-cafe-porto.ch*. Do not be put off by the couple or so chairs and tables outside – the inside is quite magnificent and full of surprises. One half of the front room is covered with a grand, wooden-beamed ceiling, with chandeliers and mirrors, while the other part has a fireplace dated 1803 and a counter full of the most delicate pastries, cookies, etc; there are other side rooms, too. The menu is rather limited.

Moderate–inexpensive

La Tinera, Via dei Gorini 2, **t** 091 923 52 19. In the basement of a building just off Piazza della Riforma, this has a typical Ticinese ambience with wooden-beamed ceilings, pots and pans and wine around the walls, and wooden tables and chairs. The menu offers an array of set meals, Ticinese- and Lombard-influenced, as well as daily specials.

Ascona

Ascona and Locarno, from their respective locations on either side of the Maggia River, could be described as twin towns; but, in reality, they have little in common. **Locarno**, by far the larger of the two, has its attractions – particularly in the Old Town – and it plays host to a film festival (*see* box below). But Ascona, with a population of just 5,000, is a magically pretty town and most visitors choose to stay here.

Its narrow streets and lanes, dominated by the church's towering spire, meander down, converging with the long and narrow piazza that separates the lake from the town itself. This piazza, the main meeting place of Ascona, is lined with an eclectic array of hotels, restaurants, bars and shops. Adding to the town's peaceful charm, the authorities have made a determined effort to restrict the use of cars insofar as possible. However, you do have to yield to the swans and ducks. It is the place to relax, order a cool drink and admire the tranquil and very appealing panorama: pretty villas; yachts, motor boats and lake steamers sliding gracefully over the water; the unusual Brissago Islands; and, wherever you rest your gaze, tree-lined slopes cascading freely into the lake shore. It is no wonder that Ascona has artistic and cultural traditions dating back to the Middle Ages and Renaissance eras. Notwithstanding that, it was at the end of the 19th and beginning of the 20th century that this tiny town, known as Borgo, reached its cultural climax. At that time, an influx of philosophers, anarchists and other free-thinkers such as Herman Hesse, James Joyce and Carl Gustav Jung were attracted here. These, and others, have made the hill overlooking Ascona, Monte Verità (Mountain of Truth), famous in its own right.

Around the Town

The main attraction of Ascona is the pretty town itself, with its delightful pastel-coloured buildings on the famous piazza adjacent to Lake Maggiore and the maze of tiny lanes directly behind it with their boutiques, exclusive shops and galleries.

Notwithstanding that, there are several cultural attractions that are worth exploring. For example, the tourist office itself is housed in the beautifully Baroque **Casa Serodine**. Otherwise known as the Casa Borrani, its stucco decorations by Giovanni Battista Serodine (1587–1626) – brother of the painter Giovanni Serodine (1594–1631) – give it the most elaborate façade of any secular Swiss building.

Locarno International Film Festival

This festival, *www.pardo.ch*, has been held annually since 1946. The Piazza Grande serves as an open-air theatre for 8,000 viewers. The most prestigious award, the Golden Leopard prize, is given to the best film in the international competition.

Getting to and around Ascona

See 'Getting to Ticino', p.263 for directions to Locarno. Ascona is either a short drive across the Maggia River, or take the no. 1 bus from just outside Locarno railway station.
Ascona is so small it is easy to **walk** everywhere.

The majestic bell-tower of the **Chiesa Parrochiale SS. Pietro e Paolo** (Saints Peter and Paul Parish Church) dominates not only the adjoining Piazza San Pietro, but also Ascona itself. Look closely at the side facing the lake and you will find the commune's coat-of-arms featuring St Peter's keys and the papal tiara. Although first mentioned in 1264, most of what you see today dates from the 16th century. Inside, there are three magnificent paintings created by Giovanni Serodine between 1600 and 1630, some 15th-century frescoes and a choir enclosed on three sides.

Another church worthy of investigation is located to the northeast, closer to the more modern part of town. The **Chiesa Mater Misericordiae** (Church of the Collegio Papio) dates from the 14th and 15th centuries and is consecrated to Santa Maria della Misericordia. It has an attractive interior, with pride of place belonging to the main altar's polyptych, a unique work dating from 1519 by Giovanni Antonio de Lagaia, a painter from Ascona. The adjacent **Collegio Papio** (Papio College), was bequeathed by Bartolomeo Papio (1526–80) in his will, and Pope Gregory XIII subsequently commissioned the architect Pellegrino Pellegrini to create it. Begun in 1584, it took four years to complete, and features a magnificent cloister with two sets of arches decorated with numerous heraldic coats-of-arms, most of which belong to cardinal-archbishops from Milan – the jurisdictional power of the era. These days the college is a private school.

Ascona has three entirely different types of museum, in quite different locations. The **Museo Communale d'Arte Moderna** (Modern Art Museum) is arguably the most important and is situated just to the west of the tourist office. Housed in an attractive 16th-century *palazzo*, it got its start in 1922 when members of a large artists' colony here donated one of their works – 65 in all – to create a future museum. The main collections are those of the foundations Marianne Werefkin and Richard and Uli Seewald. The Russian Marianne von Werefkin, a joint founder of the Munich Expressionist Blaue Reiter movement, has 70 of her works and 160 sketchbooks here. Look, also, for impressive works by Utrillo, Klee and Franz Marc.

On the other side of town, just behind the Hotel Eden Roc, is the small **Museo Epper**. Opened in 1980, this small museum preserves the artistic heritage of Ignaz Epper (1892–1969) and his wife Mischa Epper-Quarles Van Ufford (1901–78), who settled here in

Museo Communale d'Arte Moderna
Via Borgo 34,
t 091 759 81 40,
www.museoascona.ch;
open Tues–Sat 10–12 and 3–6, Sun and hols 3–6;
adm

Museo Epper
Via Albarelle 14, **t** *091 791 19 42; open Tues–Fri 10–12 and 3–6, Sat–Sun 3–6*

1932. Ignaz is highly thought of as a major figure of Swiss Expressionism, whilst Mischa's sculptures and drawings belong to the more classical French tradition.

Those wishing to learn more about the eccentricities and unusual ideas of those visionaries who flocked to this region beginning in the late 19th century should definitely head for the **Fondazione Monte Verità** (Monte Verità Foundation). This was both the residence and HQ of the 'Co-operative vegetarian colony Monte Verità', and exhibits documents by the utopian visionaries from the north (see p.276) on universal concepts such as truth, anarchy, social utopianism, purification of the body, psychology, dance, music and literature. Take a stroll in the park, also, to the Casa Selma – the 'Russians' House' and the old showers used by the residents – and see the circular painting *The Clear World of the Blessed*, by Elisar von Kupfer, in the recreated wooden house of the Chiaro Mondo dei Beati.

Fondazione Monte Verità
Via Collina,
t 091 758 40 40,
www.monteverita.org

Lake Excursions

No visitor to Ascona can ignore the presence of Lake Maggiore, and two excursions should definitely be considered. Firstly, take a trip to the **Brissago Islands**. They have an ancient history, with Roman remains and the ruins of an early 13th-century church being found there. In 1885 they were purchased by Baroness Antonietta Saint Leger, who built a fine residence and invited her many painter, writer, sculptor and musician friends as guests. More interestingly, for visitors today at least, she turned the larger of the two islands into an exotic garden featuring plant species representative of the Mediterranean, subtropical regions of Asia ranging from China to Korea, southern Africa, North, Central and South America as well as Australia and parts of Oceania. On the small island the spontaneous vegetation is kept in its natural state.

⭐ **Brissago Islands**
t 091 791 43 61,
www.isolebrissago.ch;
adm

Farther afield but not actually visible from Ascona is the charming Italian town of Stresa, and its own Borromeo Islands are certainly worth a visit.

Navigazione Lago Maggiore
www.navigazione laghi.it

All of these places can be reached on the lake steamers of the **Navigazione Lago Maggiore**, departing from Ascona.

ⓘ **Ascona >**
Ente Turistico Lago Maggiore:
Casa Serodine,
t 091 791 00 90,
www.maggiore.ch; open Mar–Oct Mon–Fri 9–6, Sat 10–6, Sun 2.30–5; at other times of year Mon–Fri 9.30–12.30 and 2–5.30, Sat 11.30–3.30

Guided Trips and Tours in Ascona

Trenino, t 078 676 16 00, is a tourist train that takes you on an interesting tour of Ascona. Climb aboard across from the Hotel-Restaurant Elvezia on the Piazza G. Motta.

Festivals in Ascona

Late June/early July: the **New Orleans Jazz Festival**, *www.jazzascona.ch*, completely takes over the piazza.

Mid-July: Festival of Ascona – top art events.

Aug: music weeks in Ascona.

Where to Stay in Ascona

*****Eden Roc**, t 091 785 71 71, www.edenroc.ch (*luxury*). Located just to the east of the piazza on the lake, this is undoubtedly the hotel of choice in Ascona. Totally refurbished in 2001, it has the ambience of a beautiful Italian *palazzo* with its original paintings and works of art co-existing gracefully with unique furnishings. Its 48 deluxe rooms, 33 luxury suites and 3 presidential suites follow this style and you can choose from three restaurants, including the classically French Eden Roc – from whose terrace you can watch the sun set over the lake – and the creative La Brezza. There are three pools: indoor, indoor/outdoor and outdoor and, of course, the lake itself, as well as a water-skiing school and boats for hire; also various health facilities and the Clarins Beauty Farm. The hotel also offers a free shuttle service to and from the train station in Locarno.

***Al Porto**, Piazza G. Motta, t 091 785 85 85, www.alporto-hotel.ch (*moderate*). Behind an attractive façade on the piazza; 36 elegantly bright and modern rooms – ask for a lake view. Also a fine restaurant and a pleasant garden.

***Tamaro**, Piazza G. Motta, t 091 785 48 48, www.hotel-tamaro.ch (*moderate*). Right on the famous piazza, this offers charming, stylish accommodation in 51 traditionally decorated rooms, some with a lake view. The restaurant is worth a visit for its gracious architecture.

Eating Out in Ascona

Grotto Baldoria, Vicolo S. Omobono 9, t 091 791 32 98, www.grottobaldoria.ch (*moderate*). Tucked away in one of the side streets off the piazza; the menu is whatever the chef decides he is going to cook that day. The ambience is pleasing and the fare inexpensive.

Elvezia au Lac, Piazza G. Motta 15, t 091 791 15 14, www.hotel-elvezia.ch (*moderate*). A great place for lunch or dinner, with an extensive selection of pizza, *antipasti*, soups, pasta and risotto, as well as meat and fish dishes.

Centovalli

There may be no towering well-known peaks here, but the Centovalli – valley of a hundred valleys – is still hugely impressive and very beautiful. Starting just west of Locarno/Ascona, with the magnificent village of Intragna as its gateway, this deep, wide valley twists and turns. The Melezza River is joined along its way, from north and south, by waterfalls and tributaries from valleys too numerous to count. Past the border with Italy at Camedo it widens greatly and becomes known as the Valle Vigezzo, before dropping steeply down to the strategically important Italian town of Domodossola.

History

These valleys have always been remote, and life for the villagers extremely difficult. In fact, a connecting road wasn't built until the late 1800s, and it wasn't until later, in 1923, that the quaint Ferrovie Autolinee Regionali Ticinesi (FART – an unfortunate acronym) train line was opened between Locarno and Domodossola, becoming

Getting to and around the Centovalli

See 'Getting to Ticino', p.263, for directions to Locarno. From Locarno take the **FART train**, *www.cento valli.ch*; the platform is underneath the regular station in Locarno. The train runs along the length of the valley to Domodossola, Italy. Other options are to **drive** or take the **bus**, but the road is difficult in places and you'll miss out on some of the spectacular views that the train ride offers (*see* box below).

the international rail connection between the important Gotthard and Simplon railway lines. This is known as the Centovallina in Switzerland and the Vigezzina in Italy.

Historically, families here have been both interconnected and large, with male children named mostly after the saints of the different parishes – and life merely a matter of survival. People's sole recreation was on church feast days where Mass, at which the women sat behind the men, was followed by a processional celebration for the particular saint being honoured. Work, too, was a problem, and these hardy Ticino men had to look to other places to gain financial rewards. Many gained a reputation as highly proficient chimney sweeps (*spazzacamini*) and took their skills as far afield as Venice, even developing their own language so that they could communicate with each other secretly. Others gathered chestnuts and roasted them in town squares. More went to work in the port of Livorno, Italy, whilst some ventured as far away as California and Australia.

These days, unlike many places in Switzerland, the Centovalli has very little commercialization and this adds to its attraction.

Intragna

Intragna is the largest village here and, despite being close to such cosmopolitan towns as Locarno and Ascona, retains an entirely different ambience. The use of local stone in construction makes it look older than it actually is; the village is dominated by the 17th-century 226ft (69m) bell-tower of the **San Gottardo church** – claimed to be the highest in all Ticino. Interestingly, its church records show just how closely knit families were here. They

Ferrovie Autolinee Regionali Ticenesi (FART) Train

The reality is that a car, or even a bus, doesn't give you the best views of the valley. This honour undoubtedly goes to the curious **Centovallina trains**, which have large picture windows and a better route, generally with two services an hour. Note, too, the very old and strange carriages – more like tramcars – that sit as museum pieces outside some stations. On its 34-mile (55-km) journey between Locarno and Domodossola, it passes 83 bridges and tunnels and negotiates tight curves and steep slopes to the highest station at an altitude of 2,743ft (836m). The varied scenery, with the river dividing the valley, is captivating.

indicate that not once, in the 200 years of recorded marriages until well into the 1800s, did a member of the dominant Selmina/ Salmina family marry a person from outside Intragna. In truth, there isn't too much to see, but a walk around the core area outside the San Gottardo church is interesting, not least for the extremely narrow cobble-stoned streets, hardly wide enough for a car to pass along. It is the best place to base yourself for exploring the Centovalli.

Monte Comino

Some of the valley's captivating scenery can be enjoyed on the short FART train trip from Intragna to Verdasio – just three stops – where a short, sharp walk uphill from the station takes you to the

Monte Comino
t 091 798 13 93,
www.comino.ch

Monte Comino gondola car station. In six minutes the gondolas will take you from 1,804ft (550m) at Verdasio to 3,773ft (1,150m) at Comino, on the north side of the valley. From here there really are wonderful views, both back down to the valley and to distant snow-capped peaks. Just 85ft (26m) higher there is a strange little shrine, dating from the second half of the 15th century, home to the revered Madonna della Segna, whose festival day is 6 July.

**Ristorante Alla
Capanna**
t 091 798 18 04,
www.monte-comino.ch

Although there are signposts to the larger Monte Comino mountain hotel and restaurant, a far more interesting option is to go around and down from the gondola car station to the tiny **Ristorante Alla Capanna** – actually the highlight of the trip. It is only open from March to October, and the charming couple that run it rely on solar power for lighting and power and wood for heating. They invite you into their home to either eat in their little dining room or out on the south-facing terrace, and the fantastic home-made dishes more than compensate for the limited selection. The specialities here are a Ticino cold meat dish, risotto or a typically regional polenta. Wash it all down with a glass or two

Tourist Information in Intragna

There isn't a tourist office in Intragna, but the tourist offices in Ascona, see p.278 and Locarno, Via B. Luini 3, t 091 791 0091, have information on the Centovalli. Also see www.procentovalli.ch and www.intragna.ch.

Where to Stay and Eat in Intragna

Antico, Via Cantonale, t 091 796 11 07, www.hotelantico.ch (*inexpensive*). This charming hotel is in the heart of the village directly in the shadow of the San Gottardo bell tower. The 26 rooms have an old-fashioned feel, as do the public areas. The wooden-beamed dining room has an impressive brick fireplace and antiques decorate the walls. It is separated from the well-stocked, cosy bar by a curved archway. There is a private courtyard, a pool and small children's playground. The hotel's **restaurant (*moderate*) is the best option in the village. For a cost of CHF 30 you can get a three-course dinner – maybe even cooked by the owner himself – consisting of a choice of warm or cold starter, main course and dessert or cheese.

Garni Intragna, Piazza, t 091 796 10 77, *www.garni-intragna.ch* (*inexpensive*). This is close to the Antico and has a similar feel. If you stay here you can use the facilities at the Antico. It is a steep walk up from the Intragna train station to the centre of the village, so call the hotel and they will willingly come and pick you up.

of the local red wine, Nostrano, made from a combination of Bondola and Merlot grapes.

Time, now, to work some of this extravagance off and, suitably, Comino is a fine starting point for a **hike**. The *Locarno-Ascona Dintorni e Valli* hiking map is useful as all routes are numbered, but it is not absolutely necessary as the paths are clearly signposted. The best idea is to walk back on the generally downhill main path (*sentiero principale*) to Intragna, via Selna, 2,772ft (845m), and Costa, 2,086ft (636m), a walk of about 2½ hours. From Costa either walk on down to Intragna, 1,112ft (339m), or take the easy option on the gondola car. Before setting out, study the colour posters on the walls of the Alla Capanna, as these explain to you the wide variety of flora and fauna that can – or might – be seen on these slopes.

Of course, the less energetic might decide that a little snooze on the sunny terrace of the Alla Capanna is in order, before returning to Intragna on the gondola and the Centovallina.

✪ Valle Maggia | Valle Maggia

The Valle Maggia, covering one-fifth of the canton of Ticino, is a wonderland of natural beauty that, surprisingly, remains relatively unknown. It is a series of valleys whose rivers converge at various points, cascading down to the valley floor at Cevio. From here the water flows into Lake Maggiore, some 18½ miles (30km) farther south. The mountains to the east, north and west create a virtually impenetrable barrier and yet this area has been inhabited for

Hiking in the Valle Maggia

One of the best ways to enjoy the natural attributes of the Valle Maggia to the full is by taking advantage of the nearly 435 miles (700km) of paths. These meander through magnificent scenery, including more than 40 alpine pools and lakes and numerous waterfalls. This will enable you to view the incredible array of fauna and flora indigenous to the area. You could perhaps take a bus to one village and hike to another, but be forewarned that the buses are not that frequent.

St Gothard Pass
Airolo
A2-E35
Faido

Val Bedretto
Valle Leventina

Robiei
Fusio
Basodino glacier
Mogno
San Carlo
Peccia
Sornico
Sonlerto
Foroglio
Brontallo
Cavergno
Bignasco

Val Lavizzara

Val Verzasca

Bosco Gurin
Valle di Bosco
Cevio
Cerentino
Valle Rovana
Campo
Cimalmotto
valle di Campo

Valle Maggia

TICINO

Maggia

Maggia

Avegno

Intragna
ITALY
Melezza
Camedo
Centovalli
Ascona
Locarno

Brissago

N

10 km
5 miles

Getting to the Valle Maggia

By Car
Follow the road from Ascona/Locarno that runs parallel to the Maggio River.

By Bus
From Locarno take the no. 315 to Cevio, Bignasco and Cavergno.

Getting around the Valle Maggia

By Car
If you don't have a **car** the only option here is the various **bus** routes that run between the villages.

By Bus
Bus no. 11 Cevio to Bosco Gurin. Bus no. 11 Cevio to Cerentino Paese, then bus no. 27 on to Campo and Cimalmotto. Bus no. 17 from Bignasco to San Carlo. Bus no. 39 Bignasco to Fusio, via Brontallo.

---

millennia. But life here is dictated by geography, a fact that will become clear when you visit the rural villages and hamlets.

The valley begins at **Avegno**, just a few kilometres north of Ascona and Locarno. Along here it differs from its near neighbours in that it has a wide floor that accommodates 12 villages, the inhabitants of which account for more than 80 per cent of the entire population. If you travel this way on a summer weekend, don't be surprised if the roadsides are lined with cars. This is a very popular place for people to sunbathe. Multilingual signs warn of the dangers of the extremely cold river water and of sudden surges in the water level.

Maggia

Maggia is home to the **tourist office** for the Valle Maggia. The main point of interest in the village is the remarkable Chiesa della Madonna delle Grazie. This 15th-century church, one of the oldest in the valley, is famous for its frescoes and paintings by Giovan Antonio Vanoni (1810–86), who was noted for his scenes depicting local farmers' lives.

Chiesa della
Madonna delle
Grazie
*open May–mid-Oct,
1st Sat of month, Wed
2–4, Thurs 3–5, Fri 4–6*

Cevio

Cevio is the main village in the valley and is one of the most appealing. Its square is a delight, particularly the beautifully decorated Pretorio, with its magnificent coat-of-arms. The Museo di Valmaggia is located here within two buildings – the Palazzo Franzoni and the Casa Respini-Moretti. Here you will find many

Museo di
Valmaggia
*t 091 754 13 40,
www.museovalmaggia.
ch; open April–Oct
Tues–Sat 10–12 and 2–6,
Sun 2–6*

exhibits that relate the history, social development and lives of the farmers and shepherds of the valley.

Val Rovana

Cevio is also the ingress to the Val Rovana to the west. Before it splits into two valleys the terraced fields of **Linescio** – created by farmers to exploit every inch of available land to grow rye and potatoes – are prominent in the landscape. Then, just after, there is the split into the **Valle di Bosco** to the north and the **Valle di Campo** to the south, both of which run due west and end near the Italian border. **Bosco Gurin**, nestled at the end of the former, at 4,944ft (1,507m), is the highest village in the Ticino and, these days, is a favourite skiing destination. It is mainly inhabited by descendants of colonizers from the Valais, who passed over the foreboding mountains to the north in the 13th century. Consequently it is the only village in the canton of Ticino where the official language is Swiss-German – Gurinergerman. **Campo**, in the more southerly Valle di Campo, is notable for the large houses constructed there by returning émigrés.

Val Bavona and Val Lavizzara

A short distance north of Cevio, just past Bignasco, the Valle Maggia splits again. To the west is the **Val Bavona**, which up until the 16th century was populated year-round but these days is only inhabited from April to October and, with the exception of San Carlo, has no electricity. The main points of interest in this rugged, wild valley are the waterfalls at **Foroglio**, the tiny hamlet of **Sonlerto** and the **San Carlo to Robiei cable car**. The latter gives you a marvellous perspective of the surrounding mountains, including the **Basodino glacier**.

San Carlo to Robiei cable car
Further information at www.robiei.ch, or from the mountain station **t** *091 756 65 53, or the valley station* **t** *091 756 65 46; operates end June–mid-Oct*

The **Val Lavizzara**, to the east, is sparsely populated and has six very distinct villages, **Sornico** being the most important. Notable among the others are **Fusio**; **Mogno**, home to an interesting church designed by Mario Botta (*see* p.271) – it is elliptical in shape and was built from Peccia marble, granite, iron and glass; **Peccia**, which has the only quarry in Switzerland where white marble is extracted; and **Brontallo**, which sits precariously high off the main road. Its colourful houses, often constructed of stone, are blessed with a south-facing perspective which gives the village a Mediterranean feel.

Where to Stay and Eat in the Valle Maggia

(i) **Maggia** >
Ente Turistico di Vallemaggia: Centro commerciale, t 091 753 18 85, www.vallemaggia.ch; open Oct–May Mon–Fri 9–12 and 2–5; June and Sept Mon–Fri 9–12 and 2–5, Sat 9–12; July and Aug Mon–Fri 9–5, Sat 9–12

Albergo Basodino, t 091 754 11 01, Cevio (*inexpensive*). A pleasant hotel on the main square. Neat and tidy rooms combine with a nice bar, restaurant and terrace to create a delightful ambience.

Albergo Posta Bignasco, t 091 754 11 23 (*inexpensive*). Located about halfway up the valley at a fork in the road that leads to Robiei. This family-run establishment has a rustic ambience and clean, comfortable rooms.

Albergo Robiei, t 091 756 50 20 (*inexpensive*). Situated at the far end of the valley at an altitude of 6,562ft (2,000m), this is a convenient base for those taking the nearby cable car. You will recognize it by its octagonal shape and, though it is a little old-fashioned in style, it offers the benefit of an on-site restaurant that seats 90.

Hotel Walser, Bosco Gurin, **t** 091 759 02 02, *www.hotel-boscgurin.ch* (*inexpensive*). This hotel, which sits at the entrance to the village, offers 12 comfortable and recently renovated rooms, a charming restaurant with a fireplace offering regional specialities, as well as a sauna and fitness centre.

Graubünden

Located in the southeastern corner of
Switzerland, Graubünden is the largest
canton. Surrounded on three sides – by
Austria, Ticino (Swiss Italy) and Italy –
Graubünden is slightly different
culturally to other parts of Switzerland.

Arguably, Graubünden is Switzerland's
most attractive canton. It is very rarely
less than pretty and often quite
spectacular. The Upper Engadine is a
perfect example of the latter,
particularly so around St Moritz where
dramatic mountains surround a series
of lakes. St Moritz is a town unlike any
other, coming alive in the sparkling
winter season as the playground for the
world's jet set.

However, Graubünden isn't all about
large resorts; there are many other
lesser-known destinations that have
charm in abundance, particularly
around the Lower Engadine.

14

Don't miss

⭐ **Relaxing
experience**
Therme Spa, Vals **p.290**

⭐ **Fun funicular
excursion**
Muottas Muragl Bahn,
Pontresina **p.293**

⭐ **Unique spa**
Engadin Bad Scuol, Scuol
p.295

⭐ **Across the
border**
Nauders, Austria **p.298**

⭐ **Wild, natural
landscape**
Swiss National Park
p.300

See map overleaf

Don't miss

1. Therme Spa, Vals **p.290**

2. Muottas Muragl Bahn, Pontresina **p.293**

3. Engadin Bad Scuol, Scuol **p.295**

4. Nauders, Austria **p.298**

5. Swiss National Park **p.300**

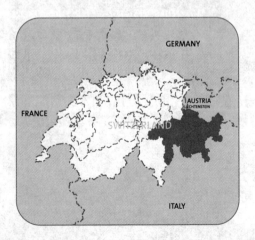

Getting to and around Graubünden

By Air

There aren't any airports in the region. If you are flying to Switzerland with the intention of heading straight to Graubünden, the most convenient airport to fly to is Zürich's **Kloten International Airport**, *www.flughafen-zuerich.ch*.

By Car

Chur (the canton's capital) is best reached from the north (from St Gallen) and south (from Lugano) on the A13 motorway, and from destinations in eastern Switzerland by way of the A3/A13 motorways. From Chur, lesser roads lead to all other parts of Graubünden. (An alternative route from Lugano to St Moritz is detailed below in 'By Bus'.) Otherwise, there are no motorways in the canton and the roads, often incorporating passes, can be scenic but on the slow side.

By Bus

Travelling by **postbus**, *www.postbus.ch*, is the most interesting option from Lugano. The bus leaves Lugano and enters Italy before joining Lake Como at Menaggia and continuing up the western side of the lake and then crossing it towards Chiavenna and the border with Switzerland. After that the road ascends quickly and steeply through the Maloja Pass, before passing the series of lakes leading to St Moritz.

By Train

From all destinations in Switzerland the best and fastest train services run to Chur, from where trains either continue to, or connect with, other destinations in Graubünden.

Graubünden's history stretches back to the pre-historic era, and recent archeological digs have yielded evidence of Bronze Age settlements dating from between 1800 to 800 BC. The Rhaetians, however, were the first inhabitants of the valley to leave conclusive proof of their presence here. It is also known that in 15 BC the Romans occupied the whole of Rhaetia, governing it as a province. The current capital, Chur, was then known as Curia.

Subsequent to the Romans the diocese of Chur took control of parts of the area. The League of God's House was founded in 1367, which was followed soon after by the Grey League (Grauer Bund), because of the basic grey clothes commonly worn by its members, and in the next century the League of Ten Jurisdictions in 1436. In 1471 the three leagues formed an alliance and this was the first step towards the formation of a canton, but that came centuries later. The eventual name given to the canton, Graubünden (Grisons in French), was from the name Grauer Bund.

Early in 1499 the Habsburgs took control of the region but they were defeated by the alliance of the three leagues at the Battle of Calven. However, peace didn't last. Later that year, the alliance, with help from the Old Swiss Confederacy, finally completed the rout of the Habsburgs during the Swabian War, and the subsequent Treaty of Basel granted almost complete independence to the Swiss Confederacy.

In 1526 the bishop of Chur lost jurisdiction and by 1798 this area became the canton of Graubünden under the Helvetic Republic,

14

Graubünden | Introduction

Getting to and around Vals

By **car**, travel via the motorway to Chur and exit at Tamins. Continue west on Route 19 via Flims to Ilanz before heading south down the pretty valley to Vals.

From the Lake Geneva region and the Valais it's a bit more complicated as you have to drive the length of the Valais to Andermatt and on to Ilanz via Disentis before entering the valley to Vals. The problem is that in winter this route will most probably be inaccessible as some passes will be closed, but in the summer it's spectacular, if slow.

By **train** and **postbus**, from all destinations in Switzerland except the Lake Geneva region and the Valais, it's necessary to take a train(s) to Chur and then change to one to Ilanz, where a postbus, *www.postbus.ch*, will be waiting to take you through to Vals.

From the Lake Geneva region and the Valais it's necessary to take the train(s) via Disentis to Ilanz to connect with the postbus.

Once you're in Vals, it's small enough to **walk** around.

---

but with the name of Raetia. Finally, in 1803, it became a canton of Switzerland, the largest in the country, and its coat-of-arms incorporates the coats-of-arms of the original three leagues.

Vals

With a population of just about 1,000, whose Roman Catholic Walser descendants migrated here from the Valais in the 12th century, Vals sits at an altitude of 4,107ft (1,252m). Vals is a curious place – a Walser-German-speaking enclave in the Romansch-dominated Val Lumnezia (Valley of Light) – which merits investigation. Its remoteness is in itself an attraction, as it is only accessible by a 12½-mile (20-km) road along a narrow, winding valley from the town of Ilanz.

As you approach the village a huge factory will remind you that, even without knowing it, you will most probably have tasted the water that Vals is famous for. Like everything else here, the Valser mineral-water factory – which can be toured – is communally owned.

⭐ **Therme Spa**
*www.therme-vals.ch;
open mid-June–mid-
April daily 11–8
(opening times differ for
hotel guests); adm,
(free to hotel guests),
recommended to book
tickets in advance*

The Spa

It is water that brings people here, but rather than bottled water it is the waters of the **Therme Spa** that are the attraction. The spa is located within an incongruous-looking group of modern

Romansch Language

It is the combination of Rhaetian and Roman influences that bequeathed to the area its distinctive culture and language. Romansch, spoken in this part of Switzerland, is the fourth official language of Switzerland, after German, French and Italian and, more accurately, is actually a general term for a group of dialects of the Rhaeto-Romance family. Another area to use variations of this language is northern Italy. There are even two variations of Romansch in the Engadine: Puter in the Upper and Vallader in the Lower. Even though less than 40,000 consider it their first language and it is spoken by less than 1 per cent of the population, it was given 'official language' status as one of the four national languages in 1938 and declared an official language of the Confederation in 1996.

buildings just past the factory. Most of these buildings were built in the 1960s and collectively form the **Hotel Therme Vals**, that is marketed as a one–five-star hotel. The thermal baths, which are fed by two natural springs, are immediately behind the hotel.

In 1986 the Thermalbad Vals AG company (100 per cent owned by the community) commissioned Peter Zumthor, an architect from Haldenstein, to construct a new bathing complex. In 1998 the spectacular landmark was registered as a protected building.

Built into the mountainside, with alpine flowers sprouting from the meadows on the roof, Zumthor used 60,000 Valser quartzite slabs to produce an interior that is as elegant as it is simple. The ambience here is one of quiet and peacefulness, where people can 'rediscover the primal experience of bathing, cleansing and relaxing in water, the sensation of water on one's skin, at various temperatures and in various settings'.

The facilities include a fire pool, an ice pool, a flower-scented pool, indoor and outdoor pools, a rough-hewn spring grotto and steam and sweat-bath rocks. Treatments are an important aspect of the spa. The 'Therapie' area offers treatments such as a natural sea mud pack and a stone massage, where warm stones are placed on the body. These, and any number of other enticing experiences, are available as single treatments or as part of a package.

The Village

Although the spa is the primary attraction in Vals, there are many outdoor activities on offer. There are **skiing** opportunities in winter and the chairlift opens up **hiking** paths in the summer, particularly up to the Zerfreilasee to the south. Take time, too, to walk around the charming village, to the south of the imposing water fountain and the Gasthof Edelweiss. As might be expected from the village's history, the old, dark-coloured wood buildings are reminiscent of those found in the Valais.

Where to Stay and Eat in Vals

(i) **Vals** >
Visit Vals: Poststrasse,
t 081 920 70 70,
www.vals.ch; open
Mon–Sat 9–11.30
and 2–5

*/**** **Hotel Therme Vals, t** 081 926 80 80, www.therme-vals.ch, (*inexpensive–moderate–expensive*). This has more than 140 rooms in four buildings, but the ones of choice are the 40 newly designed 'Temporaries'. Dinner in the Roter Saal – the best restaurant – is CHF 55 extra, but a slightly cheaper option is to take the half-board option where you dine at the Chessi Restaurant. Use of the spa facilities is included in your stay, and night-bathing is available to hotel guests on certain days of the week.

Gasthof Edelweiss, t 081 935 11 33, www.edelweiss-vals.ch (*inexpensive*). Located in the village square, opposite the water fountain, this is a more typical Swiss building. The hotel has just ten bedrooms that are a little basic but are comfortable and clean.

Getting to and around the Upper Engadine Valley

By **car**, the Upper Engadine Valley, in the far southeastern corner of Switzerland, is not that easily reached from other parts of the country. From Ticino it is easier to travel through Italy and arrive in the Upper Engadine via the Maloja Pass.

Trains arrive at St Moritz, often involving a change at Chur, from all other parts of Switzerland. You can then catch connections to Pontresina and the Bernina Valley, and Ardez.

Most other destinations in the Upper Engadine have to be reached by postbus, *www.postbus.ch*.

Upper Engadine Valley

St Moritz

The Upper Engadine is synonymous with St Moritz, which has a worldwide reputation as a glitzy, glamorous destination for the jet set. The town, and the three lakes that radiate from it, are located at an unusually high altitude of over 6,089ft (1,856m). The town is advertised as 'St Moritz – Top of the World'. Consequently, the area is blessed with a climate that bathes it in sunshine for an average of 322 days annually, making it the sunniest spot in Switzerland. It is said that it has a 'Champagne climate'.

St Moritz was originally famous for its therapeutic springs, which have been known for almost 3,500 years and were first recorded in 1466 BC. So revered were their powers that in 1519, Pope Leo X promised full absolution to every Christian visiting the spa of St Moritz. MTZ Medizinisches Therapiezentrum Heilbad St Moritz is the place that will meet your needs these days.

MTZ Medizinisches Therapiezentrum Heilbad St Moritz
Piazza Paracelsus 2,
t 081 833 30 62,
www.heilbad-stmoritz.ch

Despite its famous springs, St Moritz grew very little over the centuries, and had a population of merely 200 as late as 1830. That changed quickly, however, 30-odd years later as St Moritz was the birthplace of alpine winter tourism in 1864 and sport in 1884. It has hosted two Winter Olympic Games, in 1928 and 1948, and is the only place in Switzerland ever to stage them. It has also been the location for numerous winter sports world championships.

And it is in winter that St Moritz is seen at its glamorous best. Attracting a cosmopolitan, affluent, chic and elegant clientele from around the world, it accommodates them stylishly in a glittering array of luxury hotels. **Skiing**, of course, is de rigueur, but St Moritz has an eclectic array of other winter activities as well. Curious activities take place on the frozen lake, including show jumping, polo and horse racing (even over hurdles), the latter being held on three Sundays in February. Golfers will not be disappointed either. Europe's oldest and biggest tournament on snow is played here each January. And, so you won't lose your balls, they are red.

Luftseilbahn Corvatsch
t 081 838 73 73,
www.corvatsch.ch

As for other attractions in the area, there is a cable car within easy reach of St Moritz. The **Luftseilbahn Corvatsch** will take you up

Where to Stay in St Moritz

(i) **St Moritz >**
*Via Maistra 12,
t 081 837 33 33,
www.stmoritz.ch; open
mid-Dec–mid-April,
mid-June–mid-Sept
Mon–Fri 9–6.30, Sat
9–12.30 and 1.30–6.30,
Sun 4–6; mid-
April–mid-June, mid-
Sept–mid-Dec Mon–Fri
9–12 and 2–6, Sat 9–12*

*****Badrutt's Palace**, Via Serlas 27, t 081 837 10 10, *www.badrutts palace.com* (*luxury*). This hotel is a city landmark and is considered the place to be by celebrities and royalty since its opening in 1896. It offers 159 rooms and 38 suites, with amazing views of the Alps or the lake. There is a luxurious spa, the fabled King's Nightclub and an array of gourmet restaurants.

****Steffani**, Sonnenplatz, t 081 836 96 96, *www.steffani.ch* (*expensive*). A delightful building in the heart of town, this hotel is run by the third generation of the Märky family. It has 56 lovely rooms and 5 suites, an indoor pool and sauna, the Lapin Bleu and Le Mandarin restaurants, three bars and a nightclub.

***Corvatsch**, Via Tegiatscha 1, t 081 837 57 57, *www.hotel-corvatsch.ch*

(*inexpensive*). This small family-run hotel has a typically alpine ambience. Its rooms are pleasant and it has a restaurant.

Eating Out in St Moritz

Restaurant Jöhri's Talvo, Via Gunels 15, St Moritz/Champfèr, t 081 833 44 55, *www.talvo.ch* (*very expensive*). Housed in a delightful traditional Grison residence dating from 1658, this restaurant has two Michelin stars. Roland and Brigitte Jöhri have created an ambience that complements the marriage of French gastronomic cuisine and local regional specialities that they serve. Each dish – and there are many to choose from – is creatively prepared and served, of course, with an appropriate glass of wine. The wine is chosen from a well-stocked cellar that specializes in fine vintages from Switzerland, France, Italy and Spain. Eating here is an experience to be savoured.

to the mountain station at 10,837ft (3,303m), where you get a lovely panorama of the three lakes below. Narrow, long and enveloped by mountains, these stretch from their origin at St Moritz to a point just before the dramatic drop of the Maloja Pass down towards Italy. Upon these peaceful waters, regardless of the weather, you will see fishermen, both from the shore and in boats, angling for their supper.

Pontresina

Pontresina is a small, attractive village and is an ideal place to use as a base for local excursions.

If you take the train back to Punt Muragl Staz, you will find the **Muottas Muragl Bahn** (MMB), a rather curious little funicular that raises you up to the **Berghotel Muottas Muragl**, a hotel and restaurant situated at an altitude of 8,058ft (2,456m) (*the hotel is closed until December 2010*). Its terrace offers some of the finest views in Switzerland, with the subtly colourful scene of St Moritz and the lakes that meander away from it towards the Maloja Pass directly below you. The snow-white peaks of the higher mountains tower in the distance, casting a long shadow over icy glaciers that

Muottas Muragl Bahn
*t 081 842 83 08,
www.muottasmuragl.ch*

Getting to and around Pontresina

By **car**, Pontresina is just a very short drive from St Moritz, just past Muottas Muragl after entering the Bernina Valley.

By **train**, Pontresina is just three stops away from St Moritz, along the Bernina Valley line.

The village is small, so you can get around on **foot**.

lie off the valley leading to the Bernina Pass to the left. This journey is worth it for the views alone, but lunch at the restaurant is pleasant or, alternatively, visit in the evening, have dinner and marvel at the sunset.

From this base you can take a little exercise. The views continually evolve on an interesting hike around, not up, the mountain to **Alp Languard**. This take about 2½ hours and along the way there are enlightening perspectives of the wall of peaks, the loftiest of which is Bernina at 13,284ft (4,094m), across the valley. Among these mountains are massive glaciers with the largest, Vadret da Morteratsch, nearly reaching the valley floor. At Alp Languard there is a restaurant for refreshments, before you make your descent, by chairlift or on foot, to Pontresina.

Another excursion just a short distance down the valley from Pontresina gives you the chance to explore more high peaks. The **Diavolezza-Bahn** cable car (the cable car station is next to the Bernina Diavolezza railway station, which is on the line from St Moritz and Pontresina), with a capacity of 125, will whisk you to the top of Diavolezza, at 9,770ft (2,978m). At the top there is a couple of restaurants, a souvenir shop and a sun terrace, where you'll find Europe's highest outdoor Jacuzzi. In the summer months you can join a guided tour to learn more about the awesome glacial formations and the peaks that frame them.

(i) Pontresina >
Kongresszentrum Rondo, **t** 081 838 83 00, *www.engadin-stmoritz.ch; open mid-April–mid-June Mon–Fri 8.30–12 and 2–6, Sat 8.30–12; mid-June–mid-Oct Mon–Fri 8.30–6, Sat 8.30–12 and 3–5, Sun 4–6; mid-Oct–mid-Dec Mon–Fri 8.30–12 and 2–6, Sat 8.30–12, mid-Dec–early April Mon–Fri 8.30–6, Sat 8.30–12, and 3–5, Sun 3–5*

Where to Stay and Eat in Pontresina

****Hôtel Walther, t** 081 839 36 36, *www.hotelwalther.ch* (*luxury*). A magnificent, turreted, white building, this hotel has a belle époque ambience. It has the Aqua Viva spa, pool and mountain bikes. Half-board Plus includes a breakfast buffet, afternoon tea and cakes and a five-course dinner in the gourmet restaurant. *Closed from mid-April–mid-June, mid-Oct–mid-Dec.*

***Steinbock, t** 081 839 36 26, *www.steinbock-pontresina.ch* (*expensive*). In a 17th-century pastel-coloured Engadine house next to the Walther, whose pool facilities guests here can use. This hotel has 37 rooms, including one junior suite, and the cosy Colani Stübli restaurant serves Engadine specialities.

Berghotel Muottas Muragl, t 081 842 82 32, *www.muottasmuragl.ch* (*inexpensive*). Accessed only via the Muottas Muragl Bahn (MMB), this has a traditional mountain ambience and a charming restaurant. (*Closed until December 2010.*)

Lower Engadine Valley

The Lower Engadine is in the far eastern part of Switzerland that adjuts into, and is surrounded by, Austria and Italy. It is a by-product of the frequently torrential Inn River; the valley is flanked to the north by the Silvretta range and to the south by the Lischana mountains. Geographical peculiarities have made it remote from other parts of Switzerland.

The Lower Engadine has not succumbed to the demands of tourism. Its mountains are not scarred with cable cars or railways and you will not find any celebrated towns here. What you will find are pure alpine panoramas and a place where you can explore the glorious beauties of unsullied nature to your heart's content. In the unspoiled villages you will see many houses decorated with *sgraffito* – the elaborate artwork found on the exterior of houses throughout the Engadine.

Scuol

Scuol, a town with less than 2,000 inhabitants, has creatively built upon the local phenomenon of healing waters and revolutionized the traditional concept of the spa.

The Spa

Engadin Bad Scuol
t 081 861 20 00,
www.engadinbadscuol.
ch; open daily
8am–10pm;
adm, valid for 2½ hours
Roman-Irish Bath: open
daily 9–9; adm, including
unlimited admission to
the bath and sauna
landscape; reservations
need to be made 24 hours
in advance
Therapy Centre: t 081
861 20 04

The Engadin Bad Scuol is unique in Switzerland, and offers a complete body and mind experience. It comprises different parts: the **bath and sauna landscapes**, the **Roman-Irish bath** and the **therapy centre**, where waters from the Luzius, Sfondraz, Bonifazius and Lischana springs are used to treat any number of ailments.

The **bath and sauna landscapes** make up the majority of the spa. The centrepiece of the **bath landscape** complex is a large, round, indoor pool, equipped with several water fountains, where the water is maintained at a relaxing 93.2°F (34°C). Arranged around this are several smaller pools, including the popular Jacuzzi. Next, you will find a brine pool, at 95°F (35°C), whose waters contain 2 per cent natural salt from the springs of the United Swiss Rhine Salt-Works. However, as brine has the capacity to damage several minerals and stays on the skin, it is advisable to remove spectacles and/or jewellery, and to shower immediately afterwards. The cold-water pool is a chilly 64°F (18°C), but the most unusual pool is outside, reached via an interior channel where you pass through weather-protecting strips. Circular like the large pool, it is sub-divided into three concentric rings. The outer ring is a 'Lazy River' with concrete Jacuzzi beds built into the walls, and the two inner rings have Jacuzzi jets; the water is a warm 93.2°F (34°C). It is an amazing experience to lay there luxuriating in the water while the snow gently falls around you blanketing the nearby mountains. If all of this gets too much, there is a solarium inside with wonderfully comfortable lounge chairs: the perfect place for a little snooze.

The **sauna landscape** is just off the bath landscape. This is a mixed-sex area and you must dispense with your swimming costume. The only thing that accompanies you further is a towel, although this generally is carried over the arm – not wrapped around you. People of other cultures, particularly North Americans, might tend to believe that this can give rise to pruriency. To the Swiss, however, it is as natural as going to a normal swimming pool, and there is absolutely no embarrassment. An outside sauna gives out 203°F (95°C) of heat; if that leaves you in need of a cooling-off, you can follow up with a dive into the open-air cold pool with a coldwater cascade. At just 64°F (18°C), it is an exhilarating and chilling experience. Along the side of that pool, but back inside, is a glass-encased solarium with comfortable lounge chairs offering complimentary refreshment from a refrigerator filled with bottles of the spa's own natural water.

The **Roman-Irish bath** is a wonderfully sensual experience. At the reception area you will be given a toga to replace your bathing costume and a pair of rubber slip-ons to prevent you slipping on the wet tiled floors. The baths take 2½ hours to pass through, and it is also a mixed-sex area. Having changed, you start with two increasingly hot dry saunas 129.2°F (54°C) and 158°F (70°C), which are followed by a shower and an invigorating soap and brush massage – usually performed by a masseuse on the men and by a masseur on the women – that stimulates circulation and peels the skin. Your massage done, have a quick shower and head for the Vapour Baths with the first at 107.6°F (42°C) and the second at 118.4°F (48°C). Shower again and it is time for complete relaxation in two quite large baths, 96.8°F (36°C) and 93.2°F (34°C) respectively. The latter is, rather like a small swimming pool, entered via the steps that encircle it, and capped by an intriguing domed roof decorated with rather exotic paintings of mermaids. The penultimate stop – and you will not want to linger long – is the 64.4°F (18°C) Cold Water Pool. After you shower yet again an assistant will escort you to the Resting Place. There you will lie for half an hour or so, wrapped in warm towels on contoured air-beds, listening to the soft sounds of nature emanating from the ceiling.

Schloss Tarasp
t 081 864 93 68,
www.schloss-tarasp.ch;
guided tours daily June,
early July 2.30, 3.30; until
late Aug 11, 2.30, 3.30, 4.30;
until mid-Oct 2.30, 3.30; at
other times of year Tues
and Thurs 4.30; adm

The Castle

Another sight of national significance within the valley, and one whose commanding site makes it difficult to ignore, is the **Schloss Tarasp** (Tarasp Castle). In years past, many castles were scattered throughout the Inn Valley, although most are now just ruins. But not Schloss Tarasp, constructed atop a hill directly in front of the village around the middle of the 11th century by the Tarasp family. Subsequent centuries brought family feuds, battles and other upheavals that occasioned correspondingly frequent changes in ownership, sometimes leaving the castle unattended and in disrepair. Stability finally came, however, in 1900 when Dr K. A. Linger, owner of a Dresden cosmetic and pharmaceutical company, purchased it for CHF 20,000. While this was a huge sum at the time, it only represented the beginning of the expense necessary to renovate, restore and furnish the castle. Sadly, Dr Linger died in 1916, shortly before the castle was ready for him to move into. And that presented another problem. Although Dr Linger had bequeathed the castle and its contents to August III, King of Saxony, he declined to take possession in light of the financial burden associated with its upkeep. Resolution was reached when the castle was offered to, and accepted by, an old friend of Dr Linger's, the Grand Duke Ernst Ludwig of Hesse and the Rhine, who had at his disposal the necessary financial means to fund what would be costly ongoing expenses. A grandson of Queen Victoria and brother of the last Empress of Russia, the Grand Duke spent as much time as he could manage during the remainder of his life at Tarasp. At present, the castle is owned by one of his descendants, Princess Margareta von Hessen.

Outdoor Activities

Winter sports enthusiasts will want to consider basing themselves around Scuol. Here, a combination of cable cars, chair and skilifts are available to whisk you to a total of 50 miles (80km) of pistes. Snowshoeing, ski-touring, tobogganing, cross-country skiing and skating are also popular activities. Sledges are available for hire from the top of the Ftan-Prui chair-lift. There are also more than 31 miles (50km) of prepared **winter hiking trails** in the Scuol, Bad Tarasp-Vulpera area.

Mountain hiking is popular in this area. In fact, spread throughout the valley are in excess of 621 miles (1,000km) of mountain pathways that facilitate access to all areas of the countryside. The trails, naturally, go up and down hill, but also through dales, meadows and pastures and alongside countless rivers. One of the more enticing hikes runs from **Ftan** to **Guarda**, over a ridge along the mountain. On the slightly more than 2-hour walk, you will be treated to exhilarating views and visit two villages with considerable and contrasting charms. In Ftan, situated at an altitude of 5,413ft (1,650m), the population of 450 is dispersed over a fairly wide area and residents use their cars to get around. Guarda, which in English translates to 'look', is quite different. Here,

Activities in Scuol

(i) Scuol >
next door to the bus
station, t 081 861 22 22,
www.scuol.ch; open
early June–late Oct
Mon–Fri 8–6.30, Sat
9–12 and 1.30–5.30, Sun
9–12; late Oct–mid-Dec
Mon–Fri 8–12 and 2–5,
Sat 2–5; rest of year
Mon–Fri 8–12 and
1.30–6, Sat 2–5

Engadin Adventure, t 081 861 14 19, www.engadin-adventure.com. Offers professionally guided white-water rafting, mountain biking and mountain scooter trips in this region.

Where to Stay in Scuol

****Belvédere, t** 081 861 06 06, www.belvedere-scuol.ch (expensive). Right in the village centre, this gracious hotel has an attractive façade and pleasant gardens with a nice outside pool. Each of the 72 modern and spacious rooms are individually designed, and some have alpine views. There's also a superb restaurant, cosy piano bar and a wellness centre and spa.

****Schlosshotel Chastè**, Sparsels, **t** 081 861 30 60, www.relais chateaux.ch/chaste (expensive). Found in the shadow of the imposing castle.

Throughout the hotel, and its 11 rooms and 7 suites, pine panelling combined with slightly more modern furnishings make for a warm and comfortable ambience. Also a wonderful restaurant and a well-equipped, on-site health club.

***Engiadina**, Rablüzza 152, **t** 081 864 14 21, www.hotel-engiadina.ch (moderate). Near the village centre – 3mins from the spa – in a traditional house that has been cleverly converted, with many of its 12 rooms furnished in Swiss pine.

Where to Eat in Scuol

Schü-San, t 081 864 81 43 (moderate–inexpensive). Incongruously, this pleasant Chinese restaurant and bar overlooks the main pool of the spa. It has a wide-ranging menu including vegetarian dishes, lots of curry and house specialities.

cars must be left in a car park below the village, the village clinging as precariously to its traditions as it does to the mountainside. Its attractions are twofold: breathtaking vistas of the valley below and mountain peaks in the distance; and interesting examples of sgraffito. The sheer number of these enchanting houses found here and their incredible beauty have earned Guarda the nickname 'Museum Village' and, in fact, this has been recognized by the Swiss government as a place of national significance.

If the idea of walking back does not appeal to you, take a bus from Guarda down to Guarda railway station where you can catch the train back to Scuol.

(44) Nauders Nauders, Austria

The village of Nauders in Austria is just a short bus trip or drive from Scuol and is an interesting place to visit in summer. In the Austrian Tyrol, under the shadow of surrounding snow-capped mountains, two lovely villages stretch towards the horizon and, at the point of their divergence, a quaint village clings to the lower slopes that rise between them. Nauders, on the Reschen Pass at 4,528ft (1,380m), is a fascinating contrast to its Swiss cousins.

This is still an active farming community, many of the barns prominently display medallions proudly announcing awards received for prized cattle. Quite incongruously, there is a predominance of hotels, and rather nice ones at that. On closer inspection these have many of the amenities – such as pools, saunas, health clubs and fine restaurants – that you would expect to find in far larger resorts. The reality is that Nauders is in fact a resort village – but with a difference: it successfully combines a working-farm village lifestyle with the infrastructure necessary to attract an international clientele.

Not only is Austria a little more laid back than Switzerland, but prices in general are also quite a bit lower.

Around the Village

Besides exploring the village, which is an absolute delight, the **Schloss Naudersberg** is worth a visit. First documented in 1239 as the seat of the Masters of Nauders, it was the seat of a county court from 1300 to 1919. Subsequently abandoned and on the verge of ruin, it was purchased in 1980 by the Köllemann family who have been restoring it ever since.

The main summer tourist activity in Nauders is **hiking**, and the tourist office offers the *Bike- und Wanderkarte Nauders* and a brochure detailing information about walks and hikes around the village. The brochure will tell you that there are no less than 38 marked (strangely 1 to 36 and 40 and 47) hiking trails around the village – and very well marked they are, too. The trails are classified as either blue (very easy, suitable for children and older people), red (moderate) or black (quite difficult). Beware, though, that the classifications have been made by mountain folk with sturdy constitutions and legs like mountain goats. For example, Route 6 (blue) going up to the Grosser Mutzkopf via the Grüner See (suitable, but cold, for bathing) could not be classified as a leisurely stroll. To be fair, though, apart from a few steep stretches, the trek goes mostly through pastureland and could not either be classified as mountaineering. And the views – across a panorama that takes in three countries – are stupendous. You will see, immediately to the south, the Reschenpass, beyond which lies the Reschensee reservoir and the Italian South Tyrol. Further around and towards the west, there's a marvellous view back down the Lower Engadine valley towards Scuol in Switzerland.

On your wanderings you may notice huge piles of firewood stacked at random intervals. Following Nauders tradition, 132 local families have the rights to the wood, but not to the land, on the slopes around the village. What's more, these rights are tied to a particular property and the fireplaces – up to two – located within that property. Each designated fireplace owns an entitlement to 283 cubic feet (8 cubic metres) of wood. Woodsmen are responsible for cutting the wood, piling it and replenishing the forest; the recipients of the wood must transport it to their homes.

Schloss Naudersberg
Alte Strasse 1,
t (01143) 05473 87 242,
www.schloss-
nauders.com; guided
tours in German
Sun and hols 11, Tues,
Thurs, Fri 4.30, Wed 5;
adm

14

Graubünden | Nauders, Austria

ⓘ **Nauders >**
*Tourismusverband
Nauders:
Dr-Tschoggfey-Str. 66,
t (01143) 05473 87220,
www.nauders.com;
open summer Mon–Fri
9-12 and 2–6, Sat 9–6,
Sun 9–12; at other times
Mon–Fri 9–12
and 2–5*

Where to Stay and Eat in Nauders

★★★★Mein Almhof, t (0043) 05473 87313, *www.meinalmhof.at* (*moderate*). With well-equipped rooms, a fine restaurant, an indoor pool and a health club. The delightful owner Hans Kröll takes great care to ensure that all of your needs are met. Full board recommended.

Into the South Tyrol

A short excursion into Italy should definitely be on everyone's itinerary. You may be surprised to find that this part of Italy, the **South Tyrol**, is very Austrian in character. That is because it used to be part of Austria, but was handed over to Italy at the end of the First World War. The main attraction in South Tyrol is rather unusual. In the course of the development of an area reservoir, a small village was evacuated. Yet, rising forlornly from the calm waters that have claimed the town, is the top portion of the village church spire, a single reminder of the inhabitants and faith of that community. This eerie scene is one that is often photographed – especially on a clear day with snow-capped peaks in the background.

Swiss National Park

⭐ **Swiss National Park**

The Swiss National Park (Parc Naziunal Svizzer) is the only national park in Switzerland. It was opened in 1914 and is the oldest national park in Europe. What's more, it has the most stringent environmental protection rules of any park in the European Alps. Covering 65sq miles (169sq km), it is entirely free of human intervention.

The park is mountainous. Approximately half of it is wasteland, a quarter alpine grasslands and the remaining quarter forest and mountain pines. It is home to a wide variety of flora and fauna, some of which only survive here. The visitors' centre organizes wildlife-watching excursions and a number of other trips.

Tourist Information in Swiss National Park

ⓘ **Swiss National Park >**
*Besucherzentrum,
Zernez, t 081 851 41 41,
www.nationalpark.ch;
open June–Oct daily
8.30–6; winter limited
opening times; adm*

The Swiss National Park Centre in Zernez offers exhibitions, a children's discovery trail and a five-language audio guide. They will also provide you with information on hiking trails, weather conditions, etc.

Where to Sleep and Eat in the Swiss National Park

Hotel Parc Naziunal, Il Fuorn, Zernez, t 081 856 12 26, *www.ilfuorn.ch* (*inexpensive*). This is the only hotel in the national park. It offers comfortable rooms with pine and larch décor. The restaurant offers classic game specialities as well as trout.

Getting to and around the Swiss National Park

The Swiss National Park occupies land east of the St Moritz to Scuol road, and is bisected by the road running east of Zernez through the Müstair Valley. By **car** from St Moritz it's a direct road to Zernez. From Chur you come over the Flüela Pass to Susch, before making the short trip south to Zernez. From Zernez drive through the Müstair Valley. Parking is only permitted in official parking areas.

By **train** from the direction of St Moritz it's a direct line to Zernez. From Chur it's necessary to change at Ardez and then get a connection to Zernez.

From Zernez a **postbus**, *www.postbus.ch*, runs through the length of the Müstair Valley stopping at the Hotel Park Naziunal, Il Fourn.

The only way of getting around the park is by **hiking**, but as it's at an altitude of between 4,593ft (1,400m) and 10,498ft (3,200m) hikes should only be undertaken by those fit enough to handle the conditions.

Samnaun

Samnaun is one of the most unusual and curious mountain villages in Switzerland. Unusual, in that it is tucked away in the far eastern corner of the country – in a valley with four other villages – almost surrounded by Austria. In fact, historically, it has always been far easier to reach Austria than to get out to the Inn Valley and then on to the road to St Moritz and other parts of Switzerland. Even today, the road down to Switzerland – as opposed to going via Austria – is very poor and dominated by curving tunnels that often have room for just one car.

It is this geographical quirk that, in the late 19th century, led to Samnaun's curiosity value today. At that time, the Swiss government tried to impose taxes on Samnaun's trade with Austria. The citizens of the valley, though, rebelled; and using the argument that as they, effectively, could not trade with the rest of Switzerland, they refused to pay Swiss taxes. The end result is that Samnaun is now a tax-free village. This is its main attraction and the reason why most visitors come here.

Shopping in Samnaun

Shopping dominates everything in the very narrow, steep valley of Samnaun, and prices are far lower than in the rest of Switzerland, starting with much cheaper petrol as you enter (or leave) the village. The only real problem is where to look first. In reality, the majority of the over 50 stores are quite small and the range of goods for sale other than alcohol and tobacco is rather limited. The best, and largest, shops are found grouped together near the Hotel Post in the centre of the village, just across from the tourist office. For upscale watches and jewellery go to the **Bijouterie**; **Parfüm-Kosmetik** sells duty-free designer perfume and cosmetics; the **Duty-Free-Center** offers a wide range of sports watches, cigars, alcohol and spirits and accessories such as Victorinox etc.; and **Sport Mode-Boutique** has large choice of fashionable sportswear featuring every major international designer label, not to mention the biggest selection of skiing and hiking boots, climbing gear and other such outdoor equipment.

Bijouterie
t 081 868 57 34

Parfüm-Kosmetik
t 081 861 92 95

Duty-Free-Center
t 081 868 57 35

Sport Mode-Boutique
t 081 861 93 30

14
Graubünden | Samnaun

Getting to and around Samnaun

By **car** there are just two approaches to Samnaun from other destinations in Switzerland, both of which converge at Susch. From St Moritz the road runs via Samedan and Zernez, and from Chur via Davos and Klosters over the Flüela Pass to Susch. From Susch the road follows the Inn Valley passing Guarda and Scuol on the way to Martina where, soon after, a rather difficult road rises up to Samnaun.

From wherever you come from in Switzerland **train** services stop at Scuol. From there it's necessary to take a **bus** to Martina, the border stop with Austria, and then another bus on to Samnaun.

Samnaun is a small village so you can just **walk** to where you need to get to once there.

Euro-Center
t 081 868 58 80

Hangl family
www.hangl.ch

Snow-how-Center
t 081 861 93 30

All of these stores, and the **Euro-Center** petrol station at the entrance to the village, are owned and operated by the **Hangl** family, who operate similar facilities at Ischgl, just across the border in Austria. As several of the brothers have made a name for themselves in the international ski-racing scene, it is also appropriate that they run the **Snow-how-Center**, where you can rent, or buy, anything that you will need for any winter sport activity.

Sport and Spa Activities

At an altitude of 5,905ft (1,800m) and with a ski area situated between 4,593ft (1,400m) and 9,514ft (2,900m), this valley has over 124 miles (200km) of ski trails, making it a **winter sports** paradise. The area is served by 40 lift facilities including the unique Twinliner double-decker cable car. In the summer the narrow alpine valleys have more than 155 miles (250km) of groomed hiking trails.

Alpen Quell Erlebnisbad
t 081 868 57 07;
www.alpenquell.ch

The **Alpen Quell Erlebnisbad** is a wonderful combination of indoor pool and other water and health facilities.

Event in Samnaun

ⓘ **Samnaun ›**
Samnaun Tourismus:
Dorfstrasse 4,
t 081 868 58 58,
www.samnaun.ch;
open Mon–Fri 8–6, Sat
10–12 and 2–5.30

Late Nov: Clau Wau, *www.clauwau.com*, is an annual event where Santas from around the world compete in teams of four, in various events, to see which will be declared the best in the world.

Where to Stay in Samnaun

★★★★Sport u. Wellness Post, Dorfstrasse 9, **t** 081 861 92 00, *www.wellnesshotelpost.ch* (*expensive*). Located in the centre of the village. It offers 52 spacious and elegantly furnished rooms and equally sumptuous public areas. It has a health and beauty area with sauna, solarium and whirlpool, and the trendy Why Not nightclub.

★★★Vital-Hotel Samnaunerhof, Dorfstrasse 48, **t** 081 861 81 81, *www.samnaunerhof.com* (*moderate*). This is an interestingly designed hotel

in the upper part of the village. It has 24 rooms that vary in size, but are modern and up-to-date. Extensive facilities include a health and fitness centre with a range of treatments on offer. It has an à la carte restaurant, pizzeria and a duty-free shop.

★★★Camona, Dorfstrasse 47, **t** 081 861 82 82, *www.camona.ch* (*inexpensive*). This is a pleasant little hotel with just 11 rooms, which is located in the upper part of the village. It has a pizzeria with a nice outside terrace.

Eating Out in Samnaun

Schmuggler Alm, **t** 081 861 82 00, *www.schmuggleralm.ch* (*expensive–moderate*). Situated a little way past the upper part of the village. A combination of restaurant, pizzeria and bar, this place has a delightful ambience and is an après-ski favourite. Serves favourites such as fondue and raclette.

Getting to Müstair

By **car** from St Moritz it's a direct road to Zernez, while from Chur you come over the Flüela Pass to Susch, before making the short trip south to Zernez. From Zernez drive the whole length of the Müstair Valley to the convent, which is right next to the Italian border.

By **train**, from the direction of St Moritz it's a direct line to Zernez; from Chur it's necessary to change at Ardez and then get a connection to Zernez. From Zernez a **postbus**, *www.postbus.ch*, runs through the length of the Müstair Valley to the convent.

Convent of St John
t 081 851 62 23,
www.muestair.ch

Convent of St John, Müstair

The history of the Convent of St John dates back over 1,200 years. It is considered that there was an abbey here around the year 780, established by a bishop of Chur, possibly at the behest of Charlemagne, in an era when many such places were being constructed. Due to its strategic location controlling the alpine pass to Italy, it was also fortified. In the early 9th century a series of frescoes were painted here and later, during the 11th and 12th centuries when the church was expanded, more were added and even painted over the old ones. Sometime in the early 12th century, although first written confirmation wasn't until 1167, the monastery converted to a convent.

The Swabian War was actually started here and in 1499 the Habsburgs looted the convent. Around 1500 it was changed from a single-nave Carolingian building to a three-nave late Gothic-style church. Not long after, the Ilanzer Articles weakened the powers of the bishops of Chur and consequently reduced the income of the convent.

During the 20th century restoration work exposed mural work and in 1983 UNESCO recognized them as 'Switzerland's greatest series of figurative murals, painted *c.* 800, along with Romanesque frescoes and stuccoes' and the Convent of St John was declared a UNESCO World Heritage site.

There is also a small museum here as well as a shop, where many products originating in the convent's kitchens, needlepoint workshop and woodshop are available for purchase.

There are actually nine rooms available at the convent and you can enjoy meals with other guests. You are encouraged to participate in monastic prayer and the Eucharist. The priest in charge is also available to answer any spiritual questions or concerns that you might have.

Language

The languages used in Switzerland are German (spoken by about 65% of the population); French (about 20%); Italian (about 7%); and Romansch (around 1%, in the canton of Graubünden). German is spoken in a Swiss-German dialect (*Schwyzerdütsch*), in itself very different from other German dialects. High German is the written language.

You will find that most people in Switzerland can speak English, especially people working in the tourist industry and those in large towns and cities.

All words and phrases translated below are in the following order: German, French and Italian.

Pronunciation

German

Vowels

Simple vowels in German are either long or short. They are always long when doubled or followed by *h*, and mostly long when followed by a single consonant. They are, as a rule, short when followed by a group of consonants.

short *i* as *i* in 'it'; **long** *i* as in 'machine'
short *e* as in 'let'; **long** *e* as in 'late'
long *a* as in 'alms'
short *o* as in 'not'; **long** *o* as in 'no'
short *u* as in 'put'; **long** *u* as in 'rude'
short *ä* as in 'fell'; **long** *ä* as in 'mare'
ie as English *ee*
ö as *ur* in 'urn'
ü as German *i* with rounded and protruded lips
e at the end of a word is always pronounced, as an 'er'
äu and *eu* as *oi* in 'boy'

ei and *ai* as *ei* in 'height'
au as *ow* in 'how'

Consonants

Most German consonants are pronounced as in English. Here are some exceptions:
ch as *ch* in 'loch'
j as *y* in 'yes'
s as *z* sound in 'rose'
sp and *st* as *shp* and *sht* when at the beginning of a word
th as English *t*
v as English *f*
w as English *v*
z as English *ts*

French

Vowels

a/à/â between *a* in 'bat' and 'part'
é/er/ez **at end of word** as *a* in 'plate' but a bit shorter
e/è/ê as *e* in 'bet'
e **at end of word** not pronounced
e **at end of syllable or in one-syllable word** pronounced weakly, like *er* in 'mother'
i as *ee* in 'bee'
o as *o* in 'pot'
ô as *o* in 'go'
u/û between *oo* in 'boot' and *ee* in 'bee'

Vowel Combinations

ai as *a* in 'plate'
aî as *e* in 'bet'
ail as *i* in 'kite'
au/eau as *o* in 'go'
ei as *e* in 'bet'
eu/œu as *er* in 'mother'
oi between *wa* in 'swam' and *wu* in 'swum'
oy as 'why'
ui as *wee* in 'twee'

Nasal Vowels

Vowels followed by an *n* or *m* have a nasal sound.

an/en as *o* in 'pot' + nasal sound
ain/ein/in as *a* in 'bat' + nasal sound
on as *aw* in 'paw' + nasal sound
un as *u* in 'nut' + nasal sound

Consonants

Many French consonants are pronounced as in English, but there are some exceptions:

c followed by *e, i* or *y*, and *ç* as *s* in 'sit'
c followed by *a, o, u* as *c* in 'cat'
g followed by *e, i* or *y* as *s* in 'pleasure'
g followed by *a, o, u* as *g* in 'good'
gn as *ni* in 'opinion'
j as *s* in 'pleasure'
ll as *y* in 'yes'
qu as *k* in 'kite'
s between vowels as *z* in 'zebra'
s otherwise as *s* in 'sit'
w except in English words as *v* in 'vest'
x at end of word as *s* in 'sit'
x otherwise as *x* in 'six'

Italian

Italian words are pronounced phonetically. Every vowel and consonant (except *h*) is sounded.

Vowels

a as in English 'father'
e when unstressed is pronounced like *a* in 'fate', when stressed can be the same or like the *e* in 'pet'
i as the *i* in 'machine';
o like *e*, has two sounds, *o* as in 'hope' when unstressed, and usually *o* as in 'rock' when stressed
u as *u* in 'June'

Consonants

Consonants are the same as in English, except:

c when followed by an 'e' or 'i', is pronounced like the English *ch*
g is also soft before 'i' or 'e' as in *gira*
z as English *ts*
sc before the vowels *i* or *e* become like the English *sh*

ch as *k* in Chianti
gn as English *ny*
gli as the middle of the word 'million'

Useful Phrases

hello (informal) *hallo/grütsi salut ciao*
hello (formal) *guten Morgen bonjour buongiorno*
goodbye *auf wiedersehen au revoir arrivederci*
sorry *entschuldigung désolé scusi*
please *bitte s'il vous plaît per favore*
thank you *danke merci grazie*
good *gut bon/bonne buono/a*
how much? *wie viel? combien? quanto?*
yes *ja oui si*
no *nein non no*
WC *toilette toilettes toeletta*
men *Herren hommes signori*
ladies *Damen dames/femmes signore*
help! *Hilfe! au secours! aiuto!*

General

Do you speak English?
Sprechen Sie Englisch?
Parlez-vous anglais?
Parla inglese?

I don't understand
Ich verstehe nicht
Je ne comprends pas
Non capisco

I don't know
Ich weiss nicht
Je ne sais pas
Non lo so

I would like...
Ich möchte...
Je voudrais...
Vorrei...

Speak more slowly
Bitte sprechen Sie langsamer?
Pourriez-vous parler plus lentement?
Parla lentamente

What is your name?
Wie heissen Sie?
Comment vous appelez-vous?
Come si chiama?

My name is...
Mein Name ist...
Je m'appelle...
Mi chiamo...

Transport

I want to go to...
Ich möchte nach... fahren
Je voudrais aller à...
Desidero andare a...

When is the next...?
Wann ist der nächste...?
Quel est le prochain...?
Quando parte il prossimo...?

What time does it leave (arrive)?
Wann fährt er ab (kommt er an)?
A quelle heure part-il (arrive-t-il)?
A che ora parte (arriva)?

From where does the train leave?
Wo fährt der Zug ab?
D'où part le train?
Da dove parte il treno?

How long does the trip take?
Wie lange dauert die Reise?
Combien de temps dure le voyage?
Quanto tempo dura il viaggio?

Single/return ticket
Einfache Fahrkarte/Rückfahrkarte
Un aller simple/aller et retour
Un biglietto semplice/andata e ritorno

Accommodation

a single room
ein Einzelzimmer
une chambre pour une personne
una camera singola

a twin room
ein Zimmer mit zwei Betten
une chambre à deux lits
una camera con due letti

a double room
ein Doppelzimmer
une chambre pour deux personnes
una camera doppia

with shower/bath
mit Dusche/Bad
avec douche/salle de bains
con doccia/bagno

Numbers

one *eins un(e) uno(a)*
two *zwei deux due*
three *drei trois tre*
four *vier quatre quattro*
five *fünf cinq cinque*
six *sechs six sei*
seven *sieben sept sette*
eight *acht huit otto*
nine *neun neuf nove*
ten *zehn dix dieci*
twenty *zwanzig vingt venti*
thirty *dreissig trente trenta*
forty *vierzig quarante quaranta*
fifty *fünfzig cinquante cinquanta*
sixty *sechzig soixante sessanta*
seventy *siebzig soixante-dix settanta*
eighty *achtzig quatre-vingts ottanta*
ninety *neunzig quatre-vingt-dix novanta*
hundred *hundert cent cento*

Days

Monday *Montag lundi lunedì*
Tuesday *Dienstag mardi martedì*
Wednesday *Mittwoch mercredi mercoledì*
Thursday *Donnerstag jeudi giovedì*
Friday *Frietag vendredi venerdì*
Saturday *Samstag samedi sabato*
Sunday *Sonntag dimanche domenica*

today *heute aujourd'hui oggi*
yesterday *gestern hier ieri*
tomorrow *morgen demain domani*

Months

January *Januar janvier gennaio*
February *Februar février febbraio*
March *März mars marzo*
April *April avril aprile*
May *Mai mai maggio*
June *Juni juin giugno*
July *Juli juillet luglio*
August *August août agosto*
September *September septembre settembre*
October *Oktober octobre ottobre*
November *November novembre novembre*
December *Dezember décembre dicembre*

Further Reading

Barber, Hoyt, *Secrets of Swiss Banking: An Owner's Manual to Quietly Building a Fortune* (Books for Business, 2002).
  How to safely conserve your wealth in Switzerland.

Bonner, Roger, *Swiss Me* (Bergli Books, 2008).
  Humorous stories about the Swiss.

Church, Clive H., *Politics and Government of Switzerland* (Palgrave, 2004).
  One of the few English-language studies of contemporary Swiss politics.

Fossedal, Gregory A., *Direct Democracy in Switzerland* (Transaction Publishers, 2007).
  An overview of Switzerland's institutions and democracy.

Glueck, Michael Wells, *Living Among the Swiss* (iUniverse, 2002).
  The author's personal views on Swiss society.

Habicht, Peter and Prack, *Fredy Lifting the Mask* (Bergli Books, 2001).
  Everything you need to know about Basel's famous carnival.

Habicht, Peter, *Basel – A Centre at the Fringe* (Merian Verlag, 2008).
  A comprehensive guide to the history of Basel.

Lievano, Sergio Hoi, *Your Swiss-German Survival Guide* (Bergli Books, 2006).
  Guide to how to understand, and be understood, in Swiss-German.

Oertig-Davidson, Margaret, *Beyond Chocolate: Understanding Swiss Culture* (Bergli Books, 2002).
  An in-depth review of Swiss habits and culture.

Reynolds, Kev, *Alpine Points of View* (Cicerone Press, 2004).
  Collection of alpine photographs.

Reynolds, Kev, *Walking in the Bernese Alps* (Cicerone Press, 2008).
  A guide to hiking and trekking in this beautiful region.

Reynolds, Kev, *Walking in Ticino* (Cicerone Press, 1992).
  A guide to hiking and walking in the Ticino.

Reynolds, Kev, *Walking in the Valais* (Cicerone Press, 2007).
  A guide to hiking and trekking in the dramatic region.

Rushton, Andrew and Fekete, Katalin, *Swiss Cookies, Biscuits for Christmas and All Year Round* (Bergli Books, 2008).
  Recipes for traditional Swiss biscuits and cookies.

Sharp, Hilary, *Tour of the Matterhorn* (Cicerone Press, 2009).
  A guide to walking routes around the famous Matterhorn.

Sloan, John C., *The Surprising Wines of Switzerland* (Bergli Books, 1996).
  A comprehensive guide to Swiss wines.

Style, Sue, *A Taste of Switzerland* (Pavilion, 1992).
  Some of the very best of Switzerland's recipes and cooking traditions.

Index

Main page references are in **bold**. Page references to maps are in *italics*.

Dedication

For Bernard and Rita Esquenet; far more than just life-long friends, the brother and sister I never had of my own.

Also for Georgina Ellis and her family, for all the care and love she, and they, gave to my mother, Carrie, in her last years.

1st edition published in 2010

Cadogan Guides is an imprint of
New Holland Publishers (UK) Ltd
London • Cape Town • Sydney • Auckland

New Holland Publishers (UK) Ltd
Garfield House
86–88 Edgware Road
London W2 2EA

80 McKenzie Street
Cape Town 8001
South Africa

Unit 1, 66 Gibbes Street
Chatswood, NSW 2067
Australia

218 Lake Road
Northcote
Auckland
New Zealand

cadogan@nhpub.co.uk
www.cadoganguides.com
t +44 (0) 20 7724 7773

Text copyright © Norman Renouf 2010
Copyright © New Holland Publishers (UK) Ltd 2010

Front cover photograph: Traditional Swiss chalet © Guenter Fisher/Photolibrary.
Back cover photograph: High alpine peaks above Saas-Fee © Norman Renouf.
Photo essay photographs: pp. 1, 4, 6 bottom margin/bottom centre, 8, 9 top, 11 top, 12, 13 top, 14 bottom, 16 © Norman Renouf; p. 3 margin © Murattaner/iStockphoto; p. 3 main © Patrick Ward/Corbis; p. 5 © Manchan/Photolibrary; p. 6 top margin © Chaikin/shutterstock; p. 9 bottom © Kruyshaar/shutterstock; p. 10 © Saas-Fee/Saastal Tourism; p. 11 bottom © imagebroker/Photolibrary; p. 13 bottom © awdebenham/iStockphoto; p. 14 top © 100zax/iStockphoto; p. 15 © Steve Vidler/Photolibrary.
Maps: © Cadogan Guides, drawn by Maidenhead Cartographic Services Ltd
Cover design: Jason Hopper
Design: Sarah Gardner
Editor: Clare Hubbard
Proofreading: Dominique Shead
Indexing: Isobel McLean

Printed and bound in Italy by Legoprint
A catalogue record for this book is available from the British Library

ISBN: 978-1-86011-433-5

Switzerland
touring atlas

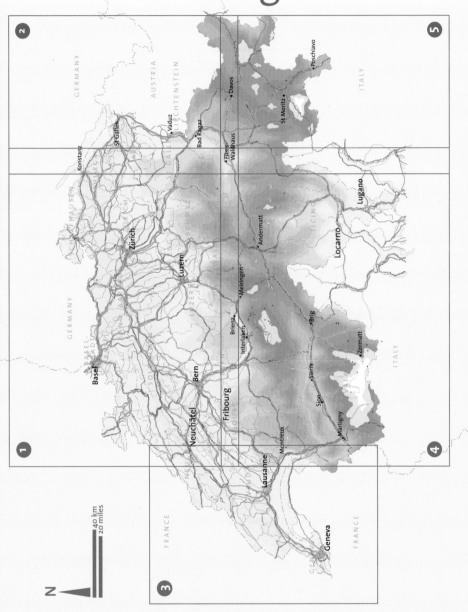

N

40 km
20 miles

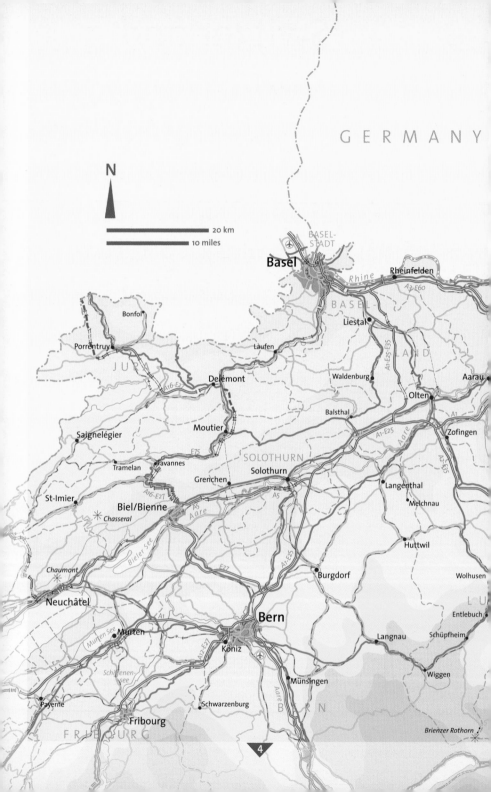

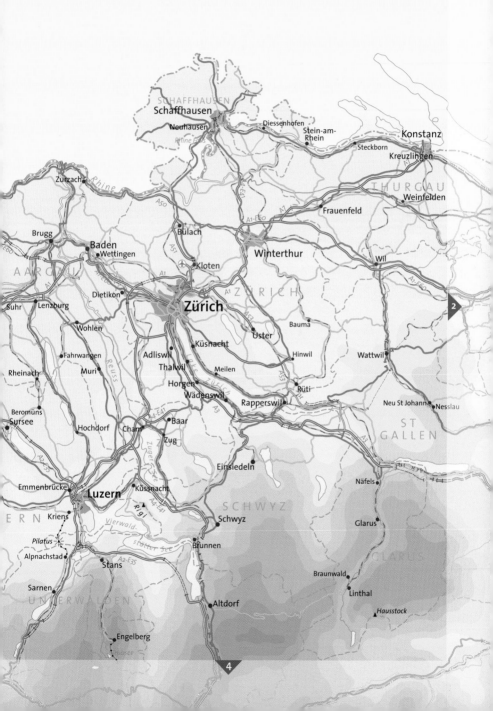

N

20 km
10 miles

Konstanz

Boden See (Lake Constance)

Kreuzlingen

GERMANY

Romanshorn

Arbon

Rorschach

St Gallen

A1-E60

Heiden

Gossau

Lustenau

Herisau

Altstatten

APPENZELL

A13-E43

Urnäsch

Appenzell

Schwägalp

Säntis

Buchs

ST GALLEN

Vaduz

A13-E43

Walenstadt

LIECHTENSTEIN

AUSTRIA

A9

Sargans

Maienfeld

Bad Ragaz

Schiers

Landquart

A28-E43

Samnaun

Küblis

Flims-Dorf

Tamins

Weissfluhgipfel

Klosters

To Nauders (Austria)

Chur

Flims
Waldhaus

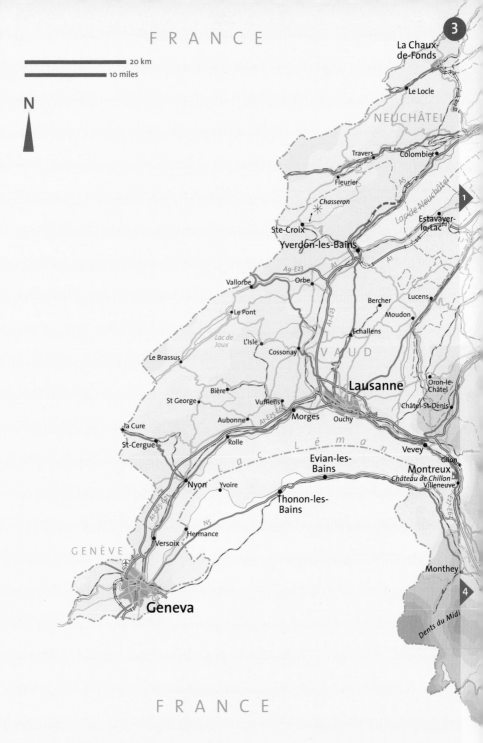